SAP® Solution Manager Enterprise Edition

PRESS

SAP PRESS is a joint initiative of SAP and Galileo Press. The know-how offered by SAP specialists combined with the expertise of the Galileo Press publishing house offers the reader expert books in the field. SAP PRESS features first-hand information and expert advice, and provides useful skills for professional decision-making.

SAP PRESS offers a variety of books on technical and business related topics for the SAP user. For further information, please visit our website: www.sap-press.com.

Michael Klöffer, Marc Thier
Performing End-to-End Root Cause Analysis Using SAP Solution Manager
2007, 80 pp.
978-1-59229-189-2

Torsten Sternberg, Matthias Friedrich
SAP Solution Manager Service Desk – Functionality and Implementation
2008, 135 pp.
978-1-59229-214-1

Gerhard Oswald
SAP Service and Support
2006, 304 pp.
978-1-59229-089-5

Markus Helfen, Michael Lauer, Hans Martin Trauthwein
Testing SAP Solutions
2007, 367 pp.
978-1-59229-127-4

Marc O. Schäfer, Matthias Melich

SAP® Solution Manager Enterprise Edition

Galileo Press

Bonn • Boston

ISBN 978-1-59229-271-4

© 2009 by Galileo Press Inc., Boston (MA)
2nd Edition, updated and revised

2nd German Edition published 2008 by Galileo Press, Bonn, Germany.

Galileo Press is named after the Italian physicist, mathematician and philosopher Galileo Galilei (1564–1642). He is known as one of the founders of modern science and an advocate of our contemporary, heliocentric worldview. His words *Eppur si muove* (And yet it moves) have become legendary. The Galileo Press logo depicts Jupiter orbited by the four Galilean moons, which were discovered by Galileo in 1610.

Editor Florian Zimniak
English Edition Editor Justin Lowry
Translation lexsys Language Consulting, *www.lexsys.eu*
Copy Editor Ruth Saavedra
Cover Design Jill Winitzer
Photo Credit Masterfile/Bill Frymire
Layout Design Vera Brauner
Production Editor Kelly O'Callaghan
Typesetting Publishers' Design and Production Services, Inc.
Printed and bound in Canada

Contents at a Glance

Contents

11 Integrating Partners in the SAP Global Support Backbone 503

Foreword by SAP Global Service & Support

Following the success of the first SAP Solution Manager book, we are pleased to present this second, completely reworked edition, entitled *SAP Solution Manager Enterprise Edition*. SAP constantly provides its customers and partners with new ways of driving innovations and adapting quickly and flexibly to the market, while at the same time reducing *total cost of ownership* (TCO) and minimizing risks. Constantly enhancing the SAP product portfolio not only boosts SAP's strategic importance; it also increases the company's responsibility for its ecosystem. SAP is committed to providing its customers and partners with end-to-end, comprehensive support and maintenance for their software-based business processes and services, both today and in the future.

To achieve this, our board area *Global Service and Support*, in particular, is dedicated to developing, providing, and improving best practices, processes, methods, services, and tools. We have consistently promoted appropriate measures in all areas of service and support to better meet the needs of our customers and partners in the SAP ecosystem. Close cooperation with our customers and user groups is an invaluable asset in achieving this, and we would like to take this opportunity to thank all of those groups involved. At many of our events, customers invest time beyond their own particular needs to report problems. SAP Solution Manager demonstrates that SAP is listening, understands these concerns, and reacts accordingly.

As the key to achieving end-to-end solution operations in a globalized and technologically heterogeneous environment, *SAP Enterprise Support* provides a cross-solution offering that includes technological and application components, partner solutions, and customer-specific enhancements (*custom code*). With the standards for end-to-end solution operations and the Run SAP implementation methodology, we provide real-life processes to help you to operate your solution smoothly.

SAP Solution Manager Enterprise Edition is the central platform for meeting this commitment, and is the backbone for our customers and partners to ensure the optimal operation of SAP-based customer solutions and services.

SAP Solution Manager Enterprise Edition features services, methods, and tools to fulfill our commitment to providing end-to-end support for business processes and open integration in the ecosystem. In this context, industry standards such as the Application Management processes described in the IT Infrastructure Library (ITIL) are becoming ever more important.

These offerings, especially services, place great emphasis on scalability. Only by "productizing" our offerings and standard consulting services can we support our customers and partners in all sizes of companies — small, medium-sized, and large.

The current version of SAP Solution Manager Enterprise Edition features improved standardization, user-friendliness, and collaboration in the ecosystem. This enables SAP to provide end-to-end, comprehensive support and maintenance for our customers' and partners' software-based business processes and services, today and in the future.

Finally, we would like to sincerely thank the authors for this book full of collective experiences for our customers and partners. We hope that it gives you, dear readers, lots of valuable information about SAP Solution Manager Enterprise Edition and that you can apply the practical examples to your own projects.

Gerhard Oswald
Member of the SAP AG executive board

Dr. Uwe Hommel
EVP SAP Active Global Support

Foreword by the German-Speaking User Group (DSAG)

It's hard to believe that two years have passed since I wrote the forward to the first edition of the SAP Solution Manager book. If you think this being the second edition makes it easy to write a new forward, you're sadly mistaken.

SAP Solution Manager 4.0 is still SAP Solution Manager 4.0, but the list of enhancements is enough to cover the next three release levels of our favorite service and support infrastructure and possibly more. This may be why SAP Solution Manager 4.0 has been renamed *SAP Solution Manager 7.0 Enterprise Edition*, or perhaps simply too much time has elapsed for an SAP solution to still have the same name. I can't help but smile when I see such a mouthful, especially because SAP usually communicates only in cryptic acronyms.

Nevertheless, *Enterprise Edition* reflects the most important changes to the SAP support model in 2008, namely *Enterprise Support*. SAP's new support offering has given rise to a lot of discussion over the past weeks and months, and many customers have come to realize that there is still unchartered territory on their SAP Enterprise Support maps. But one thing is certain: Enterprise Edition is the only solution that can help reduce risks and lower total cost of ownership. I would like to thank the authors for going beyond SAP Solution Manager and addressing the subject of Enterprise Support in the first chapter. Even though this subject could (and will!) fill several books and cannot be discussed exhaustively here, any information about it is useful to us as SAP users. If you continue to Chapter 2, which introduces SAP Solution Manager, and compare the first and second editions (or even better, log onto your SAP Solution Manager and think back to the "good old days" of just two years ago!), you'll see that a lot has changed.

Some readers will recognize the content, because one of the reasons for this mass of ideas, enhancements, and improvements is the outstanding collaboration between the Service & Support Infrastructure user group in the CCC/Service & Support work group of the *DSAG* and SAP Solution Manager product management and development, which has developed over time. Together, we have launched the *Work Forces* collaboration model, which has been beneficial to both sides.

Ideas, suggestions for improvements, and concepts are compiled, checked, modified, and adjusted to meet requirements in small specialized workshops of teams composed of committed representatives of SAP user companies, with a wide variety of real-life know-how and requirements, and highly motivated SAP specialists.

Another important Work Force component is the regular usability workshops, in which new or improved tools are scrutinized by the most critical eyes in the world, namely, those of end users. At the ends of these meetings, both parties usually acknowledge that a great deal has been achieved in a short time. Even in this age of email and virtual meetings, forums, and marketplaces, some things are still best discussed face to face.

As an SAP user and member of the DSAG board, I would therefore like to especially thank our dedicated members and our colleagues at SAP. You have accomplished a lot for us users.

In a rapidly changing IT world, somewhere in the tension between Goethe's "The Sorcerer's Apprentice" (you know, "...the spirits that I called") and requirements resembling Shakespeare's *As You Like It*, we can be sure that collaboration on SAP Solution Manager will continue successfully. The journey is its own reward.

In the next edition, I'm sure we'll be amazed again by all of the new developments. But until then, there's no time to rest. If you've not already done so, off to your computer! For if you don't move with the times, time will pass you by.

Have fun reading this book. It's worth the effort.

Andreas Oczko

SAP CCC manager, arvato systems | Technologies GmbH

Member of the DSAG executive board and responsible for the Operations/Service & Support area

Introduction

Since the first edition of this book was published, there have been many changes in the SAP Solution Manager. Even the title of this new edition reflects a significant change — the new *SAP Solution Manager Enterprise Edition* version. Readers received the first edition with great interest. We are especially pleased by this interest, and with being able to present the innovations of the past two years in the overall context of SAP Solution Manager Enterprise Edition in these pages. This includes an explanation of integrated partner solutions. You will become familiar with new concepts such as the *Business Process Change Analyzer* and the *Solution Documentation Assistant*, as well as familiar content and content that has been adapted to meet new requirements.

What is SAP Solution Manager? and *Why do I need SAP Solution Manager?* are among the questions that occupy a lot of minds, and even trouble a few. We have tried to answer these questions on a conceptual and strategic level and on a practical and application-specific level.

To do so, we interviewed experts at SAP, and customers and partners, who all gave us the benefit of their personal perspectives, and we would like to sincerely thank them for doing so. The intense, constructive cooperation with these people while writing this book, but above all development requests and concept revisions, is what has enabled us to turn SAP Solution Manager Enterprise Edition into the standardized platform for application management and collaboration that we want to present to you in this book. We hope to be able to continue, and build on, this close working relationship in the future.

The book is composed of three sections, each with a different focus and target audience:

Layout of the book

► A short section (**Chapters 1** and **2**) explains the concept of *SAP Enterprise Support* and the entire spectrum of SAP Solution Manager Enterprise Edition, in general, explains the basic functions and main content, and places SAP Solution Manager Enterprise Edition in the context of ITIL (*Information Technology Infrastructure Library*) application management. This section gives CIOs and management an overview of the capabilities and strategies employed by SAP Solution Manager and provides an outlook on future development in an *executive summary*.

▶ The second section (**Chapters 3** to **9**) takes the application management structure introduced in the first section, and goes into the details of the SAP Solution Manager functions in each phase. This largest section is for project teams that require detailed information about the functionality of individual scenarios.

▶ The third part of the book (**Chapters 10** and **11**) uses customer success stories (**Chapter 10**) to explain the benefits of SAP Solution Manager Enterprise Edition in practical applications. **Chapter 11** deals with the importance of SAP Solution Manager for partners such as value-added resellers and software partners. The **appendix** contains a bibliography, information about all of the authors who contributed to this book, and further sources of information.

Overview
Chapter 1 provides a brief overview of SAP Enterprise Support, and explains the role that SAP Solution Manager Enterprise Edition plays as a platform for this new SAP support offering.

Chapter 2 clarifies the strategic significance of SAP Solution Manager as a platform for application management and collaboration between the customer, partner, and SAP.

After these predominantly strategic and summarizing chapters, **Chapter 3** explains in greater detail the structure of ITIL application management introduced in Chapter 2 and describes SAP Solution Manager Enterprise Edition functions that can be used throughout the requirements, design, build and test, deploy, operate, and optimize phases.

The objective of **Chapter 4** is to put the requirements phase in the SAP Solution Manager context. Among the topics are *SAP business maps* and the SAP Solution Manager content provided in the *Business Process Repository* (BPR). It also explains the new *Solution Documentation Assistant* function.

To be able to make the most of the available support in the design phase of application management, you need to understand functions such as the Business Blueprint and Roadmaps. These and other functions are described in **Chapter 5**.

Chapter 6 explains the challenges of the build and test phase, in which the Business Blueprint and Test Management are implemented.

Knowledge transfer and production preparation are typical tasks of the deploy phase. **Chapter 7** introduces functions and processes that support you here. The *solution* concept in SAP Solution Manager is one of the topics discussed in detail in this chapter.

SAP Solution Manager contains major functions such as Solution Monitoring, System Administration, Solution Reporting, Incident Management, and Root Cause Analysis to provide reliable, cost-effective support for your solution during the operate phase. **Chapter 8** introduces these functions and shows you their processes in detail.

Chapter 9 concludes the application management life cycle and shows you how to use SAP Solution Manager to take advantage of SAP knowledge and experience when upgrading, for example. This chapter also focuses on processes that help you maintain your solution, together with SAP, in a targeted, transparent, and comprehensible way, with particular emphasis on the concept of Change Request Management.

In **Chapter 10**, 12 customer success stories demonstrate how customers have implemented SAP Solution Manager in practical situations, throughout the entire process life cycle.

Since partners also play a vital role in the SAP ecosystem, **Chapter 11** discusses the integration of partners into SAP support processes, which not only increases their quality, but also adds value.

The **appendix** contains information on the wide variety of knowledge transfer offerings for SAP Solution Manager.

This book is designed so that you can read it cover-to-cover or refer to specific chapters as needed. We hope this book will give you a comprehensive, consistent grasp of SAP Solution Manager Enterprise Edition and enable you to recognize the benefits it can provide and new application scenarios that are possible at your company. We are confident that you will profit from our suggestions and be inspired to learn more. If you have any questions, comments, or criticism, please feel free to contact us by sending an email to the addresses given in Appendix D.

Acknowledgments

Such a comprehensive book is the product of collaboration at many levels over the course of the project. Many people have assisted the authors by providing the information necessary for us to be able to present the concepts, strategy, and content of SAP Solution Manager Enterprise Edition in book form.

We especially would like to thank:

▶ Gerhard Oswald, member of the SAP AG executive board

▶ Dr. Uwe Hommel, Executive Vice President, SAP Active Global Support

▶ Helmut Fieres, Vice President, Service and Support Infrastructure

And also:

▶ Andreas Oczko for his invaluable collaboration and close support on behalf of the DSAG

▶ Nilgün Atasoy, Doreen Baseler, Hartwig Brand, Paul Daniels, Ralf Debus, Werner Huff-Hübner, Marina Marscheider, and Anja Flint for their active support

▶ Christoph Albrecht, Werner Arlt, Anette Asmus, David Birkenbach, Michael Demuth, Daniel Emmert, Matthias Friedrich, Stefanie Fritsche, Susanne Glänzer, Roland Hamm, Andreas Heidtmann, Dominik Held, Sigo Henkel, Nikolaus Hertz-Eichenrode, Thomas Holz, Ulrike Hormann, Walter Kirchgässner, Johanna Klemm, Armin Kösegi, Dieter Krieger, Wulf Krümpelmann, Udo Lang, Martin Lauer, Reiner Markheiser, Gordon Leslie McDorman, Michael Meyer, Christoph Nake, Stefan Raffel, Erwin Rojewski, Thomas Schröder, Rüdiger Stöcker, Marc Thier, Eric Wannemacher, Heinrich Wegener, Steffen Weinstock, and Heinz Wolf for their enthusiastic, patient, and attentive reading and their productive criticism

▶ Susan Boser for her enduring commitment to proofreading and correcting the manuscript and for supporting the project as a whole

▶ Our families, partners, and children for their patience and understanding

SAP Enterprise Support provides an end-to-end, consistent, and integrated quality assurance process across technological boundaries and SAP applications. This process is based on stable and proven standards that incorporate both partner solutions and customer-specific enhancements.

1 SAP Enterprise Support

Technological progress allows business transactions to be handled more rapidly than ever before. Thanks to globalization and new technologies, you can benefit from value networks, capture new markets, and enter into partnerships to develop innovative products and services. Value networks fundamentally alter the balance between internal and external activities. They require an extremely flexible and agile IT landscape built on a stable platform. To keep up with these increasing demands, you have invested in applications that can be integrated with and operate on SAP's Business Process Platform. Such investments have allowed you to bring together your partners, suppliers, and customers in an effective value network (see Figure 1.1).

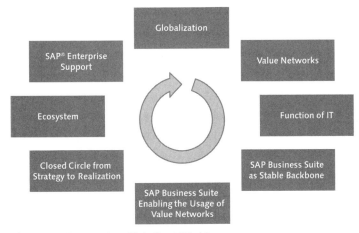

Figure 1.1 Tensions in a Globalized World

In today's global economy, your IT infrastructure has a major bearing on your business success. You wish to protect your investment, minimize your exposure to business risks, and strengthen your basis for growth. Ideally, your entire system landscape of SAP software and partner solutions should be protected.

Increased
requirements

Your IT landscape has become a critical factor for the success of your business. IT support requirements have grown accordingly. In many cases, SAP applications have become more important in your infrastructure, and unite business-critical applications in a framework that is the backbone of your company. As a result of the enlarged application portfolio in many companies, as well as business processes that reach beyond company boundaries, and the use of new technologies such as on-demand applications, many customers have expressed a desire for comprehensive, one-stop support. SAP's answer to this is its end-to-end, holistic support offering, SAP Enterprise Support.

SAP Solution Manager Enterprise Edition is the platform for SAP Enterprise Support, so the opening chapter of this book about SAP Solution Manager Enterprise Edition provides some information about the scope and benefits of SAP Enterprise Support. This background information will help you better understand the individual functions and the overall concept of SAP Solution Manager Enterprise Edition.

1.1 Integrated Quality Assurance Process

SAP Enterprise Support is a holistic offering that supports your business processes from beginning to end, protecting your investments in SAP software and opening the door to the opportunities for growth presented by the global economy.

Service partners
for the SAP
company platform
and beyond

SAP Enterprise Support covers not only SAP applications; the service offering applies to your entire platform, including business-critical customer and partner solutions.

Studies have revealed that 67% of business-critical business applications experience downtime exceeding nine hours per month,[1] despite the fact

---

1   The Standish Group International Inc.: *Extreme Chaos*. 2000.

that success today depends on information technology that works. A central point of contact between customers and SAP and an integrated concept for your entire SAP solution help you reduce this downtime and minimize the risk it poses to your business.

With SAP Enterprise Support, SAP is committed more than ever to the success of your business. SAP establishes a support infrastructure and support standards that enable you to optimize operations throughout your entire extended SAP software landscape. The SAP standards for efficient software operations set new standards. You benefit from comprehensive support services with the industry-leading IT support provided by SAP.

Deeper engagement

SAP Enterprise Support is the key to integrated, standardized, end-to-end business solutions. The focus of SAP's new offering is on enabling customers to manage their system landscapes and applications in a comprehensive, solution-oriented manner throughout the entire life cycle. SAP Enterprise Support offers an end-to-end, consistent, and integrated quality assurance process that reaches beyond all technological boundaries and spans the entire application landscape. This process is based on stable and proven standards for application management that incorporate both partner solutions and customer-specific enhancements (*custom code*). All vendors can be integrated into SAP's support ecosystem, the SAP global support backbone. This helps ensure an application management approach that encourages collaboration between all parties involved in a customer solution.

Platform support

By combining the integrated quality assurance process and standardized application management, you can, among other things, create transparency in your outsourcing contracts, and track and verify their fulfillment. Customers also require such transparency to enable innovations in their solutions and to fulfill professional and technical requirements, without neglecting previous investments. The validity and success of this approach has been proven repeatedly in the past in large enterprises, with the *SAP MaxAttention* support offering. With SAP Enterprise Support, this level of commitment is now available to all customer segments. In particular, SAP Enterprise Support will become the new standard for *Customer Centers of Expertise* (CCoEs; see also Section 1.5). Several components are combined in SAP Enterprise Support (see Figure 1.2), which is examined in greater detail in the sections below.

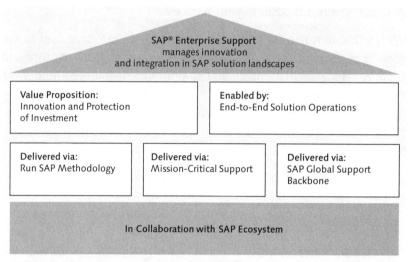

Figure 1.2   SAP Enterprise Support

Value proposition   SAP Enterprise Support allows innovation to be accelerated by making continuous improvements and hiding complexity. The emphasis is on protecting investments. With its new offering, SAP aims to help you reduce your total cost of ownership, and risks, in relation to the operation of SAP software.

This is achieved by applying consistent standards throughout the entire life cycle of a solution (life cycle management), monitoring business processes, managing custom developments, ensuring remote supportability, and sophisticated diagnostic functions.

1.2   Focus on Reducing Risks

The new business models in the global economy have resulted in larger, more closely integrated value networks. This has major benefits in terms of flexibility but also means IT landscapes are becoming more complex.

The cause of this increasing complexity is the growing number of applications and architectures, combined with interfaces between applications, all of which are indispensable to make efficient use of new value networks. However, this complexity also increases business risks. According to a study conducted by the Economist Intelligence Unit, IT complexity is the most common cause of system downtime.[2] There is also a direct correlation between complexity and increased frequency and duration of system problems, 30% of which cannot be solved within 24 hours.[3]

Complexity increases business risks and costs

SAP Enterprise Support enables you to cope with complexity and significantly reduce business risks associated with operating software. SAP Enterprise Support offers the following advantages:

Proactive risk management

▶ *Continuous quality checks* to proactively determine and eliminate potential problems before business risks arise

▶ 24/7 access to the support advisory center, where experts provide assistance, and problem solution management is available for high-priority problems

▶ Service-level agreements with specified times for initial responses and corrective measures to reduce radically the time taken to solve high-priority problems and major errors in the project

▶ Effective collaboration between SAP, its partners, and its customers on the basis of the SAP global support backbone, to reduce the time taken to solve problems

The key criterion to avoid or minimize risks is comprehensive, easily accessible documentation for the entire solution that is universally recognized as the single, reliable source of definitive information (*single source of truth*). In SAP Solution Manager Enterprise Edition, SAP provides a platform to implement, validate, and operate your solutions.

Single source of truth

Companies must recognize that the response to IT projects and solutions is shaped by opinions, feelings, and impressions, which are generally

---

2   Economist Intelligence Unit Ltd.: *Coming to Grips with IT Risk*. March 2007.
3   Forrester Research Inc.: *Optimizing SLA Performance*. 2006.

formed on an emotional level, from a departmental perspective — not the wider perspective of the overall solution. They can only overcome this challenge by continuously monitoring projects and solutions on the basis of ratings and facts to expose any problems.

A culture in which all parties involved have confidence and all stakeholders are supported must be fostered to achieve this. In such a culture, it is unacceptable to not make critical problems visible. The entire range of abilities and skills across the organization can be drawn upon to solve the problem promptly only if it is visible.

That is why a single operational management center, to manage and monitor both projects and operations, must be introduced. This control center must perform the following tasks:

▶ Agree on and document the scope of changes and their technical specifications

▶ Allocate duties and responsibilities

▶ Track the project status and any problems that have to be documented and rated as Top Issues

▶ Define and adhere to procedures that specify, for example, that a problem does not exist if no support messages or issues exist

SAP Solution Manager provides a number of functions to support the operational management center with these tasks:

▶ Quality Management (see Section 3.2)

▶ Project Management (see Section 5.2)

▶ Solution Documentation and a Solution Documentation Assistant (see Sections 5.3 and 4.3)

▶ Test Management (see Section 6.2)

▶ Business Process Monitoring (see Section 8.2.2)

▶ Incident Management (see Section 8.7)

▶ Issue Management (see Section 8.4)

▶ Accelerated SAP (ASAP) implementation methodology (see Section 5.1.2)

▶ Run SAP method for implementing end-to-end solution operations (see Sections 1.6 and 5.1.1)

1.3   Lower Operating Costs by Standardization

As a result of global competition and growing pressure on margins, IT operating costs are being scrutinized more closely.

Reducing the total cost of ownership is another goal of SAP Enterprise Support. This can only be accomplished by standardizing processes and then monitoring them to ensure that they are executed properly (*process compliance*). It is also important that resources are deployed in the best possible way and bottlenecks are identified quickly. This requires the integration of all operational units.

The pressure to achieve efficiency and effectiveness in IT has never been higher. Companies with a first-rate IT environment can achieve lower than average costs. Such performance differences are also influenced to a large extent by qualifications and experience, but a lack of standards and a failure to use proven ways of doing business (*best practices*) can also increase costs. SAP Enterprise Support can help you reduce your IT operating costs by using consistent, established best practices and mature tools.

SAP has defined comprehensive operating standards for SAP Enterprise Support that reflect the experience of more than 35 years of providing support. SAP Enterprise Support also includes the Run SAP methodology for implementing standards for end-to-end solution operations. You can optimize your IT landscape in the framework of proven best practices for solution operations. They contain the following elements:

Using tried and tested best practices and tools

▶ Blueprint for optimized IT operations in respect to scalability, performance, consistency, and high availability throughout the entire SAP software landscape

▶ Industry-leading support processes for business-critical applications to reduce the time taken to solve problems

> ▶ Fully integrated change and quality management tools that you can use to consistently maintain high quality levels and establish a process of continuous improvement—to make changes with minimum downtime

Reducing operating costs

Research by the Americas' SAP Users' Group (ASUG) and benchmarking studies by SAP have revealed that operating costs of companies with first-rate IT operations are up to 55% lower than those of their competitors.

SAP Enterprise Support can help you lower your operating costs by replacing tools and services from third parties and giving your IT staff higher-value tasks.

You can reduce the amount of effort needed for testing, and thereby avoid downtime, which in an ERP system costs on average €5,000 per minute, by coordinating change management in the system landscape.[4]

All implementation projects are subject to budgetary and time constraints, so you cannot expect an implemented solution to be optimized for operations the moment it goes live. Potential for optimization only becomes evident once the solution is operational; generally, there is a savings potential of over 30% in terms of data expansion, response times, and business process acceleration.

You can use the tools and monitoring functions in SAP Enterprise Support to establish optimization processes across organizational units and locations. To work together within the company, employees need to be able to see the same data and the same information, and be able to trace problems and the results of attempts to solve them.

To make this a reality, SAP Enterprise Support offers holistic platform support and integrated solutions for Change Request Management and quality management.

Central view

SAP Solution Manager Enterprise Edition provides you with a central view of the Transport Management System in your solution — across technological boundaries.

---

4 BMC: *Maximizing DB2 Performance and Availability*. 2006.

This information can be the basis for comprehensive integration validation and consistent planning and execution of tests. In test management in particular, this means you can tell in advance precisely which business process will be affected by a given change. When performing integration validation, you can optimize certain parameters, for example, performance, data expansion, and business processes, before implementing the project as a solution and operating it live.

These processes adhere to the SAP standards for E2E solution operations and can be implemented using established Run SAP methodology procedures.

1.4 Optimizing Business Advantages

A key criterion for optimizing business potential is the automation of business processes. Exceptions (for example, storage bottlenecks, incomplete deliveries, or missing material in production) must be monitored closely to optimize the service level and production process.

Automation

A single solution across several application components and databases usually exhibits certain inconsistencies. When operating this type of solution, the extent of inconsistencies must be measured and rated, in terms of the speed with which queues, interfaces, automated workflows, and background jobs can be processed. Exceptions and disruptions must be kept to an acceptable level.

To achieve this, it is essential to create 100% transparency for the solution and ensure that all business processes are monitored — particularly if the solution is composed of custom developments and partner applications as well as SAP applications. This includes transparency of the *key performance indicators* of business processes. All queues, interfaces, workflows, and background jobs must be monitored, and data consistency must be ensured at all times. To facilitate smooth operations, SAP Enterprise Support provides functions that encourage efficient processing, for instance, the *Custom Development Management Cockpit* (see Section 5.5), and checks for adapting modifications and determining the maintainability of custom developments.

Key performance indicators

1.5 Achieving Innovation Without Disrupting Operations

You must be able to regularly update your application and technology components to ensure stable operation of your IT solution. These updates must be consistent so they can be implemented in the production system without disrupting business processes. A solution can only bring added value to a company if this is ensured.

Updates

SAP satisfies this requirement by continuously updating established best practices for all industry solutions, legal changes, and application and technology components. Such updates are made available in SAP enhancement packages (EHPs) and legal change packages (LCPs). Corrections for all components are also regularly shipped in Support Packages (SPs).

Reducing costs and risks

To ensure that your solution is continuously improved, potential costs and risks associated with implementing Support Packages, legal change packages, and SAP enhancement packages must be reduced. Costs result mainly from resolving conflicts with customer-specific enhancements and customized use of the software, as well as testing after changes are implemented. Risks arise from side effects that could not be foreseen when the decision was made to make the change.

To gain added value for the company from available updates, you need a detailed understanding of both the potential of the SAP software and the company's business requirements. The following points are central to accomplishing this goal:

▶ A *Customer Center of Expertise* (CCoE) for operating core business areas

▶ An efficient, reproducible, and transparent procedure for resolving conflicts

▶ An automated and cost-effective procedure for testing business processes

▶ A cost-effective and rapid procedure for creating test landscapes

▶ Less downtime in production landscapes

SAP Enterprise Support helps you here with its comprehensive, holistic approach to quality assurance that aims to ensure that changes can be made with minimal risks and minimal downtime.

Integrated and holistic quality management

Such changes must be made in a well-managed and controlled manner for each technology stack and application component in a solution. The groups in a typical support organization for technology and applications are usually structured on the basis of the expert knowledge in each area. This often means that many groups exist in different branch offices. It is often not possible for one expert team to manage changes independently, because applications depend on the technological basis, and business processes usually involve several application components. Even changes to the infrastructure, for example, the network, storage system, or databases, can affect applications.

All changes for all components in a solution must therefore be visible to a quality manager, who monitors the entire change process, from the change request to development, testing, and transfer to production.

Quality manager

SAP Solution Manager Enterprise Edition — the platform for SAP Enterprise Support — provides several new functions to enable a quality manager to perform this function:

▶ A central transport mechanism and a change control system to track changes across all technology stacks and application components, and intervene as required.

▶ Integration of all development environments in the central transport system (see Section 9.1 and 9.2).

▶ Central test plan management for your core business processes.

▶ Risk-based assessment of test effort, using the *Business Process Change Analyzer*, which analyzes the impact changes will have on business processes, before you import the changes into the test systems. This tool identifies risks quickly and easily (see Section 6.2).

▶ The role of the quality manager, who can verify which tests have been performed and the status of these tests for the whole company, in SAP Solution Manager. The quality manager has a central overview of the progress of projects in the *Change Management* work center, and can decide whether the criteria of the quality gates have been met.

▸ An integrated validation process (*integration validation*) for solutions that can be used to analyze the effects that planned changes will have on critical business processes, including test planning and execution.

In addition to these new SAP Solution Manager Enterprise Edition functions, SAP Enterprise Support changes a familiar role to satisfy the changed requirements. The manager of an SAP Customer Competence Center (SAP CCC) was mainly concerned with analyzing and solving isolated problems in IT operations. The manager of a Customer Center of Expertise (CCoE) can actively manage innovations, monitor the quality of the entire solution centrally, and maintain an up-to-date overview of the software being used, with the functions of SAP Solution Manager Enterprise Edition

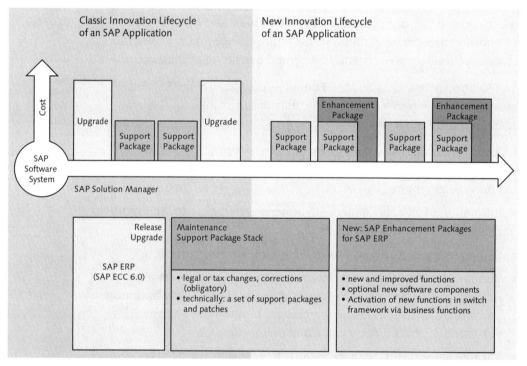

Figure 1.3 Changes in the Innovation Cycle of Applications

Companies of all sizes have applications that need to be integrated. Companies must change over to a service-oriented architecture (SOA) for a strong competitive position. You need a stable platform and higher-level support to drive such innovation processes. Innovations to the SAP software platform are usually implemented using SAP enhancement packages, third-party applications, and custom developments. SAP Enterprise Support makes it easier for you to introduce innovations using the SAP enhancement package architecture.

You regularly implement consistent updates that improve the technology platform, enhance application components, and encompass legal changes (see Figure 1.3).

The cost of implementing innovations is far lower with the SAP enhancement package architecture, because change management has been optimized in SAP Solution Manager Enterprise Edition, and factors that have a negative impact on business, for instance, downtime, are reduced.

SAP Enterprise Support and end-to-end solution operations are indicative of SAP's commitment to support technical enhancement. Customers are given the tools and information they need to better manage custom code and custom enhancements.

Innovation through third-party solutions and custom developments

Innovations can be achieved throughout the entire life cycle of your SAP platform, with minimal disruption to operations. A stable platform allows you to protect the investments you have made with ongoing innovations and strengthen your competitive position in a rapidly changing business environment.

1.6   Run SAP Methodology

Run SAP, the implementation methodology for end-to-end solution operations, is used to implement standardized processes for solution operations. The Run SAP methodology (see Figure 1.4) contains SAP standards for end-to-end solution operations within companies' business units and IT departments. These standards cover the requirements of both business process experts and IT specialists. Each of the standards contains proven methods for handling individual tasks, recommendations on using different tools in SAP Solution Manager, and information about training and services that help you implement the standard. For example, there are standards for managing change requests and changes, ensuring data integrity and transaction consistency, managing data volume, handling exceptions, monitoring business processes and interfaces, performing root cause analyses, managing and monitoring systems, and installing upgrades.

Project phases The Run SAP methodology Roadmap guides you through the following five project phases in standardizing and implementing solution operations:

- ▶ Assessment and planning of scope
- ▶ Designing operations
- ▶ Configuring operations
- ▶ Going live
- ▶ Live operations and optimization

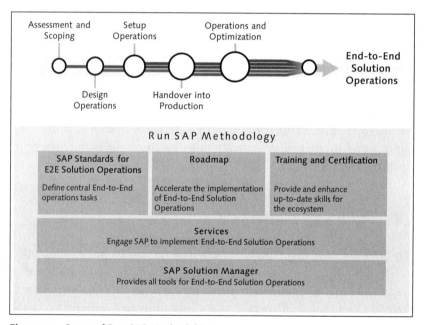

Figure 1.4 Scope of Run SAP Methodology

In addition to the Roadmap, the Run SAP methodology is composed of tools, services, training, and certification. The training courses deal with the four core competencies for end-to-end solution operations: root cause analysis, change control, business process integration and automation, and technical upgrade management. The courses and services are listed in the global catalog for services and training.

1.7 Supporting Business-Critical Processes

Another SAP Enterprise Support component supports business-critical processes. This offering provides continuous quality checks, explicit service-level agreements, clearly defined contact persons (*support advisory center*), and root cause analyses on a 24/7 basis.

Supporting business-critical processes requires rapid support, consulting, and knowledge transfer from experienced SAP experts, as well as services to ensure continuous optimization and quality assurance. This is done by the SAP Solution Manager collaboration functions.

Errors must be eliminated quickly and effectively to avoid costly downtime. If problems occur when your core business processes are performed, you need the appropriate expert knowledge immediately. With SAP Enterprise Support, you can access SAP Support's knowledge resources and cooperation technology to solve your problems as quickly as possible. SAP Enterprise Support also has global *incident management,* provided by SAP Active Global Support (SAP AGS) (see Section 8.7).

Global incident management

When you purchase standard company software, you outsource the provision of applications and technologies to a vendor, in this case SAP. You may then not always have in-depth knowledge of the technology and, in particular, application development in all areas of your company. You need standards and contractual agreements to operate, optimize, and update your software landscape. Such agreements can also stipulate that in the event of certain urgent problems, experts respond within an agreed response time. Your support partner must therefore provide the following services:

Service level agreements

▶ Perform root cause analyses within defined time limits, including an on-demand service provided by SAP experts or SAP's application and technology partners

- Provide fast and appropriate support from experts and developers via the SAP global support backbone
- Include partners and their products in incident management for priority 1 problems
- Carry out regular emergency exercises and tests of escalation procedures

The service-level agreements for SAP Enterprise Support stipulate times for initial responses and corrective measures. For example, if priority 1 problem messages are reported because a production system has gone down, SAP agrees to respond within one hour and initiate a corrective measure within four hours of receiving the message. If priority 2 problems are reported, SAP agrees to respond within four hours of receiving the message.

Corrective measures and action plans

Corrective measures are measures taken to eliminate a software error, devise a workaround solution, or define an action plan. An action plan includes regular updates, with the following information:

- Solution process status report
- Plans for next steps to solve the problem
- Activities that you or your partners are required to carry out
- Results of measures taken so far
- Date and time of the next status update
- Schedule for future activities by SAP to solve the problem

Support advisory center

SAP has established a network of *support advisory centers* for SAP Enterprise Support customers. The support advisory center is your central point of contact for all business-critical problems. It escalates your issues and provides 24-hour access to SAP's support control center. The support advisory staff can contact back-office support colleagues at all times, irrespective of where in the world the required experts are. The support advisory center also helps your organization plan and perform *continuous quality checks,* and makes recommendations to help you optimize the performance of your applications.

Continuous quality checks

SAP Enterprise Support continuously analyzes and evaluates your technical solutions and central business processes. Service engineers then recommend measures that you can take to optimize your processes and operations. For instance, SAP can check your system configuration and make recommendations on how to optimize parameters. To do so, SAP draws on its extensive knowledge database and up-to-date tried and tested procedures. The efficiency gains made in securing your operations free up resources for innovations and projects with high potential for added value. As part of continuous quality checks, you receive service reports. These reports include an action plan and recommendations with the following contents:

▸ Identification of technical risks and optimization potential

▸ Guidelines for smooth implement or upgrade projects

▸ Recommendations on how to improve system performance, availability, stability, and data consistency

1.8 SAP Global Support Backbone

The *SAP global support backbone* is composed of SAP Solution Manager Enterprise Edition, SAP Service Marketplace, and the SAP service infrastructure. It is the technical basis of SAP Enterprise Support. The 24-hour availability of SAP partners in the SAP global support backbone enables you to obtain a fast solution from SAP or its partners for all problem messages, from a *single point of contact*.

This collaboration gives SAP partners, such as value-added resellers, access to the same support processes, information, and tools that are available to SAP Active Global Support. If, for instance, you operate an SAP partner product in your IT landscape and encounter an error, you can perform a root cause analysis in your SAP Solution Manager, search for SAP Notes, and create a message and send it to SAP. The service engineers at SAP will carry out a more extensive root cause analysis. If the analysis reveals, for example, that a data inconsistency has occurred in the SAP partner software, the SAP service engineer can forward the message directly to the partner. Thus, the partner is directly involved in the message process and can use SAP's tools to perform root cause analyses and find a solution. The partner can send the solution to the customer directly, and publish it as an SAP Note in the SAP Support Portal. The

Collaboration in the SAP ecosystem

customer can track the status of the message at all times in SAP Solution Manager (see Figure 1.5).

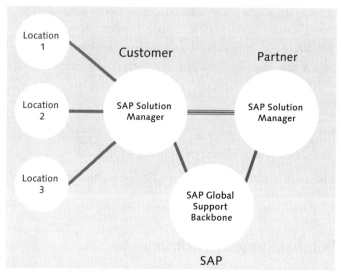

Figure 1.5 Collaboration in the SAP Ecosystem

1.9   SAP Enterprise Support – A New Offering for a New IT World

Comprehensive offering

According to leading industry analysts, SAP Enterprise Support is the logical next step in the development of SAP's support services with which SAP responds to both its customers' needs and the growing complexity and increased integration of IT systems. SAP Enterprise Support offers holistic life cycle management for both SAP solutions and partner and third-party applications. It supports continuous innovation and effective protection of investments.

Market leader

Thanks to SAP's extensive experience and comprehensive support infrastructure, potential problems can be identified in advance and avoided, root causes can be analyzed quickly, and operating costs can be reduced. The combination of more than 35 years' experience, continuous exchanges with customers and user organizations, and looking after the needs of over 75,000 customers has convinced SAP that SAP Enterprise Support offers the right level of support for every company, no matter what size.

SAP undertakes a clear obligation to support your business-critical industry solutions. With more than 5,000 technicians in SAP Active Global Support and more than 6,000 developers in 40 countries, there is always enough staff on hand to provide effective support for your business-critical processes, 24 hours a day, 7 days a week.

Quality and commitment from SAP to your success

In this way, your company can continue to grow in today's business environment and work toward new achievements.

SAP Solution Manager Enterprise Edition facilitates efficient application management and collaboration with SAP. This chapter provides an overview of the functional areas of SAP Solution Manager, and describes how it is embedded in the SAP support infrastructure.

2 Concept of SAP Solution Manager Enterprise Edition

The main task of a company's IT organization is to ensure that its business processes run smoothly. Ongoing operations must be stable, because existing applications must always be available and secure at reduced cost. The IT organization also has to support changes to stay competitive in the marketplace and react flexibly to changes in market conditions and other external factors. There is a conflict of interest between stability and flexibility.

Stability and flexibility

Your company is not the only one facing this problem. Almost all companies must address it. As a partner to its customers, SAP is also familiar with these issues, and has built up considerable expertise over the years to help companies like yours resolve this conflict of interest. How can you apply this expertise to your company?

This is what SAP Solution Manager Enterprise Edition does. As explained in Chapter 1, it is the central platform for SAP Enterprise Support. It enhances SAP Solution Manager, with which you are already familiar, supporting new requirements and options of SAP Enterprise Support while continuing to provide the existing application functions. SAP Solution Manager Enterprise Edition and SAP Solution Manager are synonymous in this book.

As well as providing the platform for SAP Enterprise Support, SAP Solution Manager Enterprise Edition enables you to optimize the processes in your IT organization and manage IT projects. SAP Solution Manager

Enterprise Edition provides support throughout the entire life cycle of your IT solution, and provides business-process oriented, transparent information for application management (see Figure 2.1). It also provides access to SAP knowledge in three ways:

▶ *Tools* to manage the tasks associated with your SAP solution. These include functions for managing changes, central monitoring, and the *Service Desk* for end user support.

▶ *Content* gives you examples of good solutions and methods that you can use as templates for your own projects. There are *Roadmaps*, for instance, for implementation and upgrade projects, templates for the flow of business processes, and process descriptions for IT organization tasks.

▶ *Services* provided by SAP experts are supplied by SAP Solution Manager where possible. For example, the *SAP business process management* service, which is a tool-based concept to ensure that your mission-critical business processes run smoothly. For an overview of the services provided with SAP Solution Manager, see Section 8.6.

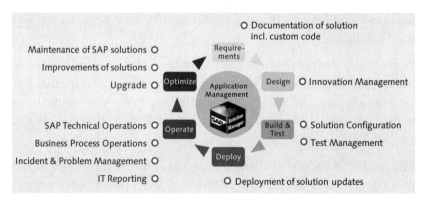

Figure 2.1 Complete Life Cycle Coverage

SAP Solution Manager supports six basic knowledge transfer concepts:

▶ **Integrated solution approach**

Mutual interdependencies and interfaces

Business processes don't usually run on only one software component. For example, a process for managing sales orders might have one component to receive the order, one for logistics, and another one for invoicing. To fully support the business process, all of the relevant components must be taken into account. Interdependencies and the interfaces between the components are just as important as the activities of the individual components.

▶ **Support throughout the entire life cycle**
The life cycle of software applications spans several phases: from initial deployment, through day-to-day operation, to continuous improvement, which can, in turn, involve the introduction of new or changed business processes. The software life cycle is continuous. Viewing individual phases in isolation typically leads to results that require major corrections later. The interdependencies between the phases are also relevant. For example, it is useful in live operation to know how business processes were implemented. To optimize a solution, you need information about the current operation status. This is why an integrated approach that spans the entire life cycle is indispensable.

Integrated approach

▶ **Business process orientation**
IT organizations provide services for a company's departments. Because each department typically has few IT experts, it is important to communicate the planning and results of IT services in a language that is easy to understand. A business process orientation facilitates transparent communication and understanding of IT services between IT staff and the user departments.

Coherent communication

▶ **Openness**
SAP customers also use applications from other suppliers. Software with additional features that are not part of SAP solutions, as well as competitor products are, to a certain extent, also integrated into business process management systems. To support the customer solution from beginning to end, such non-SAP products must also be covered to avoid delays in determining the cause of a problem and resolving it.

Products from third-party suppliers

▶ **IT governance**
Functions that already exist in SAP NetWeaver components or in products from SAP partners, for example, should not be retrofitted in SAP Solution Manager. SAP Solution Manager concentrates on planning the tasks to be completed, coordinating the use of existing tools, and documenting the results. SAP Solution Manager is a central plat-

Planning, controlling, monitoring

form for controlling IT processes that plan, control, and monitor the performance of activities.

▶ **Transparency**

Transparent documentation is fundamental to understanding activities and making correct decisions. Transparency is also becoming a more frequent legal and auditing requirement (for example, the Sarbanes-Oxley Act). In its transparent documentation, SAP Solution Manager collects all information required and makes it centrally available (see Figure 2.2).

SAP Solution Manager provides support for application management and collaboration with SAP based on these six key concepts. This applies to SAP customers and, in the event of hosting or application management outsourcing, to their IT service providers. Chapters 3 to 9 explain in detail how you can implement these concepts.

SAP strives to reduce the level of customer involvement in managing their SAP solutions as much as possible and to provide efficient support through SAP Services. SAP Solution Manager makes both of these goals achievable. In line with SAP's Accelerated SAP (ASAP) offerings, which are available to customers free of charge, SAP customers and partners can access the central SAP Solution Manager platform without having to pay extra.

Figure 2.2 Transparency in SAP Solution Manager

2.1   SAP Solution Manager as a Platform for Application Management and Administration

SAP Solution Manager assists you in application management. What exactly does this mean? To answer this question, we must first explain the scope of application management. Then we will show you which tools and content are available in SAP Solution Manager to complete the tasks in each phase of the application management life cycle.

The term *application management* comes from the *IT Infrastructure Library* (ITIL) environment. ITIL is the de facto service management standard, and includes planning documentation and the provision and support of IT services. ITIL is composed of several basic elements, including *service delivery*, *service support*, *infrastructure management*, and *application management*.

ITIL

Application management is a comprehensive support approach in the application environment, and spans the entire life cycle of IT solutions, from concept to phase-out. ITIL divides the life cycle into six phases:

▶ **Requirements**
Collection of requirements for new applications or for adapting existing applications

Application management life cycle

▶ **Design**
Conversion of requirements into detailed specifications

▶ **Build**
Application configuration and creation of an operating model in accordance with specifications

▶ **Deploy**
Transfer of any changes and the operating model into the existing, live IT landscape

▶ **Operate**
Provision of IT services required for ongoing operations

▶ **Optimize**
Analysis of service-level fulfillment and possible start of activities to improve results

Now we'll look at how SAP Solution Manager can help you perform activities in these phases.

2.1.1 Requirements

Collecting
requirements

Requirements is the first phase of the application management life cycle. In this phase, the requirements for changing the IT solution are collected and analyzed. These modifications can be functional or technical changes or suggestions for improving the usability of the solution. Individual requirements are approved or rejected. The type and scope of the requested change influence the rules used in the approval process. SAP Solution Manager supports this process with two scenarios: *Incident Management* and *Change Request Management*.

The *Service Desk* in SAP Solution Manager is an interface for end users and key users, primarily for troubleshooting. Because change requests are frequently made by system users, it makes sense for these requests to use the same interface. In this way, users can describe their requests via a familiar and easy-to-use interface.

Change Request
Management

Once a request has been entered in SAP Solution Manager, the approval procedure (part of SAP Solution Manager's Change Request Management function) starts. You classify the request to determine the approval procedure. The request passes through the appropriate approval procedure with documentation of the relevant information and decisions. At the end of the process, the request is approved or rejected.

It is important to have detailed information on the current status of the solution before approving change requests. What systems and business processes are affected by the change? How were these business processes implemented? Why? The answers to these questions are also in SAP Solution Manager, which already contains a description of your current solution. If you have not yet used SAP Solution Manager to document your solution, you can analyze your existing systems and generate documentation of them with the solution documentation assistant. You can also include information about third-party products in your decision.

2.1.2 Design

Translating
requirements into
a conceptual
design

After the request is approved, it is transformed into a project. This transformation begins in the application management life cycle *design* phase. This phase transforms the request into a detailed conceptual design, or *Business Blueprint* (see Section 5.4), in which general conditions for the implementation project and details for subsequent configuration of the systems are specified.

SAP Solution Manager provides project plans, or *Roadmaps* (see Section 5.1), that you can use as templates for your projects. A roadmap includes a structured list and descriptions of activities required for the project. This allows even customers and consultants with little experience to manage projects efficiently. Roadmaps also contain *Accelerators*, which are, for example, checklists or a link to tools that allow even experts to perform tasks better and more easily. Reporting functions in SAP Solution Manager enable you to monitor the current project status.

A wide variety of information accumulates for the project when defin- Scenarios ing the Business Blueprint in the design phase. One of the main tasks of SAP Solution Manager is to structure this information meaningfully. Because the goal is to implement or change business processes, structuring is based on these business processes: Scenarios are groups of related business processes. These, in turn, consist of process steps that can be performed in different systems (see Figure 2.3). The main advantage of this approach is that it is not limited to individual technical components. It covers the entire process, across systems, and takes account of dependencies between components.

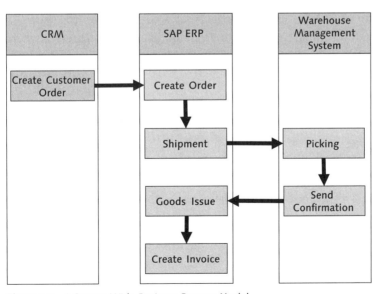

Figure 2.3 A System-Wide Business Process Model

Modeling future business processes is the first important task in the design phase. You determine how the individual business processes run in your company and what process steps will be performed in which components. This modeling can be carried out directly in SAP Solution Manager, or you can model in a professional graphic modeling environment and put the models in SAP Solution Manager.

You don't have to model from first principles. You can start with the results of the analysis of the current situation performed in the preceding phase. Adapt the result of the current analysis to the new requirements. SAP also provides a lot of business process templates in SAP Solution Manager. These templates are based on the experience of SAP and many customers from different industries. You can put these templates in your project and adapt them to meet your requirements to accelerate the modeling process in SAP Solution Manager (see also Section 4.2).

The next step is to assign the detailed information of the business processes, and their corresponding process steps, to the business process structure created. This includes configuring functions provided by SAP and setting up and configuring other software, such as your company's custom developments or software from third-party suppliers. This information is required for the subsequent realization of your project (see Section 6.1). When all required information has been collected and correctly stored, SAP Solution Manager has a complete, central Business Blueprint document. Everyone involved in the project can then access all of the information they require. This avoids incorrect information leading to inconsistencies and conflicts.

2.1.3 Build and Test

The Business Blueprint is the basis of the subsequent *build and test* phase. The specifications created must now be implemented in the applications. This includes configuring applications, checking whether the Business Blueprint was correctly and completely implemented, and implementing the operational model to run the solution effectively later.

You can configure the applications from SAP Solution Manager using the business process model in which you put the project information in the preceding phase. You always have direct access to its specification when configuring a business process or process step.

The customer-specific settings required to implement the specifications are configured directly in the applications. You can access the tools you need from SAP Solution Manager. This is especially useful to configure settings in several applications for your project, because you can access all required configuration objects from one central location. You also receive an overview of which activities have been completed and which have yet to be performed.

Business process configuration is also supported by the content of business process templates. In addition to the process models you used in the previous design phase, the templates include information about how each component has to be configured to implement the model. This saves you time searching for application settings.

Business process templates

Once you have configured your business process, you must check your settings. This test is usually performed in a quality assurance system, not in the system in which the settings were made. The settings are copied to the test system by software logistics. The changes made can be tracked by performing and logging approval procedures. This is another SAP Solution Manager Change Request Management function (see Section 9.1).

The next steps are to plan and carry out testing. You first identify the scope of the test to be carried out. Then create test cases to be performed, and provide the required test systems and data. Finally, carry out the tests and evaluate the results. SAP Solution Manager supports you throughout this process by providing functions such as the *Test Workbench* for managing tests and integrating other testing tools.

Test

As well as configuring the business processes, you must ensure during the build and test phase that these processes will run correctly by setting up an operational model. This model includes the creation and implementation of technical monitoring and reporting concepts, the configuration of user support, and data backup and recovery concepts. You can perform many of these tasks directly in SAP Solution Manager. SAP Solution Manager also provides a Roadmap, *Run SAP* (see Section 5.1), for configuring the solution operation. This includes information and checklists to help you learn from others' experiences, avoid mistakes, and configure your operating processes optimally.

2.1.4 Deploy

Live implementation of changes

Once you have successfully implemented and tested the requirements, the last step of the project is to implement them in production. This is the *deploy* phase of the application management life cycle, which involves the technical transfer of changes. Interruption of ongoing operations is to be avoided as far as possible. The users affected must be informed about the changes so they can use the improved solution optimally.

The settings are also transferred to the production landscape by software logistics tools, like the transfer to the quality assurance system, and by the SAP Solution Manager Change Request Management function.

Knowledge transfer

Knowledge transfer is as important as the transfer of settings, in the deploy phase. Users must learn how to use the new or changed business processes. Show the users the options available, and how to avoid mistakes, before the changes go live. The SAP Solution Manager *E-Learning Management* function (see Section 7.2) can help you do this.

2.1.5 Operate

Uninterrupted ongoing operations

After the implementation of the project goals comes the *operate* phase, the most important phase of the application management life cycle. Even though companies must make changes, day-to-day operations must continue to run smoothly. This is the goal of this phase. The IT organization must help users when they have problems, monitor the status of the IT solution and fulfillment of agreed service levels, and plan and perform system maintenance.

Users in your company having problems with the IT solution must receive help quickly to avoid a negative impact on business processes. SAP Solution Manager provides substantial support in this area. Problem messages are collected centrally in the Service Desk. For SAP components, a message is automatically sent from the application to SAP Solution Manager. System data is transferred at the same time, to help problem analysis.

The Service Desk shows the staff in your support organization, or your contracted IT service provider, the problem descriptions. Simple problems can be resolved immediately. You can search a *solution database* for similar cases in your company and SAP Notes. Existing solutions can resolve many problems quickly (see Section 8.7).

Solution database

If the simple solution search is not successful, you have two other options at your disposal. The first option is to use analysis tools to determine the root cause of the fault. For example, you can use the *Root Cause Analysis* function in SAP Solution Manager (see Section 8.8). Other tools can also be integrated, including those from the *Computing Center Management System* (CCMS) of SAP components. The second option is to forward problem messages to SAP Active Global Support for additional analysis and correction by SAP experts.

The administration of systems is another important aspect when it comes to keeping an IT solution running. To ensure system availability, many activities must be carried out on a regular basis, such as checking whether updates or background processes run correctly and whether system performance is satisfactory. The tools required for this generally are provided by the respective components. To avoid problems, you must check all activities to determine whether they were performed as scheduled. SAP Solution Manager provides functions for *Central System Administration* (CSA; see Section 8.1.1) for this purpose. Activities are then centrally logged for control purposes.

Central system administration

Another way of preventing interruptions is to use *technical monitoring*. Here, the current status of the IT solution is analyzed at regular intervals to proactively respond to irregularities before they affect day-to-day operations. SAP Solution Manager's technical monitoring process primarily utilizes technical warnings created in the connected systems by the CCMS monitoring infrastructure. Even warnings from application business logic, such as entries in the application log, can be integrated into Business Process Monitoring.

Technical monitoring

You can define different views to obtain a clearer overview of the warnings and their possible effects. Views graphically display warnings that relate to certain groups of systems or to the process steps of a specific business process. As such, your employees can filter out the data they need to complete their specific tasks. SAP Solution Manager also takes you from the warning itself to analysis tools that allow you to investigate a problem more closely and resolve its cause. For cases where the administrator also needs access to expert application knowledge to resolve a problem, additional information and contacts are stored for *Business Process Monitoring* of business processes to improve the quality and speed of the troubleshooting process (see Section 8.2.2).

Reporting Examining development over time is just as important as monitoring the current status so that trends can be detected and appropriate steps can be taken if necessary. This is where SAP Solution Manager's *Solution Reporting* function comes in. Solution Reporting allows you to use the data in SAP Solution Manager to assess system availability over a given period of time and the extent to which the agreed upon service levels were reached. You also have the option of flexibly creating and running your own reports.

Issue Management *Issue Management* is another function in SAP Solution Manager that you can use during the operate phase. This function helps you manage complex problems, or *issues*, that arise in your IT organization. One such issue could be resolving a problem that was discovered while monitoring. With Issue Management, you can centrally document issues, assign tasks and employees to an issue, add services and document their results, and address project-specific questions to SAP experts. Everyone involved in the solution process can access context-sensitive information to ensure that the issues are processed efficiently (see Section 8.4).

SAP Solution Manager also assists you in the operate phase by providing content in the form of business practices, which describe how activities in this phase can be performed.

2.1.6 Optimize

Implementing improvements If service levels are not fully met during the operate phase, improvements are made to the solution in the *optimize* phase. Improvements include measures to optimize software, as well as processes in the IT organization and in day-to-day operations. Here, the performance of maintenance activities, the installation of Support Packages and upgrades, and the provision of SAP Services are especially targeted.

SAP HotNews and *Support Package Stacks* are among the services SAP provides for SAP system maintenance. Support Package Stacks are released on a regular basis and include software corrections. SAP HotNews is composed of very high-priority SAP Notes that describe the solutions to problems that can cause system failure or a loss of data in the SAP system. Building on the knowledge of your solution, SAP Solution Manager filters out the Support Packages and SAP HotNews relevant to your situation. You can start the change implementation process in SAP Solution Manager immediately, make the change at a later time, or ignore it altogether. Whatever decision you make will be documented for later reference. Additional tools are used for the implementation process, such as Change Request Management and software logistics tools (see Section 9.1).

The *Maintenance Optimizer* function makes SAP Solution Manager a central control element for transparent and reproducible planning and implementation of all maintenance-related activities. The following are some of the functions the Maintenance Optimizer offers for maintaining your applications:

End-to-end maintenance of the software solutions

▶ Preconfigured, end-to-end processes for managing and maintaining the entire SAP landscape

▶ A central access point for planning and implementing all maintenance-related activities

▶ Primary source for all Support Packages and SAP enhancement packages that you received as part of your maintenance contract or license agreement

The maintenance functions allow you to control your software environment from a central location while managing ABAP and Java-based service software. Centralized monitoring functions for SAP applications provide maximum risk control for implementation and operation. This enables your SAP support team to implement corrections and enhancements more efficiently and reduce maintenance costs.

Improving IT processes is the second aspect of the optimize phase, for which SAP offers you a comprehensive range of services. These services are essentially supplied as part of the SAP support offering chosen by your company. *SAP Solution Management Optimization* services, for exam-

Improving processes

ple, focus on improving process flows, securing data consistency, increasing system availability, and avoiding performance problems. Most of the services can be used via SAP Solution Manager, because it provides much of the information required to perform the service in question. SAP Solution Manager is also the perfect platform for documenting the results of a service. These results are then made centrally available to everyone involved. Services generally are provided by SAP experts remotely or on site. Some of the services are available as *self-services*, meaning you can perform these services in your company without any outside intervention from SAP.

For a complete list of SAP services, see the SAP service catalog at *http://service.sap.com/servicecatalog*.

Upgrade

Another way to optimize your solution is by upgrading one of its components. Here, functional changes typically are made in addition to the basic technical upgrade, carried out similarly to the software maintenance procedure above. Functional changes are then also implemented in a project, as described at the beginning of this chapter in the requirements, design, build and test, and deploy phases of the application management life cycle. The optimize phase therefore does not signal the end of application management, but marks a new beginning of the life cycle.

2.2 Transparency

Another important aspect in addition to carrying out the individual activities in the six phases of application management is transparency. To be able to make the right decisions regarding your IT strategy, you need information on the status of your IT solution. Auditors also require information about who completed which tasks or changes and at what time. This largely has to do with meeting legal requirements. All of this information is gathered throughout the entire application management life cycle and must be organized and prepared.

Central data collection point

SAP Solution Manager serves as a central data collection point. This allows you to obtain an overview of your entire solution: what components are available, what their release level is, what clients are allocated to which component, and what Support Packages were installed. All of this information is required to define a release and maintenance strategy, for example. The information is also always up to date, because component data is automatically updated in SAP Solution Manager when the component changes.

In addition to being able to access the technical data for each component, SAP Solution Manager provides an overview of the implemented business processes: the processes that are supported by IT, how the processes run, and which process steps are executed by which component. This information is very important because it allows you to detect dependencies between your IT organization and business departments. What business processes are affected when a component malfunctions? What components need to be prepared if a particular activity is expected to considerably increase the volume of a business process?

You often have to be able to trace the configuration of an IT solution. **Documentation** Legal requirements such as the Sarbanes-Oxley Act or stipulations in the pharmaceutical industry require documentation of various activities along with the person who approved and performed them. This information is also necessary from the standpoint of internal quality assurance to check completeness and accuracy. For example, it can be useful to know what tests were performed with what results.

Another aspect of traceability has to do with why a business process was set up to run the way it does today. This can be relevant to problem analysis in IT support or when carrying out an upgrade project. Answers to such questions can be quickly found based on the documentation of finished projects as part of the solution in SAP Solution Manager.

Finally, your IT organization must be able to verify the services it provided for each department and determine their level of quality. Here, SAP Solution Manager provides support in the form of reporting options. Reporting options range from fully preconfigured reports such as *SAP EarlyWatch reports* through reporting templates that you can adapt to meet your individual needs (Service Level Reporting, for example), to the creation of completely individualized reports. If your company uses *SAP NetWeaver Business Intelligence* for your reporting infrastructure, you can transfer the relevant data there as well.

2.3 SAP Solution Manager as a Collaborative Platform

Using the tools and information provided by SAP Solution Manager as previously described will allow you to meet the application management requirements for your SAP solution. Here, too, teamwork boosts productivity, which is why supporting collaboration among customers, partners, and SAP is another important aspect of SAP Solution Manager.

The main advantage of collaboration is that people working in different areas with different expertise can help each other by sharing their expertise, which ultimately leads to better and faster solutions. If you want to improve the performance of an SAP solution, for example, you can optimize processes, change technical parameters, install higher-performance hardware, improve network infrastructure, or initiate other measures. SAP experts can also be consulted to guarantee a fast and effective solution for your particular task.

Accessing information

In a productive team, all team members must have access to the information they need to complete their tasks. This applies to technical, solution-based information, including details on the components and their associated business processes. Information on the project status is also required to be able to recognize synergies in a timely manner and to avoid redundancies, for example. SAP Solution Manager already has this information, thereby making it the central platform for collaboration (see Figure 2.4). Distributed projects especially profit from the central platform because important data is not saved locally, making it easy for other project participants to find.

In addition, SAP Solution Manager facilitates easy access to application systems used by experts to complete tasks and make changes. This further accelerates the speed at which experts can work, allowing the project to be successfully concluded much sooner.

Adding external experts

You can use SAP Solution Manager to collaborate in projects within your IT support organization or an *SAP Customer Competence Center* (CCC). This is why SAP Solution Manager supports projects of all sizes, from smaller projects to large implementation and upgrade projects. In some cases, you might not have the knowledge you need or the necessary resources to complete a project. When this occurs, you can rely on external support for your project. External experts can also be incorporated in the project with SAP Solution Manager.

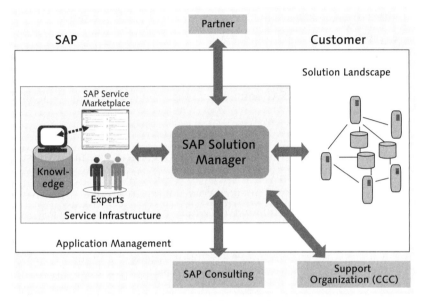

Figure 2.4 SAP Solution Manager as a Collaborative Platform

SAP Solution Manager not only promotes collaboration between experts from SAP, their partners, and your organization, but also allows for the delivery of special services to be automated, thereby increasing efficiency and ultimately lowering service costs.

Below is a list of some of the SAP service areas that use SAP Solution Manager to support efficient service deliveries:

► **SAP Active Global Support**
SAP Active Global Support and *Business Objects Support* experts can offer you a wide variety of services to implement a fail-safe, productive, and profitable solution, including online tools, on-site consultation, remote maintenance, and around-the-clock support from anywhere in the world.

SAP service areas

► **SAP Consulting**
SAP Consulting assists you in answering questions ranging from strat-

egy development and solution design, through implementation, all the way to continuous optimization.

▶ **SAP Custom Development**
SAP Custom Development specialists help you plan and implement customer-specific development enhancements to SAP solutions.

▶ **SAP Education**
SAP Education's product portfolio ensures that decision-makers, consultants, project team members, and end users in your company are in full command of SAP solutions so that you can fully leverage your SAP investment.

▶ **SAP Managed Services**
SAP experts will operate your system for evaluation purposes, during the implementation phase or throughout its entire life cycle, whichever you prefer. This eliminates your having to make a large investment in personnel and hardware while lowering overall IT costs and minimizing your investment risk.

Outlook These advantages underscore SAP Solution Manager's influence, which will become even more pronounced for SAP and customers alike in the future. Service-oriented architectures will increase flexibility in managing business processes. Many applications, including those from external providers, will be interlinked. Users have different options for accessing the systems, including portals, Microsoft Office applications, and mobile devices, all of which incorporate an increasing number of technologies that must be managed by the IT organization. In addition, cost savings on the part of existing customers, coupled with the rising number of mid-sized SAP clients, point to the trend of IT organizations becoming smaller.

Continuous support The goal of SAP's service and support strategy is to better assist customers trying to overcome this challenge. This encompasses continuous support for business processes from beginning to end, even if external applications are affected or included. Here, services are offered with an approach that is as customized as possible to improve customer value. To successfully implement this strategy, SAP provides a highly efficient support infrastructure with the SAP global support backbone (see Section 1.8 and 11.1). SAP Solution Manager is an essential part of this infrastructure.

2.3.1   Principles of an Effective Support Infrastructure

The support infrastructure provides the technical foundation for performing support services and for delivering services. Experts are given access to the information and systems they need, while communication between customers and SAP is improved. For experts to be able to efficiently complete the tasks assigned to them, a support infrastructure must meet six basic requirements, which are explained in detail in Figure 2.5. It must be proactive and bidirectional, accessible from a remote location, centrally located, complete, standardized, and secure. Fulfilling all of these requirements is fundamental for providing effective, high-quality support services.

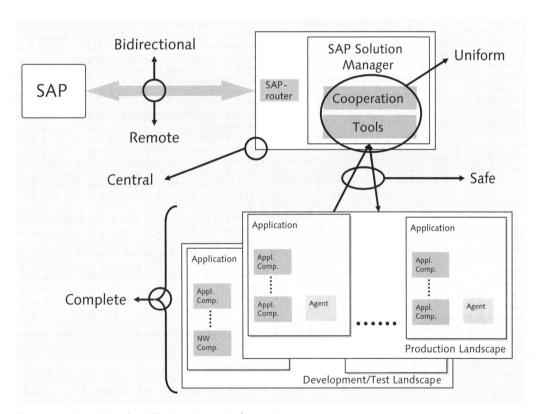

Figure 2.5 Principles of an Effective Support Infrastructure

Proactive and bidirectional approach

In the past, the customer typically initiated communication when support was needed. If a problem occurred, the customer notified Support and the issue was consequently resolved. As you can see, this approach was largely reactive. Efficient support, however, requires that communication be *proactive*, with possible malfunctions detected before they become real problems. This has a very positive impact on reducing downtime. Establishing such a proactive approach necessitates the regular exchange of information, both from the customer to SAP and vice versa. SAP Solution Manager has the capability to facilitate this exchange.

Complete solution

Whenever external experts work on your projects or assist you in solving problems, different systems invariably must be used. These systems can be development, test, or production systems, depending on the status of the project. Every application that controls your business processes can be affected. This includes not only applications from SAP, but applications from other providers as well. To secure the smooth operation of business processes across different systems and quickly discover the cause of interruptions, an efficient support infrastructure must be in place that covers your *entire solution*. Here, too, SAP Solution Manager lends a helping hand by linking all affected applications.

Standardized process

What application or technology is used to provide a service is immaterial; what matters is that the service be *standardized* if at all possible. Only in this way can high-quality services be realistically offered to a large number of customers. You, the customer, also profit from your familiarity with standardized SAP Services, because you do not have to constantly adapt to changes. Standardizing these services requires a central platform for coordination purposes—a platform such as the one provided by SAP Solution Manager.

Central location

To complete the assigned tasks, some of which involve different technologies, experts must have access to various tools. For distributed customer solutions such as service-oriented architecture, these tools may be located in different systems. Because external experts do not have a complete overview of your customer solution when they begin, it can be quite difficult to find the required tools, which consequently wastes time. To provide efficient support, your system landscape must have a *central access point* that can be used to acquire specific information on the solution and quickly access the required tools. SAP Solution Manager provides this central access within the SAP environment.

The large number of customers makes it impossible for SAP experts to provide every type of service and support on site for the customer. In addition, travel expenses would needlessly increase the end price. Another downside to physical travel is the fact that it impedes the problem-solving process from a time standpoint, especially when an urgent response is required. As such, the support infrastructure must give experts access to the required tools and information at the customer site from a remote location. *Remote access* to SAP Solution Manager and the tools and information provided by it occur via the SAProuter.

Remote access

To ensure that incorrect changes are not made to the system and to reduce the risk of a problem, *authorization levels* must be applied to the accounts of different system users to establish a clear *segregation of duties*. This can be achieved by following the authorization concepts of the individual applications. However, many areas, such as the operating system, make it quite difficult to give particular experts the exact level of authorization they need to complete their tasks. In this instance, it is simpler and more efficient for the service and support infrastructure to impose basic read-only access rights for critical areas of live applications. If an additional change must be made at this point, it should be kept as confidential as possible to avoid any abuse of change authorizations. On the other hand, documentation must be provided for the changes that were made, when they were made, and by whom.

Security

2.3.2 Role of SAP Solution Manager in the SAP Global Support Backbone

This section describes exactly how SAP Solution Manager is integrated into the SAP global support backbone and SAP support infrastructure and which tasks it assumes there. The support infrastructure is composed of not only SAP Solution Manager, but also the *SAP Service Marketplace* and other support systems for maintaining customer information, which are not accessible to customers.

The SAP Service Marketplace (*http://www.service.sap.com*) is a portal where SAP customers can find comprehensive, detailed information on the lat-

Components of the SAP support infrastructure

est version of SAP products and services. The information published here typically is of a general nature and is identical for all customers. The SAP SUPPORT PORTAL area of the SAP Service Marketplace provides access to support functions and services such as SAP Notes Search or the creation of customer messages. Customers can use these basic functions directly from the SAP Service Marketplace.

Additional benefits are provided by using SAP Solution Manager. By exchanging detailed information about the customer's solution, SAP Solution Manager and the SAP Service Marketplace ensure that the customer's processes are efficient.

Additional support systems for managing support processes are available at SAP. These systems, for example, include information on what support agreements you, the customer, have finalized with SAP. Based on this information, a decision is made on the services you are entitled to as outlined in your maintenance contract. Customers do not have access to these support systems. This system information is available in SAP Solution Manager and the SAP Service Marketplace accordingly.

Unlike the other components of the SAP support infrastructure, SAP Solution Manager is not deployed in-house at SAP (unless it is managed for you by *SAP Managed Services*). Rather, SAP Solution Manager is installed right on your premises or at one of your contracted IT service providers. Having close proximity to your SAP solution, and including a great deal of information on it, enables SAP Solution Manager to act as a bridge between your company and the support and services provided by SAP. In this way, you can use SAP Solution Manager not only as a pure information exchange platform, but also as a provider of services tailored to meet your specific needs.

2.3.3 Collaboration Processes

How does SAP Solution Manager promote collaboration between you and SAP? This question can be answered best by using the collaboration process examples listed below.

The Service Desk in SAP Solution Manager was described as an end user support tool in Section 2.1.5. This, however, is not the only way in which SAP offers assistance in solving problems.

A number of problems arise at several SAP customers. It is possible that the problem you currently are having has already been successfully resolved at another customer site. SAP describes solutions in the form of *SAP Notes*, which can be accessed on the SAP Service Marketplace. From the Service Desk in SAP Solution Manager, you can search for a specific SAP Note to help you solve your problem. When you search for SAP Notes, the information available in SAP Solution Manager is automatically taken into account. This can include details on a particular component and the release and Support Package version of the application. Having such integrated access to information provided by SAP can help you find the solution to your problem faster.

Message processing

If you don't find an SAP Note that addresses your problem, and you cannot solve the problem on your own, you can take advantage of an additional opportunity to collaborate with SAP by forwarding the message from the Service Desk to *SAP Active Global Support*. Here, the message does not have to be manually reentered on the SAP Service Marketplace. As well as receiving the actual message, members of SAP Support are sent additional information provided by your SAP Solution Manager to further assist the experts in analyzing your problem. This collaboration between you and SAP Support accelerates message processing as well (see Section 8.7).

The maintenance process initially described in Section 2.1.6 is also a form of collaboration between you and SAP. SAP provides you with collections of software corrections for various components and releases. SAP Solution Manager shows you which corrections are relevant to your solution. Applying the respective Support Packages and *Support Package Stacks* to your solution eliminates the risk of encountering the same problem already solved at another SAP customer site.

Maintenance process

SAP experts support you with the delivery of services. SAP offers a comprehensive range of services that help you manage special tasks and optimize processes. Services are delivered using SAP Solution Manager (see also Section 8.6).

Service delivery

SAP Solution Manager first gives you an overview of the services relevant to your solution. At this point, you can directly select a service you need. Experts from SAP or a qualified partner then deliver the service and document the results, their procedure, and any changes made to your system landscape or business processes in SAP Solution Manager. You can access these results in SAP Solution Manager at any time in the form of reports, which also include recommendations for additional activities. The information is then centrally available to all recipients and can be accessed at any time. If you require this information a short time later, being able to readily access it will help you avoid having to needlessly repeat analysis work. In the long term, comparing the results of individual services will allow you to detect trends.

Issue Management   You can use the *Issue Management* function in SAP Solution Manager for follow-up activities in connection with the delivery of a service. Here, information on more complex problems with regard to your IT organization and the activities related to it is centrally collected. This process was already described in Section 2.1.5. SAP experts can also be called on to solve an issue.

Whenever you request expert assistance for an issue, your request is sent to SAP together with information about the issue. This description helps SAP find the right expert, considerably reducing the time that would otherwise be required. Even greater time savings are therefore possible when analyzing the problem. A significant time saving can be achieved when analyzing problems. When the experts assigned to you access your SAP Solution Manager, they quickly receive an overview of the details surrounding your issue and learn what activities have already been performed by each of your employees, what services have been used, and what results have been attained thus far.

SAP Solution Manager also facilitates collaboration between your experts and the experts at SAP throughout the course of the project. This applies not only to Issue Management, but also to larger implementation and upgrade projects (see Sections 8.4 and 9.4).

Implementation and upgrade projects   All technical information related to your projects is stored in SAP Solution Manager. Having access to this information allows external experts to check the current status of your project at any time, therefore improving their level of integration and increasing the quality of the project's outcome. External project team members can also create project information from other locations, such as in their office at SAP. This further reduces project-related travel costs.

In addition to providing access to project documentation, SAP Solution Manager acts as a direct gateway to individual application systems on which the actual activities of the project are carried out. Included among these activities are detail analyses, application customizing, and testing (see also Sections 6.1 and 6.2). This not only improves the efficiency of your internal project team members, but also the efficiency of external experts, such as those from *SAP Consulting*.

2.3.4   SAP Services

SAP offers many services. To provide a clearer overview of these services, they have been organized within a service portfolio. One aspect of this portfolio is the phases of an IT solution life cycle in which a service is delivered (plan, build, and run):

▶ **Plan**
The services assigned to the planning phase are carried out before an SAP solution is implemented. The main challenges in this phase include the business and IT strategies, business process design, and the design of the system and application architecture.

▶ **Build**
All the services needed to implement your technical requirements in the software solution are assigned to the building phase. Examples include services for interfaces, migration, and support, which provide assistance during the transition to live operation.

▶ **Run**
With the majority of customers running live SAP solutions, this is a particularly important phase and is where standard support services come in, alongside services for optimizing and managing the technical infrastructure and the SAP solution.

The second aspect of the service portfolio has to do with the level of commitment the customer wants from SAP.   Range of services

▶ **Enablement**

An SAP solution cannot be used effectively unless users understand its structure, features, and how it works. SAP offers a number of courses and separate certification options to transfer this knowledge.

▶ **Quality management**

SAP provides quality assurance services to make sure your IT projects are completed on time and within budget, analyzes existing SAP solutions, and makes recommendations for optimizing or extending them.

▶ **Expert guidance**

SAP assigns the expert you need to assume complex tasks and work with you directly in your SAP system to solve the problem at hand.

▶ **Complete execution**

In cases where SAP assumes full responsibility for tailoring SAP software to your requirements, it can provide all of the services from one source — from project management, through technical implementation, to running the SAP solution. SAP will also implement large parts of an IT project if required.

This portfolio gives you a good idea of the services that are available to assist you in various situations. You can also choose the level of support you would like to receive from SAP. For the complete SAP service portfolio, go to *http://www.sap.com/services/portfolio/index.epx*. Additional information on specific services can be found in *SAP Service and Support*.[1]

Service packages
Individual services are grouped into packages that provide you with SAP's support offerings.

▶ **SAP Enterprise Support**

SAP Enterprise Support provides support when you introduce *end-to-end solution operations* and offers a coherent quality management process for all technology stacks and application landscapes, with the aim of optimizing the availability and performance of your business processes (see Chapter 1).

▶ **SAP MaxAttention**

SAP MaxAttention was developed for customers who prefer a cus-

---

1 Oswald, Gerhard: *Service and Support*. 3rd edition. SAP PRESS, Bonn. 2006.

tomized approach to support and maintenance. Customers who opt for this level of assistance can freely combine services to put together a Support Package that meets their exact needs. SAP MaxAttention aims to present customers with as much support as possible, which is why on-site teams are a key element of this offering. Additional elements include services from the SAP portfolio and service-level agreements.

▶ **SAP Safeguarding**
SAP Safeguarding is an analysis, tool, and service portfolio for minimizing the technical risk and expense associated with implementation, upgrades, migrations, and operation of your IT landscape. SAP Safeguarding services help you manage your core business processes, offering you risk management and service planning solutions.

In addition to these service packages, you can select services from the portfolio to best meet the requirements of your specific situation.

"Productization" is an important aspect of services. A new service can initially be provided only by experts, who are often considerably involved in development. SAP then systematically gathers its know-how and makes the service available for customers and partners. Although experts can only assist a few customers at first, their knowledge is subsequently transferred, and the service is further standardized and partially automated using tools in SAP Solution Manager, for example. This productization of services facilitates a fast and efficient transfer of knowledge, and lowers the cost for services that can be standardized while maintaining the level of service quality at the same time. Service delivery resources can also be used for new, customer-specific services offered by SAP to greatly contribute to your company's ability to differentiate itself on the market.

The *SAP EarlyWatch Alert* service aptly illustrates the different stages of productization. In the mid-1990s, SAP offered a consulting service that proactively analyzed performance. It built on its experiences to develop a remote service called SAP EarlyWatch Alert. An SAP service engineer would connect to the customer system remotely and check the system using a standardized service procedure. The service became much more widely available as a result. By 1998, it was being offered to all custom-

SAP EarlyWatch Alert

ers twice a year as part of standard support. Further productization saw the service become automated. Today, most customer systems generate SAP EarlyWatch Alerts, which are collected by SAP Solution Manager for use in conjunction with reporting functions, for example (see Section 8.2.3).

Because not all SAP Solution Manager functions and scenarios relate to precisely one application management phase, but rather some are of a cross-phase nature and geared more toward the entire life cycle, such functions are explained in this chapter at the beginning of the application management life cycle.

3 Cross-Phase Functions and Concepts in SAP Solution Manager

This chapter introduces the second part of the book, which covers in more detail the SAP Solution Manager functions outlined in Chapter 2. Chapters 4 to 9 give in-depth descriptions of the phase-specific scenarios. We will begin, however, by looking at the cross-phase concepts.

One of the main reasons integrative concepts now play such a prominent role in IT is because IT solutions are becoming ever more complex. If we take an example from the automotive industry, it becomes clear that this trend is not unique to the software industry but has become the general norm. Even today, multi-speed gearboxes remain much simpler to manufacture than automatic ones, but automatic gearboxes are much easier for drivers to use. The fact that this technology has been embraced differently in different regions undeniably indicates that no single solution suits the whole market. It also shows that differentiation (such as semi-automatic gearboxes and special automatic gearboxes for commercial vehicles) can tap new potential. In the IT industry too, all market players must make it their goal to take the strain off *business users* as much as possible and permit them the degree of automation required for their day-to-day work.

SAP has recognized this need and offers a *service-oriented architecture* concept that facilitates this goal and allows business users to run IT solutions in portals or from their familiar office environment.

Differentiation

Manageable complexity

SAP Solution Manager's central, integrative role makes necessarily complex IT solutions manageable and transparent, enabling project managers and business users to specify the required level of automation and centralization.

Furthermore, SAP Solution Manager links business and IT. Centered around business processes, it enables users to navigate from the original business process model and its documentation right down to the technical level, providing anyone who implements, uses, or owns a process with all the relevant information.

Process-centric view

SAP Solution Manager is designed to address a need frequently expressed by users and analysts: the need for a holistic view of software solutions that ceases to revolve around functions and software components and concentrates instead on processes and integration; the need to turn the spotlight away from the actual technology and focus instead on its significance for customers, helping them realize their business processes effectively and efficiently.

This is why end-to-end processes are at the heart of SAP Solution Manager. They integrate software from other vendors and, above all, let you take an active role in integrating the phases of a software solution's life cycle. The following scenarios illustrate why these end-to-end processes are so critical.

3.1   The Work Center as the Central Access Point for SAP Solution Manager

As system landscapes grow ever more complex as a consequence of heterogeneous systems and more complex solutions, your company needs a well-oiled support model.

SAP standards for solution operations

By creating the SAP standards for solution operations, SAP's aim was to foster closer working relationships with customers and partners so that standardized processes and workflows for supporting system landscapes could be defined to enable all parties to exchange experiences and reach a common level of understanding of the operations and support requirements for the future.

The outcome of these collaborative efforts can be found on the SAP Service Marketplace at *www.service.sap.com/supportstandards*. They offer numerous best practices that address a range of topics and their significance in complex processes, for example increasing complexity, rising costs and risks, poorer quality, and required resources. These best practices are the result of more than 30 years' experience providing SAP support.

A generic organizational model helps you identify employees, together with their teams and allocated tasks and roles, who are incorporated into the support process. The SAP standards for solution operations help you define and optimize processes both within and outside the team (for example, SAP Support).

Employees and their daily workflows are brought together using the SAP Solution Manager application platform. This process is supported by the new work center concept.

3.1.1   Role-Based Access to Functions

Compared with the previous SAP Solution Manager user interface, the main benefits of the work center are its ease of use and the fact that it provides users with central, role-based access to all the work areas they need. Standardized navigation and fast access to required information provide greater assistance to users as they go about their daily tasks.

Each work center is divided into three navigation levels that give you access to your work areas within SAP Solution Manager. A navigation bar is provided for main navigation. You navigate at a detailed level in the contextual navigation area and perform your daily tasks in the content area (see Figure 3.1).

You can call up the work centers assigned to you using tab pages in the navigation bar on the user interface. Navigation is single-level. The tab pages guide you to your daily activities and enable you to complete function-related tasks within the work center.

Navigation bar

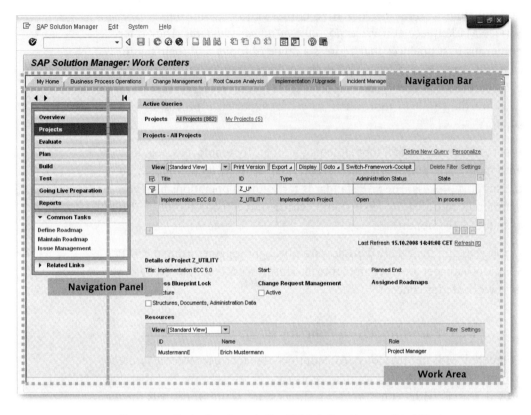

Figure 3.1 Navigation Areas in the SAP Solution Manager Work Center

Work centers support task-specific activities, for example, message processing in Incident Management and creating new change requests or maintenance transactions in Change Request Management. The contextual navigation area gives you access to all of the functions, transactions, and evaluations you need to complete your particular activities.

Contextual navigation area

The contextual navigation area is the central navigation element of every work center. It provides the following:

► Access to views in the chosen work center

► Access to the work center's common tasks and functions

► Access to related links, that is, information and functions that are in some way related to the work center

You access task-specific information and functions using the second navigation level, namely, the work center views. The content area of the work center is guided by the view you select. This area contains all information relevant for the user.

Navigation area views

If, for instance, you use SAP Solution Manager to implement a system in the company, the Implementation/Upgrade work center gives you access to the following views: OVERVIEW, PROJECTS, EVALUATE, PLAN, BUILD, TEST, GOING LIVE PREPARATION, and REPORTS (Figure 3.2).

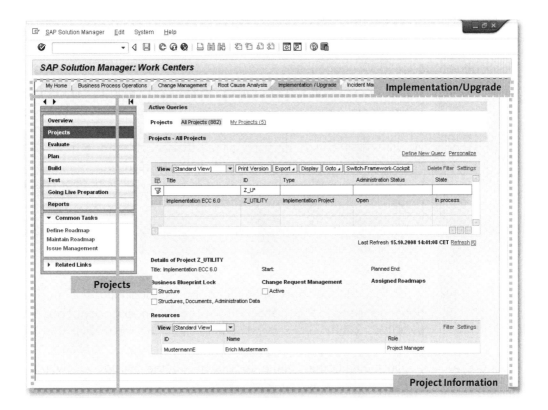

Figure 3.2 Example – Overview Navigation Area in the Implementation/Upgrade Work Center

To call up an overview of your current project, navigate to the OVERVIEW view. The content area displays a list of projects that are relevant for you. When you select your project, all related detailed information is shown. Furthermore, you can navigate to the project's configuration or administration.

Common tasks

Common tasks are the activities you need to carry out most frequently when working in a role-based work center. For example, defining and editing a project Roadmap is a common task when a project is being implemented and is therefore included in the work center. You can call up the DEFINE ROADMAP and MAINTAIN ROADMAP activities using a link in the work center.

Related links

The RELATED LINKS area in the navigation bar contains hyperlinks to additional useful information and functions relevant for the chosen work center.

Test and production systems for an implementation project are usually not available at the outset of the project. Therefore, the test system in which tests will be performed and the production system in which the go-live will take place must be managed at a later point in time. The SYSTEM LANDSCAPE link is provided in the Implementation/Upgrade work center to enable administration of these systems to be accessed centrally.

Content area

The content area of the work center is guided by the view you select. Task-specific information and functions are displayed as *object lists* or *service maps*.

Object lists

When you select an entry in an object list, additional detailed information is displayed in screen areas known as trays. To limit the information displayed to what you need and obtain a clearer overview of all information, you can collapse irrelevant trays and expand the relevant ones. This display method can be found, for example, in the OVERVIEW view in the Implementation/Upgrade work center.

Service maps

Service maps provide you with assistance in completing certain tasks and provide additional information in the form of further explanations and icons that you can use to call up corresponding functions. Service maps are displayed, for example, in the TEST view in the Implementation/ Upgrade work center (Figure 3.3).

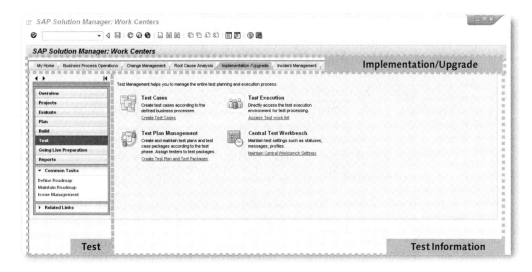

Figure 3.3 Example – Test Navigation Area in the Implementation/Upgrade Work Center

3.1.2 Available Work Centers

You have access to the following work centers in SAP Solution Manager:

▶ SAP Solution Manager Administration

▶ Implementation/Upgrade

▶ Solution Documentation Assistant

▶ System Landscape Management

▶ System Administration

▶ Change Management

▶ Job Management

▶ System Monitoring

▶ Business Process Operations

▶ Incident Management

▶ Root Cause Analysis

▶ SAP Engagement and Service Delivery

▶ Test Management

SAP Solution Manager Administration

The *SAP Solution Manager Administration* work center provides central access to the SAP Solution Manager Self-Diagnosis function as well as all of the other functions you need to manage SAP Solution Manager scenarios. The work center is divided into the following views: OVERVIEW, SOLUTIONS, PROJECTS, SYSTEMS, USERS, and ADMINISTRATIVE TASKS.

The SAP Solution Manager Administration work center enables you to perform all administrative activities in all SAP Solution Manager phases — implementation, operation, and optimization.

Central access to all projects, solutions, and systems

The SAP Solution Manager Administration work center provides you with central access to all projects, solutions, and systems. The work center enables you to rapidly create and configure new projects, solutions, and systems, and make changes to them if necessary. In addition, it gives you direct access to User Management to ensure that daily work activities flow smoothly.

The results of the last self-diagnosis and the status of processing are provided in summary form in the SAP Solution Manager Administration work center so you can immediately identify any errors occurring in SAP Solution Manager and its solution landscape and take appropriate action (see also Section 8.1.2).

Implementation and Upgrade

All technical and system-relevant information related to your projects is stored in SAP Solution Manager in the Implementation/Upgrade work center. This information can be of use when you are implementing and upgrading your solution. The work center is divided into the following views: OVERVIEW, PROJECTS, EVALUATE, PLAN, BUILD, TEST, GOING LIVE PREPARATION, and REPORTS.

You can obtain information about the current status of your project at all times in the Implementation/Upgrade work center. The central storage location for all activities and results relevant for implementations and upgrades in SAP Solution Manager creates transparency so you can track project progress and ensure that quality levels are maintained throughout the entire project life cycle.

Thanks to its transparency, this approach provides an overview of project work that solves problems experienced previously, for example, decentralized storage of preliminary concepts, Business Blueprints, and technical specifications; documentation of business processes; and documentation of customer-specific settings, test concepts, and training materials. Furthermore, it allows you to exploit synergies to work more effectively in your project and ensure that knowledge is transferred once the project is complete.

Overview of project work

The work center addresses these problems by guiding you through all phases of your project and creating transparency over all project events with the central storage location.

Finally, the REPORTS function enables you to obtain a snapshot of your project situation and report on the current status.

Solution Documentation Assistant

If you have not yet documented your existing business-critical processes, you navigate to all of the functions you need to analyze your solution landscape using the *Solution Documentation Assistant* work center (see also Section 4.3). The ANALYSIS PROJECTS, ANALYSES, and RULE DATABASE views help you automatically analyze your system landscape.

The task of making manual entries with several different tools and the time and resources associated with creating subsequent documentation were identified as cost drivers for customers and partners. Existing synergies can be exploited by using the existing SAP Solution Manager infrastructure and retrieving data automatically with the SAP EarlyWatch Alert function.

All information about existing analysis projects is displayed in the ANALYSIS PROJECTS view. This includes the project to be analyzed, the analysis results, and relevant details such as SYSTEMS, PERIODS, and GLOBAL SETTINGS. The upload function in this work center allows you to transfer the results to a project for further processing in the Implementation/Upgrade work center.

Analysis projects

System Landscape Management

The System Landscape Management work center provides central access to all of the functions you need to manage your system landscape. The work center is divided into the following views: OVERVIEW, SYSTEM MANAGEMENT, DOWNTIME MANAGEMENT, and TRANSPORT MANAGEMENT.

In the OVERVIEW view, the availability status of the systems is shown using icons. Depending on which query is active, you can select from a list of your systems together with corresponding information. When you make a selection, detailed information is provided, including the product version, main instance, and software component. You then choose the link to navigate directly to the next screen on which you can manage the system landscape.

Downtime Management

Using the respective functions in the DOWNTIME MANAGEMENT view, you can make transparent plans for security audits or system restarts. You can access the functions to define transport routes using the navigation options in the TRANSPORT MANAGEMENT view. Additional functions, for example the SWITCH FRAMEWORK COCKPIT or AUTOMATED TECHNICAL CONFIGURATION can be called up using the respective links.

The switch framework cockpit is a central point of access to the switch framework settings for your system landscape. You can use it to activate shipped business functions or deactivate them if they are reversible. The cockpit also provides you with a view showing the current status of all business functions. You can automate and standardize connections between systems in the SAP Business Suite by choosing the AUTOMATED TECHNICAL CONFIGURATION link. Once you have selected your project, the possible connections are displayed, and you can activate them at the touch of a button.

System Administration

Administration

The System Administration work center helps you complete administrative tasks associated with the solutions, systems, and instances in your system landscape. You can complete such activities either by calling up the ADMINISTRATION TOOLS and USER MANAGEMENT views directly, which contain all of the traditional administrative transactions, or by using TASK MANAGEMENT. The latter not only brings together tasks that were created in other SAP Solution Manager applications, for example, in Job Scheduling Management or Issue Management, but also incorporates tasks you have scheduled as part of central system administration.

In addition, you have the option of creating tasks in Task Management and optimizing system administrative processes, for instance, by delegating tasks to the work centers.

Change Management

The Change Management work center is the direct access point for all of the functions you need to make changes in your systems and handle them in the best way possible. The work center is divided into the following views: OVERVIEW, PROJECTS, CHANGE REQUESTS, CHANGE DOCUMENTS, HOTNEWS, MAINTENANCE OPTIMIZER, LICENSE MANAGEMENT, QUERIES, and REPORTS.

A summary of all important objects is provided in the OVERVIEW view. To ensure that any tasks that you have created or that have been assigned to you can be handled by a colleague in your absence, members of your organizational unit are able to view them. You can process your tasks by calling them up directly with a link.

The PROJECTS view provides you with the current status of changes to an ongoing project or a solution. Information such as current status, active phase, milestones, and quality gates is brought together and displayed in visual form. Additional detailed information is shown in the processing list.

You can view change requests or change documents using the link provided in the overview or by going to the corresponding views, namely, CHANGE REQUESTS and CHANGE DOCUMENTS. To process a change request or change document, choose the links shown in the list.

The HOTNEWS function belongs to the functions for managing change requests in SAP Solution Manager. Before you create a new change request, you can use the HOTNEWS view to see solution-related SAP Notes that explain how to avoid or solve problems that might lead to loss of data or SAP system downtime.

Maintenance
optimizer The purpose of the *Maintenance Optimizer* view is to help you with the product-related maintenance of your system landscape. A processing list shows all product maintenance activities that have already been requested. You can request new transactions in the COMMON TASKS area using the NEW MAINTENANCE TRANSACTION link.

If you are not authorized to carry out maintenance, you can view the current status of your product license and maintenance certificate in the LICENSE MANAGEMENT view. You can trigger the maintenance certificate to be requested, updated, and distributed automatically directly from this view.

You can use the task list to complete your open tasks and activities. Detailed information about each task, for instance, its current status and its maintenance cycle or status, is available from the task list. You use the Task Manager to implement it.

Personalized
queries
In the QUERIES view, you can save your own profile so that you do not have to filter for your required settings every day. By using personalized queries that provide your specific data each day, you can avoid long and laborious searches.

The REPORTS view in the Change Management work center allows you to analyze data and output it centrally.

Job Management

The Job Management work center provides central access to all of the functions you need to enter, document, schedule, and monitor background jobs. The work center is divided into the following views: OVERVIEW, JOB REQUESTS, JOB DOCUMENTATION, JOB MONITORING, TASK INBOX, and REPORTS.

If you want to request a new job or make changes to the function of a job or scheduling sequence in daily operations, you use the JOB REQUESTS view. If the request has been approved via the workflow process, it must be fully documented. You have direct access to the JOB DOCUMENTATION view, where you can maintain information, for example, about organizational units, systems, or error handling.

For jobs that have been scheduled already, you can choose between JOB MONITORING as a reactive monitoring function or CENTRAL PROCESS SCHEDULING and JOB SCHEDULING as a proactive monitoring function. JOB MONITORING provides you with the monitoring status using alerts. If you opt for CENTRAL PROCESS SCHEDULING and JOB SCHEDULING, you can define your own queries that inform you of the status of scheduled jobs.

Note that the JOB MONITORING function is directly dependent on the Business Process Operations work center. To be able to use job monitoring in the Job Management work center, you must first make the basic settings in the Business Process Operations work center.

Dependencies

Activities relating to Job Scheduling Management that you or your colleagues have entered or intend to enter using Task Management can be found in the TASK INBOX view. In this view, you can enter a task or choose a link to navigate directly to a task to complete it.

System Monitoring

The System Monitoring work center provides central access to all functions required to monitor systems. The work center is divided into the following views: OVERVIEW, SYSTEM STATUS, ALERT INBOX, PROACTIVE MONITORING, CONNECTIVITY MONITORING, JOB MONITORING, SELF DIAGNOSIS, SETUP, and REPORTS. All monitoring information from the individual views is summarized in the overview.

The SYSTEM STATUS view provides you with an overview of the status of system availability in the form of icons. Detailed information about the instance, server, and status is displayed when you select a system.

Incoming alerts with the current status are displayed in the ALERT INBOX. From there, you can view additional information about the reasons for an alert, which helps you to analyze problems. Directly from an alert, you can create a service desk message containing all relevant details, reset the display of the alert, or confirm that it has been processed.

Alerts

The PROACTIVE MONITORING view allows you to verify the status of your systems before alerts are generated. A range of system-specific monitoring tools enable you to continuously check the status of ABAP and Java application servers before alerts have been generated. In addition, you can monitor selected RFC connections and the status of background jobs centrally.

The SELF DIAGNOSIS function is used to run background consistency checks on processes and configurations and draw attention to any impairments to important functions with critical alerts (see also Section 8.1.2).

Reports The work center provides you with access to the most essential reports, for example, SAP EarlyWatch Alert and Service Level Reporting, so you can output monitoring data centrally (see Sections 8.2.3 and 8.2.4).

Business Process Operations

The Business Process Operations work center provides central access to all of the functions you need to monitor your business processes and interfaces. The work center is divided into the following views: OVER-VIEW, SOLUTIONS, BUSINESS PROCESSES, ALERT INBOX, DATA CONSISTENCY MANAGEMENT, DATA VOLUME MANAGEMENT, and REPORTS.

Monitoring data for solutions and processes The work center allows you to display the currently available monitoring data for your solutions and business processes using alerts. You can change the alert mode if you want to filter the monitoring data on display.

Detailed information about a solution or business process is shown when you select the respective entry in the processing list. The information pertaining to solutions is divided into business scenarios and processes; for business processes it is further subdivided into process steps and technical interfaces. The graphic function displays all available information in aggregated form.

Alerts You can use the ALERT INBOX to process or confirm alerts directly. It allows you to display OPEN ALERTS or the CURRENT STATUS.

▶ OPEN ALERTS shows the alerts you have not yet analyzed and confirmed.

▶ CURRENT STATUS shows the current alerts relating to the last data collection.

In addition, you are given an overview of planned and delivered services and data volume management. The DATA CONSISTENCY MANAGEMENT view gives you an insight into the business process monitoring alerts that concern data consistency and help you analyze data consistency.

The REPORTS view offers a central place where the most important reports for business process and interface monitoring are provided.

Incident Management

The Incident Management work center provides central access to all of the functions you need to enter and process messages. The work center is divided into the following views: OVERVIEW, MESSAGES, QUERIES, and REPORTS.

Message processing

This work center provides you with a summary of messages, sorted according to status and the function assigned to your business partner. In addition to the messages that you have created or for which you are assigned as the processor, your organizational unit is able to see all other messages as well. This ensures that messages are processed even if the processor is absent.

As a message processor, you can navigate to the MESSAGES view, where all messages are shown in the processing list. Message processing opens when you select a message from the list.

You can save your own profile so that you do not have to set your required filters manually each time. To do so, you choose the QUERIES view. By using personalized queries that provide the particular data you require each day, you can avoid long and laborious searches.

Personalized queries

The work center provides access to the reporting functions and allows you to output your data centrally in the REPORTS view, for example, SOLUTION-SPECIFIC REPORTS.

Root Cause Analysis

The Root Cause Analysis work center provides central access to all end-to-end and component-specific tools of solution manager diagnostics. These tools can be used to analyze errors across the entire landscape, regardless

Analysis tools

of the technology in use. The work center offers structured access to the tools, from end-to-end root cause analyses (end-to-end workload analysis, end-to-end exception analysis, end-to-end trace analysis, and end-to-end change analysis) and system-specific analyses (for example, change reporting or CA Wily Introscope) to host-specific or database-specific analysis tools such as the file system browser, OS command consoles, or database monitoring. The range of filter options allows you to group different systems according to user requests and needs and use them in the analysis.

In addition, you can configure and perform error analyses on the tools for root cause analysis directly from the Root Cause Analysis work center. The work center offers a number of tools and a self-diagnosis function for this purpose.

SAP Engagement and Service Delivery

The *SAP Engagement and Service Delivery* work center is the central access point for SAP support staff and the starting point for providing a service to customers using the corresponding Service Session (automated checklist) on the basis of assigned issues. All important information about the overall situation surrounding the customer solution(s) is provided in the work center. This information includes all services that have already been performed or are planned (see Section 8.6), existing issues and Top Issues (see Section 8.4), the scope of the respective customer solution (processes and systems, current projects), and the current status of the systems (SAP EarlyWatch Alert services performed). Central access to service reports is possible; that is, you can choose a link to navigate directly to the SAP Service Marketplace message belonging to the service, where you can give feedback on a service provided by SAP.

Service report   The outcome of an SAP service is a report containing both an account of the analyses that have been performed and detailed, mainly technical recommendations (tasks) to resolve the issues. Together, the tasks for one or more issues or Top Issues form the action plan, which schedules and prioritizes the recommendations and assigns persons or groups. Because the issues, Top Issues, and tasks are all SAP Solution Manager objects, they not only exist as part of the service report but can also be distributed to the employees responsible as tasks. It is also possible to monitor their status.

In the work center, you can manage all Top Issues centrally, define corresponding action plans, and work your way through them with services. This is why the SAP technical quality assurance manager works in this work center. This person's duties include ensuring that issues are assigned to planned services and that the focus of services is set correctly.

The REPORTS view allows you to gain a quick insight into the status of issues, Top Issues, and SAP Enterprise Support engagement for reporting purposes.

Test Management

The Test Management work center provides central access to all test activities in SAP Solution Manager. The work center is divided into the following views: OVERVIEW, TEST PREPARATION, TEST PLAN MANAGEMENT, TESTER WORKLIST, TEST EVALUATION, SETTINGS, and REPORTS.

The work center views reflect the overall process flow for integration testing. Solutions and projects can be taken as the foundation for testing. The OVERVIEW offers you a central, aggregated view of all information that is shown in the individual work center views.

Process flow

You make your preparations for test activities in the TEST PREPARATION view. On the basis of projects or solutions, it is possible to enter test cases in or assign test cases to the business process structure of the Business Blueprint or the Solution Directory. By doing so, you lay the foundation for creating or editing test plans in the TEST PLAN MANAGEMENT view. This is also the view in which you create test packages and assign them to testers.

Test preparation

If you have been assigned to a test package as a tester, you access your test cases either by choosing the MY ASSIGNED link in the TESTER WORKLIST area in the OVERVIEW view or from the TESTER WORKLIST view directly. The processing list shows the test packages that have been allocated to you. By choosing links, you can enter processing mode directly, for example, to enhance existing documents, enter or track the status of enhanced messages, or close test cases.

The Test Management work center provides you with access to the TEST EVALUATION and REPORTS views so you can evaluate test progress and additional test data.

If you would like to adjust the basic settings for integration testing, you can do so in the SETTINGS view. The icons allow you to make settings for the Test Workbench and business intelligence (BI) reporting.

3.1.3 My Home

The My Home work center is a personalized, central entry point for your daily work in SAP Solution Manager.

My Home aggregates all information and tasks from the work centers assigned to you so you can see them at a glance. The work center is divided into the following views: OVERVIEW, WORK, and REPORTS.

Overview The OVERVIEW view of the My Home work center brings together all of the information that is presented in the overviews of the work centers assigned to you. You can personalize the standardized default to limit the scope of the OVERVIEW to the information relevant for you by hiding irrelevant information and composing your own particular layout. Once you have personalized your My Home work center, you only see the information and activities you need for your daily work.

Central entry points to different communities, for example, the SAP Developer Network (SDN), wikis, and other forums, are in the pipeline for My Home.

3.1.4 Configuring the Work Centers in SAP Solution Manager

SAP has restricted the necessary configuration steps to two areas — services and roles — to enable you to configure your work centers quickly and with a minimum of technical difficulty.

The SAP Solution Manager Implementation Guide takes you through the steps to activate the services and manage the authorization roles for your existing role concept. This simple enhancement means your previous configuration remains unaffected.

This approach allows you to avoid major additional expenses for consulting services or training and enables your IT department to incorporate new company areas into the SAP Solution Manager concept.

3.2 Integrated and Consistent Quality Management

Controlled and quality-assured change management is a key element in highly integrated solution landscapes to ensure that SAP applications are highly available and operate reliably. Throughout the entire life cycle of an SAP solution, most changes and enhancements are made at the application level. They involve transferring custom software developments or Customizing settings made within the scope of projects or customer-defined shipment cycles to production operation. Such changes require a traceable, standardized IT process that covers planning, approval, development, testing, and finally release into production. Using such a standardized IT process minimizes the risk of adversely affecting productive business processes.

The following section aims to clarify the demands placed on a quality management process by taking the example of a software development project, namely the *Manufacturer Claims Monitor*. The Manufacturer Claims Monitor is an application that is based on service-oriented architecture (SOA). It enables end users to enter complaints to a manufacturer, view their status, and track returns to the manufacturer in the SAP NetWeaver Portal. The complaints data comes from SAP Enterprise Resource Planning (ERP). The end user displays the data by following guided procedures modeled on the basis of SAP NetWeaver Composition Environment (SAP NetWeaver CE).

Example: Manufacturer Claims Monitor

Figure 3.4 presents the software solution landscape for this software development project. It consists of a three-system landscape composed of a development system, quality assurance system, and production system for SAP NetWeaver Portal, SAP NetWeaver CE, and SAP ERP.

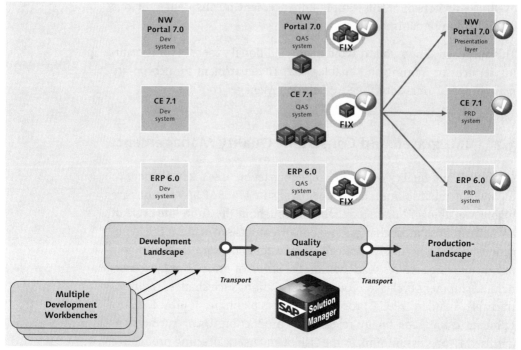

Figure 3.4 Transport Landscape for the Manufacturer Claims Monitor

It is essential that these three operational system landscapes are brought together in a single process to achieve a high level of quality in the software development. This is the only way to bring about 100% transparency of changes. To meet this challenge, SAP Solution Manager offers the following functions for the quality assurance process:

▶ **Quality Gate Management**
The aim here is to manage the quality assurance process in a directed and traceable way, guided by full transparency of changes and their impact on production.

▶ **Transport Management**
The purpose of this is to manage changes and their logistics centrally so they can be made across technological boundaries and application components. Every development environment is integrated via the central change and transport control system.

▶ **Test Management**
Test management guarantees the continuity of end-to-end business processes via central test planning. A central quality manager validates test execution and completeness.

The software development project is divided into four phases for the quality management process: scope, build, test, and deploy. The phases are separated by *quality gates* (Q-Gates). Using the Q-Gates, the quality manager and quality advisory board can check and document the progress being made in a project. A Q-Gate represents a milestone in a project and includes a check on the results of the preceding phase. You can record the necessary results and requirements placed on a given software development project in checklists and documents.

Phases and Q-Gates

The scope phase marks the beginning of every software development project. Its purpose is to ensure that within the scope of the project, the tasks essential to achieving a successful outcome are carried out. In projects, both the architecture and technical requirements are verified. The scope phase starts with the approval of the Project Begin Q-Gate.

Scope

To complete this phase and move onto the next phase, build, the change requests must be complete and their scope and level of priority defined. The quality manager should not initiate the Q-Gate centrally until all change requests have been agreed upon by the user department and approved. When the Q-Gate is triggered, the scope of the project is frozen, and time and resources required for the project are committed in planning. Once the quality advisory board has verified the quality criteria, the Q-Gate can be approved. The build phase can then begin.

The build phase sees the start of the actual development process. In the example of the *Manufacturer Claims Monitor*, a given number of transport requests is created in all three development systems involved in the project, and these are furnished with development objects (see Figure 3.5). The development objects are processed in different development environments. Whereas the Change and Transport System (CTS) previously supported ABAP objects only, the enhanced CTS as of SAP NetWeaver 7.0 SP14 also allows you to include non-ABAP objects in transport requests (see Section 9.2.1). All of these transport requests are functionally interdependent, which means the transports must be

Build

imported into downstream systems synchronously to guarantee that they work correctly.

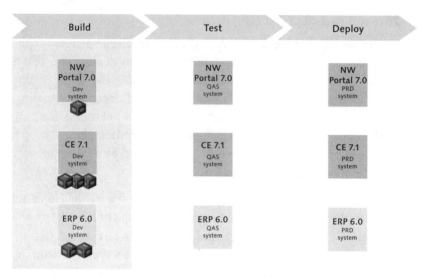

Figure 3.5 Transport Requests Are Created on the Basis of the Enhanced CTS for the Manufacturer Claims Monitor for Each Transport Route

The next phase can only be triggered once software development is complete and *unit tests* have been performed. In addition, test cases must be created, and the potential impact the changes may have on the existing productive solution must be known. The impact must be analyzed from both a functional and performance perspective. Using the *Business Process Change Analyzer* (see Section 6.2.2), you can check whether the software development impacts core business processes and, if so, which ones. Only at this stage is it possible to fully assess the central test plan for the user, integration, regression, and performance tests.

Test   Once the quality manager and advisory board have approved the Q-Gate between the build and test phases, the block on importing into test systems is lifted. This is the first time individual changes or projects can be imported into test systems and activated. The test team must successfully work through the test cases defined previously (for example, user test and integration test). If they encounter errors, they must take appropriate corrective measures and ensure that the test cases are assigned to newly created transport requests in the respective development systems.

Assigning corrections to the project makes it easier for the administrator to subsequently transport the corrections to the test systems and prevents possible inconsistencies (see Figure 3.6).

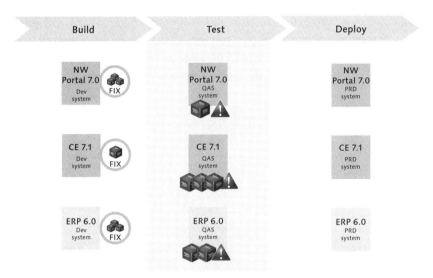

Figure 3.6 Central Test with Error Correction for the Manufacturer Claims Monitor

The test phase is only considered complete when the following test results have been accomplished:

1. The user test has been carried out in its entirety, and the user department has approved the solution. This indicates that the development meets the expectations and requirements of the user department.

2. The integration test has been completed and has shown that the business process works end-to-end, uninterrupted by system boundaries.

3. The regression test has confirmed that the productive core business processes affected still function properly.

4. The performance test has proven that the solution meets the agreed upon requirements in terms of response times and scaling.

A final check must confirm that all corrections and error repairs have been imported into the test system and tested. The quality manager is only free to trigger the next Q-Gate once the project scope has been released for production operation in its entirety.

Deploy   If the quality advisory board also deems the Q-Gate to have been passed successfully, the deploy phase is activated, and the block on importing into production systems is lifted. The person responsible for software logistics can now carry out the import. In the deploy phase, the project can only be imported as a whole, that is, with all changes and corrections (see Figure 3.7). This ensures that all transport requests in the project are imported into the production systems fully and in the right order. The implemented project is formally concluded by the last Q-Gate when it goes live successfully.

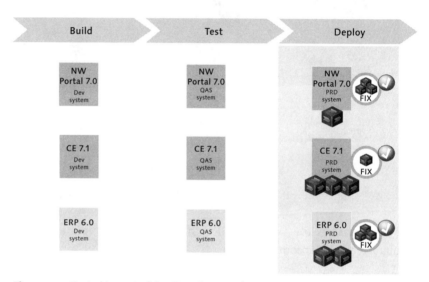

Figure 3.7 Central Import of the Manufacturer Claims Monitor Project into Production

Success criteria   To conclude the project, the success criteria for stable and high-performance operations of the software solution must be met. These are *key performance indicators* (KPIs), for instance, verifying that the number of incidents and corrections is not unusually high compared with other solutions. The project team can only be fully disbanded once responsibility for operating the solution has been transferred to the support organization. The quality manger can document this event formally in the Q-Gate and then, with the agreement of the quality advisory board, draw the project to a successful close.

Section 9.2 contains a detailed description of the quality gate management functions, including central transport management. Test management is explained in detail in Section 6.2.

Before a project begins, you collect and evaluate all functional and nonfunctional requirements during the requirements phase. SAP also provides support in this phase in the form of content and tools.

4   Requirements Phase

The following sections present tools and functions in the SAP Solution Manager environment that assist you in the requirements phase. At this stage, your primary concern is to evaluate scenarios and their respective business processes and check their viability for your project. In the SAP Solution Manager environment, you can use *SAP Business Maps* for knowledge transfer and more detailed process analysis. Their content is stored in the *Business Process Repository* (BPR), SAP's process library. This includes content designed specifically for implementations that you can use in your projects.

In many projects, however, you need to first analyze which transactions and processes are currently in use so you can define the project scope. For this purpose, SAP Solution Manager Enterprise Edition includes the Solution Documentation Assistant, which performs automated analyses to enable you to detail your core business processes in a Business Blueprint quickly and efficiently.

4.1   SAP Business Maps

SAP Business Maps give valuable support to partners and customers. They provide a platform for knowledge transfer, act as a communication channel, and encourage SAP, its partners, and customers to use a common language. They also illustrate how SAP applications support business processes from different industries and the added value they create.

Communication medium

SAP's business maps provide graphical overviews of the business processes found in companies. They help organizations envision, plan, and implement business solutions that are coherent, integrated, and comprehensive. They are based on best practices and build on the collective experiences of SAP, its partners, and customers. Focusing on industry-specific processes, SAP Business Maps help you compose comprehensive business solutions that are compatible with innovative software technologies.

SAP updates its business maps once a year and adapts them to new business and technical requirements. This aligns the solutions with the latest developments. The first level provides an overview of a given industry's core business processes. The second level provides detailed insight into the special functions required for each process.

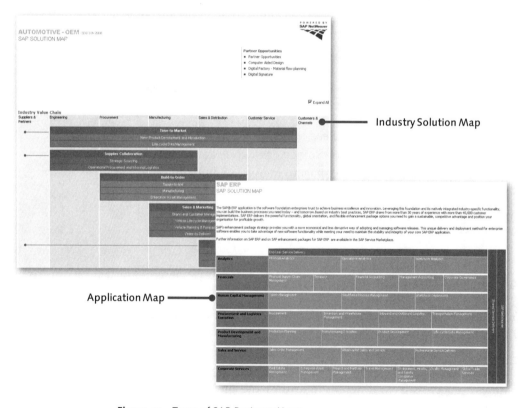

Figure 4.1 Types of SAP Business Maps

4.1.1 Solution Maps

Solution Maps are available in two formats. *Industry Solution Maps* give a graphical illustration of industry-specific scenarios based on a company's value chain, and *Application Maps* map one particular SAP application. Both formats let you navigate across multiple levels, enabling you to access detailed information for individual business processes and call up descriptions or more information (see Figure 4.1).

Formats

Industry Solution Maps

Industry Solution Maps (Figure 4.2) present the typical core processes found in a given industry in an easy-to-understand graphical form. Their explicit purpose is to give a clearly structured illustration, with differing levels of detail, of all the main duties that a company or authority has to carry out. Industry Solution Maps focus on scenarios and highlight an organization's critical core processes and most important functions.

Typical core processes

SAP has produced Industry Solution Maps for 50 industry segments, including three different segments for the automotive industry: manufacturers, suppliers, and sales and service. The first level shows a company's core competencies for each element of the value chain, such as research and development, broken down into individual business scenarios, such as New Product Development and Introduction. Cross-industry issues for human resources (HR) and financials are shown as basic functions not linked to a specific value chain.

The second level of an Industry Solution Map contains a descriptive text for each business scenario, other relevant detailed information, and links to related topics.

A *business scenario* is composed of various processes and process steps. Whereas business scenarios may vary in different industries, the processes and process steps may be the same. Systematically breaking down scenarios into smaller units like this allows individual components to be reused. Additionally, a business scenario contains information about the business objectives and key performance indicators (KPIs) associated with the scenario. The business processes that make up the scenario each have a description and state that SAP or a partner solution supports the

Business scenarios

process. You can also see whether these solutions are currently available or will be part of a future software release.

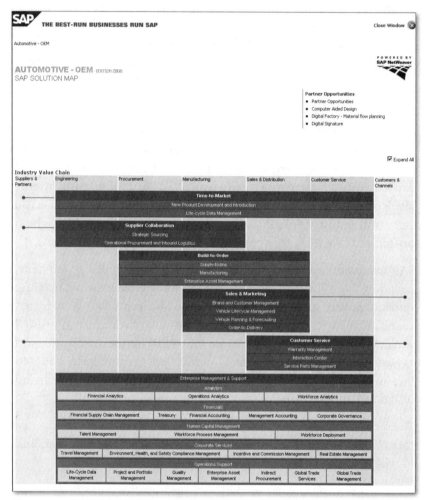

Figure 4.2 Example of an Industry Solution Map

There are also links to technical process variants and configuration variants, which correspond to the processes in SAP Solution Manager and indicate that implementation documentation is available for the process. They form the interface to SAP Solution Manager.

Application Maps

SAP Application Maps depict cross-industry SAP applications and provide navigation options across multiple levels (Figure 4.3). The Application Map is structured along process categories or key functions (vertically) and process groups (horizontally).

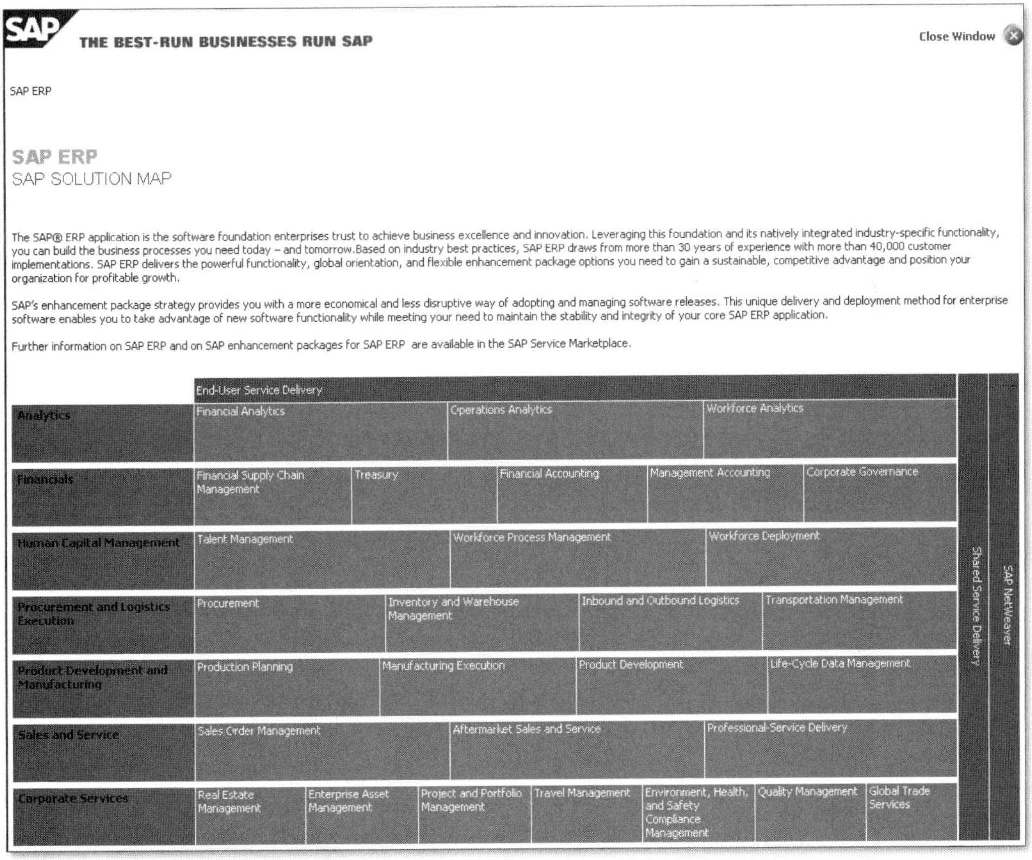

Figure 4.3 Example of an SAP Application Map

Additional information associated with a particular process group, such as business objectives, is also linked to the respective process groups (for instance, Quotation & Order Management). On the second level, you can navigate to the process view and individual process steps, where you will

Presentation levels

find the business processes and a process description, as well as information about availability and product assignment. At the process level, Application Maps also contain technical process variants, each of which represents an element from SAP Solution Manager and thus shows the processes for which implementation content is available. In many cases, you can navigate directly from the configuration variants to the component documentation (see Figure 4.4).

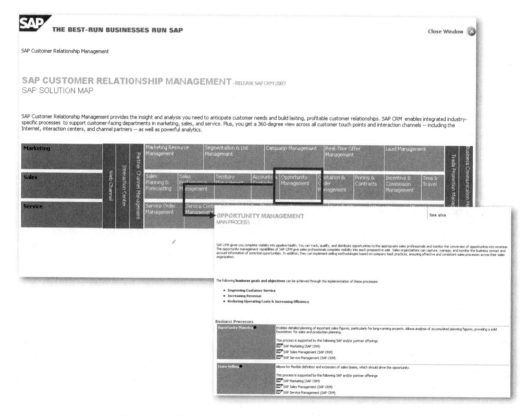

Figure 4.4 Navigation Process Group • Process

4.1.2   SAP Solution Composer

Customer-specific Solution Maps

To offer customers a flexible solution, SAP has developed *SAP Solution Composer* in addition to the Solution Maps. You can use this intuitive software to design customer-specific Solution Maps. Regardless of whether you are drawing up a new Solution Map from scratch or customizing one of the SAP Solution Maps, SAP Solution Composer lets you visualize an organization's business processes and plan new IT solutions. It is also easy to incorporate additional information such as documents, graphics, and links. The result is the perfect blueprint for a specific company, which can be saved in several formats and displayed using Microsoft PowerPoint, for example. Because SAP Solution Composer also contains all of the SAP Business Maps, it can be used to plan and map internal as well as inter-enterprise partnerships.

SAP Solution Composer is a PC-based tool, which you can download free of charge at *http://www.sap.com/solutions/businessmaps/composer*. It contains all types of SAP Business Maps, which you can download along with the tool and use to create or modify your own Business Maps. Besides planning implementation projects, you can use the tool for defining, documenting, and communicating your business solution requirements. It produces a tailor-made solution and implementation plan, which your company can use to align processes and supplement them with content from SAP.

SAP Solution Composer offers a wide range of functions that enable you to do the following:

Functions

▸ Modify existing Solution Maps and create new ones.

▸ Assign business goals and objectives, products and solutions, KPIs, user-defined attributes, and documents.

▸ Assign roles, business documents, and other records.

▸ Export content into different formats (Microsoft Office, HTML).

Customers can use personalized Solution Maps to figure out the status of their current IT landscape, with or without help from SAP or SAP partners. They can apply this information to analyze strengths and weaknesses and determine which solutions SAP and SAP partners provide for any weak points identified.

4.2 SAP Solution Manager Content – Process Orientation and Accelerated Implementation

This section provides you with more details of SAP Solution Manager content: What challenges do companies face when implementing IT solutions? What is SAP Solution Manager content? How can the content benefit my company? Where can I get more information?

4.2.1 Challenges

Optimizing value chains · Innovation, time-to-market, and efficiency are the traits enterprises currently have to possess if they want to retain and boost their competitive strength. Optimizing value chains has become a major objective, demanding a greater emphasis on individual business processes. In its role as a pacesetter, IT must be able to address changes in the value chain flexibly and quickly and provide swift and effective methods for implementing business-process-centric software.

An implementation project typically is composed of the following phases: Business Blueprint, realization (configuration), testing, final preparation, and go-live and support. Process models (available in the Business Process Repository [BPR]) help you define and model company-specific business processes for the Business Blueprint; configuration information and best practices offerings provide support when you implement the business processes in the system. The content provided by SAP should be regarded as a template for implementing business processes. You can incorporate company-specific features, regarding business processes, as well as the settings required in the software solution, quickly and efficiently during the implementation project.

4.2.2 Content and Structure

Business Process Repository · The BPR is a structured directory containing a wide range of business processes. All the scenarios and processes are available centrally and provide a starting point for modeling company-specific business processes. They are grouped by topic or content.

The meta model for this approach to business process modeling has three levels (see Figure 4.5):

- ▶ Scenario
- ▶ Process
- ▶ Process step

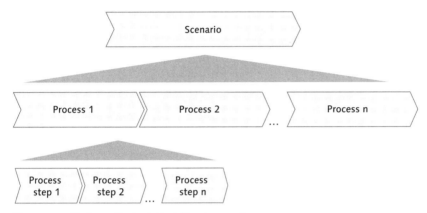

Figure 4.5 Business Content Modeling Approach

Processes are combined to form scenarios that represent general business processes. Every industry for which SAP offers a solution has various scenarios depicting business practices in the given industry. SAP Solution Maps, which describe the business practices of a particular industry against the backdrop of the respective value chain, show what implementation information is available in SAP Solution Manager for the relevant business processes. Several alternatives are available for implementing a process (for example, invoice processing can be implemented with SAP ERP or SAP CRM). Furthermore, there is a wide range of cross-industry processes that are typical of human resources (HR) or accounting departments, for instance.

The focus is on implementing IT solutions, which primarily includes, as already described, support for business processes. Besides business-related scenarios and processes, technical scenarios are also available, which can form a basis for new business solutions (such as setting up reporting concepts) but which are also relevant for a company's technical processes, particularly in the field of IT (IT services, for example).

The BPR is divided into two main areas (see Figure 4.6). The first area, called ORGANIZATIONAL AREAS, contains all available processes. For the

BPR structure

purpose of simplification and ease of use, this section is arranged to correspond to the elements of a generic value chain (such as sales, marketing, and purchasing). The second area contains cross-scenario basic settings as well as all the scenarios and processes, grouped by INDUSTRY SOLUTION AND APPLICATION (SAP ERP, SAP CRM, SAP SCM, and so on).

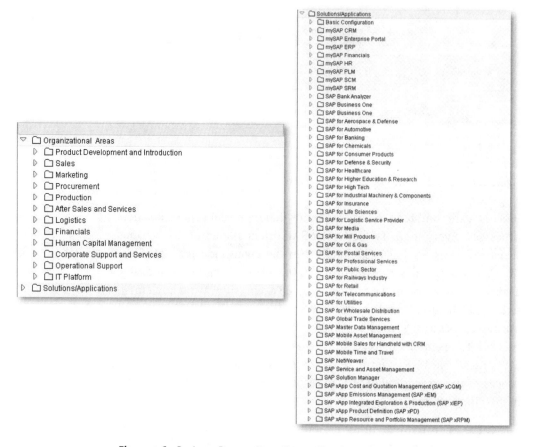

Figure 4.6 Business Process Repository – Structure

4.2.3 Implementation Content – Information Categories

Information for the Business Blueprint and implementation phases is supplied for each of the levels in the BPR (scenarios, processes, process steps).

The business significance and structure is described for every scenario and every process. This descriptive text covers the business context of a process as well as its detailed structure. It also contains information about the (technical) requirements for the selected object and about the results. In addition to the business description, the detailed structure makes it easier to understand a business process by portraying it as a flow chart (component view; see Figure 4.7). The graphic displays the process based on the software solutions used.

Scenario and process descriptions

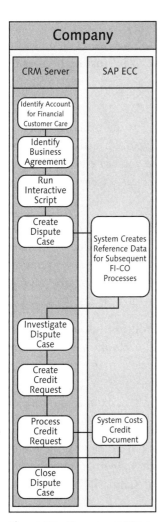

Figure 4.7 Component View

SAP Solution Manager automatically derives the graphics from the defined scenario structure or process structure, as seen by the user in the navigation tree. Structures you have defined yourself are also depicted accordingly.

Documents as well as graphics can be exported from SAP Solution Manager and used elsewhere in project documentation for the Business Blueprint.

Implementation information

The process level contains concrete information regarding implementation: Which Customizing entries are required? What is the best sequence in which to make the settings? Which additional settings have to be made in the system? Which transactions are relevant for the process in question?

This information is available in Transactions SOLAR01 and SOLAR02, on the CONFIGURATION and TRANSACTIONS tabs for the process selected. From here, SAP Solution Manager lets you navigate directly to the Customizing settings for the relevant system, where you can enter the necessary data in the right order efficiently and effectively (see also Sections 5.4 and 6.1).

Additional documentation in Customizing gives you a better understanding of the business context of the system settings you need to make, thereby enabling you to tailor them flexibly to your company's requirements. Where necessary and practical, this kind of implementation information is also provided for scenarios and individual process steps.

Basic settings

Basic system settings that you have to make during implementation, regardless of the business process concerned, are summarized in the *basic settings*. Because they apply to all scenarios, they can be found at the level of the component on which the business process is based. Basic settings also include Customizing settings, transactions, and further explanations.

Portal roles

Scenarios and processes can be grouped to form portal roles. A role therefore is composed of scenarios and processes for a given group of users. The BPR contains configuration information for standard roles. Because roles often include multiple scenarios and processes, they are stored in the context of the relevant component (like the basic settings).

4.2.4 Product-Dependent Content

SAP Solution Manager content is constantly evolving, partly in a process of continuous improvement and partly to reflect developments in the associated software products.

Content is valid for certain releases. To account for this, different content versions are created and shown in accordance with the selected software constellation (that is, which products go with which release). A visual distinction is also made: Content that is available but is not active for a selected product context is shown in light gray. You can display all of the available versions and their software components and releases for every scenario and process.

Versioning

4.2.5 Outlook

Value chains and their business processes continue to change in a dynamic economic environment. Software solutions are always evolving. The BPR, for its part, acknowledges such developments. SAP optimizes and enhances the content and modeling approach at regular intervals.

SAP's focus on business requirements has resulted in a service-oriented approach to software development (service-oriented architecture). Business processes therefore represent the central starting point for identifying and defining services. In this regard, the BPR plays a significant role in helping you establish service-oriented IT solutions.

Information about the currently available content is displayed in the online version of the BPR (*https://implementationcontent.sap.com/bpr*), shown in Figure 4.8. You can call up the scenarios and processes along with descriptive information and graphics for the selected objects.

The BPR is especially significant in SAP Solution Manager Enterprise Edition. The content of the BPR is used here to create a Business Blueprint on the basis of the automated analyses performed by the Solution Documentation Assistant (see Section 4.3).

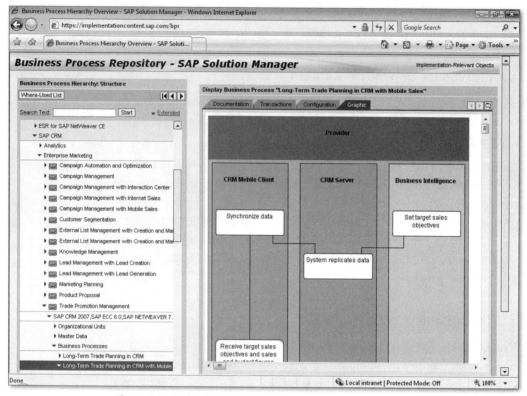

Figure 4.8 Online Version of the BPR

4.3   Solution Documentation Assistant

The Solution Documentation Assistant enables you to automatically evaluate business processes in SAP Solution Manager. It helps you prepare upgrade projects, evaluate new functions, and analyze custom developments. You can, for instance, determine which business processes are being used actively in production systems and view this information graphically to help you identify standardization potential and optimize your business processes.

Above all, existing customers already operating a productive solution can benefit from the capability to create solution documentation for their existing solution quickly and efficiently with the Solution Documentation Assistant. Its scope, however, is not limited to the initial creation of solution documentation; you can also use it to continuously verify and update your solution documentation. In this sense, the Solution Documentation Assistant makes a lasting contribution to the reduction of your operating costs as well as the transparency of the solution.

Identification of core business processes, a process supported by the Solution Documentation Assistant, is divided into the following process steps (see Figure 4.9):

> Identifying core business processes

▸ Document the system landscape.

▸ Automatically assign the results of the analysis to a process structure.

▸ Create the Business Blueprint.

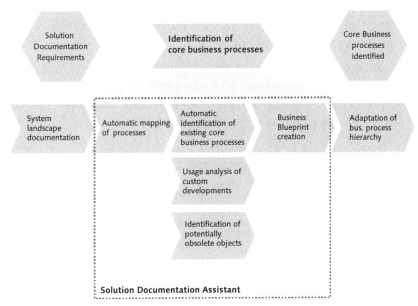

Figure 4.9   Identification of Core Business Processes

This new SAP Solution Manager function cuts the time you need to achieve the goal of making solution documentation available centrally in SAP Solution Manager for all of your core business processes. This centralized documentation can then serve as a *single source of truth* and support you when you explore other SAP Solution Manager scenarios based on this information. For example, this solution documentation can

> Central access

help you establish business process monitoring (see Section 8.2.2) or use the Business Process Change Analyzer (see Section 6.2).

4.3.1 Documenting the System Landscape

You have three possible entry points when it comes to entering the components of the landscape of the managed systems that you want to document:

▶ Transfer existing system documentation from previous implementation or upgrade projects.

▶ Transfer documentation from existing solutions in SAP Solution Manager.

▶ Use previously undocumented solution and system landscapes that are already in production operations.

If the managed systems in your system landscape are already connected to SAP Solution Manager, no further action is required. If the systems have not yet been connected, enter them in Transaction SMSY (Solution Manager System Landscape, see Section 5.2.5).

4.3.2 Automatically Assigning the Results of the Analysis to a Business Process Structure

Sources You can use the Solution Documentation Assistant to automatically analyze your business processes and draw on different sources to reuse existing process documentation:

▶ Documentation from existing implementation and upgrade projects in SAP Solution Manager

▶ Documentation for SAP partner products

▶ Documentation from existing solutions in SAP Solution Manager

▶ Documentation for SAP standard processes in the BPR, which is integrated into SAP Solution Manager

Check any existing documentation from existing projects or solutions. If no documentation yet exists, create a project in SAP Solution Manager (see Section 5.2) to create the documentation automatically with the Solution Documentation Assistant.

The existing structures and data from projects and solutions are copied to the analysis projects. You can also base the analysis projects on imported data from a different SAP Solution Manager system.

The analyses show the outcomes in relation to structures. In addition, all data used is comprehensively analyzed, which means the outcome of an analysis may reveal objects that are not assigned to the structure but nevertheless are used productively. This approach ensures that all objects that are used productively appear in the solution documentation.

Structure-based mapping

The analysis findings are presented in such a way that they can be used for considering higher-level business aspects as well as taking a more detailed look at the analyzed objects, for instance, transactions or reports. The Solution Documentation Assistant distinguishes between objects that result from productive data or data created for test purposes. The analysis findings can be transferred from the Solution Documentation Assistant to the underlying Solution Manager project at the touch of a button. The project can be updated in this way.

When analyzing productive solutions, you can verify the correctness and consistency of existing documentation at reasonable intervals. Because the solution acts as the source in this case, you are not required to create a Solution Manager project before you start the analysis. If the analysis reveals that the existing solution documentation needs to be updated, you can create a new project from within the analysis and copy the analysis findings to it. This poses no threat to the productive solution, which can be updated at a defined time by transferring project data to the solution under controlled circumstances.

Updating and consistency check

You also have access to the analysis results in the form of an extensive HTML report.

You can call up all activities relevant to working with the Solution Documentation Assistant from the Solution Documentation Assistant work center (see Figure 4.10).

Work center

The Solution Documentation Assistant work center presents several views to enable you to manage analysis projects, process analyses and their results, and process check steps in the rule database.

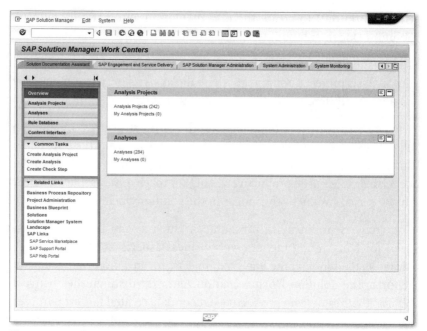

Figure 4.10 Solution Documentation Assistant Work Center

Views The following views are provided:

- An OVERVIEW that gives you fast access to your current projects and analyses.

- ANALYSIS PROJECTS to provide a detailed view of all analysis projects and the analyses that you have created for a given project. You can open the view on an individual analysis project so that you can view and edit its analysis structure and check rules.

- ANALYSES to allow you to see all analyses in detail. You can search for particular analyses and open a view showing the findings of a given analysis.

- A RULE DATABASE to allow you to see all the check steps that exist. You can create, edit, and delete check steps here.

- The CONTENT INTERFACE enables you to export or import analysis projects or check rules as files. For instance, you can use this function to import and use analysis projects provided by SAP partners.

The work center supports you with guided procedures when you are creating analysis projects and analyses. It also allows you to create check steps: Guided procedures

▶ **Create Analysis Project**
You create a new analysis project on the basis of a Solution Manager project, a solution, or an imported analysis project. You can also call up the guided procedure from the view for analysis projects.

▶ **Create Analysis**
You create a new analysis on the basis of an existing analysis project and plan the time it is to be performed. You can also initiate the guided procedure from the view for existing analyses.

Analysis Project

The Solution Documentation Assistant offers you a view showing the structure and details of an individual analysis project. You can use the view to display and edit the check rules that are assigned to the nodes in the analysis structure, for example.

In the analysis, check rules enable nodes in the analysis structure to be rated. Check rules denote check sets and check steps belonging to a structure node, for example a business process.

The Solution Documentation Assistant work center displays the check rules of an analysis project in the CHECK RULES area of the detailed view of the analysis project (see Figure 4.11). Check rules are automatically copied from the source (project, solution, or imported data) when you create the analysis project. You can edit and extend check rules to increase the quality of the analysis. Check rules

The check rules are split into two levels:

▶ Check sets
▶ Check steps

In the analysis, check sets enable nodes in the analysis structure to be rated. This rating is based on the results of check steps that have been assigned to the check sets. You are free to choose how many check steps Check sets you assign to each check set. In turn, you can assign as many check sets as you like to each structure node.

Check step
A check step is an object to be analyzed, for instance, a transaction, a report, or an SQL statement. The check step is the smallest unit in the check rules.

A threshold value is assigned to check steps and is taken as a rating criterion for analysis purposes. For example, you can define that the CREATE DOCUMENT check step can only be rated as productive if it is executed more than 100 times a month.

Rule database
The rule database provides an overview of all available check steps including ones that have not been assigned to analysis projects. You can use the rule database to search for check steps and display detailed information for them. You can also edit the check steps and create new ones.

Analysis structure
The view of an individual analysis project shows the analysis structure, for instance, as it appears on the basis of the underlying Solution Manager project, and the check rules that are assigned to the nodes in the analysis structure.

Analysis structure
The work center depicts the structure of an analysis project as a tree in the ANALYSIS STRUCTURE screen area. Some of the nodes in the structure are abstract. Their purpose is to organize the items listed below them, namely, concrete business scenarios or processes and their individual steps. Examples of such nodes include:

▸ Organizational units

▸ Master data

▸ Business scenarios

▸ Business processes

The other nodes represent concrete business scenarios, business processes, and process steps. Their names stem from the underlying Solution Manager projects, solutions, or imported analysis projects. This type of node might, for instance, represent the process for creating a purchase order.

These nodes are assigned with check sets to which check steps are assigned. Such steps enable the nodes to be rated when analysis is performed. The attachment symbol is displayed in the structure next to all of the nodes that have been assigned to check sets already (see Figure 4.11).

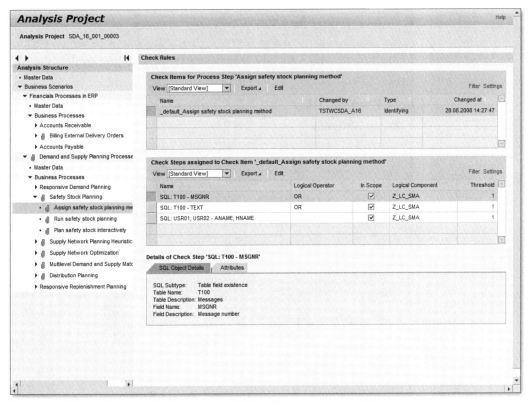

Figure 4.11 View of an Analysis Project in the Solution Documentation Assistant

The hierarchy of the analysis structure is also taken into account when the results of the analysis are determined, which means a business scenario groups together the rating results of all of the business processes that belong to it, and a business process groups together the results of all of the process steps that belong to it.

The Solution Documentation Assistant gives you a detailed view of the results of an analysis. The analysis results are arranged according to the following aspects and presented on the corresponding tabs (see Figure 4.12):

Analysis results

▸ **Structural Result Display**

▸ **Analysis Result Summary**

A summary of the analysis results, looking in particular at the success of the analysis and the use of objects, for example, SAP or customer-specific transactions and reports.

▸ **Graphical Overview**

Pie charts enable you to see at a glance the extent to which certain results occur in the analysis structure rating and check rules (see Figure 4.12).

▸ **Analysis Setting**

▸ **Error Statistics**

View of the errors that can occur when analysis takes place.

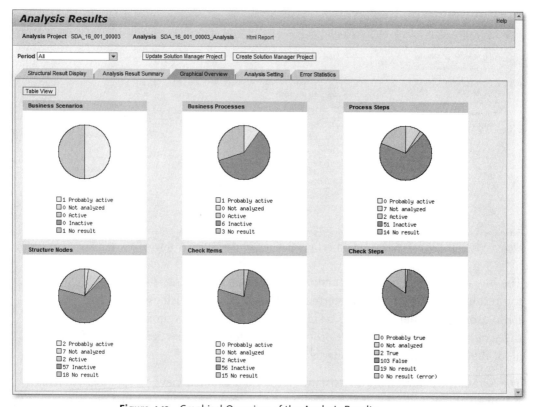

Figure 4.12 Graphical Overview of the Analysis Results

The following additional functions are available:

▸ The results overview can show either the results for all periods cov- ered by the analysis or just one period.

Results overview functions

▸ You can transfer the analysis results to the underlying Solution Man-ager project. Update rules are provided to help you transfer the results.

▸ You can present the analysis results as an HTML report.

4.3.3 Updating Analysis Results in a Project or Transferring Them to a Solution

Once you have successfully completed an analysis project, you can update the data in your Solution Manager project at the touch of a button. You are free to edit the resulting Business Blueprint if necessary (see Section 5.4). You transfer the project to your solution documentation using the standardized procedures for implementing solutions (see Sections 5.3 and 7.1).

In the design phase, you use the findings from the requirements phase to specify precisely how your application or IT operating processes are to function and which IT applications should be used to map the processes. This chapter describes the SAP Solution Manager functions that support you through this phase.

5   Design Phase

A 2004 university study on project management found that only 43% of all projects reflect their clients' strategies, and only 13% boost the value of the IT solution. Furthermore, one quarter of all projects begin with insufficient resources.

To enable you to deal with impending bottlenecks quickly and efficiently, it is essential that you have professional, transparent project management procedures and a clearly defined project scope. With these in place, you will be able to safeguard your company's investments, deploy resources for specific objectives, set priorities, and ensure that everyone involved in a project communicates well.

Transparent project management

SAP Solution Manager's role during this phase is to provide you with *Roadmaps* — proven procedures for project management — and structure project management activities clearly using tools such as project administration functions. SAP Solution Manager also helps you draw up a well-defined, transparent conceptual design (Business Blueprint) for your project.

5.1   Roadmaps – Professional Project Guidance

SAP Roadmaps provide methodical frameworks for SAP projects. They give a structure to results and activities and provide the tools, services, and other methodical procedures that are recommended or required to help you achieve your objective. Special *accelerators* in the Roadmap structure help you with certain project tasks by providing templates, examples, standards, product information, or best practices, for example. Besides the know-how presented in a Roadmap, you can use the activities and their descriptions to plan and organize your projects. The accelerators help you reduce the time, expense, and risks associated with implementation projects.

Roadmaps

SAP has compiled Roadmaps for various purposes: The *ASAP Implementation Roadmap* for implementations, the *SAP Upgrade Roadmap* for upgrades, and the *Global Template Roadmap* for working with templates and global rollouts. In the Run SAP Roadmap, SAP continues to provide a method for introducing end-to-end IT operating processes in a company or group. The following section introduces the Run SAP Roadmap and the ASAP Implementation Roadmap.

5.1.1 The Run SAP Roadmap

Scope of Run SAP

The *Run SAP* method was developed to meet the requirements of IT operations on the increasing complexity of IT solutions (landscapes and software products). The scope of Run SAP includes:

▸ Best practices for end-to-end IT operating processes, that is, *SAP Standards for Solution Operations*

▸ A training and certification program to ensure a minimum standard of knowledge

▸ An extensive service offering to ensure support from SAP experts for parts of the implementation project

▸ Tools in SAP Solution Manager that enable or support the IT operating processes in a highly integrated way

▸ The Run SAP Roadmap itself, which maps implementation methodology and merges the different Run SAP components

Using the methodology in the Run SAP Roadmap it is possible to implement end-to-end IT operating processes or to adapt existing processes to new requirements (ASAP implementation projects, SOA). In general, a Run SAP subproject should be defined for each implementation project because the IT operating processes normally have to be adapted when new components are implemented.

The Roadmap is oriented toward the typical project phases and is constructed as follows:

- ▶ Planning (assessment and scoping)
- ▶ Design
- ▶ Implementation
- ▶ Preparations for go-live (handover to production)
- ▶ Production operation
- ▶ Optimizing operations

End-to-end IT operating processes can be implemented in individual subprojects within the scope of Run SAP. Accordingly, Figure 5.1 shows the Roadmap as viewed from the project.

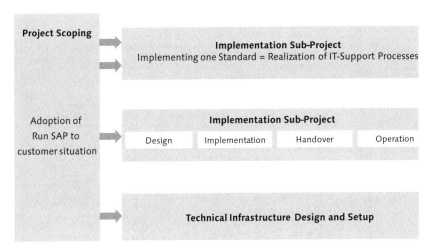

Figure 5.1   Schematic Diagram of Implementation with Run SAP

In the first phase of a Run SAP project, you adapt the holistic Run SAP Roadmap to your customer's situation to define a project plan for further procedures. You then define the individual, end-to-end IT operating processes as independent subprojects, implement them, and go live with them. This is useful because the individual processes and functions must be available at different times if the Run SAP project is based on a parallel ASAP implementation project. For example, a working Change Request Management process is required before the actual implementation phase of the ASAP project begins, while an end-to-end incident management process does not have to be available until the end of the implementation phase if a lot of problems are identified in the test phase.

Technical infrastructure

Furthermore, for the technical infrastructure you must also check the extent to which new sizing, redistribution, or higher availability is necessary as a result of introducing and adapting IT operating processes (technical infrastructure design and setup).

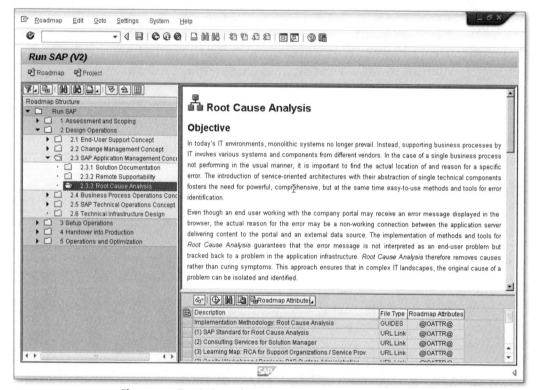

Figure 5.2 Run SAP Roadmap in SAP Solution Manager

Structure of the Run SAP Roadmap

Figure 5.2 shows the structure of the Run SAP Roadmap in SAP Solution Manager. You can call up a Roadmap in SAP Solution Manager with Transaction RMMAIN or via the Implementation/Upgrade work center. Each phase has different work packages in which individual topics are summarized. The DESIGN OPERATIONS, SETUP OPERATIONS, and OPERATIONS & OPTIMIZATION phases include the work packages END USER SUP-

PORT, CHANGE MANAGEMENT, SAP APPLICATION MANAGEMENT, BUSINESS PROCESS OPERATIONS, and SAP TECHNICAL OPERATIONS, to which the individual, end-to-end operating standards are assigned as topics. You can call up the current Run SAP Roadmap on the SAP Service Marketplace at *service.sap.com/runsap*.

Phase 1: Assessment and Scoping

In the initial phase of the Run SAP Roadmap, requirements are analyzed to identify the operating processes relevant for you. You then prioritize the planned processes and define the scope of a possible Run SAP project. Once the technical dependencies have been evaluated and an initial evaluation of qualifications has been performed, a project plan is suggested, which contains the work packages and a rough schedule. The project plan also contains the recommended training and workshop programs, a service plan, and a rough estimate of expenditure.

Requirements analysis

The RUN SAP area on the SAP Service Marketplace provides a tool that you can use to easily create a typical project plan based on your details. This plan gives you an initial overview of work packages, schedules, and SAP support offerings, and can serve as a very good basis for further discussion with SAP or your implementation partner.

If you want to be certified as a *Customer Center of Expertise* (Customer CoE), a quantitative review of the present IT operating processes is also carried out in this phase, and the project plan contains all work packages required for certification. Certification as a Customer CoE takes place once the Run SAP project is completed.

Customer Center of Expertise

Phase 2: Design Operations

The first part of the design operations phase is to review the present operating process for each selected topic (as-is analysis). You then evaluate your requirements and match them to the present situation (fit/gap analysis). This then results in a blueprint of the process together with a detailed project plan that also contains a concrete estimation of expenditure.

Phase 3: Setup Operations

Implementation In the third phase, you implement and test the defined IT operating processes. The required training and workshop programs also take place. At the same time, you install the required technical infrastructure and integrate it into the processes. As the central element, this includes integrating tools from other providers and setting up SAP Solution Manager.

Phase 4: Handover to Production

Before the new or changed IT operating processes are deployed, you make sure that all processes have been implemented and tested as planned and that the necessary tools have been installed and set up. You also have to ensure that employees in the IT organization have been trained in the new processes and tools, and that they can operate the solutions. A transfer phase should be defined for the time after deployment so that the project team can still support the organization in the event of start-up difficulties.

Phase 5: Operations & Optimization

After deploying new and changed IT operating processes, your main focus is to ensure that operations run smoothly. The process may have to be adapted in the event of disruptions. You should aim to continually optimize the processes because the potential for improvement increases as the end user and IT operation become more familiar with the solution.

If you made plans for certification as a Customer CoE in the initial phase, now is the best time to obtain certification from SAP.

5.1.2 ASAP Implementation Roadmap

Scope of the Roadmap The ASAP Implementation Roadmap represents many years of SAP project experience. It covers the entire implementation process, taking into account project management concerns as well as functional and technical issues, and has a result-oriented, structured form. The ASAP Implementation Roadmap offers the following:

- It covers processes and best business practices for implementing every possible combination of SAP applications from the SAP Business Suite.

- It provides a framework for project management that fully complies with the *Project Management Institute Project Management Body Of Knowledge* (PMI PMBOK) industry standard.

- It covers all of the activities necessary for implementing SAP solutions and applications, with particular emphasis on planning and executing projects, recording requirements, configuration, developing and testing customer solutions, and preparing for go-live.

- It gives clear recommendations for projects that intend to provide one or more of their services at a global level. Global sourcing can result in significant savings in all kinds of projects.

- It covers technical aspects of the implementation process, such as planning and designing the infrastructure, setting up the system landscape, and installing and configuring software.

The ASAP Implementation Roadmap is divided into five phases:

Phases of the ASAP Implementation Roadmap

Phase 1: Project Preparation

In this phase, the team initiates, plans, and prepares your SAP project. You define the main features of your project plans, agree on project standards, draw up a schedule, and assemble the project team. This is also the time when you agree on the implementation scope and make plans for the technical requirements and infrastructure.

Phase 2: Business Blueprint

In this phase, the project team reaches a common understanding of how your enterprise wants to conduct its business operations with the SAP application. The result is a Business Blueprint, a collection of scenario-related and detailed process requirements that outlines what you want the system to do. This document also highlights any gaps for which you need to develop functional specifications. This phase is considered to be complete when the stakeholders have approved the business requirements in the Business Blueprint.

125

Phase 3: Realization

In this phase, the requirements that were laid out in the Business Blueprint phase are implemented in the development system and tested in the test system. In large projects, you can break down the implementation process into a series of cycles to give you more control over how the business processes are configured, developed, and tested. Integration testing is conducted during the configuration stage to ensure that the system is ready to go live. During this phase, the project team also puts together solution-related documentation and training materials.

Phase 4: Final Preparation

In this phase, the team finalizes plans for cutover activities, data transfer, and production operation. Training is provided for end users, and system tests are conducted (performance, load, and infrastructure tests). Any critical open items should be addressed during this phase. By the end of this phase, the solution is ready to go live, and a support organization is in place to support it.

Phase 5: Go-Live and Support

In this phase, the project team switches from a preproduction state to a production environment, monitors the first few weeks of production operation, and resolves any problems that may arise. The project is completed during this final project phase.

The *Roadmap phases* (level 1) contain *deliverable groups* (level 2), which group together deliverables. To reflect Project Management Institute (PMI) terminology, we have introduced the term *deliverable group* (which replaces the *work packages* that can be found in the Run SAP Roadmap). A deliverable group, identified by the prefix *DG*, bundles logically related deliverables. Figure 5.3 shows the deliverable group 2.4 DG: Business Scenario Requirements with deliverables such as 2.4.3 Business Scenario Definition.

Deliverables   Each phase also includes a number of *deliverables* (level 3), which are bundled as deliverable groups. Every deliverable can be subdivided into two elements. One element describes individual deliverable components, known as *outputs*. Outputs are indicated by the prefix *O* and displayed at level 4. The Business Blueprint contains a special section for business processes, which describes business and technical requirements and other specifications for a solution. Each one of these elements is an output.

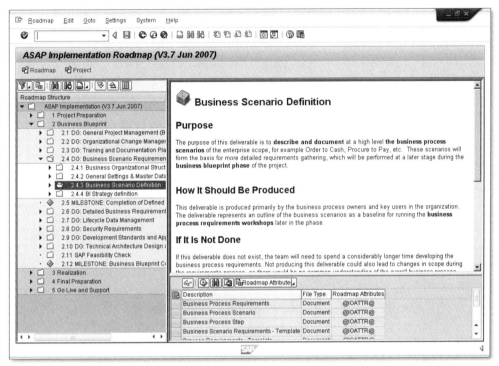

Figure 5.3 ASAP Implementation Roadmap in SAP Solution Manager

The second element of a deliverable description is the *method*, identified by the prefix *M*. A method contains *activities* and *tasks* that the project team has to complete in order to create the output and, in turn, generate the deliverables. Activities (level 4) and tasks (level 5) provide this level of detail. An activity groups a number of tasks for achieving certain project objectives, whereas a task describes the steps to be completed by individual project team members. Both levels include *accelerators*, which help you accelerate your project activities. As an alternative to using the structure view, you can access your Roadmap from the entry screen (see Figure 5.4). It shows the Roadmap phases and their deliverable groups, as well as additional *milestones* and services that you can order from SAP Active Global Support to help you expedite your implementation project.

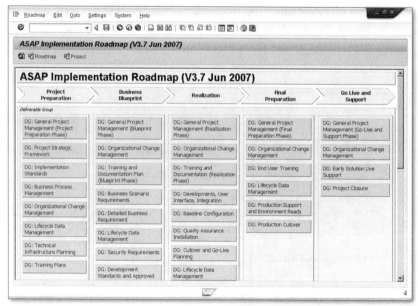

Figure 5.4 Entry Screen for ASAP Implementation Roadmap (Without Services or Milestones)

The advantages of this new structure are obvious: Project managers can better manage deliverables and therefore better monitor the current status of the project.

5.1.3 Working with the Run SAP and ASAP Implementation Roadmap

The Roadmap structure is divided into *phases* and *work packages* or *deliverable groups* and *topics,* or *deliverables*, *outputs*, *activities*, and *tasks*, which you can find on the left of the screen (see Figure 5.2 and Figure 5.3). On the top right, you can see topics, which describe the outputs, as well as the activities and tasks that result in these outputs.

On the bottom right, you can see the accelerators. They include examples, templates, and links to the SAP Help Portal and supplementary information on the SAP Service Marketplace, that is, additional material that can speed up your implementation project.

The Roadmap itself contains accelerators, describing how SAP Solution Manager enables project teams to achieve their implementation objectives in each project phase.

Auxiliary materials

The Run SAP Roadmap generally provides you with the following accelerators to introduce end-to-end operating standards:

Materials for implementation with Run SAP

▶ **Documentation of the standard**
Each standard contains best practice descriptions of specific tasks, explanations of which tools should be used in SAP Solution Manager, and available training and service offerings from SAP, which support the implementation of the standard.

▶ **Implementation methods for the standard**
The documents describe the steps required to define, implement, and deploy end-to-end operating processes and adapt them to new scenarios.

▶ **Documentation of industry-specific operating topics**
Special best practice documents can be selected using an attribute filter (see below) for many industries, for example, retail, utilities, or banking. These documents relate to industry-specific features of IT operations, for example, mass data processing or period-end closing.

All the phases of the ASAP Implementation Roadmap are supported by SAP Solution Manager tools. You can use the following materials:

Materials for implementation with ASAP

▶ **Phase checklist for SAP Solution Manager activities**
A phase-based checklist showing which SAP Solution Manager transactions support which type of Roadmap task or activity.

▶ **Solution Manager usage outline**
A general overview of all of the transactions relevant for SAP Solution Manager. It describes which tab pages have to be edited and which fields must be completed for certain deliverables to be achieved.

In addition to accelerators, every structure node has the following attributes, which makes it easier for project teams to find information:

Attributes

▶ **Subject areas**
All subjects are assigned to one or more subject areas, which represent the different fields of knowledge and experience in the implementation project. Examples include business process requirements,

design, configuration and testing, organization change management, and training.

▶ **Flavors (variants)**
A flavor, or variant, shows which area of the structure is relevant for a specific solution. Selecting a variant allows you to generate a solution-specific view of the Roadmap, showing only the content that applies to the solution that your team is implementing. You choose the variant when you create a project in SAP Solution Manager and define the solution scope (see Section 5.2).

▶ **Roles**
The ROLE attribute shows which roles are involved in the tasks, activities, or outputs. The role description supplies expert knowledge for various project team roles, such as business consultant or project manager.

You can combine these attributes to define your own filters that display the information you want to find, such as which business process requirements an application consultant has to compile for the SAP CRM application.

5.1.4 Delivery and Availability of Roadmaps

Roadmap formats   All SAP Roadmaps are available in English only and in two formats, each with different features:

▶ **Integrated in SAP Solution Manager**
In general, you would opt for this format if you want to use Roadmaps actively in your projects, say, to create project documentation or indicate the processing status. This format also enables you to record issues or problem messages in good time for problems that threaten to jeopardize your business processes. Integration with Issue Management (see Section 8.4) and the Service Desk (see Section 8.7) allows you to organize and subsequently analyze how to deal with a problem.

▶ **HTML version on SAP Service Marketplace**
This format is used primarily by teams that need offline access to Roadmaps. This may be the case before SAP Solution Manager is installed or for project team members who cannot access SAP Solu-

tion Manager while in the field. You can download the latest version at *http://service.sap.com/roadmaps.*

The HTML and SAP Solution Manager versions differ as follows:

Differences

▶ HTML Roadmaps cannot be edited, modified, or filtered.

▶ Whereas SAP Solution Manager requires a separate server or instance, the HTML Roadmaps are simpler to install and use. The content can be displayed with any browser and the appropriate Microsoft Office applications.

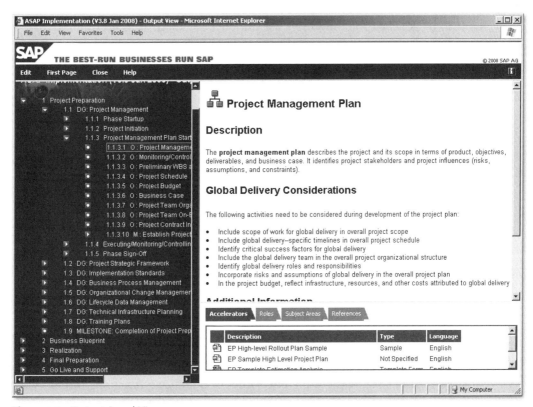

Figure 5.5 Output-Based View

Despite its restricted features, the HTML version does offer different views. In addition to the whole structure, you can display output-based (see Figure 5.5), method-based, or product-based HTML views, for instance, for the SAP NetWeaver Exchange Infrastructure, SAP NetWeaver

HTML version views

Portal (ASAP), Retail, Utilities, or Banking (Run SAP). The views focus on specific areas from the overall structure. Which view you select depends on project-specific requirements. The project manager can select a view — and consequently the level of detail for the project — depending on whether you work on the basis of tasks or outputs. The filtering options mentioned above (output-based, method-based, or complete view) are also available in the *Roadmap Authoring Environment* (see Section 5.1.5) and project-specific Roadmaps (Transaction RMMAIN).

5.1.5   Editing Roadmaps

Impact of modification

Roadmap editing tools let you create your own project methodology. Their flexibility enables you to design Roadmaps that suit your company's needs, with a structure that you can adapt as required, and in the right language. Furthermore, you can tailor SAP Roadmaps to your own requirements to reduce the amount of editing required and to set up your Roadmap more efficiently.

Before you decide to extend SAP Roadmaps or design your own Roadmap, we recommend that you consider the implications of changing SAP content. The content is shipped every six to eight months. To keep your Roadmaps in sync with the SAP content updates, your team would need to update them at the necessary intervals. To make this more straightforward, you should keep a detailed log of all the changes that your team makes to a Roadmap, so that you can consolidate these modifications more easily with the updated version of the SAP Roadmap.

The content of SAP Roadmaps can be changed only in copies of the respective header data, structure, and documents. As such, you copy and then change the relevant Roadmap rather than modifying SAP originals.

Resources

The Roadmap editing environment offers two functions to help your team adapt SAP Roadmaps and create new ones:

▸ **Roadmap Repository for defining Roadmaps (Transaction RMDEF)**
This is where you define header data for a Roadmap, such as its name and attributes (flavors, roles, subject areas). The attributes are used for

filtering information in an SAP Solution Manager project. Whereas partners tend to develop their own methodologies, customers will more likely use SAP Roadmaps supplemented with their own content.

▶ **Roadmap Authoring environment for editing structures and creating an entry screen (Transaction RMAUTH)**
This is where you structure your Roadmap or make changes to copied structures (see Figure 5.6). Any documentation that you create or change in the TOPICS and ACCELERATOR areas is stored in a local SAP NetWeaver Knowledge Warehouse (SAP NetWeaver KW) system, which provides the document management functions (see Sections 5.3 and 5.4).

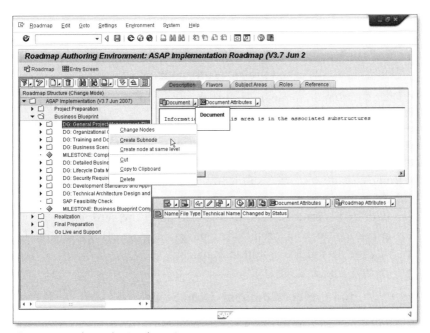

Figure 5.6 Editing the Roadmap Structure

To classify the Roadmap content in more detail for subsequent project work, you assign attributes to the individual structure nodes and accelerators. You can also create your own entry screen to give you a phase-by-phase overview of your project's key aspects.

5.2   Project Administration as the Cornerstone of Project Preparation

Scope of the phase

The design phase is the time for planning, defining, and preparing your implementation project. As you have already seen, the ASAP Implementation Roadmap is a generic guide that walks you through all of the necessary steps, regardless of the objective, scope, and priorities of your particular project. By the end of this phase, you will have reached the first milestone and achieved the following:

▸ Defined the project charter and project objectives

▸ Clarified the scope of the implementation

▸ Documented the project plan

▸ Defined a schedule and budget for the project

▸ Documented and approved project standards

▸ Identified and assigned project team members

▸ Drawn up requirements regarding the design of the system landscape

Clarifying this general project data at an early stage provides a solid basis for implementing your software successfully and running your project efficiently. The Project Administration transaction (SOLAR_PROJECT_ADMIN) and the PLAN view of the Implementation/Upgrade work center in SAP Solution Manager contain support functions for managing project standards and team members, basic scheduling, and setting up the system landscape for your project. The project manager is responsible for entering the data in SAP Solution Manager.

5.2.1   Initial Project Administration Screen

Project types

The initial project administration screen gives you an overview of all the projects in SAP Solution Manager. It is your central point for all project administration tasks. In addition to implementation projects for SAP applications and industry solutions, you will find other types of projects, including:

- *Template projects* for creating global templates as a starting point for global rollouts or SAP partner solutions
- *Upgrade projects* for upgrading a solution
- *Maintenance projects* for continuous solution maintenance and change request management (see Section 9.1)

An example implementation project is described below to illustrate the project administration functions in more detail. You can easily apply this information to other project types, because the functions in SAP Solution Manager are essentially identical for all types of projects.

5.2.2 Creating an Implementation Project

Implementation projects are for realizing independent projects that will be used only within the SAP Solution Manager system. This means that you set up and execute the project locally; you cannot transport projects of this type.

After specifying a project name and title, you begin defining general data. Initially, this involves GENERAL DATA. On this tab page (see Figure 5.7), you enter information about the responsibilities of project managers and the language that will be used throughout the project and to map business scenarios[1] and business processes[2] later. Once you have saved the project, you cannot change the language. In the project description, you can outline the main features of your project by documenting the business case, objectives, and preliminary plans for resources, scheduling, and budgeting.

We recommend that you use the templates supplied as accelerators in the ASAP Implementation Roadmap. They are in the Roadmap structure under 1. PROJECT PREPARATION – 1.1 DG: GENERAL PROJECT MANAGEMENT – 1.1.3. PROJECT MANAGEMENT PLAN START-UP.

Templates as accelerators

---

1 The term *business process* is used in SAP Solution Manager; subsequently, it is also referred to as *scenario*. The equivalent term *business scenario* is also used in the documentation of these scenarios.

2 The term *business process* is used in SAP Solution Manager; subsequently, it is also referred to as *process*.

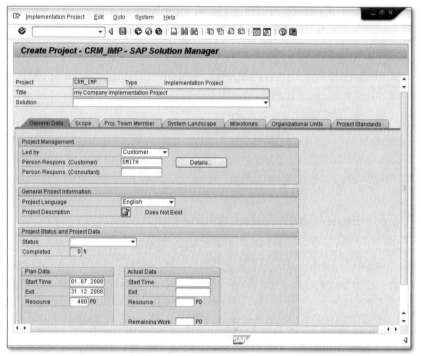

Figure 5.7 Input Screen for General Project Data

5.2.3 Setting the Project Scope

The project scope specifies which applications are to be implemented. It is based on an as-is analysis and customer-specific requirements. Purpose-designed tools such as SAP Solution Composer supply initial approaches and results for evaluating and presenting the business benefits of an SAP solution. You specify the project scope in more detail in the Business Blueprint phase. For more information, see Section 5.4.

The scope you define in the Project Administration transaction determines which (implementation) method is to be used for the project and — if the implementation project is based on templates — which templates are to be used as a foundation.

On the ROADMAP SELECT tab page, you select the current version of the ASAP Implementation Roadmap for your implementation project. You can also select solution-specific variants and the CORE ASAP variant, which describes the cross-solution ASAP methodology. For example, for an SAP CRM implementation project, you choose version V3.7 JUNE 2007 with the variants (flavors) MYSAP CRM and CORE ASAP (see Figure 5.8).

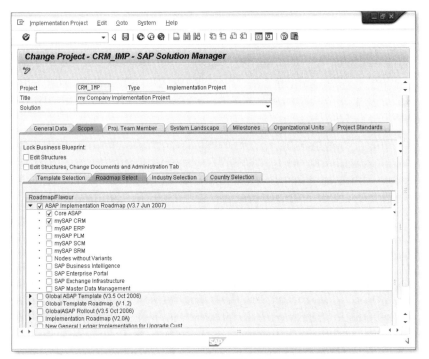

Figure 5.8 Roadmap Selection in Transaction SOLAR_PROJECT_ADMIN

You can now use the selected Roadmap for your specific project, which means you can enter statuses and notes in the Roadmap, assign employees to individual work items, create messages and project documentation, and add keywords. You can generate views for particular project team members, keywords, roles, and subject areas, which gives every project team member the option of restricting the Roadmap structure.

Project-specific use

The templates selected for the scope are not discussed further here, because they are not relevant for our example project. Templates are used in the *global rollout* scenario, which involves using templates to set up a rollout project as an implementation project.

5.2.4 Assigning Project Team Members

You assign resources in the Project Administration transaction in preparation for allocating project team members' responsibilities for editing the Roadmap, creating the Business Blueprint, and configuration. Project team members refer to users created in USER ADMINISTRATION (Transaction SU01). Team members are assigned roles that contain all of the authorizations they require to complete their tasks in the project. SAP Solution Manager offers customizable roles for the following groups: application consultants, development consultants, basis consultants, and display-only users.

Project authorizations

All project team members have change authorization for the whole project. However, you can restrict processing in subsequent project transactions (Business Blueprint, configuration) to team members assigned to the respective business process. You do so by setting the RESTRICT CHANGES TO NODES IN PROJECT TO ASSIGNED TEAM MEMBERS indicator on the PROJ. TEAM MEMBER tab.

Changing the project team

Once you have assigned employee IDs, you can use them for filtering the process structure in the Business Blueprint and Configuration transactions. This means that the scope for editing can be limited to the information relevant for the project team member. To accommodate organizational changes over the course of a project, you can replace or remove team members centrally. Subsequent changes to the project are thus kept to a minimum, while a history of all changes guarantees complete reproducibility.

You can also enter additional organizational data on the Milestones and Organizational Units tab pages. This data is optional; it is for information purposes only and is not included in reporting.

Two other vital elements of project administration involve setting up the system landscape and defining project standards, both of which are explained in the following sections.

5.2.5 Structuring the System Landscape

Elements of the system landscape

A well-planned, effective system landscape is essential for accessing systems connected to SAP Solution Manager during the Business Blueprint, configuration, and testing phases. SAP Solution Manager also takes into account that a complete system landscape is not usually available at the start of a project, even though you must be ready to begin working on the conceptual design in the Business Blueprint.

This section introduces the basic parameters that are integral to the project. Refer also to the system matrix in Figure 5.9.

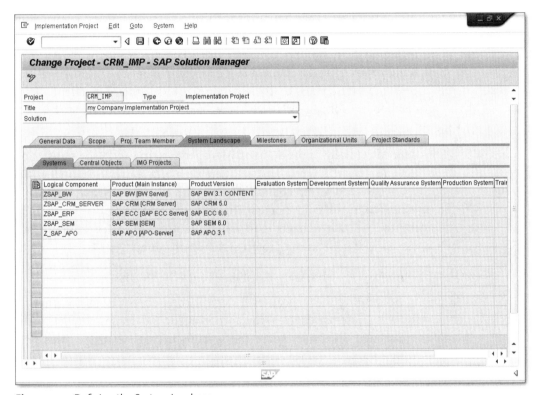

Figure 5.9 Defining the System Landscape

A logical component groups together different systems with the same SAP product release (more specifically, main instances and product versions) so you can standardize their usage across the system landscape in projects and subsequent operational solutions. The system and client combinations assigned to a logical component are usually linked by transport routes. The combinations have a specific function, or *system role* within the system group: This role is indicated in the column headings DEVELOPMENT SYSTEM, QUALITY ASSURANCE SYSTEM, and PRODUCTION SYSTEM. In practice, other names are often used to express this very abstract concept, such as *installed base*.

When the current situation was reviewed in our example project, logical component ZSAP_ERP was assigned, based on the product version SAP ECC 6.0. Physical systems are assigned later in the project. You can use the SYSTEM LANDSCAPE function to test whether working RFC connections have been established. This function also checks system compatibility regarding the minimum requirements for communication with SAP Solution Manager. The assignment of logical component ZSAP_CRM_SERVER points to future plans to implement SAP CRM. Other dependent logical components for SAP APO, SAP SEM, and SAP BW will be added.

Central definition of logical components
For logical components to be used consistently in projects, they must be defined centrally in the Solution Manager System Landscape transaction (SMSY). This lets you manage system data efficiently, use suitable RFC connections to set up communication with the systems, and group systems into logical components. This task usually falls to a system administrator. All that remains is to assign the relevant logical components, using input help, in the project system landscape.

Advantages
So what is the advantage of using logical components?

▶ Decoupling the logical level (logical component) from the physical level (systems) enables you to document the process model in the Business Blueprint before the systems become available. This flexible approach reflects real-life practices, where development, quality assurance, and production systems seldom are available at the start of a project. You can then add the systems gradually without affecting the process model definition.

▶ Using logical components centrally allows them to be used consistently in other projects, for instance.

▶ Changes you make centrally to logical components can be seen automatically in all projects that use the components. This is the case, for instance, when a quality management system is added subsequently for test purposes.

▶ Logical components are also suited to presenting third-party products and legacy systems. This means you can map all of your business processes in one integrated process model, regardless of whether they run on SAP or non-SAP software.

▶ Logical components enable you to manage complex, distributed system landscapes relatively easily; system dependencies are visible at a glance, as are options for navigating to the relevant systems, which depend on the system roles.

For each project, you usually record all of the logical components with the relevant SAP and non-SAP products that are required to run the solution being implemented.

Working with the system landscape

The logical components also have another function: They control the selection of business processes in the subsequent Business Blueprint phase. There are two approaches:

▶ **Top-down approach**
Initially, you do not record a system landscape. In the subsequent Business Blueprint phase, you select the relevant scenarios or processes from the complete range of SAP solutions. In this case, the system proposes the necessary logical components and adds them to the project system landscape. If the required releases are higher than those in your existing project system landscape, you can choose earlier releases by selecting logical components with older product versions. In this case, however, you have to check manually that the selected scenarios or processes run on the different product versions. This procedure is advisable for new implementations.

▶ **Bottom-up approach**
You record the *existing* system landscape for the project. In the Business Blueprint, the system automatically proposes only scenarios and processes that can run in your current system landscape. You can also add scenarios and processes that require higher product versions. The system automatically proposes the logical components required for these and adds them to the project system landscape. This procedure is advisable if the system landscape is already documented, for instance, for reviewing the current situation in preparation for upgrading.

This is an iterative process that you keep repeating until you have worked out the best possible solution for your current system landscape. The system always checks that your project system landscape contains the minimum components needed to run the selected solution.

5.2.6 Defining Project Standards

Documenting and approving project standards is another important aspect of the project preparation phase. It enables you to ensure that all project team members apply the same standards consistently later in the project, resulting in better communication during the project and facilitating evaluation.

You define certain project standards in the Project Administration transaction: standard status values, keywords, and documentation types. Keywords can be used in subsequent phases to filter the project scope by team, subproject, or scenario. Standardized documentation types with templates help you compile documentation in the Business Blueprint and configuration phases. Status values give you an effective means of monitoring how work is progressing in different project phases.

SAP supplies default values for documentation types and status values. You can also tailor these standards to your requirements or define your own standards.

Documentation types

You might use the following types of documentation:

- ▶ Management summary for each scenario or process
- ▶ Documentation for scenarios, processes, master data, and organizational units
- ▶ Test document
- ▶ Configuration document
- ▶ Templates for functional and technical specifications such as program enhancements, interfaces, and data transfer

Which types of documentation you actually use will, of course, vary greatly from project to project. As such, the above list is intended only as a guide. We recommend, however, that you do not include project management documents such as meeting minutes.

The ASAP Implementation Roadmap is a valuable resource when you are defining project standards for documents: In the Roadmap structure, under 1.3 DG IMPLEMENTATION STANDARDS – 1.3.1. IMPLEMENTATION PROJECT STANDARDS – 1.3.1.2 O: PROJECT DOCUMENTATION STANDARDS, you can access the SAMPLE DOCUMENTATION MAP accelerator. It gives details of the process model levels for which you can use standard documentation types.

Accelerators for project standards

You always use the following procedure to create and add project standards:

Creating project standards

1. You check whether the project standards provided by SAP (for example, documentation types and respective templates) can be used in your project and, if necessary, define new ones. You do so in a central repository, accessed using the PROJECT TEMPLATE button. You can define one status profile for each documentation type, specifying which status values are permitted and the sequence in which they may be set when documents are edited. Status profiles are also used for digital signatures, which is particularly helpful to customers working in validated environments. You define status profiles in Customizing for SAP Solution Manager.

2. Next, you copy the relevant standards from the central repository to the project-type-specific repository for documentation types. These documentation types become the common repository for the respective project types, that is, for all implementation projects. In the project itself, you initially classify them as *unused*.

3. To use implementation project standards in an actual project, you copy them to your project as *available* standards. Restrict the selection to the documentation types that are actually to be used in the project (see Figure 5.10).

Any documentation created during the project is stored in the SAP NetWeaver KW component integrated in SAP Solution Manager. You simply need to define the storage context for each project. This controls which version of a document (such as language and release) is used for editing. Besides the default customer namespace proposed for the context (enhancement /KWCUST), you can use an existing customer namespace or request a separate one from SAP. The document context

Documentation context

also protects documents against unauthorized changes, because you can include it specifically in the authorizations for project team members. This is not usually necessary for standard implementation projects.

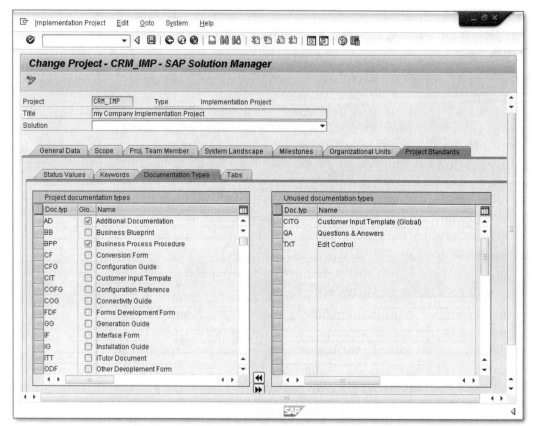

Figure 5.10 Used and Unused Documentation Types

On the TABS tab page, you can specify which tab pages are to be available for a project in the Business Blueprint and Configuration transactions. You can indicate tab pages that are not required as hidden (invisible); however, we recommend that you keep the default settings for recording the change history.

You now have a basis for working on the project during the Business Blueprint phase.

5.3   Documentation of Solution

IT landscapes are regularly maintained throughout their life cycle and adapted to new business requirements if necessary. The planning and reporting for the respective initiatives are therefore an important instrument for operating the solution successfully. Detailed documentation of the existing solution is the basis for efficient planning and reporting. You must completely and accurately describe the individual components in your solution landscape as well as the business processes. This documentation is referred to frequently during the implementation project and later when operating the solution.

A good approach to modeling your solution is to first concentrate on some core business processes. These are the processes that are particularly important for the economic success of your company. Disruptions to these processes have an extraordinary effect on the success of your business.

Core business processes

To create the documentation, you should first concentrate on the system that performs the most important steps in the process. This system is also described as a *critical system* for a business process because the failure of the system greatly impairs the process. Because the later operation of the system essentially focuses on the critical systems, particular care is required to describe these systems and the corresponding process steps. Next, you integrate the description of the other systems involved, the subsequent process steps, and the interfaces used, until all interfaces that transfer critical data for the business process have been documented.

Critical system

The documentation of the business processes initially includes the individual process steps. It should be described in a standardized format. As well as the actual process, you also document more detailed information, for example, the roles involved or possible dependencies. Table 5.1 contains a template for documenting business process steps. In addition to describing the individual process steps, the documentation presents information about the whole process, such as the purpose of the process or relevant key performance indicators (KPIs).

Process Step	Name of Process Step
Description	\<Short description of the business process step (target state)\>
Who performs the step?	\<Responsible role or function to perform the step\>
When is the step performed?	\<Fixed date or triggering event\>
What information or documents are required?	\<Documents with information required to perform the step (paper or system documents)\>
Which tool is used?	\<System function used (dialog, batch, or program) or other required media\>
What is the result of the activity?	\<Generated/changed data and documents (if relevant: who is the recipient?)\>
Comments	\<Reference to further information; business processes used; critical factors\>
Specifications for master data	\<Which master data is required and how is it replicated?\>
Specifications for reporting	\<Information required for reporting\>
Specifications for system configuration	\<Required Customizing settings or system configuration (including customer development requirement)\>
Who is involved/date	\<Name of project team members who created the documentation\>

Table 5.1 Template for Documenting Business Process Steps

The business process documentation is generally created as part of an implementation, maintenance, or upgrade project. You create it using the Business Blueprint (SOLAR01) and Configuration (SOLAR02) transactions in SAP Solution Manager in particular, both of which can be accessed from the Implementation/Upgrade work center. More detailed information about documenting your solution with these transactions is provided in Sections 5.4 and 6.1. You can obtain more support for documenting your existing solution from the Solution Documentation Assistant (see Section 4.3).

The system documentation contains technical information about the system, for example, the product and release, the server and database on which it is installed, the software components it contains and their Support Package level, the clients that are configured, and how you can connect to them (see Figure 5.11). It also contains information about the corresponding system landscape (development, quality assurance, and production system) and the respective transport routes of software logistics.

System documentation

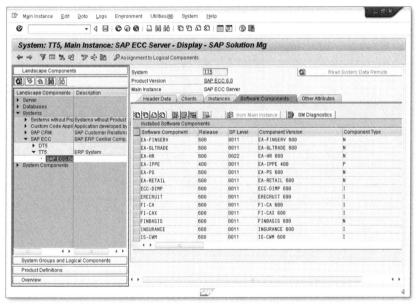

Figure 5.11 Displaying System Documentation

The documentation of the systems in the solution landscape is generally created automatically for SAP applications and applications that are registered in the *System Landscape Directory* by connecting the systems to SAP Solution Manager. It is also possible to manually enter the data for non-SAP applications in the System Landscape Solution Manager transaction (SMSY) in SAP Solution Manager. This transaction can be reached through the System Landscape Management work center.

Many people require the information in the solution documentation to complete their tasks. However, different data is required depending on

Solution views

the person's role. SAP Solution Manager therefore provides different solution views (see Figure 5.12).

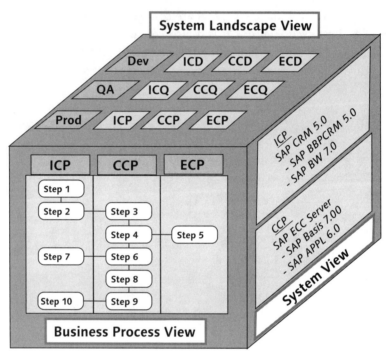

Figure 5.12 Solution Views

Business process view

The *business process view* shows the core business processes. The process steps contained are each assigned to logical components (products or product versions). You use this view in projects, in particular, to store the project documentation in a structured way.

System view

The *system view* focuses more on technical aspects. It contains all systems and logical components that are operated by a certain organization. This view makes it possible to view the system and its product versions and software components in detail. A connection to the business process view and system view is created by assigning business process steps to systems.

The *system landscape view* arranges all logical components to be operated and monitored in system landscapes. This view defines the relationships between production and nonproduction systems (for example, development and quality assurance) in a system landscape and in particular, the transport rules relevant for monitoring changes. Therefore, this view is particularly relevant for software logistics tasks.

System landscape view

The topic of traceability is becoming increasingly important not only due to legal regulations such as the Sarbanes-Oxley Act and the requirements of the Food and Drug Administration (FDA), but also in light of general IT governance. In close collaboration with customers, SAP has introduced new functions for traceability management in SAP Solution Manager Enterprise Edition.

Traceability

Traceability management extends the options of SAP Solution Manager in the document management and editing project structure areas.

The digital signature plays an important role in document management in a regulated environment. You can use a digital signature to sign electronic documents digitally. When you process digital data, a digital signature has the same function as a written signature on printed documents. Digital signatures uniquely identify the signer of a digital document.

Document management

Digital signatures can be used in a wide range of scenarios, enabling you to:

▶ Confirm that a document has been read or approved (for example, approval of final document versions for Business Blueprint documents)

▶ Protect the integrity of data (for example, signatures on tester notes or other documents for auditing purposes)

SAP Solution Manager Enterprise Edition offers new functions that make it possible to trace changes.

New functions in SAP Solution Manager

▶ When digitally signed documents are displayed and printed, the signature is always displayed or printed automatically. To ensure the security and integrity of your data, this function cannot be suppressed.

▶ Document history has been extended to show all information about the history of changes to documents, including the digital signature processes.

▶ Document reporting has been extended.

Editing the project structure

To facilitate working with project structures in a regulated environment, new functions have also been provided with SAP Solution Manager Enterprise Edition.

▶ For example, you can lock structure nodes that you have finished editing in the project structure, for example, in the Business Blueprint (Transaction SOLAR01). This is especially important if the steering committee of the project has approved a structure. By locking these structure nodes, you can prevent project members from making changes to the project structure at a later date. To ensure the security and integrity of the data, you can use the digital signature to identify the user who has locked the nodes.

Locking a structure allows the tabs of the structure, for example, DOCUMENTATION, to be changed.

▶ If you have finished editing tab data in the project, you can lock the areas of the tab and therefore prevent other project members from making changes. Depending on the structure nodes, you can lock and unlock entries on the following tabs (tabs can also be locked with a digital signature):

  ▶ Gen. Documentation

  ▶ Proj. Documentation

  ▶ Administration

  ▶ Transactions

  ▶ End User Roles

  ▶ Configuration

  ▶ Test Cases

  ▶ Development

  ▶ Training Materials

To facilitate transparent documentation of your projects and to provide information exactly where it is needed, you can assign customer-specific attributes to the project at different levels. You can define these attributes for structure nodes in the project structure or assign attributes to certain objects.

Free attributes

Depending on the object, the following tabs are available for assigning attributes:

- GENERAL: general information about the object and assignment of keywords
- CONNECTIONS: assignment of documents
- OTHER ATTRIBUTES: customer-specific attributes and their assignment
- HISTORY: editing history

After editing the attributes, you can lock them so that it is no longer possible for other project members to make changes.

The attribute values of an object are assigned to the combination of object and logical components. If you use the same object with the same logical component again in the project, the system automatically adopts the assigned attribute values so that you have centralized access to integrated system documentation.

5.4 Business Blueprint – Conceptual Design for Your Solution

The purpose of the Business Blueprint phase is to outline the current situation as identified during workshops so you can compile a Business Blueprint documenting the target state of the solution being implemented and the resultant requirements. The conceptual design drawn up by the project team members therefore describes how your enterprise wants to map its business processes using SAP and non-SAP systems.

This phase also entails the following steps:

- Refining the original project goals and objectives
- Finalizing the overall project schedule

▶ Implementing Organizational and Change Management

▶ Defining functional standards for and documenting customer developments

▶ Defining the requirements for the authorization concept, security policy, and end user training concept

▶ Planning the system environment for operations

In SAP Solution Manager, you can draw up your conceptual design in the Business Blueprint transaction (SOLAR01). It provides valuable support, especially for mapping and documenting the processes with regard to implementation. This function can be found, for example, in the PLAN view in the Implementation/Upgrade work center.

5.4.1 Mapping Customer-Specific Solutions

Integrating existing processes

Implementation projects can have very different starting points. Some projects have only a broadly defined scope and use the implementation content shipped with SAP Solution Manager as a starting point for the implementation project. Other projects may be based on the results of the analysis of the Solution Documentation Assistant (see Section 4.3), ARIS process models, or Microsoft Visio diagrams. Irrespective of the starting point, the goal is always to find the optimal way of integrating or setting up existing processes as part of a harmonized, overall implementation concept.

The team usually holds a series of workshops to gradually break down the requirements from solution level to business process level. The ASAP Implementation Roadmap offers methodical support for this task in the *Business Solution Requirements* and *Detailed Business Requirements* deliverable groups.

Process structure

In the Business Blueprint transaction, you depict your solution as a structure based on scenarios and processes (process structure) with three levels: business scenarios, and their sublevels, business processes, and process steps. Organizational units, which show how your enterprise is organized, and master data complete the scenario definitions. These elements are also referred to as *structure items*. If you work with additional levels, we recommend that you incorporate virtual levels using naming conventions for prefixes (short names or numbers). Your project work will be easier if you adopt no more than five levels to the SAP Solution Manager three-level concept. The process-centric view you draw up for the Business Blueprint is the basis for all subsequent project stages, including configuration, testing, and operations. The work you put in here pays off in later project phases: You can systematically prevent integration gaps in the transition from one project phase to the next.

It is not generally advisable to structure your model using functional units such as organizations, business departments, persons responsible, or SAP components. You can take account of such aspects by assigning keywords, which enable you to generate views for specific groups of users by filtering the Business Blueprint and configuration information.

The *Business Process Repository* (BPR, see Section 4.2) in SAP Solution Manager provides predefined implementation content for all of the applications and solutions in the SAP Business Suite. It includes the business scenarios and processes supported by the respective application, relevant business descriptions, assignments to SAP functions in the form of transactions and URLs, for example, and settings for configuring the business processes.

Predefined content

The implementation content portrays an SAP application or industry solution, allowing you to familiarize yourself with the details of a given solution. Building on this content in your project reduces the time and effort you spend on implementing and tailoring the solution as part of an upgrade project, for example. Always check the usage of the following sources in order:

▶ **Use of predefined implementation content from BPR to set up process structure**
We recommend that you start by evaluating the scenarios, processes and process steps, master data, and organizational units proposed by SAP (SAP reference elements). On the STRUCTURE tab page, use the input help to select the elements that correspond to your implementation scope (see Figure 5.13).

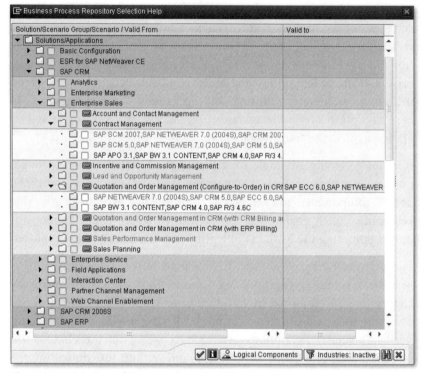

Figure 5.13 Selection of Scenarios from the BPR

The input help shows scenarios from SAP CRM – Enterprise Sales. Each individual scenario, such as CONTRACT MANAGEMENT, contains combinations of products representing the minimum requirements for running the scenario (indicated as VALID FROM). If the system landscape currently defined in the Project Administration transaction supports the scenario (bottom-up approach), the version is displayed in bold, or otherwise in gray. You can also select grayed out versions; the system advises you if you need additional system components to run the given scenario and automatically compares the project system landscape with proposals for logical components. This procedure is the same as the top-down approach discussed in Section 5.2.5. To display details about selecting reference elements and comparing the system landscape, click the information icon. When you select SAP reference elements, all assignments of documentation, transactions,

Customizing settings from IMG activities, and test cases are copied to your project automatically.

Depending on the solution and demand, SAP implementation content is available in different languages. Check whether the language you require is available and search for the concepts in English, if necessary.

Because customers almost always need to make some adjustments, you can rename and reassign reference elements, or copy them and add your own content (such as project documentation and process graphics) to develop custom variants. In addition to the above options, you can insert new process steps without losing the information about the origin of the processes. Keeping the links to the original SAP reference elements equips you for future upgrades, enabling you to use comparison functions to identify and copy new features and changes that are relevant for the upgrade.

For information about the implementation content available, see the SAP Service Marketplace: *http://www.service.sap.com/solutionmanager* • Downloads • Overview of the current implementation content.

▶ **Reuse of processes from operational solutions**
Not all customers who use SAP Solution Manager start by implementing new solutions. Customers who deploy the Business Process Monitoring functions for an operational solution must have already defined processes, which they can reuse in an implementation project. They need only assign the operational solution to the project. This enables them to select existing processes using input help and copy them to their project. The downside of this approach is that customers cannot compare processes against SAP reference processes at a later date.

▶ **Use of reference elements from other subprojects**
In some cases, reference elements can be reused from other projects to map the process structure, reducing the time and effort required to describe the processes. Other projects can therefore be used as a source of data for the process structure. If you use SAP reference elements to build the master structure, you can follow a two-stage procedure to copy any changes made to these elements from the master project to a subproject.

▶ **Definition of custom structure items**

You can also set up a partial or complete process structure without using reference elements. However, in this case you will not be able to compare your processes against SAP reference processes at a later stage, for example, to see upgrade-related changes. We recommend, therefore, that you investigate the possibility of referring to, that is, initially copying, SAP reference elements at least at the process level, even if you change the elements radically later on for your specific project. However, you always have access to comparison functions, which highlight changes to SAP reference elements that are relevant to a particular project and allow you to copy them if necessary. If you do not use SAP reference elements, you have to make all assignments yourself that qualify a structure item in more detail, such as transactions and IMG (Implementation Guide) assignments for configuration. You can delete redundant reference elements that you have copied from the BPR, provided you have confirmed that they are definitely not needed. If you cannot confirm this, or if certain processes might be implemented in a subsequent phase, we recommend that you use the scoping functions to hide processes that will be implemented from the project scope later on.

Master data
You assign general, cross-scenario master data (such as material masters and business partners) directly to the implementation project (MASTER DATA structure node) above the scenarios. You define scenario-specific master data below the respective scenario. The same applies to ORGANIZATIONAL UNITS. Universal master data also includes general settings such as countries and units of measurement.

Multiple use of structure items
If a structure item appears more than once in the project structure, it is advisable to define a master structure item, such as a dominant process, as a template for other processes. If you change the master process, you can transfer changes easily to the copied processes (ADJUST TO ORIGINAL on the STRUCTURE tab page).

Organizationally, it is important to allocate persons responsible for the individual structure items in the process structure. Particularly in the case of cross-functional processes, clearly defined responsibilities are critical for efficient communication during the project, both when processes are mapped and if they are changed subsequently. You maintain information concerning team member responsibilities and other administrative data such as keywords on the ADMINISTRATION tab page. Convenient reporting options are available in SAP Solution Manager for this data at all times (Transaction SOLAR_EVAL).

In our example project, the process structure is based on predefined SAP implementation content from the BPR. Detailed documentation is added to the project gradually to describe the requirements. Figure 5.14 shows the project structure.

5.4.2 Documenting the Target State

In the Business Blueprint phase, you expand on the process structure by adding descriptions of business objects (master data and organization) as well as scenarios and processes. By assigning functions to the SAP system world (as transactions, for instance), you define how the business processes run in the system. If you use predefined implementation content from the BPR, you can access business scenario and business process documentation on the GEN. DOCUMENTATION tab page. You must not change this documentation during implementation projects. If you need to create project-specific documentation for the Business Blueprint, use the PROJ. DOCUMENTATION tab page. From the TRANSACTIONS tab page, you can call transactions, URLs, and programs to navigate to the relevant applications. This means you can start conducting initial tests on these functions in the blueprint phase.

The Business Blueprint should contain the requirements for the solution being implemented. This includes the actual scenario and process documentation, which records the current situation, the requirements, implementation options, and the process flow displayed graphically in some cases. A functional vulnerability analysis can supply input for requirements regarding enhancements and customer developments (including interface definition, program developments, and data transfer). Furthermore, you can record requirements for end user training, as well as for setting up authorizations and end user roles.

Requirements

Specifying the requirements therefore gives you a firm and comprehensive basis for implementing your solution. You can draw on SAP or customer-specific documentation types and templates that you defined in

Project Administration (Transaction SOLAR_PROJECT_ADMIN; see Section 5.2) and thereby ensure that the documentation process observes project standards. Project team members can refer to precompleted sample documents for a clear and consistent illustration of *how* to fill out the documents.

When you create project documentation in SAP Solution Manager, you can use the documents in various ways (see Figure 5.14).

Figure 5.14 Process Structure and Requirements Documentation

Storage — Documentation is stored in the SAP NetWeaver KW component integrated in SAP Solution Manager. The following information refers to processes but also applies to other structure items in the project structure. You can:

▸ Use the templates defined in the Project Administration transaction to create new documents

▸ Create references to existing documents, that is, link to a particular document at a different place in the structure. This option is useful if, for example, a process is used in multiple scenarios and the process documentation is applicable to all of the scenarios.

- Copy an existing document. This option is useful if processes or scenarios are similar but not identical. You can use documentation for a similar process as a basis for tailoring the documentation for other processes. You need fewer resources to create documents, but the number of documents to be managed in SAP NetWeaver KW increases.

- Upload documents and therefore integrate existing information from a central repository

- Insert web links to documents that were created in a different (external) repository, such as an intranet or file server, and for which migration is not economically feasible. This option has performance-related advantages too for all types of materials that require substantial memory space, such as web-based tutorials. Although such materials are stored locally, you can still incorporate and access them centrally via SAP Solution Manager.

- Check documents in and out. You can check documents out to edit offline. Checked out documents are automatically locked against editing in SAP Solution Manager until they are checked in again.

- Use documentation from SAP or a template in your project documentation. Documents from SAP and templates are displayed on the GEN. DOCUMENTATION tab page; they must not be changed during implementation projects. You can refer to these documents from the project documentation. We recommend this option if you do not want to change the documents but want to include them in the Business Blueprint document. Alternatively, you can copy documents, which is recommended if you need to tailor standard documentation.

Under SETTINGS • USER SPECIFIC…, you can define user-specific settings in a separate window. These settings govern which tab pages are displayed or hidden, as well as editing and display options for documents.

User-specific settings

Besides documenting the steps involved in scenarios and processes, you can also use graphics to display the actual process flows. A graphic lets you store information that cannot otherwise be depicted in the process structure due to the structure's linear nature. The graphic on the tab page of the same name gives you insight into the composition of scenarios and processes, logical components, and non-SAP products running the processes in question (where appropriate), as well as the relationships (synchronous and asynchronous) between process steps. One advantage of SAP Solution Manager is that it automatically proposes basic scenario and process graphics based on the process structure, which you can revise if necessary. For detailed modeling, you can embed graphics created in external modeling tools into your project as a separate type of documentation, such as a process graphic.

Defining document owners

As with the project structure model, you need to assign project team members as document owners; they need not be identical to the process or scenario owners. On the PROJ. DOCUMENTATION tab page, owners set the predefined status values to reflect the current editing status and thus create a basis for analysis. You can display change data for documents at any time by clicking the ATTRIBUTE button and then the HISTORY tab.

You can create an interim or final version of your conceptual design at any time by generating a Business Blueprint document. You indicate any documents that you want to be included as BLUEPRINT-RELEVANT. The Business Blueprint document includes information such as:

▶ Business areas

▶ Requirements regarding master data, organizational units, scenarios, and processes that are to be realized

▶ Components required

▶ Scenario and process graphics

Creating document parts

One of the many options for generating documents is creating document parts. By selecting a suitable documentation type (such as *Management summary*), you can merge (interim) status reports maintained by the document owners to form a complete management document.

If necessary, you can also include the project description and other project planning documents in the Business Blueprint by assigning them to the project documentation accordingly.

Blueprint sign-off

The Business Blueprint phase ends with the *Blueprint sign-off*. The Business Blueprint is frozen at a particular point and signed off by process owners and IT managers from the individual departments. You freeze the blueprint by setting a lock in the Project Administration transaction. This specifically prevents changes being made to the process structure, blueprint-relevant documents, or administrative data (SCOPE tab page). Subsequent changes must be requested explicitly and systematically via the Change Request Management procedure.

5.5   Customer Developments

The functions supplied with standard applications do not always cover a customer's requirements completely. For this reason, additional functions are developed in some projects or existing functions are changed. Developments like this can either be made directly by the customer, by another company or by the SAP Custom Development organization. In the following section, we generally talk of customer developments, regardless of whom a customer has commissioned to make the development.

Customer developments can be programs that are implemented in SAP applications, independent applications that are operated in addition to an SAP application and that are connected to it via interfaces, or changes to existing standard applications (modifications). Various development environments are available for development, such as the ABAP Development Workbench, SAP NetWeaver Developer Studio, SAP NetWeaver Composition Environment, or development environments from other providers.

Although customer developments were previously discouraged because they significantly increased the time and effort required for maintenance, the general opinion today is very different. Based on open integration technology such as that supplied by the SAP NetWeaver technology platform, it is possible to develop applications that exist outside of the standard SAP application but that are integrated as if they were part of the SAP application. You can implement new business processes quickly and flexibly by combining and orchestrating enterprise services developed by SAP, partners, or in your company, and add logic and a suitable user interface.

Enterprise services

The users of your solution expect the required functions to be available, regardless of whether they are provided by a standard application or a customer development. To meet this expectation, your IT organization

Standardized operation concept

must ensure that a standardized operation concept exists for the entire solution. The customer development must therefore be introduced to this concept. Therefore, certain aspects must be considered at the start of the development. The customer development can subsequently be operated and maintained efficiently only if the results of the development project, such as program code, data structures, configuration, and documentation, are well structured and documented. This applies not only to new customer developments, but also to enhancements from previous projects. A detailed analysis of the existing developments is first required here to identify necessary activities and possible improvement measures. The existing analysis functions in the *Custom Development Management Cockpit* (CDMC) are introduced in the following section.

Supporting customer developments is often more complex than supporting standard applications. This is mainly because a standard application is generally used by more customers than a customer development, so more support experience is available for the standard application. The problem is compounded if the persons involved in the development project have left your company or the partner involved is no longer available. Therefore, proper documentation of the customer development is essential. It is important that you at least have the specification of the development project, a list of the development objects involved, and the required configuration settings. Section 5.5.2 discusses important information on documenting customer developments in SAP Solution Manager.

5.5.1 Analysis of Customer Developments

As described in the previous section, many SAP customers modify or enhance their SAP standard software in some way. Some customers enhance reports that are specific to their company, for example, while others implement entirely customer-specific (internally or externally developed) add-ons. Using customer developments and modifications, customers can model their business processes according to their market requirements. Customer developments and modifications are therefore unavoidable in a company, and as a result, there is generally a large number of customer-developed objects or modified SAP standard objects.

However, requirements change so quickly these days that many customer-developed objects and modifications to SAP standard objects sooner or later become outdated. Experience shows that after just a few years, a third of customer developments are no longer in use or have been modified, not only because of changed requirements, but also because new versions of SAP standard software are supplied, which contain objects that are equivalent to customer developments. This can lead to an unnecessarily high, particularly unjustified, maintenance cost that in turn leads to high operating costs for the customer.

It also becomes difficult for customers to keep track of all these modifications to the standard system and customer developments. The high costs incurred when upgrading or importing Support Packages is an important consequence of the increasing number of modifications and customer-developed objects. Before the system is upgraded to a newer SAP release or a Support Package is imported, all customer developments must first be inspected and adapted manually; then all objects must be tested individually to ensure that they will not cause any problems in the new context.

Upgrades

The Custom Development Management Cockpit (CDMC) is SAP's latest approach to analyzing how customer developments are used and identifying which of these are obsolete. It then assesses the effect of an upgrade or Support Package installation on the customer developments.

Custom Development Management Cockpit

The CDMC is a function in SAP Solution Manager Enterprise Edition that supports customer-specific solutions in all phases of application management, particularly in the requirement and design phases and in the optimization phase (see Chapters 4, 5, and 9). In the requirements and design phases, customers identify the core business processes in their company. The CDMC supports them during this phase by identifying and analyzing how customer developments are used (based on the call statistics provided by the system). At the same time, customer developments that are obsolete are identified.

In the optimization phase, customers must ensure that the planned changes are implemented consistently. The CDMC provides support for upgrade projects not only by reducing the number of obsolete customer-specific developments, but also by accelerating the upgrade enormously. This is because customers only adapt the customer developments if they are absolutely necessary. The CDMC provides support for project planning because

Optimization phase

it is possible to make an early estimate of expenditure for adapting the relevant object types necessary for a more recent release. The customer therefore profits from improved and more reliable planning, and shorter project terms that lead to greater savings on the project costs.

The Custom Development Management Cockpit indicates the quality and scope of the customer developments and therefore consists of two components.

1. In *clearing analysis* (CA), the use of customer objects is analyzed and obsolete objects are identified. The results of this clearing analysis are the ideal starting point for clearing these developments. Detailed instructions guide the customer through the *clearing process*.

2. *Upgrade/change impact analysis* (UCIA) identifies the technical effects of an SAP upgrade or the installation of a Support Package on customer-developed objects, and makes it possible to produce an estimate of the time and effort required to adapt these objects.

The CDMC can be called up in the Implementation/Upgrade work center in SAP Solution Manager (see Figure 5.15 and Figure 5.16).

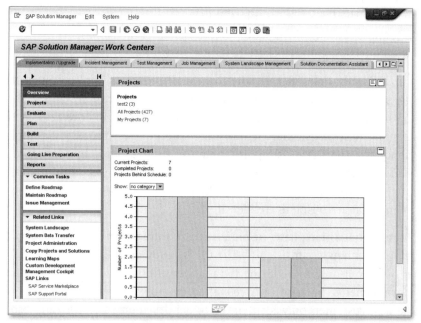

Figure 5.15 SAP Solution Manager – Work Center: Implementation/Upgrade

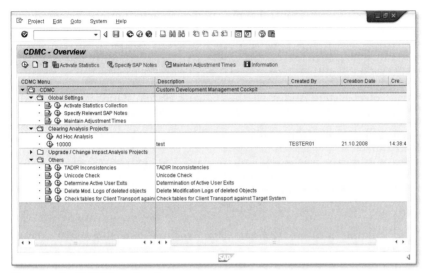

Figure 5.16 CDMC Overview Screen

Figure 5.17 shows the system landscape in a clearing analysis project.

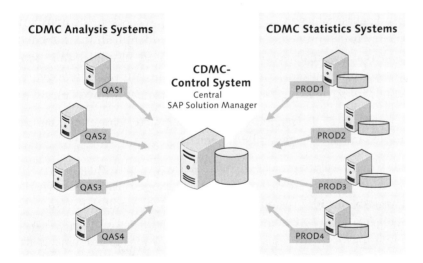

Figure 5.17 System Landscape in a CDMC Clearing Analysis Project

In the statistics system, the statistical data, such as executed transactions, is gathered and saved in CDMC database tables. All project-related analyses are performed in the corresponding analysis system. The control

System landscape

165

system includes the control center where all activities are triggered and monitored. The systems are connected by remote function call (RFC). Several pairs of statistics and analysis systems can be assigned to a control system.

In a typical system landscape, the statistics system stands for the production system, the analysis system corresponds to the consolidation system, and the platform for the control system is SAP Solution Manager.

Clearing analysis phases

The clearing analysis has five phases (also see Figure 5.18):

The *project settings* phase includes tasks such as defining the system landscape and displaying the relevant SAP Notes.

The activities in the *data collection phase* include collecting statistical data in the statistics system and identifying the customer-developed objects and the modified SAP objects in the analysis system. The collected statistical data is then imported from the statistics system into the central system.

In the *analysis phase*, domain duplicates in the customer namespace and empty database tables are identified, the syntax is checked, the transport frequency is determined, inactive objects are identified, the extended runtime is analyzed, objects without a reference are identified, and a top-down and bottom-up analysis are performed. The latter constitute central functions for recognizing used and unused customer-defined objects.

The results can be viewed in the *display phase*. Here, various options are available for displaying and filtering the data.

Clearing process

The clearing analysis project is concluded with the *clearing process*. In this process, objects are deleted from the customer namespace (Z*, Y*, and namespace with a customer-specific prefix), or modifications to standard objects in the SAP namespace are removed. The clearing process is different for these two cases. Obsolete modifications to SAP objects are removed using SAP standard tools, whereas obsolete objects that are assigned to the customer namespace are physically deleted according to SAP clearing guidelines. To optimize the clearing process, each clearing tool used by the customer should correspond to the standard SAP deletion process as provided in the ABAP Workbench. This means that when a master object is deleted (for example, an object of type PROG), all other dependent objects (for example, text elements) must be deleted automatically. This ensures that all relevant objects are really deleted. Otherwise, dependent objects would remain in the system even if they are no longer used and then be found by later clearing projects. This process of deleting and restoring (accidentally deleted objects) for obsolete objects is described in the clearing instructions.

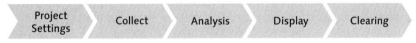

Figure 5.18 Clearing Analysis Phases

The system landscape in an upgrade/change impact analysis project is displayed in Figure 5.19.

Upgrade/change impact analysis project

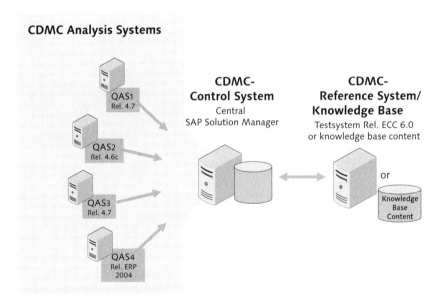

Figure 5.19 System Landscape in a CDMC Upgrade/Change Impact Analysis Project

The upgrade/change impact analysis project is also managed in the control system. The analysis systems and reference system are from the same project, but different product versions. In the analysis systems, objects developed by the customers are analyzed to find out how the change to SAP objects affects them. The reference system shows the system in

167

which the upgrade or other planned change has already been made so that the SAP objects appear in this system in the changed version. When the effects are analyzed, this version is compared to its unchanged counterpart, which is saved in the analysis system.

In a typical system landscape, SAP Solution Manager is the platform of the control system. The role of the analysis system can be taken over by a quality assurance system. The reference system is represented by a nonproduction system such as a test system or the knowledge base.

When defining the project landscape for an upgrade/change impact analysis, you can choose between a reference system and a knowledge base. The knowledge base provides an alternative to the reference system. You use it to collect the SAP objects that are changed by your upgrade. Thanks to the knowledge base, companies can calculate the budget required for the upgrade project and decide if they want to perform a test upgrade.

Upgrade/change impact analysis phases

The upgrade/change impact analysis has three phases (also see Figure 5.20):

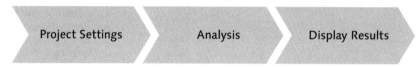

Project Settings   **Analysis**   **Display Results**

Figure 5.20 Upgrade Change Impact Analysis Phases

The *project settings* phase involves tasks such as defining the system landscape, displaying or recording SAP Notes relevant for the upgrade, and estimating the time and effort required to adapt the individual object types. In the second phase, various analyses are performed. For example, a list of all SAP objects used by customer developments is created, and the SAP objects used by customer-developed objects and changed during the upgrade are identified. Finally, the SAP objects of the current active version in the analysis system are compared to their new counterparts in the reference system. The CDMC assesses the effect of each change to an SAP object and classifies the affected customer objects by effect. Once the comparison is finished, the results of the analysis can be displayed in the last phase. The CDMC environment offers various options for displaying and filtering data, as well as the option of assigning a processor to each object, whereby a specific person is authorized to analyze the object in detail and decide how to proceed as regards this object.

Furthermore, the clearing analysis and upgrade/change impact analysis program calculate the time and effort required to adapt customer-developed objects that use SAP objects. This calculation is based on the comparison results and the estimates for time and effort specified in the first phase.

Estimation of time and effort

In the results list, each customer-developed object is classified according to the probability of it having to be changed:

▶ A green traffic light means the object does not have to be changed due to the planned upgrade or change.

▶ A yellow traffic light means the object probably has to be changed.

▶ A red traffic light means the object probably has to be adapted to ensure that it functions correctly after the upgrade or change.

Classifying the affected customer developments provides a basis for a more exact estimation of the time and effort required to adapt the objects.

CDMC provides a high degree of transparency of customer developments and modifications, and contributes to making great savings on maintenance and project costs.

5.5.2 Documentation of Customer Developments

To document customer developments in SAP Solution Manager, you use the same functions as to document projects (see Sections 5.3 and 5.4). Whether you add the documentation to an existing project or create a new project for the customer development depends primarily on the scope of the development. If the customer development involves changing just one business process step in an existing project, you can assign the documentation of this development in the Business Blueprint (SOLAR01) and Configuration (SOLAR02) transactions to the relevant process step. For larger developments, however, we recommend that you create a separate project for the customer development (see Section 5.2). This is also advisable if the development is to be used in several projects or systems.

A frequently asked question is, Which parts of the project are actually affected by customer developments? This information is relevant for operating the solution during the project and once the project is completed. The parts of the project are identified using keywords, which are first defined in SAP Solution Manager. SAP generally recommends that the keywords in Table 5.2 are used for customer developments.

Keyword	Name
SAP_EXT	SAP with enhancements
SAP_MOD	SAP with modifications
CUST	Customer development

Table 5.2 Keywords for Identifying Customer Developments

The keyword *SAP with enhancements* should be used for business process steps in which the standard function of an SAP application has been enhanced using an existing enhancement option (for example, implementing a Business Add-In [BAdI]). *SAP with modifications* identifies objects created by a change to the original SAP code. The keyword *customer development* is assigned to the objects in the project structure that you or another company completely developed and that do not contain any standard SAP code.

If a customer development is not based on an SAP NetWeaver system, but was instead developed using another development environment, the corresponding system cannot always be automatically connected to SAP Solution Manager. Therefore, it may be necessary to define the system manually in the System Landscape Maintenance transaction (SMSY).

The defined keywords are generally available to all projects. However, you still have to explicitly define which keywords can be used in each project in the project administration for your projects. You should always assign the three keywords mentioned above to projects for documenting customer developments. Then you can assign suitable keywords in the Business Blueprint or configuration of your project to individual elements in the project structure (for example, business processes or business process steps). You can use the keywords as filter criteria when reporting on your project (see Section 5.6).

As well as the scope of the customer development, the function description is also important. You must document what the customer development does, how it is started, and how it is integrated into the standard application or other customer developments. In particular, this document must be comprehensible to persons who were not involved in the development project. For example, if a problem occurs during subsequent operation of the solution, the support staff must be able to understand the customer development to analyze the cause of the problem. To ensure this, collect all of the information required in one or more documents and add this to the particular business process step in the Business Blueprint of your project.

Functional documentation

A program can be started in three different ways. In most cases, the call is made by the predecessor via an interface. It is necessary to list the interfaces used to be able to analyze the process flow technically and to detect performance problems of interfaces in particular. For each interface, enter the technical name of the interface, the interface technology used, a description of the data exchanged, and the throughput and performance expectations. The same information is required for the interfaces that your customer development uses to call up other programs, for example, the SAP standard application.

Another option for calling up a customer development is to regularly execute a background job. To document this variant, enter the name of the job, details of scheduling (such as frequency), existing requirements or restrictions, and troubleshooting procedures. The third option for calling up the development is for a user to call it up directly. In this case, you must document which ABAP transaction, WebDynpro application, URL, Business Server Page, or program is used. Record this information on the TRANSACTIONS tab in the Business Blueprint of the project.

To safeguard development quality, you must ensure that the developed code is transported completely from the development system to the quality assurance system and later to the production system. The list of development objects affected is relevant not only in the actual development project, but also later, for example, when maintaining the solution, or in future upgrade projects (see also Section 5.5.1). To support these processes, create the list of affected development objects in the Configuration (SOLAR02) transaction of your project on the DEVELOPMENT tab (see Section 6.1.2).

Development objects

You use the CONFIGURATION tab in exactly the same way to describe the existing configuration objects of your customer development.

The customer development documentation also includes background information on the development project. This includes details of why the development project was started, which gaps it closed in the standard SAP application, and which advantages this had. Especially for modifications that require a high level of maintenance, you should also clarify which alternatives to modifying the standard application were investigated and why these were rejected. All of this information is beneficial when discussing how to handle the development, for example, when discussing whether a development can be replaced by other functions in the standard application. As with other documentation, you add this information to the relevant element in the project structure in the Business Blueprint or Configuration transactions.

5.6   Reporting – Design Phase

The amount of information available to organizations has grown rapidly. Not only do internal systems produce large volumes of data, but technologies such as the Internet and simpler interfaces to external systems have made external information much more accessible. In some cases, people are even beginning to talk of an *information overload*. Decision-makers are often flooded with information, and can only control this deluge by preparing the data adequately. Reporting has become the answer to this problem. It can be used as an information system, as well as an early warning system.

5.6.1   Reporting in Project Management

Efficient reporting provides information about the course of a project and its state. However, the data itself provides no information about whether projects are successful. Therefore, the challenge lies in preparing the information appropriately and thematically so that it can be interpreted correctly.

In project management, reporting serves a number of purposes. Its main task is to enable successful project management. Other functions include supporting communication between people involved in a project and ensuring that the project history can be traced.

An effective information policy can prevent additional project expense that would otherwise be unavoidable. The ability to trace projects can provide a valuable experience base for future projects.

Project Management

Project management provides status reports that can be prepared regularly using project-relevant data so you can get an overview at any time. You can use filters and other technical reporting tools to remove the time-consuming manual element from searching for information.

The reporting functions in project management document events that occur during a project. Actual situations can be evaluated, and project sponsors and stakeholders can be informed accordingly. Significant deviations from plans are recorded, such as recognizable errors or drawbacks in the project. The relevant project managers decide which measures to take to improve the situation. Their job is to intervene during projects and get them back on the right track by taking appropriate actions and decisions.

Management requires responding to irregularities in a project and is based on information from reporting. There are basically six options for responding to irregularities:

Management options

- ▶ Adapt the strategy
- ▶ Change the project culture
- ▶ Take structure-related measures
- ▶ Change the plans
- ▶ Take diagnosis-related measures
- ▶ Adapt the way the project is managed (reporting)

Of course, the task of project management is also to confirm project successes using data.

Communication

Communication management deals with the sharing of information within a project as well as with external communication.

173

Internal communication

Reporting plays an important role in internal project communication. Uniform project standards ensure that all project team members have access to the necessary project information. They prevent project information from being misinterpreted. Information should be prepared with specific target groups in mind. This ensures that project team members receive only the information that is relevant for their functions.

External communication

On a different evaluation level, reporting also supports external communication, for instance, with collaboration partners from other projects, stakeholders and customers, or project sponsors. Again, reporting standards that are to be observed throughout a project can be used for planning communication and distributing information.

Documentation and Reproducibility

Experience base

Regular evaluations describe how a project is progressing. Together, all of these project analyses document the project history without interruptions or gaps. This valuable information flows into an experience base, which, in turn, acts as a readily accessible source of information for future projects. This approach promises long-term improvements in the way other projects are planned and executed (see Figure 5.21).

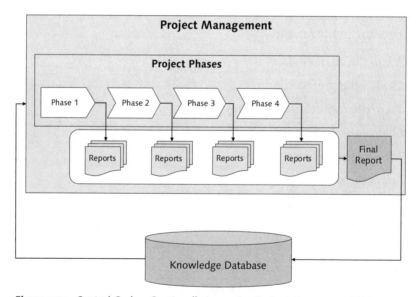

Figure 5.21 Control Cycle – Continually Improving Project Management Using an Experience Base

This loop describes a systematic process of learning from past, shared experiences to enhance efficiency in projects and project teams. The objective is to take a structured approach to learning from common experiences and document such experiences in a reusable, easy to understand form.

Prerequisites

Reporting cannot be used successfully unless certain basic conditions are fulfilled. These include both functional and organizational prerequisites:

▶ **Ease of use**
Ease of use is a decisive factor; every employee should be able to execute, use, and deal with reporting functions. The goals here are to enhance project quality and to better understand the different analysis results. Interpreting such results accurately means that fewer questions arise during a project, which contributes to high-quality and faster procedures.

▶ **Robust reporting**
Reporting is the control mechanism for a project. Without a control mechanism, a project will struggle to progress efficiently. The robustness of the reporting facility is therefore a key factor.

▶ **Reliability**
Reliability is extremely important in reporting. Current project situations cannot be analyzed without up-to-date information and measurements. The requirements regarding reliability become tougher if reports are created fully or partially automatically.

▶ **Buy-in**
If all project team members respond well to the reporting functions, the quality of project management increases. Reporting is an information medium that lives on the timeliness, completeness, and accuracy of the information that flows into the analyses. This demands a high level of discipline from all project team members when it comes to recording project-relevant data. Employees are more likely to buy into the reporting functions if, for example, they are shown how the information can benefit them.

▶ **Standards**

To improve project-controlling procedures through the control cycle, reporting procedures need to be standardized. This ensures higher quality so that lasting improvements can be made to recurring processes.

▶ **Traceability**

Besides a project's current situation, its history, or progress, is very significant. Such information is used to analyze factors that could potentially trigger problems during the project.

Using Reports

Types of reports   You can create or generate analyses and reports in different ways. A distinction is made between reports that are generated automatically and those that are prepared manually or individually.

▶ **Automatically generated reports**

Creating reports manually is time-consuming. All of the necessary information has to be gathered, in some cases from different data sources, and put into a certain textual or visual format. This format, in turn, may need to conform to whatever standard has been defined for the project.

To minimize the effort required, you can use software and predefined report templates to generate such reports.

Whereas automatically generated reports have many advantages, certain information may not be immediately obvious to the end user. For the significance of the information to be readily apparent and accessible, users need to gather and compare data from multiple automatically generated reports.

Report variants   Special report variants based on the generated reports can be used to create reports that can be configured individually. Variants enable users to create reports that extract answers to specific queries from the central database.

▶ **Manually created reports**

Reports that are prepared individually are the most time-consuming for members of the project team. Creating a report manually requires an in-depth analysis of available information. The right dependencies have to be used to put the information in a meaningful context. While predefined standards can make this task easier, manual reports will never achieve the same level of quality and efficiency as automatically generated reports.

SAP Solution Manager therefore features extensive reporting options to let you create reports efficiently. These options include customer-specific report variants, which are split into the different phases of projects and solutions. General reports are also available. Figure 5.22 depicts the comprehensive reporting features in SAP Solution Manager and thereby underpins the importance of reporting.

All rows below are within the "Project" area. Columns 1–5 (Status, Team Member, Plan Data, Actual Data, Keywords) are grouped as "Administrative Data" under the overall heading "Data in SAP Solution Manager".

Phase/Area	Category	Report	Status	Team Member	Plan Data	Actual Data	Keywords	Documents	Transaction Objects	Configuration Objects	Development Objects	Test Cases	Issues/Messages	Training Materials	End User Roles	Structure Nodes	Logical Components	Templates, Global Attributes	Test Plan	Change Requests	Service Desk Messages	Issues, Top Issues	EoDs	Accelerators
Business Blueprint Phase	Administration	General Status Analysis	X	X	X	X	X								X	X	X	X						
		Worklist		X																				
		Worklist according to status	X	X																				
		Worklist according to planned end date		X	X																			
	Object assignments	Documentation		X				X								X	X		X					
		Transactions		X				X	X							X	X	X	X					
		Issues/Messages		X				X					X			X	X		X					
		End User Roles		X				X								X	X		X					
		Dokuments and Links						X																
		Cross-Tab Analysis		X			X	X	X							X	X	X	X					
Configuration Phase	Administration	General Status Analysis	X	X	X	X	X								X	X	X	X						
		Worklist		X																				
		Worklist according to status	X	X																				
		Worklist according to planned end date		X	X																			
	Object assignments	Documentation		X				X						X		X	X		X					
		Transactions		X				X	X							X	X	X	X					
		Configuration		X				X		X						X	X	X	X					
		Development		X				X			X					X	X	X	X					
		Test Cases		X				X				X				X	X	X	X					
		Issues/Messages		X				X					X			X	X		X					
		End User Roles		X				X								X	X		X					
		Documents and Links						X																
		Cross-Tab Analysis		X			X	X	X	X	X	X				X	X	X	X					
Test Phase		Test Plan Status Analysis										X								X				
		Project Status Analysis		X				X		X		X				X	X	X	X					
Roadmap		Accelerator		X				X								X								X
		Status	X	X				X								X								
		Issues/Messages		X				X						X		X								
		Documents		X			X	X								X								
System Lanscape		Assign Logical Components														X	X							
History		History for Tabs	X	X	X	X	X	X	X	X	X	X	X	X	X	X	X							
		History for Documents						X																
Learning Map		Feedback Analysis												X										
Solution		Transactions							X							X	X	X						
		Documentation						X								X	X							
		Change Management																		X				
		Service Desk																			X			
		Issue and Top Issue Tracking																				X		
		Expertise-on-Demand																					X	

Figure 5.22 Overview of Reporting in SAP Solution Manager

5.6.2 Reporting – Business Blueprint

The Business Blueprint reports let you analyze information from your project, such as scenarios, processes, status values, project deadlines, and transactions. The more detailed your information, the broader your reporting options will be. You can analyze data for a single project or for several projects, depending on the scope of your project or the purpose of your analysis.

Report areas The Business Blueprint reports are grouped in two areas:

▶ **Administration**
For analyzing administrative information, either the general status or worklists that can be assigned to one or more members of the project team. When analyzing worklists, you can focus on specific basic data such as the status or planned end date.

▶ **Assignments**
For analyzing the assignments in the project structure (scenario, processes, and process steps). This could include documentation and transactions that were supplied by SAP or that were added over the course of the project.

Figure 5.23 shows the reports available in SAP Solution Manager for the Business Blueprint phase.

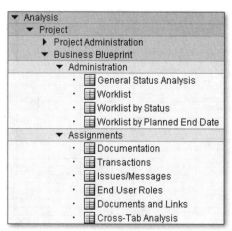

Figure 5.23 Reports for the Business Blueprint Phase from the Solution Manager Transaction: Report (SOLAR_EVAL)

In addition to the specific reports for the Business Blueprint phase, you may find other cross-phase analyses useful. These include analyses for the system landscape and the history of project data.

You can create and save selection variants for all of the reports in Transaction SOLAR_EVAL and the REPORTS view in the Implementation/ Upgrade work center; these can be executed directly and answered more quickly and accurately thanks to their reports on frequent questions. You can make selection variants available to all users, and you can also make a wide range of different settings. For example, you can pre-populate or protect input fields or indicate them as hidden or required entries.

Selection variants

The relevant rows of Figure 5.22 provide a detailed overview of the data analyzed in the different reports in the Business Blueprint phase.

Administration

The reports listed under ADMINISTRATION help you analyze administrative data. Besides the general status, you can evaluate the worklists of one or more members of the project team and focus specifically on the status or planned end date.

You can use predefined reports or execute individual ones, which you can define as standard reports, if necessary.

Examples of data you might analyze in your project include:

Reporting scenarios

▶ **Incomplete elements**
The report analyzes all elements of the project structure for which the planned project end falls within the period specified in PLANNED END and that are not 100% complete.

▶ **All completed elements**
The report analyzes all activities for which the actual project end (from the actual status information) falls within the analysis period you specified.

▶ **Individual reports**
You can run individual reports in addition to those mentioned above.

To be able to compare individual values in the analysis result to each other, you can calculate column totals.

For example, you have several open projects and find that one of the projects will probably need more time. To check the relationship between planned and current resources, you analyze all elements and activities that are not 100% complete. Next, you take the analysis results and total the PLANNED RESOURCES, ACTUAL RESOURCES, and REMAINING RESOURCES columns. The totals show you the variances.

Project Structure Assignments

Blueprint-specific assignment
All scenario and process structures must contain blueprint-specific assignments for the individual structure items. The scenario and process structure alone only provide an item-specific view of existing assignments. Assignment reporting provides a higher-level view. You can make various settings to create user-specific report variants for specific queries. You can also define the variants as standard project variants so that all team members can use them.

You can analyze the following assignments in the Business Blueprint phase:

▶ Documentation

▶ Transaction

▶ Issues/messages

▶ End user roles

▶ Documents and links

Figure 5.24 shows the documentation and transaction reports for the example implementation project CRM_IMP described in the previous sections. The associated selection screens show you the wide range of options available for creating report variants.

Displaying a report
You can display report results in two ways: as a tree structure or as a table. The tree structure gives you a quick overview and, with the same structure as the project, is instantly familiar (see Figure 5.25).

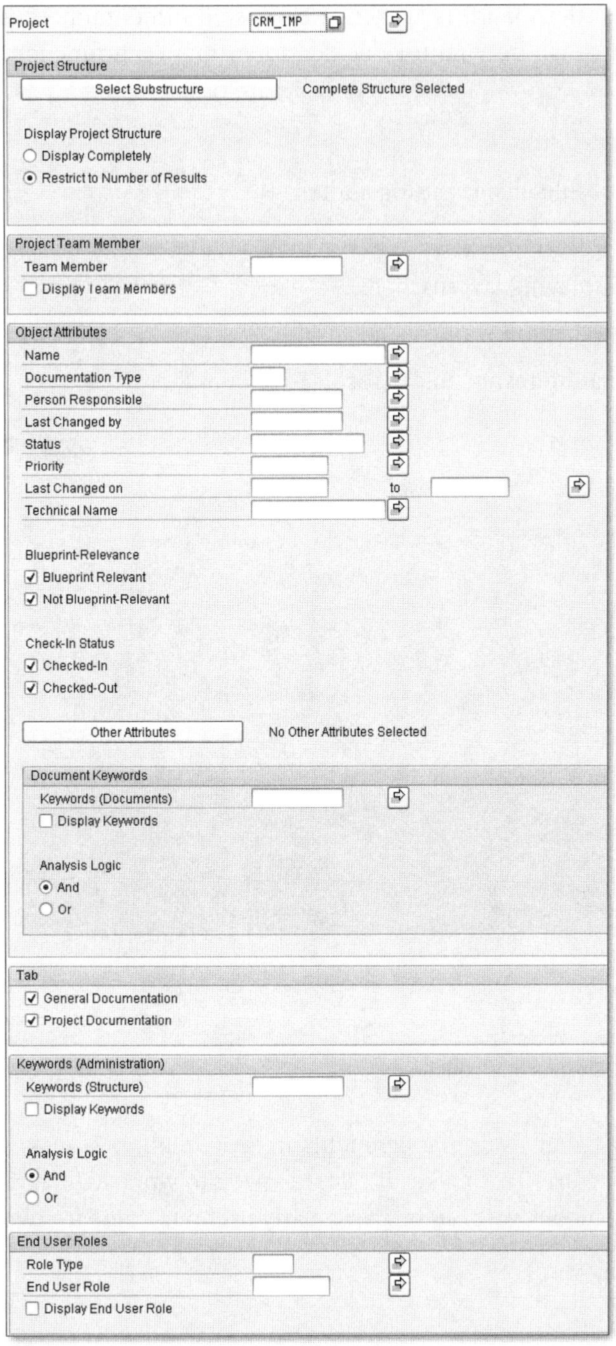

| Project | CRM_IMP | | ⇨ |

Project Structure

| Select Substructure | Complete Structure Selected |

Display Project Structure
○ Display Completely
◉ Restrict to Number of Results

Project Team Member

| Team Member | | ⇨ |
☐ Display Team Members

Object Attributes

Name		⇨
Documentation Type		⇨
Person Responsible		⇨
Last Changed by		⇨
Status		⇨
Priority		⇨
Last Changed on		to		⇨
Technical Name		⇨

Blueprint-Relevance
☑ Blueprint Relevant
☑ Not Blueprint-Relevant

Check-In Status
☑ Checked-In
☑ Checked-Out

| Other Attributes | No Other Attributes Selected |

Document Keywords

| Keywords (Documents) | | ⇨ |
☐ Display Keywords

Analysis Logic
◉ And
○ Or

Tab

☑ General Documentation
☑ Project Documentation

Keywords (Administration)

| Keywords (Structure) | | ⇨ |
☐ Display Keywords

Analysis Logic
◉ And
○ Or

End User Roles

| Role Type | | ⇨ |
| End User Role | | ⇨ |
☐ Display End User Role

Figure 5.24 Selection Screen – Documentation Report

The table, on the other hand, is attractive because it offers numerous technical functions that are vital for detailed reporting. Such functions include:

- Sorting project results
- Restricting the results display using a filter
- Totaling
- Defining and displaying layouts
- Downloading evaluation results
- Exporting evaluation results to Microsoft Excel

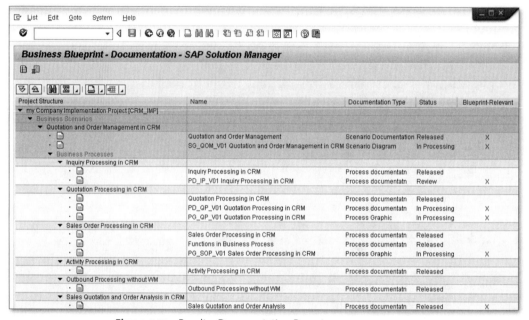

Figure 5.25 Result – Documentation Report

Comparing reports All of the reports for analyzing assignments in SAP Solution Manager have the same structure. This makes it easier for you to work with various reports simultaneously. It can be particularly useful to compare two reports, for instance.

The selection screen for analyzing the transactions assigned to structure items (see Figure 5.26) is similar to the selection screen for documents. The only difference is that document-specific attributes are replaced with transaction-specific ones.

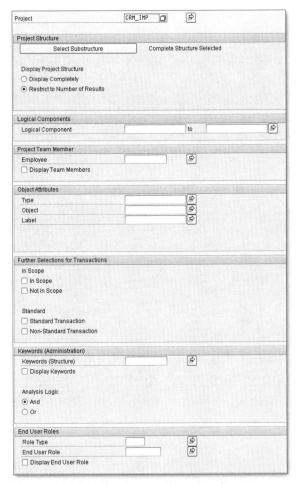

Figure 5.26 Selection Screen – Transaction Report

As with all of the assignment reports in SAP Solution Manager, there are two results lists – a tree structure and a table (see Figure 5.27).

Cross-Phase Reports

In addition to the phase-specific reports, other reports are available for analyzing data that is not specific to one phase. These include reports on the system landscape and the history of data in SAP Solution Manager.

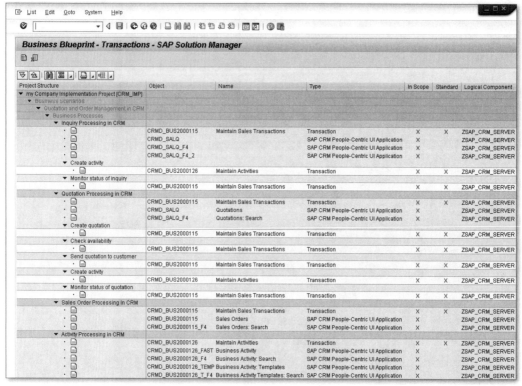

Figure 5.27 Result – Transaction Report

System Landscape

You can use the system landscape report in the planning, Business Blueprint, configuration, and test phases. It determines which components are assigned to individual process steps and in which systems they are processed. You can therefore get an overview of the systems and processes at any time.

On the selection screen, you can select the project structure and the logical components, as usual.

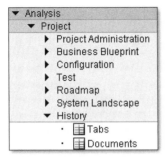

Figure 5.28 Reports for Tab Page and Document Histories

History

SAP Solution Manager logs numerous changes so they can be traced. For projects, its main purpose is to record changes to the scenario and process structure and the assigned elements. Another important aspect is the management of document histories. To enable changes to be displayed by topic, SAP Solution Manager offers two cross-phase reports (see Figure 5.28):

▶ **History of elements assigned to the structure (tab pages)**
This reports tracks assignments made during a particular period. It shows you what was changed when, where, how, and by whom (for example, it would indicate that a transaction was added to or deleted from a process).

▶ **History of documents**
Unlike transactions and configuration elements, documents are independent objects in SAP Solution Manager (transactions and configuration elements are links to objects in managed systems). SAP Solution Manager therefore logs changes to these objects as well, which you can analyze using a separate report for documents. Again, you can trace all changes made to a document and display its history. This enables you to see what was changed when, where, how, and by whom.

The purpose of the build and test phase is to implement the scenarios and processes defined in the Business Blueprint in accordance with your requirements. It entails setting up a system landscape for configuring and testing the planned scenarios and processes. This chapter describes how you can conduct your project using SAP Solution Manager.

6 Build and Test Phase

To realize the scenarios and processes you defined in the requirements phase, you use the build and test phase to set up the system landscape that will run your scenarios and business processes. You adopt the structure used in the Business Blueprint, which helps you configure your solution around your business processes and during subsequent testing activities. Implementation encompasses the following steps:

Phase-specific steps

- ▶ Continuous monitoring of project targets, especially costs, deadlines, and resources

- ▶ Active implementation of Organizational and Change Management

- ▶ Elaboration of training materials and end user documentation

- ▶ Creation of end user roles and implementation of authorization and security concept

- ▶ Elaboration and implementation of realization specifications for customer developments

SAP Solution Manager assists you in configuring your systems around your processes. You can navigate directly to the SAP Implementation Guide (IMG) in the different development systems being managed and set up the systems centrally from SAP Solution Manager. You can also document the configuration settings centrally.

Furthermore, by integrating existing testing tools, SAP Solution Manager supports you in organizing and documenting the results of a range of testing activities, from unit testing through to integration testing.

The goals of this phase are to implement the system, conduct comprehensive testing, and release the system in preparation for production operation.

6.1   Solution Configuration

SAP Solution Manager provides the central infrastructure for configuring your business processes. The project team can retrieve all of the relevant information (such as documentation) from the process structure. Remote function call (RFC) connections link you to all of the systems defined in the SAP Solution Manager system landscape so you can make settings directly in the respective systems.

6.1.1   Configuration and Documentation

Physical systems   Because you cannot configure the relevant systems until the development and Customizing systems (and quality assurance systems for subsequent testing) are connected, the system landscape matrix defined during project preparation is now supplemented by the actual physical systems, thereby completing the navigation matrix step by step. In our example SAP CRM project, this involves assigning the systems with the *development* and *quality assurance* roles (see Figure 6.1).

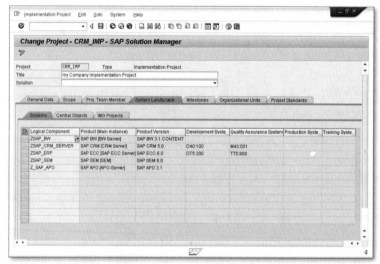

Figure 6.1   Project System Landscape, Including Development and Quality Assurance Systems

The system administrator is responsible for assigning the required SAP CRM systems and establishing a connection with them, and does so centrally in the Solution Manager System Landscape transaction (SMSY). At this point, the systems automatically become available in the project. The project manager is then only required to use SAP Solution Manager to create the respective IMG project in the SAP CRM development system. Within this project, the configuration settings are made and grouped together in transport requests (IMG PROJECTS tab page).

You configure your solution in the Configuration transaction (SOLAR02). Your starting point is the process structure that you created in the Business Blueprint transaction (SOLAR01), along with all of its assignments, which were recorded in the Business Blueprint document and approved for implementation.

If you use predefined SAP implementation content from the Business Process Repository (BPR), you can draw on the following resources during your configuration activities:

▶ **Cross-scenario configuration in configuration structure**
This entails basic technical settings, such as setting up communication links between the systems running SAP CRM and SAP ERP, as well as scenario-related settings that apply to various scenarios or processes. If you are implementing only selected scenarios from a solution, the system proposes the configuration settings relevant to your selection, which you can amend if necessary. By selecting specific industries, you can reduce the scope of the system's proposal. The settings listed on the CONFIGURATION tab page not only include individual IMG activities or groups of activities, but also configuration documents for topics such as non-ABAP components, which supplement the IMG documentation. Preconfigured *Business Configuration Sets* (BC Sets) are available for certain solutions. You can activate them in the target system and adapt them as required.

▶ **Scenario and process-specific configuration**
This refers to configuration settings that are relevant for individual scenarios and processes. The information on the CONFIGURATION tab page applies in this case, too.

Note that with the exception of the documentation, configuration settings are not shipped with SAP Solution Manager but rather with the respective application; SAP Solution Manager provides the infrastructure you require to access the system settings in the development systems being managed.

Phased configuration

With complex or lengthy implementation projects, it can be helpful to break down the configuration process into a number of phases:

▶ **Baseline configuration**
A level of configuration that has been defined and agreed upon. It contains high-priority requirements that need to be implemented quickly. The baseline generally covers the implementation of organizational units and core processes (main scope).

▶ **Final configuration**
The baseline configuration is finalized in a series of cycles. This is an iterative process in which you finish planning, configuring, documenting, and testing your process configurations. This includes working on customer developments and master data.

You can use keywords on the ADMINISTRATION tab page to classify the relevant master data, organizational units, and business processes by baseline and cycle. You also assign project resources and status values in preparation for efficient communication during the configuration phase and for process-based analysis.

Configuration documentation

There are essentially two methods for documenting configuration settings:

▶ **Documentation in the IMG project**
You document your settings directly in the IMG project for the development system and can therefore analyze the IMG project at any time. The advantage here is that you save the documentation once, centrally, in the IMG project. All processes and process steps that are customized in this IMG activity therefore refer automatically to the same configuration document.

▶ **Documentation in SAP Solution Manager**
Alternatively, you can document your settings on the CONFIGURATION tab page for the structure item in question and assign the docu-

mentation to processes or process steps that are customized in the same IMG activity. Whenever you need, a where-used list shows you where in the process structure a particular document is still assigned. Furthermore, the system logs all changes made to the documentation; different versions let you see successive document changes.

You can also combine the two methods. This enables you to generate a URL in the attributes of every document in SAP Solution Manager, which you simply copy and paste into the corresponding configuration document and call from there. In technical terms, the URL points to a *logical info object* (LOIO), which means that when the document is accessed, the system links to the most recent version in the form of *physical info objects* (PHIOs). As such, the link in the IMG documentation always refers to the current document content.

Combined method

No matter which method you opt for, as in the Business Blueprint phase, it is important to assign responsibilities and (document) status values, from the process level right down to the level of IMG activities. Particularly in the case of cross-process IMG settings, this makes coordination and communication easier. They allow for vertical integration, especially across subprojects, as well as horizontal integration, by linking process and configuration. If you compile your documentation in SAP Solution Manager, the processes and process steps make suitable levels for storing configuration settings that need documenting.

In our example project (see Figure 6.2), you can see structure areas in the top-left corner for general technical and cross-scenario configuration settings. Below these areas, you can see the process structure we defined in the Business Blueprint phase. Taking the INQUIRY PROCESSING IN CRM process as an example, the first steps have been taken to configure the process on the CONFIGURATION tab page. The default values from the BPR prove helpful here. You work through them according to your instructions and enhance them with customer-specific configuration documentation on a step-by-step basis.

Example

SAP Solution Manager lets you report on the current processing status based on the status values assigned to documents. To do so, you use the Analysis - Solution Manager transaction (SOLAR_EVAL).

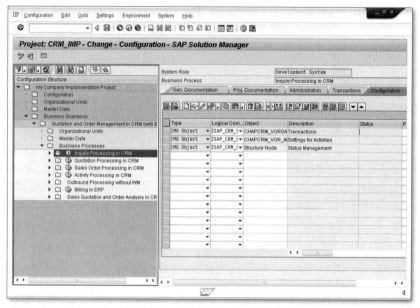

Figure 6.2 Process Configuration and Documentation

If you documented your configuration settings in SAP Solution Manager, you can create a final configuration guide in Microsoft Word format. To do so, you select either the entire structure or specific parts of it by selecting CONFIGURATION • GENERATE CONFIGURATION GUIDE .... In contrast to the Business Blueprint document, when you generate a configuration guide, the system considers only documents from the CONFIGURATION tab page.

Throughout the configuration phase, we recommend that you describe procedures so that you can compile end user documentation. Using the template for *Business Process Procedures* (BPPs) in SAP Solution Manager, you can draft step-by-step instructions for selected transactions. The description explains how the transaction is used in the context, which requirements must be met, and how the individual activities are performed — ideally on the basis of example data. Once you have filled out this form, you can include it in the process structure at the process step level, on the TRAINING MATERIALS tab page. This gives you a building block for creating training materials specifically for end users. For more information, see Section 7.2.

6.1.2   Implementing Customer Developments

You may need customer developments before you can configure your processes completely. You usually define the functional scope for enhancements to reports, interfaces, forms, user exits, migration programs, and
new developments in the Business Blueprint phase at the same time as
the functional documentation. You can supplement the scope with realization specifications, which state how enhancements are to be implemented in technical terms. You store these specifications, along with
links to objects that are to be enhanced or created specifically for your
company in the development system, on the DEVELOPMENT tab page.
The object types you can use include programs, transactions, Internet
services, BSP applications and extensions, function groups, and modules.
This assignment lets you call the relevant object directly in the development system. Again, it is advisable and useful to define responsibilities
and statuses for each object so you can monitor progress in the Analysis
– Solution Manager transaction (SOLAR_EVAL).

Complex development requirements may call for a separate development
structure. In this case, you would enter development-related documents
and objects in the new structure. You can also link the documents to
structure items that the customer development affects, such as processes.
This enables you to create different views of the same content.

Setting up
separate
development
structures

As mentioned earlier, this is also the project phase in which you implement the authorization and security concept and create end user roles.
When you define roles for end users, you can assign organizational units
or jobs on the END USER ROLES tab page. The project analysis (Transaction SOLAR_EVAL) lets you run CROSS-TAB ANALYSES, which indicate
which process steps are assigned to which transactions and end user
roles and, consequently, provide input for the roles' functional scope.
Sections 6.1.4 and 8.9 provide more information about the analysis
options available in the configuration phase.

6.1.3   Working with Messages

Queries and obstacles that arise over the course of the project should
be recorded and addressed as soon as possible. The Service Desk in SAP
Solution Manager is a sophisticated tool that enables project team mem-

bers to address implementation-related problems and queries. You can use the Service Desk for a range of tasks — from recording and classifying all types of faults (incident management) and monitoring how they are processed (where appropriate, with escalation to other departments or specialists) to resolving the problem, either by Service Desk staff or, if the problem message was forwarded, by experts from SAP Active Global Support.

In implementation projects, you can use the message function without having to configure the Service Desk completely. You set up the minimum functions by making basic settings for the Service Desk in Customizing for SAP Solution Manager; most of the settings are made automatically.

Assigning a message to a project

If messages have not been assigned, they must be assigned centrally (for instance, by project management) to a particular topic. They are assigned to the appropriate project or subproject automatically on the basis of the project context in which they are created. The message handler can be assigned centrally (by project management), locally (by topic owners or subproject managers), or directly by the message handler, who selects it from the worklist of unassigned messages. Even when used in this way, the Service Desk outperforms external tools such as Microsoft Excel when it comes to managing open error messages.

In an implementation project, the end users are project team members working during the Business Blueprint, configuration, and testing phases. The messages created here can cover a broad range of subjects, from open items and business requirements to actual error messages. You need to ensure that messages and their solutions are described in sufficient detail for third parties to understand. Although it is possible to forward messages directly to SAP, you rarely need to do so with project-related messages.

Besides being able to enter messages in the project context based on the process structure (MESSAGES tab page), employees can submit messages directly from the environment in which the problem arises, for instance, when configuring the development system. To report on messages, you can use general analyses for problem messages in the Incident Management work center and a project-specific analysis in the Analysis – Solution Manager transaction (SOLAR_EVAL).

Section 8.7 provides more information about the Service Desk and how it can be used.

6.1.4 Reporting – Build and Test Phase

As with the reports for the Business Blueprint phase (see Section 5.6), you can analyze information from your project, such as scenarios, processes, status values, project deadlines, and transactions, in the configuration phase as well. The more detailed your information, the broader your reporting options will be. You can analyze data for a single project or for several projects, depending on the scope of your project or the purpose of your analysis. Reports for administrative data as well as the objects assigned to the project structure are available.

Figure 6.3 presents the SAP Solution Manager reports available for the configuration phase. Figure 6.4 provides a detailed overview of the data analyzed in the different reports.

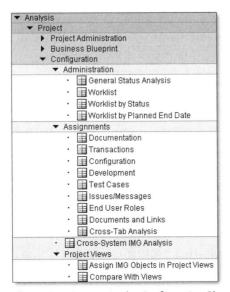

Figure 6.3 Reports in the Configuration Phase

Reporting in SAP Solution Manager — Data in SAP Solution Manager (Administrative Data)

Project / Phase	Report	Status	Team Member	Plan Data	Actual Data	Keywords	Documents	Transaction Objects	Configuration Objects	Development Objects	Test Cases	Issues/Messages	Training Materials	End User Roles	Structure Nodes	Logical Components	Templates, Global Attributes	Test Plan	Change Requests	Service Desk Messages	Issues, Top Issues	EoDs	Accelerators
Business Blueprint Phase – Administration	General Status Analysis	X	X	X	X	X								X	X	X	X						
	Worklist		X																				
	Worklist according to status	X	X																				
	Worklist according to planned end date		X	X																			
Business Blueprint Phase – Object assignments	Documentation		X				X		X					X	X		X						
	Transactions		X					X	X					X	X	X	X						
	Issues/Messages		X						X			X		X	X		X						
	End User Roles		X						X					X	X		X						
	Dokuments and Links						X																
	Cross-Tab Analysis		X				X	X	X					X	X	X	X						
Configuration Phase – Administration	General Status Analysis	X	X	X	X	X								X	X	X	X						
	Worklist		X																				
	Worklist according to status	X	X																				
	Worklist according to planned end date		X	X																			
Configuration Phase – Object assignments	Documentation	X							X				X	X	X		X						
	Transactions	X						X	X					X	X	X	X						
	Configuration	X							X	X				X	X	X	X						
	Development	X							X	X				X	X	X	X						
	Test Cases	X							X		X			X	X	X	X						
	Issues/Messages	X							X			X		X	X		X						
	End User Roles	X							X					X	X		X						
	Documents and Links						X																
	Cross-Tab Analysis	X					X	X	X	X	X	X		X	X	X	X						
Test Phase	Test Plan Status Analysis												X					X					
	Project Status Analysis		X		X			X					X		X	X	X	X					
Roadmap	Accelerator		X		X										X								X
	Status	X	X		X										X								
	Issues/Messages		X		X							X			X								
	Documents		X		X	X									X								
System Lanscape	Assign Logical Components														X	X							
History	History for Tabs	X	X	X	X	X	X	X	X	X	X	X	X	X	X								
	History for Documents						X								X								
Learning Map	Feedback Analysis												X										
Solution	Transactions							X						X	X	X							
	Documentation						X							X	X								
	Change Management																		X				
	Service Desk											X								X			
	Issue and Top Issue Tracking																				X		
	Expertise-on-Demand																					X	

Figure 6.4 Overview – Reports and Data in the Configuration Phase

Administration The reports listed under ADMINISTRATION behave the same in the configuration and Business Blueprint phases. The only difference is the data itself. All administrative data except keywords is phase dependent, which means that only keywords can be transferred from the Business Blueprint phase; no other data is transferred.

Project structure assignments In addition to the assignments from the Business Blueprint phase, the configuration phase contains the following information, which is stored in the form of assignments:

▶ Configuration

▶ Development

▶ Test cases

▶ Training materials

Taking the CRM_IMP project as an example, Figure 6.5 illustrates the report on the CONFIGURATION tab page for configuration objects that are assigned to structure items in the project.

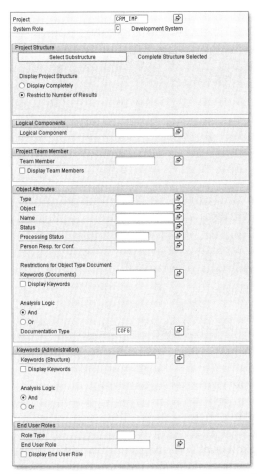

Figure 6.5 Selection Screen – Configuration Reports

The report results (see Figure 6.6) show the configuration elements assigned to the different structure items. You can also access configuration documents, which fully explain the procedure and configuration steps used in the configuration phase. The results also show the IMG objects and transactions that you can use to make the settings described.

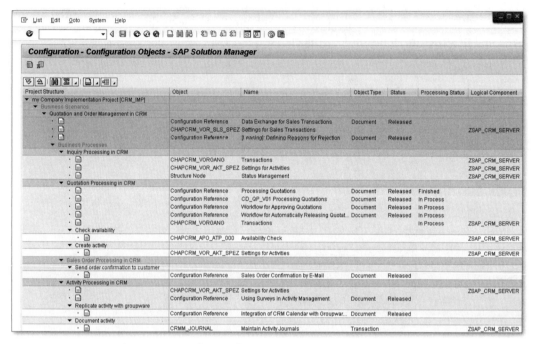

Figure 6.6 Result – Configuration Reports

As in the Business Blueprint phase, cross-phase reports are available in the configuration phase for analyzing the system landscape and the history (see Section 5.6.2).

6.2 Test Management

Before transferring your solution configuration to your production system landscape and thus making it available for your operative business processes, you must first check that all changes have been made correctly and do not have a negative impact on other business processes. SAP Solution Manager provides extensive test functions for this purpose.

6.2.1 Motivation and Approach

Why is there any need at all for SAP customers to test the business processes they model with SAP solutions? It could be argued that the SAP Business Suite — given the fact that it is used every day by countless companies and users — should really contain very few errors.

The answer to this question is multifaceted and has to do with the way SAP and, above all, you as an SAP customer coordinate and make changes to SAP solutions that have already been implemented.

Most SAP software is used to map highly integrated, often complex business processes. When it is implemented, SAP standard software is adapted to accommodate your specific business processes with the following activities:

- Configure business processes and how they are managed, for example, pricing.
- Enter the master data and attributes, for instance, vendors, materials, services, and customers, that are needed to execute business processes.
- Implement and configure software from SAP partners or third parties and integrate it with SAP solutions using standard or customer-specific interfaces.
- Where appropriate, the end users choose the user interface for running business processes.
- If required, create and implement composite applications to handle extremely customer-specific processes. These applications are based on service-oriented architectures (SOA) and use Web services to communicate with SAP Business Suite applications.
- If required, include *custom code* in SAP standard solutions to map customer-specific functions or processes.

Adapting SAP software

For the majority of SAP customers, the outcome of these activities is a comprehensive solution that encompasses complex interactions between SAP, partner, and third-party applications and interfaces, as well as custom code and customer developments (see Figure 6.7).

Comprehensive solution

Of course, your overall solution must be tested thoroughly at each SAP customer before going live. Such testing may include tests of individual functions, integration tests between SAP and non-SAP applications, scenario tests in which entire business processes are executed from beginning to end, and performance and acceptance tests on the part of end users.

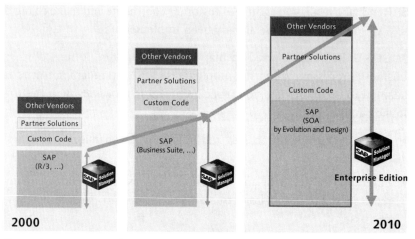

Figure 6.7 Customer Solution Landscape

Reasons for changes

After going live, there are a number of reasons you need to make changes to your SAP-centric solution. In many cases, these changes result from maintenance work or functional enhancements of business processes that are required by your user departments. Changes include:

▶ SAP Support Packages for maintaining SAP solutions

▶ SAP legal change packages to comply with changes to statutory requirements

▶ SAP enhancement packages (EHP) — functional enhancements that you can activate on an individual basis

▶ Adjustments to the existing configuration

▶ Implementation or adaptation of partner or external applications and their SAP interfaces

▶ Customer-specific enhancements and customer developments (*custom code*)

▶ Implementation or adaptation of SAP or partner composite applications using SOA Web services

These changes are the main cause of further testing activities subsequent to going live. The required tests cannot be performed entirely by the software manufacturers because the customer environment — with its configuration, master data, and interfaces — must be taken into account in all tests.

The Challenges of Test Management

A survey of member companies of ASUG and DSAG (SAP user groups for the Americas and Germany, respectively) revealed a clear consensus on the difficulty of organizing and carrying out functional tests. It identified four problem areas.

▶ Functional tests in heterogeneous system landscapes:

  ▶ Integration tests for business processes that require several SAP applications and system instances.

  ▶ Tests for interfaces that connect SAP solutions with third-party applications.

▶ Lack of analysis concerning the impact of changes:

  ▶ Changes to SAP solutions; for example, configuration changes, often impact on a number of critical business processes without the company realizing it.

  ▶ Due to a lack of options for analysis, these effects cannot be detected, which prompts many companies to put off necessary adjustments, for example, activating SAP Support Packages.

  ▶ The task of defining the required test coverage is also severely hampered by the lack of analysis options. As a result, changes are often made without all critical processes first being subjected to a regression test.

▶ Provision of test environments and test data:

  ▶ Test environments should resemble the production environment and reflect the changes to be tested as closely as possible. Due to the large volume of data and sensitivity of the data, test environments cannot be created simply by making a copy of the production system. Consequently, many companies' test systems contain obsolete configurations and data.

▶ Problems are compounded by the fact that providing suitable test data for manual and automatic tests gives rise to a number of difficulties. For example, the customer credit rating check in the order-to-cash process can only be carried out if special data conditions exist.

▶ Test automation:

▶ Whereas automated tests can reduce the number of manual testers, they require specially trained experts with knowledge and experience of the testing tools to reproduce the required dynamics in the automated test cases.

▶ Automated tests demand high levels of maintenance because changes to the SAP solution often damage the automated test cases concerned.

The response to these challenges is threefold:

▶ A *methodology* for implementing, operating, and adapting SAP-centric solutions

▶ A *test process* based on practical experience

▶ The *test functions* of SAP Solution Manager and integrated partner applications

Methodology   SAP Active Global Support has developed a methodology for implementing, operating, adapting, and enhancing SAP-centric software solutions: *end-to-end (E2E) solution operations*. Included in this methodology is a collection of proven best practices, referred to as SAP standards for solution operations (see *http://service.sap.com/supportstandards*). These are based on the experience gained through supporting numerous SAP customers. A range of standards concerning test and change management are provided here.

The Run SAP implementation methodology is recommended if you are interested in implementing E2E solution operations in phases (see Section 1.6 and 5.1.1). Its contents include overviews and detailed training, an Implementation Roadmap, and a certification program for consultancies.

The first step in the end-to-end test process (see Figure 6.8) is to identify the test coverage. Because changes to SAP-centric solutions constitute the main cause of various testing activities, you must first differentiate between the types of solution change.

Test process

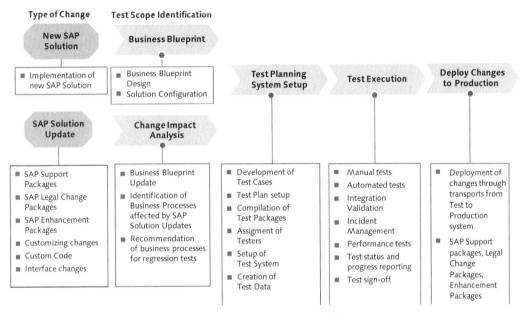

Figure 6.8 SAP Best Practices for the Test Process for SAP-Centric Solutions

When an SAP solution is implemented, for example, SAP CRM as an enhancement to an existing SAP ERP system implementation, a host of business processes are adapted, configured, and documented in the *Business Blueprint* (a catalog of the business processes in operation). The test coverage is derived directly from the list of business processes that have been adapted.

Planned changes to an SAP solution are motivated by a wide range of reasons: maintenance in the form of SAP Support Packages, functional improvements in the form of SAP enhancement packages or custom developments, changes to the configuration, and adjustments to interfaces for SAP partner or third-party applications. We recommend the following approach for identifying the test coverage: After your planned change has been approved, an initial risk assessment is carried out on the effects the change will have on existing operations. A second, more detailed risk analysis is then performed once the changes have been implemented in the development system and tested in the test system. You should use new procedures here that are capable of performing analyses on the source code and configuration at runtime (*change impact analysis*) and identifying the potential impact on critical business processes. This type of analysis allows you to determine the test coverage *on a risk basis* — only if changes impact on critical areas selected by you are new test cases created and manual testers (and potentially also automatic tests) are allocated. While this does not usually reduce the amount of effort associated with testing, it does enable test resources to be targeted more precisely at risk areas.

Planning tests and making test systems and test data available

Once the test coverage has been identified, the tests themselves can be planned. First, your user department collects the business requirements. These may then be supplemented with test requirements by the quality management department. On the basis of these requirements, manual and possibly automatic test cases are created, or existing ones are reviewed and adapted. All test cases are generally managed in topic-related test catalogs that do not yet bear any relation to a current test cycle.

For the purpose of an actual test cycle, suitable test cases are grouped together as test packages. These may be generated using risk-based methods (see above) so that test resources can be targeted at the areas that have changed. When integration tests are run on complex business processes, it is important for test sequences to be planned because every process step relies on data from the steps preceding it. You also have to assign testers to your manual test cases. Before the test cycle can begin, the test systems must be brought up to date; that is, they must resemble the production systems but with the newly added changes incorporated. This presents many companies with a major challenge because simply making a copy of the production system is often not feasible for a variety of reasons. The last step is to provide test data for the test cases. This also involves complex issues because in integration tests, process chains involving multiple steps must be tested. This requires you to plan carefully coordinated configuration, master, and transaction data.

After the tests have been planned and the test systems are available and contain test data, testing can begin. Depending on the type and scope of the test cycle, regression tests, functional user tests, or performance tests may be run. The software developers perform unit tests beforehand in the development systems.

Executing tests

At the start of the test cycle, the manual testers receive details by email of their test packages, testing period, and how to access the test systems. Automatic tests are scheduled or started directly. Every test that is executed is logged and documented with test notes. A test status is set in all cases, either manually or automatically.

If the system responds in an unexpected way during manual testing, the tester enters an *incident* (Service Desk message, see Section 8.7) in the corresponding incident management system. This does not usually take place automatically for automatic tests. Instead, if the test is canceled or a warning or error message is output, a tester qualifies the issue before an incident is reported. Each incident is described in detail and may be supplemented with screenshots before being forwarded automatically to the persons responsible, who then analyze it and categorize it as critical if necessary. Once a correction has been made in the development system, it is transported to the test system and retested.

Incident management

In light of the complexity and heterogeneity of modern software solutions, *integration validation* is recommended for particularly important business processes. This involves gathering and subsequently evaluating a substantial amount of data from the software applications that are active while a given business process is being executed. This type of validation also enables detection of concealed warnings and error messages that frequently occur on the interfaces between applications.

Integration validation

If large-scale changes are made or new software solutions are implemented, *load tests* should be performed before these are used in production. These tests simulate a situation in which a high number of users execute transactions simultaneously. They are also capable of simulating how the system responds to large data volumes.

Load tests

Throughout the entire test cycle, test coordinators monitor the test status and progress, as well as the processing status of incidents that have been reported. Once all test activities have been completed and all relevant incidents have been resolved and retested, you can schedule the *quality gate* (Q-Gate). This meeting brings together all of the parties responsible, who decide on the outcome of the tests and whether to release changes for the production system. If they reach a positive decision, you can trigger the transports and import SAP Support Packages and SAP enhancement packages in the production system.

Functions and Tools for Testing

► In SAP Solution Manager, SAP provides a central platform with tools to handle all aspects of test management and related activities. SAP Solution Manager offers test functions and tools that cover the entire cycle:

► Documentation of business processes and assignment to SAP systems

► Dynamic analysis of the impact changes have on business processes

► Planning of manual and automated tests

► Test execution, problem handling, and status reporting

► Validation of integration tests

► Management of Q-Gates

► Enhanced transport system for ABAP, Java, .NET, and C++

Additional products
This offering is supplemented by a range of additional SAP products such as SAP Test Data Migration Server, the SAP Quality Center application by HP, SAP Test Acceleration and Optimization, and SAP LoadRunner by HP, all of which are highly integrated with SAP Solution Manager. Test applications from other suppliers can be integrated with the tools provided in SAP Solution Manager using certified interfaces.

Guiding Principles for End-to-End Test Management

SAP's strategy for end-to-end test management is guided by three key principles that have an influence on the existing level of test functions and their further development:

- **SAP Solution Manager as the central platform for test management**
  SAP Solution Manager as the central platform for end-to-end testing delivers all major test functions you need to handle all aspects of test management for SAP-centric solutions — using either its own tools or those of highly integrated partner solutions.

- **Risk-based test planning**
  Continuous further development of risk-based test planning to analyze the impact of changes on critical business processes and arrive at adequate test plans.

- **More options for you, the SAP customer**
  You, the customer, have the choice of using a combination of the test tools of SAP Solution Manager and solutions from partners or third parties. You can put forward suggestions for test tools from other providers and their integration with SAP Solution Manager in the SAP user groups, DSAG and ASUG.

6.2.2 Functional Testing

From the many tools available for testing SAP-centric business processes, two options have emerged. In option 1, almost all of the test tools are provided by SAP Solution Manager, whereas option 2 relies on a combination of SAP Solution Manager, SAP Quality Center, and SAP Test Acceleration and Optimization.

Two options

Both of these options support the entire testing process, from Business Blueprint and change analyses to test requirements, planning and execution, problem handling, quality gate management, and transporting changes to the production system. In both options, SAP Solution Manager plays a pivotal role in bringing together technical and business aspects. Both options feature comprehensive test management functions and thereby offer optimum support to global enterprises for coordinating and executing tests.

You should choose between the two options on the basis of your company's particular situation and implement the existing integration and all of the tools it contains to achieve the greatest levels of efficiency and transparency in your test management activities.

Functions and Tools for Testing: Test Option 1

Almost all of the functions and tools for testing offered by option 1 (Figure 6.9) are provided by SAP Solution Manager and SAP Test Data Migration Server.

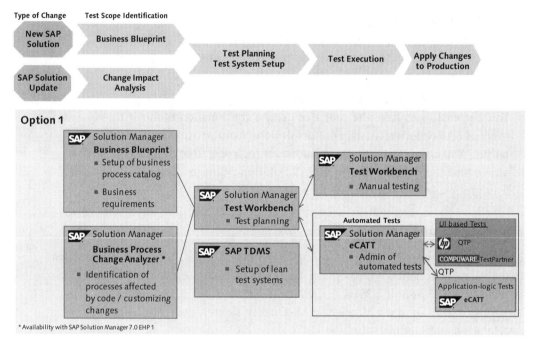

Figure 6.9 Functions and Tools for End-to-End Testing: Option 1

SAP Solution Manager – Business Blueprint

The Business Blueprint functions enable you to design, document, and hierarchically catalog your business processes (see Section 5.4). The next step is to configure or adapt the business processes in the assigned SAP application systems (see Section 6.1).

Your user departments can store their *business requirements* from a test management viewpoint. At a later time, the manual and automatic test cases are also assigned to the business processes using the Business Blueprint. This provides a holistic view of the business processes — all technical and business aspects are entered centrally using the Business Blueprint and then centrally adjusted if changes are made later.

By taking this centralized approach to designing, managing, and documenting business processes using the Business Blueprint, you achieve a significant increase in efficiency compared with a decentralized approach, which often leads to documentation becoming quickly outdated.

When you adapt an existing SAP solution, this raises the question of whether important applications or critical business processes are affected. No matter if SAP source code is adjusted due to SAP enhancement packages or customer enhancements, or if the configuration or interfaces have been changed — the question of which areas of the solution are affected by the change must always be addressed. From EHP 1 onward, SAP Solution Manager 7.0 offers a new analysis function: the Business Process Change Analyzer (BPCA), illustrated in Figure 6.10.

SAP Solution Manager – Business Process Change Analyzer

The purpose of this application is to precisely analyze the business processes that are affected by a change. To do so, you begin by creating a list of all SAP objects that are used when business processes are executed. This very detailed information is saved in the system as a technical bill of materials (TBOM). In the event of an intentional change, the SAP objects contained in the transport are compared with the SAP objects listed in the TBOMs to identify the affected business processes and areas. This allows you to schedule the required regression tests for precisely the affected areas and make well-directed use of your test resources.

Technical bill of materials

To ensure that the analysis is as accurate as possible, a static environment analysis is performed and all SAP objects used in the business process variant are recorded dynamically at run time. To record the SAP objects dynamically, you must execute your critical business processes again in a suitable system. As they are being executed, all of the SAP objects (module pools, function modules, configuration and master data tables, interfaces, and so on) that are used are recorded and entered in a TBOM that is assigned to the business process using the Business Blueprint.

If SAP Support Packages, SAP enhancement packages, custom developments, or configuration adjustments are implemented further down the line, the business processes that are affected can be identified with the BPCA. These analyses can be saved with a time stamp and contain very detailed information that can be used by subsequent test applications.

It is advisable to assign all relevant test cases to the business processes using the Business Blueprint. You can then automatically generate a test plan containing all affected processes on the basis of the BPCA – Test Workbench integration.

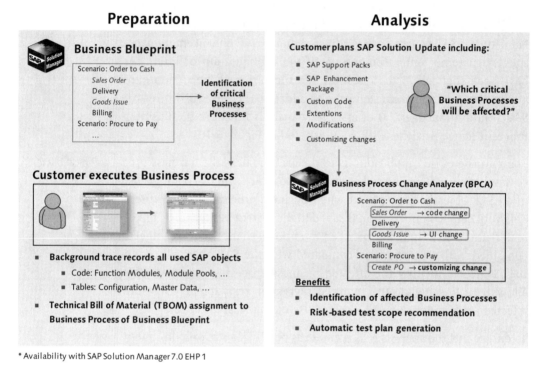

Figure 6.10 Business Process Change Analyzer

SAP Test Data Migration Server (SAP TDMS)

SAP Test Data Migration Server (TDMS) accelerates the process of automatically building test systems and other, nonproduction SAP systems. It draws on the configuration, master, and transaction data from a source system such as your production system and uses it to build the target system. In addition to creating an initial test system build, you can also add data to an existing system or replace it.

Creating a system using SAP TDMS differs considerably from simply copying a system because customers are keen to keep the volume of data in their test system much lower and avoid sensitive data or modify it. For this purpose, a number of different methods are used in SAP

TDMS. When the system is first built, the TDMS shell creation function is used to extract repository and cross-client information and create a *system shell*. In the next step, client-specific configuration data and master data can then be transferred. A range of methods are used to reduce the transaction data. For instance, you can restrict the transaction data that is transferred to one or more periods or organizational units. A flexible TDMS framework also allows you to devise your own methods. For sensitive data, for example, from SAP HR, you can apply preconfigured data anonymization methods.

Once the initial build is complete, SAP TDMS also allows specific items of data to be updated. To this end, documents from the source system can be selected and copied to the target system together with all preceding documents. This means integration tests can even be performed on complex business processes. SAP TDMS has been optimized to achieve high data throughput and performance levels while putting as little strain as possible on the source system used.

Once the test coverage resulting from the planned changes is known, you can create the test cases and test catalogs and then create and assign the test packages for each tester. In option 1, the SAP Solution Manager Test Workbench is used for this purpose.

SAP Solution Manager – Test Workbench

You can use the following functions to plan *manual tests* with the Test Workbench:

▶ **Business requirements**
When designing and documenting business processes, you can save requirements that are relevant for creating test cases.

▶ **Manual test cases**
You have the option of creating test documents that contain instructions to help manual testers perform tests. You can enter test case descriptions directly as text or create them in a word processing program and upload them to the test case. Because the number of test cases usually grows as time progresses, you can assign a range of attributes to make the cases easier to catalog and locate, for example, priority and keywords. You can also, in turn, link each test case with the above-mentioned business requirements, which means it is possible to check that all requirements have been covered in test cases.

▶ **Cataloging test cases**
Test cases can be cataloged in two ways. It is advisable to assign all test cases directly to the business processes. You do so by configuring the business processes in SAP Solution Manager at any time once the design stage is complete. If you do not want to use this function, you can use the test catalog functions of the Test Workbench instead.

▶ **Test plan**
All relevant test cases are grouped together in one or more test plans for an actual test cycle. You can create test plans by manually selecting the appropriate test cases. Alternatively, you can generate the test plan automatically using the business process hierarchy or by entering keywords.

▶ **Test packages**
Manual test cases are assigned to testers using test packages. Similar to the process of creating the test plan, you can create the packages manually from the test cases found in the test plan or generate them by selecting test case attributes. One or more testers can be assigned for each package.

▶ **Test sequences**
To run tests on complex process chains, you often require different testers with different process know-how. To this end, test packages enable test sequences to be established. For each sequence, you can define which test cases are to be performed by which testers. Only after a given test sequence has been completed successfully is the next tester notified by email that he can perform the next test sequence.

▶ **Release procedures and digital signatures**
To ensure that statutory requirements are met and to enable a formal release procedure, the Test Workbench allows you to use a release status schema. In this schema, you can define that test plans and test packages can only be used once they have been explicitly released. Once test activities have been completed, you can lock the test plan and test packages. To comply with stringent legal standards, all status activities can be documented by the respective users with digital signatures.

Planning automatic test cases

In option 1, the SAP eCATT tool is used to create automatic test cases. To test user interfaces not based on the SAP GUI, this should be supplemented with tools from partners and third parties by means of existing interfaces. These tools enable you to create automatic tests for extensive business process chains. Furthermore, Web services and their use in composite applications can also be tested.

The following functions can be used to plan automatic tests with eCATT:

eCATT functions

▶ **eCATT script**
To generate the initial test script, you execute a business process while eCATT records the SAP objects used and the activities performed by the user and then compiles a test script from them. Next, parameters are added so that test data can be used dynamically and transferred between process steps. eCATT scripts enable test results to be checked extensively. For example, after a test has been run, you can check the accuracy of data posted in the respective SAP tables using eCATT check functions. You can create eCATT scripts for SAP GUI and Web Dynpro Java user interfaces. Web Dynpro ABAP interface support is in the pipeline. You can easily create test cases for other SAP user interfaces and non-SAP applications using partner applications that are capable of being integrated.

▶ **eCATT test data container**
Test data for complex business process scenarios such as *order-to-cash* can be planned flexibly with the eCATT test data container. The test data container also allows business process variants to be executed because the creation of variants is often mapped on the basis of variations in test data in multiple test data records.

▶ **eCATT system data container**
eCATT scripts are very flexible and can be used for a range of system landscapes because they are cataloged independently of systems. The system data container reveals the logical and physical system in which the automatic tests are to be performed. The fact that system data and eCATT scripts are separated means you can change the systems to be tested without having to change the test script. You simply assign a different system data container to the test script.

▶ **eCATT interfaces**
With eCATT, it is simple to incorporate test applications from certified

partners while making use of the entire eCATT infrastructure. This provides considerable advantages throughout the entire life cycle of test cases because they can be created, managed, maintained, executed, and their results evaluated in just one environment. For instance, you can create automatic test scripts from CRM or web shop applications using partner applications that you can call up at an appropriate place in an eCATT test script. The following products are currently certified: HP QuickTest Professional, Compuware TestPartner, and Borland SilkPerformer.

Test execution and status reporting

The Test Workbench allows you to perform tests manually and automatically, enter problem messages, create test logs, and handle test status management and status reporting using the following functions:

▶ **Start of test activities**
Manual testers are sent email notifications when their test packages are available.

▶ **Manual test execution**
The test case description provides testers with all of the information they need to perform the manual tests. Thanks to the SAP system information stored in the test package, you can execute the relevant transaction or application in the allocated test system. After performing the test, you have the option of saving the test results and screenshots in a test note. The test case description can be taken as a template and supplemented with the test results. You complete your test activities by setting the corresponding test status, which forms the basis for the test coordinator's test reporting activities.

▶ **Manual execution of test sequences**
If you have defined a test sequence for a test case, only the first tester receives email notification at first. After completing the test successfully, the tester sets the corresponding test status, which triggers an email notification to be sent to the next tester in the sequence.

▶ **Automatic test execution**
You start automatic eCATT tests from the test package just like manual tests. Once the test has been executed, the application sets the test status itself. The extensive test logs are managed in the Test Workbench and can be called directly from the status reports.

▶ **Problem messages**

If problems or errors occur while tests are being executed, you can enter them directly in the integrated incident management application in SAP Solution Manager. The test case and problem message are linked to each other and can be called directly from status reporting and evaluated (see Section 8.7).

▶ **Status reporting**

The Test Workbench provides a wide range of hierarchical and list-based reports to control the status. As a test coordinator, you can use these reports to track the progress of testing at all times — even if tests are being conducted in different locations around the world — and analyze the number and priority of problems that have occurred. Further reporting options are enabled as of SAP Solution Manager 7.0 EHP 1 thanks to new integration between Test Workbench and SAP NetWeaver Business Intelligence (BI).

SAP Solution Manager supplies a range of tools for planning, executing, and analyzing functional tests. As of Release 7.0 EHP 1, the new *Test Management* work center enables web-based access to all test management functions, which means the functions relevant for each role can be made available through a single point of entry (see Figure 6.11).

SAP Solution Manager – Test Management work center

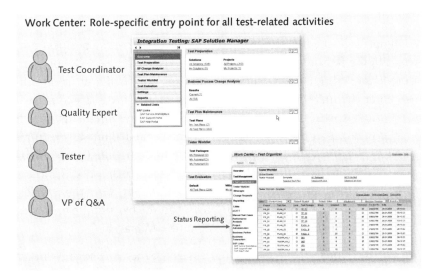

Figure 6.11 Test Management Work Center as the Point of Entry to All Test Functions

Functions and Tools for Testing: Test Option 2

The functions and tools for testing offered by option 2 are provided by SAP Solution Manager, SAP TDMS, SAP Quality Center, and SAP Test Acceleration and Optimization.

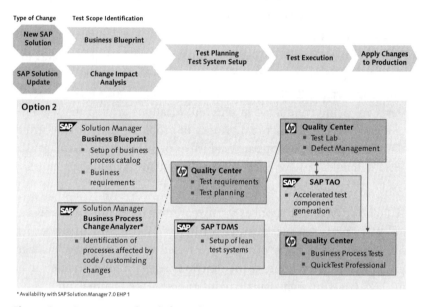

Figure 6.12 Functions and Tools for End-to-End Testing: Option 2

SAP Solution Manager – Business Blueprint

As in option 1, the first step you take here is to define the business processes in the Business Blueprint. In option 2 (see Figure 6.12), however, there is an additional key element. You can transfer the business process hierarchy to SAP Quality Center. To do so, it is necessary to furnish the processes with further test-relevant business requirements, which — after the transfer has taken place — can be expanded into test requirements in the SAP Quality Center requirements component. The official name of the interface is *SAP Solution Manager Adapter for SAP Quality Center by HP,* and it is an additional price list component. After the transfer, you can plan tests in the *SAP Quality Center* on the basis of the processes that are defined and managed in SAP Solution Manager.

SAP Solution Manager – Business Process Change Analyzer

We also recommend that you use the Business Process Change Analyzer in option 2 to analyze the impact of changes on business processes. This has various benefits. First, you can center the test coverage more precisely around the processes and components affected. Second, it is much easier for you to establish which automatic tests may potentially have been damaged by changes. You can then use SAP Test Acceleration and Optimization to rapidly regenerate the affected test components.

SAP TDMS facilitates the process of initially building a test system and then regularly updating it with test data that is representative of the business. It is described in more detail in the previous section, Functions and Tools for Testing: Test Option 1.

SAP Test Data Migration Server (TDMS)

SAP Quality Center contains all of the functions needed to manage manual and automatic tests professionally. It is made up of a range of components and boasts very sophisticated user guidance:

SAP Quality Center by HP

▶ **Requirements**
The requirements component is where you can store test requirements for the business processes. Provided the process hierarchy was created using the SAP Solution Manager adapter, you can take the requirement documents from the Business Blueprint as a starting point. On the basis of the hierarchy stored in the requirementscomponent, you can generate (empty) test cases automatically in the test plan component to be defined subsequently.

▶ **Business components**
When it comes to automatic tests with SAP Test Acceleration and Optimization, this component is highly significant for creating component-based test cases. Its functions are explained in greater detail in the section about SAP Test Acceleration and Optimization.

▶ **Test plan**
Manual test cases are created in the test plan component (see Figure 6.13). You can enter a range of attributes for each test case and describe the flow and expected results using the script. Furthermore, you can describe and present individual test steps as lists. You have the option of assigning other documents, for example, because they contain details of test data to be used or screenshots of the application being tested. Every test case can be linked to the previously entered test requirements, which means the extent to which requirements are covered remains transparent at all times.

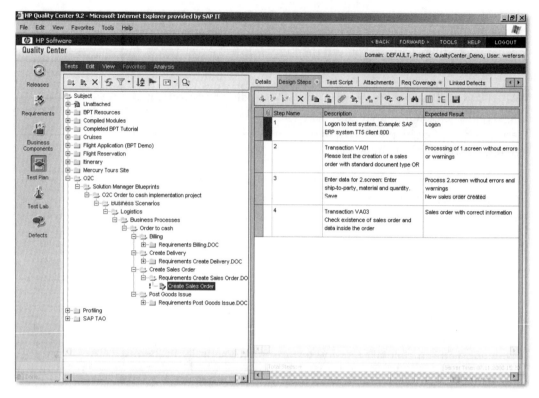

Figure 6.13 Test Plan Component of SAP Quality Center

▶ **Test lab**

You use the test lab module to define test cycles and execute the tests. You can select tests from the test plan module and present them in a completely new hierarchy. When it comes to executing the tests, you can notify the manual testers of the start of test activities by email. Using their assigned test cases, the testers can perform the tests in the respective SAP systems and enter the results directly in the test log and add screenshots if they choose. All of the tests that are performed are carefully logged and become available to you immediately for substantial analyses that can be performed straight away or later. This applies to both manual and automatic test cases. If an active interface is in place, all test results are transferred to SAP Solution Manager and can be drawn on there in all analysis tools.

▶ **Defects**

If problems arise when a test is being performed, you can use the defect component to enter problem messages directly. In turn, these messages are connected to the test case and can be assessed in the overview reports and detailed reports. As of SAP Solution Manager 7.0 EHP 1 and SAP Quality Center SP16, these problem messages can be sent by means of the adapter to the Service Desk in SAP Solution Manager, thereby ensuring that they can be further handled in an SAP context. Such synchronization is possible in both directions, that is, a *defect* can originate from a Service Desk message. It is always ensured that only one of the two messages is active and able to be processed or changed.

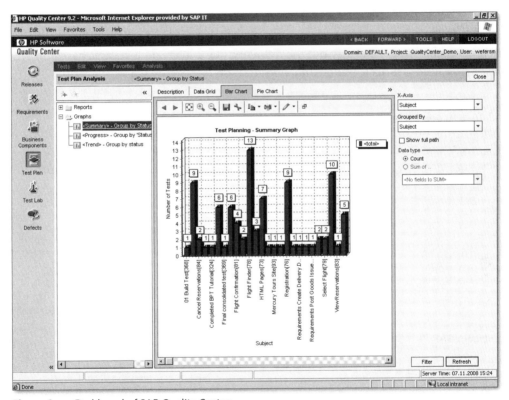

Figure 6.14 Dashboard of SAP Quality Center

You do not call up reporting, analyses, and dashboards (see Figure 6.14) in SAP Quality Center using a separate component; they are immediately available in all four components. All reports are offered as lists and in graphical form. Furthermore, you can create your own reports and flexible dashboards.

SAP Test Acceleration and Optimization Many companies aspire to using automatic test cases, particularly to handle regression tests, because such test cases present a means of reducing the number of manual testers while simultaneously increasing test coverage. Unfortunately, automatic test cases are easily damaged by changes to the user interface or the process flows of SAP applications. In turn, this leads to considerable maintenance effort for automatic test cases. This is where SAP Test Acceleration and Optimization comes in. It offers a function to automatically create test components for SAP GUI-based transactions and then model test cases based on these test components. If you want to change the user interface further down the line, it is simply a matter of regenerating the test component concerned and entering test data to repair the test case.

Creating test cases You must carry out the following steps to create test cases based on SAP Test Acceleration and Optimization (see Figure 6.15):

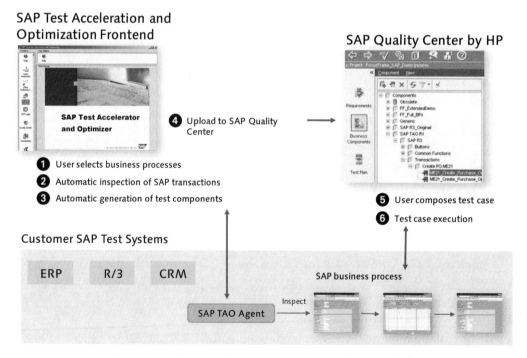

Figure 6.15 Automatically Generating Test Components with SAP Test Acceleration and Optimization

1. Identify required user interfaces for each transaction.

2. Automatically generate test components with SAP Test Acceleration and Optimization for each user interface selected in a transaction.

3. Automatically upload all generated test components to the Business Process Testing (BPT) component in SAP Quality Center.

4. Model an automatic test within the test plan component in SAP Quality Center. To do so, you select all required test components and define the flow sequence.

5. Enter test data for all relevant fields in the test case.

6. Include the test case in a test set in the test lab component in SAP Quality Center to enable the test case to be executed.

The popular *record and playback* function records a test case in one go just like a VCR. The drawback to this is that it is difficult for you to make subsequent changes or repairs to the test case, and to do so you need to know about scripting techniques. The only alternative is to record the whole test case again. Automatic test cases created with SAP Test Acceleration and Optimization are easier to adapt because they are not recorded in one go but rather consist of test components. If a test case is damaged, only the test component concerned is replaced to repair the test case and make it executable again. To do this, we recommend that you proceed as follows (see Figure 6.16):

Record and playback

1. First, you use the BPCA application to help you identify the business processes and user interfaces that are affected by changes to the SAP solution.

2. Next, you use SAP Test Acceleration and Optimization to regenerate just the test components that relate to the user interfaces concerned.

3. When you upload the test components to the BPT module using SAP Quality Center, all test cases concerned are updated.

4. The final step is to check and, if necessary, rework the test cases in respect to the required test data. In addition, the test cases concerned are consolidated again with SAP Test Acceleration and Optimization to achieve better performance.

The outcome is that the affected test cases are updated and ready to be executed.

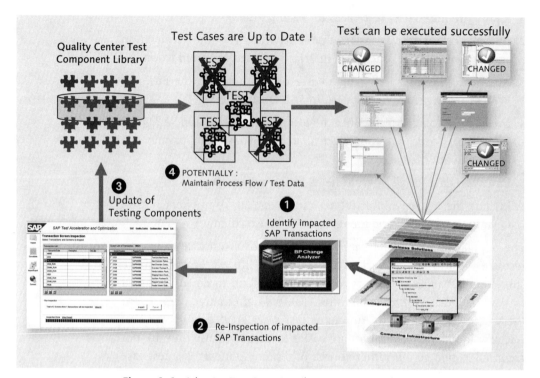

Figure 6.16 Adapting Test Cases Based on SAP Test Acceleration and Optimization

6.2.3 Other Test Activities

In addition to the functional tests described above, other test activities are available, which are described briefly in the following section.

Integration Validation

Problem Executing integrated business processes usually requires a number of SAP and partner software components that are connected to each other via interfaces. Functional tests based on manual or automatic test methods are insufficient to guarantee functional security. Therefore, we recommend that in addition to functional aspects, you validate the integrity of business process flows (*integration validation*). The following subareas should be subject to additional integration validation:

- Data consistency
- Response times
- Process integrity

The first step is to define which of the important business processes Procedure are to be validated and which key performance indicators (KPIs) are relevant for these processes. Typical KPIs include, for example, the average response time of a transaction and the system throughput per hour. These processes then undergo careful analysis from a technical perspective to ensure that all of the components and interfaces used in each process are complete. This is the basis on which the analysis and verification tools to be used are selected.

The components and interfaces identified at this stage are now subjected to detailed analysis from the following angles:

- **Response times**
  A detailed analysis of response times is carried out for each process step. Depending on the technology, a variety of tools can be used here. For the purpose of analyzing processes based on SAP GUI and the browser, end-to-end trace analysis is an integrated tool in SAP Solution Manager that allows you to isolate a single user action and gather relevant data, regardless of the technology being used. For process steps that are not interactive (interfaces or background processes), data is recorded with component-specific tools, for example ABAP trace.

- **Process integrity**
  To ensure the integrity of processes that span a number of components and interfaces, it is essential to investigate not only errors that you identify when performing functional tests, but also exceptions that are triggered when processing components connected by synchronous or asynchronous interfaces. The end-to-end trace analysis enables you to record and analyze all error situations triggered by components connected with synchronous interfaces. For components connected asynchronously, the end-to-end exception analysis provides the function you need to analyze all errors in a given period independent of component. You must monitor the interfaces closely to ensure that you have completed all asynchronously triggered actions.

▶ **Data consistency**
The process of checking data consistency is divided into two parts. First, you must ensure that the database is only updated once within a given logical unit of work (LUW). In the case of ABAP-based process steps, this can be achieved with the end-to-end trace analysis, which contains the aggregated ABAP trace function and the SQL trace function. For process steps beyond system boundaries, it is additionally necessary to safeguard the consistency of data in all of the components involved in the process step. The Data Consistency Management view in the Business Process Operations work center in SAP Solution Manager is ideally suited to this purpose for SAP systems. You must perform application-specific checks for partner applications.

Analysis The data obtained here is then taken as the basis for evaluating the KPIs defined in the first step. First, you must eliminate any identified errors while implementing the process steps and then ensure that the defined KPIs are achieved. Next, you have to ensure that the defined KPIs are achieved by taking configuration measures, making changes to your custom developments, or adjusting the interfaces to partner applications.

Once optimization has been completed, it is crucial to verify and document the improvements using the same test methodology that you applied originally. This cycle is repeated until all errors have been eliminated and all of your defined KPIs have been achieved.

Load tests

If you make important changes to an SAP solution, you should schedule load tests to address the following risks:

▶ System availability under load

▶ Functional stability under load

▶ Response times

▶ Performance weak spots in the IT infrastructure and the applications

SAP LoadRunner *SAP LoadRunner by HP* is an ideal tool to check these aspects. It supports
by HP load tests in an SAP context for the following user interfaces: SAP GUI, Web Dynpro, HTTP(S) protocols, and email protocols. SAP LoadRunner is used as follows:

- Select the business processes for the load test.

- Create test scripts to simulate user behavior.

- Perform the load test with SAP LoadRunner while gradually increasing the number of virtual users.

- Evaluate the results by comparing the simulated performance with predefined target values.

- Adjust the infrastructure or applications concerned if performance does not meet requirements. SAP LoadRunner supports this aim by pinpointing weak spots during the test and displaying them in graphical form.

- Once the changes have been implemented, the load test is repeated to verify how effective the measures have been.

SAP LoadRunner is a separate SAP price list component that you can obtain through SAP Sales.

Web Service Tests

An increasing number of SAP customers are using composite applications to enable them to introduce new and innovative business processes without changing their existing SAP solutions (for stability reasons). You achieve this goal on the basis of a service-oriented architecture (SOA) in which Web services engage in two-way communication with SAP applications without the need to modify the applications. SAP provides a large number of Web services for all SAP Business Suite applications.

Composite applications

In contrast to the SAP Business Suite solutions shipped by SAP, composite applications are only created when Web services are put to use. This, of course, leads to a requirement for testing to ensure that the new applications function properly when interacting with the Web services. SAP eCATT is a suitable tool for performing the functional tests because it allows tests to be conducted based on user interfaces and on Web services without drawing on user interfaces.

The following approach is recommended:

1. In the test system, create eCATT scripts for individual tests for each of the Web services used. The conditions in the test system should

reflect the production environment as closely as possible in terms of configuration, master, and transaction data. This first ensures that the Web services can function properly in the customer environment with the respective data. The functions provided in eCATT are ideal for the purpose of these tests.

2. The second step is to perform the functional test on the composite application using the required Web services. For this purpose, a script is created in eCATT that automatically tests all of the process steps from the end user's perspective. Other tools such as HP QuickTest Professional and Compuware TestPartner can be brought in here to help automate the test. This ensures that the wide variety of possible user interfaces can be included in the test.

3. Using a combination of individual tests for Web services, processing logic tests based on user interfaces, and a representative selection of test data, you can test modern composite applications from a functional perspective.

In the deploy phase, the application moves into live operation. Communication channels are critical during this phase because they enable the smooth transfer of information to end users.

7   Deploy Phase

The purpose of final preparation is to transfer the results of the realization phase into the live solution. All open issues concerning the final steps for going live are clarified. Once this phase has been completed successfully, the production business processes of your solution can run.

As in the build and test phase, the *Test Workbench* of SAP Solution Manager provides valuable support; the same utilities and tools can be used to test various aspects of the system, such as performance, load, and interfaces.

At this stage, the *Learning Maps* created in SAP Solution Manager are distributed to the relevant end users, who can then use them for self-study purposes to tailor content to their working environment and provide feedback on individual units or the Learning Map as a whole. Feedback can be evaluated and used to improve the training materials. For more information, see Sections 7.2 and 7.3.

Learning Maps

This phase facilitates the transition from a preproduction environment to production operation. During this phase, it is important that *support* is provided to end users, not just in the critical days after going live, but on a long-term basis as well. SAP Solution Manager's integrated *Service Desk* can be used for this purpose (see Section 8.7).

Service Desk

Before production can go live, the *cutover* plans must be implemented, which involves transferring data verified in the realization phase from the legacy system to the production system. Tested configuration settings as well as modifications and customer developments are also transported to the production system.

SAP GoingLive Check SAP recommends performing the *SAP GoingLive Check* about two months before the planned go-live date. It reduces the risks involved in implementation by proactively identifying potential problems with regard to performance, availability, and maintenance so that corrective measures can be taken promptly.

Go Live and Support In the *Go Live and Support* phase, users gain the practical experience of using a solution. This demands a well-organized user support structure that all employees can access. You can also monitor system transactions and optimize overall system performance during this phase. SAP Solution Manager offers a wide range of utilities and tools for running the solution, for example, which allow you to monitor implemented processes across all systems. Particularly during early phases of system operation, it is recommended that you analyze the system proactively using *SAP EarlyWatch*. You can identify potential problems early on, prevent bottlenecks, and monitor performance of your systems regularly and automatically by setting up *SAP EarlyWatch Alert* in SAP Solution Manager. It is also an effective tool for checking your core business processes and systems.

SAP EarlyWatch Check By running *SAP EarlyWatch Check*, a service that analyzes your operating system, database, and SAP system proactively, you can derive further recommendations and measures on how to optimize performance. For more information about SAP EarlyWatch, see Sections 8.2.3 and 8.6.

7.1 Solutions in the Solution Directory

Solution One of the challenges you face in production after completing a project successfully is preserving the knowledge gained from the project and keeping it up to date during operations. SAP Solution Manager's *solution* concept is designed to help you do this. A solution contains information about systems, software components, and business processes (scenarios), which you can transfer from your project to SAP Solution Manager. You thereby ensure that all of the information can still be accessed and consolidated further after the project has been completed (see Figure 7.1).

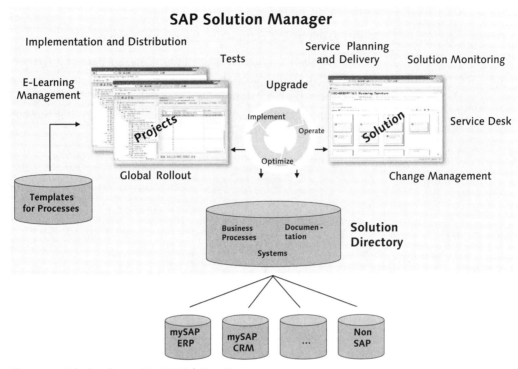

Figure 7.1 Solution Concept in SAP Solution Manager

You manage solutions in the *Solution Directory* (Transaction SOLMAN_   Advantages
DIRECTORY). Solutions offer the following advantages:

▶ **All assignments in the SAP Solution Manager project are available**

  ▶ The scenario and business process structures are transferred to the
    solution.

  ▶ Configuration object assignments are readily available.

  ▶ You can use test cases in the structure to effectively test changes
    that have been made.

  ▶ You can reuse e-learning materials from projects in the solution.

  ▶ The solution has the same system landscape concept as the project,
    which means you can reuse the structure when upgrading.

▶ **Standard presentation of solution components such as servers,
  systems, business processes, and scenarios**

▶ Improved display of graphics and diagrams

▶ Option of exporting graphics to Microsoft Office or HTML

You can distinguish two types of information: master data and transaction data that changes more often (see Figure 7.2). You can define one or more solutions in SAP Solution Manager. The master data is shared between solutions (same systems and logical components), but transaction data is usually defined for just one solution.

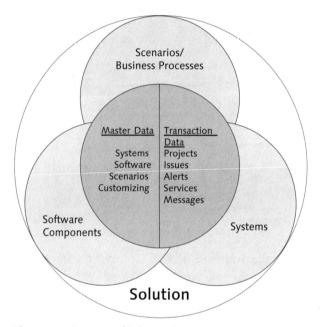

Figure 7.2 Overview of Solution Components

A solution has the following characteristics:

▶ Unique function (role)[1], for example, productive, planned, temporary, support, or demo.

▶ Authorization concept.

---

1 The function determines which systems are selected from the logical components. Only the role determines how systems are used for Business Process Monitoring and other functions. Additional systems can be integrated to include other functions (such as SAP EarlyWatch Alert, central system administration).

- Life cycle.

- Independent of other solutions.

- Business processes can be part of one solution only. Systems and logical components can be used in multiple solutions.[2]

7.1.1 Criteria for Shaping a Solution

Solutions are shaped by:

- The number of systems in the solution

- End-to-end business processes across all systems and logical components involved (including third-party providers)

- A company's organizational units (and in some cases, its structure, requirements regarding technical availability, and so on)

- Solution roles (technical function)

- Functions

  - System monitoring (number of alert objects and RFCs, limits regarding graphical display)

  - Business Process Monitoring (number of alert objects and RFCs, limits regarding graphical display)

  - Delivery of SAP services (size of data model)

- Special requirements such as hosting

- Authorization and delimitation requirements

- Definition of a "solution master" template

Other, less influential factors include:

- Number of SAP EarlyWatch Alert reports

- Business process documentation

- Problem tracking

- Change Request Management

- Service Desk (not dependent on the solution, but it affects sizing)

---

2 Changes affect all solutions in which the systems or components are used.

From SAP's perspective, solutions are shaped mainly by the scope of end-to-end business processes documented and the number of systems involved (including their function within the solution, such as system monitoring).

Complex landscape

In complex organizations, the definition of multiple solutions based on the organizational structure and specific requirements of individual organizational units is recommended. This enables customers and groups with large and complex structures to be mapped and managed more easily. However, it is essential that all business objects for one business process are included in one solution. The process must not be split across multiple solutions or (sub)processes. Small and midsize enterprises usually have one solution.

7.1.2 Working with Solutions

To continuously enhance existing solutions and meet business requirements, solutions may need to be copied within one SAP Solution Manager system or exported to other SAP Solution Manager systems.

Functions for the life cycle of solutions

The following functions are required for the life cycle of a solution:

Copying Solutions

Solutions are copied within one SAP Solution Manager system. When the source and target solutions are selected, you can specify whether you want to copy reports from SAP EarlyWatch Alert, Service Level Reporting, or other solution-relevant service data. The following restrictions apply:

▶ Issues, Expertise on Demand queries, and Top Issues are not copied.

▶ The Service Plan cannot be copied because it is uniquely assigned to a solution (the original solution).

▶ Business Process Monitoring is deactivated after the copy process and must then be reactivated manually in the monitoring session.

Exporting

When a solution is exported (Transaction SOLUTION_TRANSFER), the entire solution is copied to a *flat file*. Documentation, Issues, Top Issues,

Expertise on Demand queries, and the Service Plan can be exported. The documentation is summarized in the SAP Solution Manager system in a separate transport.

Importing

The exported flat file undergoes a consistency check when it is imported (Transaction SOLUTION_TRANSFER). This checks, for example, whether logical components with the same name already exist. A dialog box may then provide the option to transfer an exported logical component to an existing one or create a new logical component (see Figure 7.3).

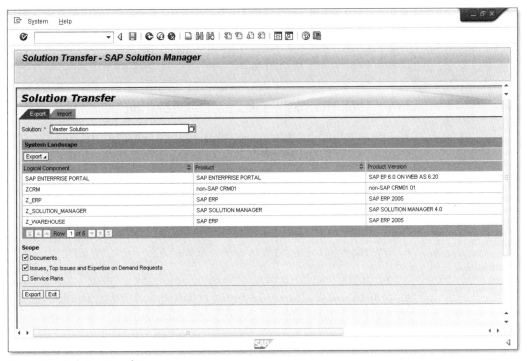

Figure 7.3 Solution Transfer

When a solution is imported, a target solution must already exist (but can be empty). The two import options REPLACE and COPY are available, which essentially determine how SAP views the new solution. When the REPLACE option is selected, data that exists at SAP for the old solution

Import options

(such as Top Issues or the service plan) is assigned to the new solution as soon as it has been made known to SAP. When the COPY option is selected, a new solution is created that is completely unknown to SAP.

Splitting

You split a solution by copying it, or exporting and importing it, and then deleting specific information from the new solution. Programs to support this process are not planned.

Changing Functions After Changing the Solution

Transferring settings for functions of SAP Solution Manager is useful only if the same systems are available after migration, which is usually only the case when companies are sold or an SAP Solution Manager system run externally is migrated.

7.1.3 Solutions as a Basis for Collaboration

The main point of reference for collaboration between SAP and the customer is a solution in which:

▶ Business processes are sufficiently documented

▶ Services are delivered that are listed in the service plan

▶ Issues are documented and tracked

▶ Expertise on Demand is available from SAP

It must be clear which of the possible solutions (if your company has more than one) is the platform for collaboration. To accommodate different requirements, three scenarios are distinguished:

1. You are using SAP Solution Manager and the solutions in line with SAP's philosophy. This allows you, as the customer, to work with SAP in the same solution and fully exploit the synergies offered by SAP Solution Manager. The service engineers, however, also make changes to the solutions during and after service delivery, for example, to document a process step more thoroughly.

2. You allow the same solution to be used, but SAP works in separate projects and business processes. This still results in synergies such as a shared service plan and Issue Tracking, but processes can no longer be documented together.

3. You do not allow shared use within the same solution, for example, due to legal reasons. As a workaround, a separate solution is created for which business processes are documented. However, this is the most unfavorable option because all synergy effects are lost. During more extensive activities, the available time is spent checking whether the stored data is up to date.

7.1.4 Consistent Use of SAP Solution Manager

Software is continually subject to changes that can be grouped into life cycle phases. These phases involve implementing, operating, upgrading, and, in special cases, rolling out solutions. Figure 7.4 shows the relationship between the life cycle phases and the resulting projects and solutions implemented.

The life cycle phases of a solution

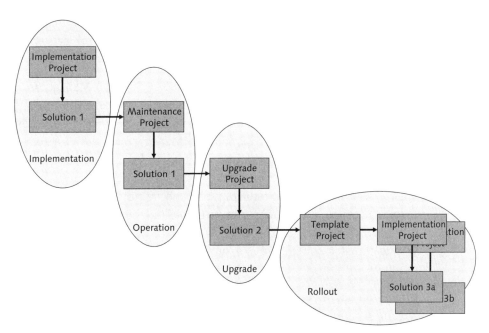

Figure 7.4 The Life Cycle Phases of a Solution

The process is as follows:

1. First, software is implemented as a project. Information from the project flows into a solution after the implementation phase.

2. Changes to the software (solution) that are identified during daily use are carried out in a maintenance project and transferred to the solution, based on a check-in/check-out mechanism.

3. The upgrade is performed as an upgrade project.

4. If a rollout is planned, a solution can be copied into a template project from which it is distributed to different implementation projects.

The key elements comprise the solution in which business processes and scenarios are documented along with central procedures for managing systems and components.

7.2   E-Learning Management – Efficient Knowledge Transfer During Projects

E-Learning Management in SAP Solution Manager is designed for customers who want to transfer knowledge to users involved in projects effectively, efficiently, and promptly.

Efficient and cost-effective
The purpose of E-Learning Management in SAP Solution Manager is to create user training courses on new and changed processes in projects or solutions and make them available to end users as *e-learning materials*. The advantage here is that SAP Solution Manager provides easy-to-use software for you to manage learning materials, reuse and update materials at any time (depending on requirements), and train users more efficiently. E-learning also reduces travel and training location expenses because users can complete training activities independently at the workplace, which reduces absence from work. It presents another attractive way to transfer knowledge and supplement project-related classroom training.

When you adapt your IT solution to meet changing requirements, you have to notify users who work with the solution daily about changes, for example, to the interface. SAP Solution Manager helps you organize learning units into a *Learning Map* and distribute materials to specific user groups in the company.

7.2.1 Creating Training Materials

You first create e-learning materials. To do so, you can use existing project documentation or other formats such as presentations. You can organize and categorize individual learning objects in SAP Solution Manager using the existing business process structure. If you have defined end user roles in your project, you can use them in E-Learning Management (Figure 7.5) to distribute information to specific end users. Every user has different training requirements. A project manager, for example, would prefer an overview, whereas a technology consultant or specialist department user would like to understand functions in detail.

Creation

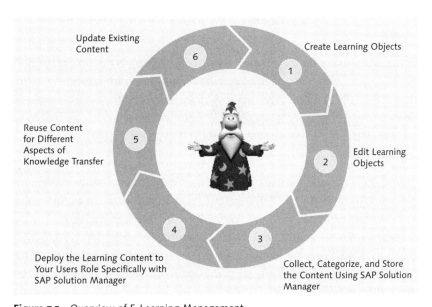

Figure 7.5 Overview of E-Learning Management

7.2.2 SAP ProductivityPak by RWD Adapter for SAP Solution Manager

With *SAP ProductivityPak by RWD Adapter for SAP Solution Manager*, SAP provides an interface to *SAP ProductivityPak by RWD*, a performance support solution. This product enables you to develop documentation (application simulations, process documentation, or training materials) with an integrated workflow and supports the exchange of knowledge between authors, experts, and users. The re-recording function allows you to create new versions and replace original screenshots with new language versions. The users access up-to-date content using a context-sensitive help function from each 32-bit application or via intranet pages.

With the adapter for SAP Solution Manager, customers who use SAP ProductivityPak by RWD can store their documentation centrally in SAP Solution Manager and edit and manage it with SAP ProductivityPak by RWD — with full use of functions from both products. Documents can be created, edited, or deleted directly from SAP Solution Manager. The integrated adapter enables you to make full use of all functions in SAP ProductivityPak by RWD. For example, you can collaborate with multiple authors, use extensive recording and editing functions, output data in various formats (HTML, PDF, Flash, Microsoft Word), and define workflows.

Project documentation

One example of where the adapter is used is in project documentation: A project team can create documentation for project configuration directly from SAP Solution Manager using SAP ProductivityPak by RWD. These documents are then integrated in SAP Solution Manager on the relevant tab pages (such as CONFIGURATION, PROJ. DOCUMENTATION, or TRAINING MATERIALS).

Creating application simulations

The adapter can also be used to create application simulations, for example, as training material. You can start recording directly from SAP Solution Manager in order to then navigate to the relevant transaction to be recorded. When recording (and any postprocessing in SAP ProductivityPak by RWD) is complete, end users can access the simulation in SAP Solution Manager on the relevant tab pages (such as LEARNING MATERIAL) or by using the functions of SAP ProductivityPak by RWD.

The adapter also allows you to add documents created with SAP ProductivityPak by RWD to test case documentation. Its integration enables you to record, create, and store these documents directly in SAP Solution Manager on the TEST CASES tab page.

7.2.3 Learning Maps: Organizing and Distributing Training Content During a Project

Edited content is collected, categorized, and stored in SAP Solution Manager. To integrate e-learning content in your project, call the Configuration transaction (SOLAR02; see Section 6.1) and navigate to the process step for which you have created a learning object. On the TRAINING MATERIALS tab page, select INSERT DOCUMENT. A dialog box appears in which you can enter a TITLE and the DOCUMENTATION TYPE (TRAINING) and set the status of the learning unit. You then save the file to your project (UPLOAD FILE). The learning object is saved in your project and displayed on the TRAINING MATERIALS tab page.

You can also define attributes for the learning object. To do so, select your learning object in the list and choose ATTRIBUTES. To help users schedule training, it is important to include a description of the learning object and the time needed to complete the training unit.

Learning object attributes

On the END USER ROLES tab page, you can also define the users for whom the process step is relevant. When doing so, you can select predefined roles from the HR organization or technical profiles, or define your own roles.

When you have saved the content in the project, you can generate a Learning Map. To do so, call the Learning Map Builder transaction (SOLAR_LEARNING_MAP; see Figure 7.6) and select CREATE. A dialog box appears in which you can enter a title for your Learning Map and define your project as the data source.

SAP Solution Manager takes the project structure and uses it to generate a proposed chapter structure. You can then enter a title for the Learning Map, a company logo, and the URL of your company's web page at the header level.

Another important function integrates the Service Desk in the Learning Map. The CREATE SUPPORT DESK LINK function displays a link in the Learning Map (see Figure 7.7), which when selected opens a new support message on an entry screen (see also Section 8.7). The message already contains certain information, and end users can add their own text if they have questions or problems regarding the Learning Map.

Integrating the Service Desk

In this way, technical problems can be reported directly to the support
organization without any integration gaps.

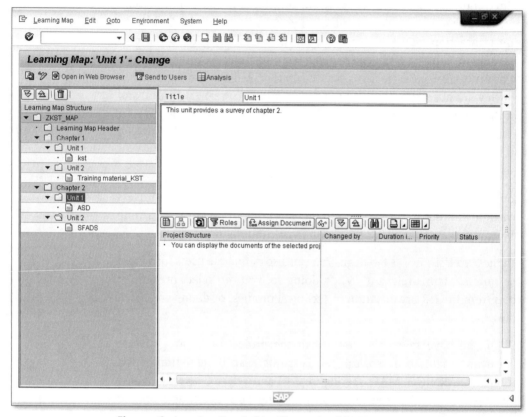

Figure 7.6 Learning Map Builder (Transaction SOLAR_LEARNING_MAP)

Chapter structure

You can change the chapter structure of the Learning Map, remove proposed chapters, and add new ones. To assign learning objects to the
chapters, you can drag and drop learning objects from the project structure at the bottom right of the screen into the relevant chapters. You can
also enter additional information for the chapters. In the web browser,
you can display a preview of the Learning Map at any time by selecting
OPEN IN WEB BROWSER.

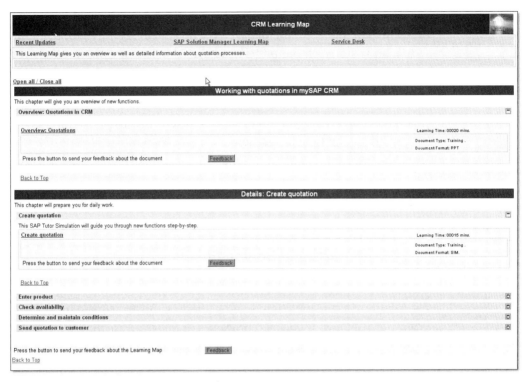

Figure 7.7 Completed Learning Map in Web Browser

To inform users about a Learning Map, you can send out email notifications based on end user roles. When you select SEND TO USERS, your email program opens and a generated text containing the URL of the Learning Map is copied from SAP Solution Manager to the clipboard. You can insert this text, adapt it, and send it to the users assigned to the selected role. This approach ensures that information is communicated efficiently to a specific audience.

The e-learning life cycle does not end here (see Figure 7.5). The Learning Map is subject to continual improvement. The feedback function in E-Learning Management helps you in this process. Learning Map users can submit anonymous evaluations and comments about the content by selecting FEEDBACK. Such information is an important element that enables those responsible to respond to requirements.

Feedback function

E-learning can be conducted at any time, directly at the workplace, with the help of SAP Solution Manager as a document server. All of the information is stored in the project and available in SAP Solution Manager. The benefits of e-learning are obvious:

▸ Existing documents can be reused easily.

▸ End user training becomes more efficient because e-learning is not restricted by time or location.

▸ Role-based distribution of information enables learning according to user needs.

▸ The feedback function enables a higher quality of training through.

7.3   Reporting – Deploy Phase

When a project is transferred to production operation in the deploy phase, one of the most important success factors is that end users know how to use new or changed processes in their daily activities. To monitor this transfer of knowledge, SAP Solution Manager provides special reporting functions.

With SAP Solution Manager, you generate Learning Maps from the existing project structure for end users' respective task areas, for example, to show the buyers in your company how to use new functions. A Learning Map provides a clear overview of the content in a computer-based self-learning course and presents information about the learning units and links to the training material (see Section 7.2) in HTML format.

Feedback   End users can evaluate Learning Maps using an HTML-based feedback option. All of the feedback from end users is saved anonymously. You can display the results of these evaluations in Learning Map Management (Transaction SOLAR_LEARNING_MAP). When doing so, you can analyze four different criteria:

▸ Number of times the Learning Map was called

▸ Individual evaluations

▸ Average evaluation

▸ Feedback on individual learning units and the overall Learning Map

The analysis provides information about the usage rate and quality of Learning Maps. It also lets you display the feedback as text. Figure 7.8 shows the results of a Learning Map analysis.

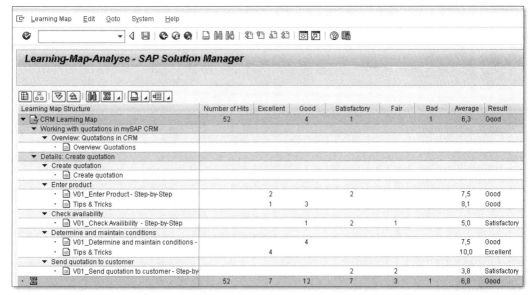

Learning Map Structure	Number of Hits	Excellent	Good	Satisfactory	Fair	Bad	Average	Result
▼ CRM Learning Map	52		4	1		1	6,3	Good
▼ Working with quotations in mySAP CRM								
▼ Overview: Quotations in CRM								
• Overview: Quotations								
▼ Details: Create quotation								
▼ Create quotation								
• Create quotation								
▼ Enter product								
• V01_Enter Product - Step-by-Step		2		2			7,5	Good
• Tips & Tricks		1	3				8,1	Good
▼ Check availability								
• V01_Check Availibility - Step-by-Step			1	2	1		5,0	Satisfactory
▼ Determine and maintain conditions								
• V01_Determine and maintain conditions -			4				7,5	Good
• Tips & Tricks		4					10,0	Excellent
▼ Send quotation to customer								
• V01_Send quotation to customer - Step-by				2	2		3,8	Satisfactory
•	52	7	12	7	3	1	6,8	Good

Figure 7.8 Results – Learning Map Analysis

The operate phase groups tasks that are performed after system startup. Most of these tasks involve system administration, system monitoring, message processing (Service Desk), root cause analysis, issue management, and service delivery.

8 Operate Phase

The high demand for new information technology over the past 30 years has accelerated the ever-growing market for software solutions. Solutions now become outdated in a matter of a few years, with solution landscapes becoming more powerful and thus increasingly heterogeneous and complex. Consequently, IT organizations responsible for maintaining solution landscapes have been under more constant pressure than almost any other department. Operating costs need to be kept as low as possible, while at the same time ensuring the stability of the solutions and the integration of new products. Despite the more complex requirements, operating costs are frequently brought down by downsizing teams or delegating tasks to central service providers that oversee many systems. Transferring the knowledge necessary to perform new tasks, substituting experienced staff, and monitoring systems efficiently are becoming increasingly difficult. The associated risks are also becoming greater.

SAP Solution Manager enables simple and complex processes to be handled automatically in many different areas, such as automated system monitoring and error notification, the collection of technical data, and report summaries based on SAP EarlyWatch Alert (EWA) and Service Level Reporting (SLR). It therefore allows you not only to react swiftly and purposefully but also to identify trends early on and take action before errors occur. Current know-how, as well as task and workflow documentation, is also integrated in many areas where administrative responsibilities and other tasks occur (Central System Administration, Solution Reporting, Business Process Monitoring).

Automation of tasks

Work center The diverse tasks within solution operations are spread out clearly across the following work centers:

- System Landscape Management
- System Administration
- System Monitoring
- Business Process Operations
- Job Management
- Incident Management
- Root Cause Analysis

The personalized user interface, ability to work centrally, automation, and efficient transfer of knowledge give experts the time they need to concentrate on their core competencies. This, in turn, allows small teams to monitor and manage complex system landscapes, while making the services they offer transparent to the end user. SAP Solution Manager therefore makes it possible to keep IT know-how inside companies or outsource it and monitor the services provided.

8.1   System Administration

System administration is a key element to ensure that your IT landscape is set up and can be monitored in the best possible way. It covers all initial and ongoing administrative tasks and activities you need to manage SAP solutions and therefore constitutes the starting point for production operations. This area contains the tools and activities that you require to guarantee that your SAP solutions operate smoothly from a technical viewpoint.

Daily system administration of SAP solutions is integrated logically here according to typical administrative tasks that, in turn, are arranged according to the respective SAP system types. SAP Solution Manager allows you to manage recurring administrative tasks centrally and ensure that they are always executed by saving them as recurring tasks to be completed. This simplifies the system administrator's tasks and lowers costs in production operations.

SAP Solution Manager provides all of the fundamental functions you need to manage your SAP landscape. In addition to a user management function, it offers all tools to monitor both ABAP and Java elements in the IT landscape, as well as functions to manage instances, databases, and output devices (for example, printers), start and stop systems, and archive data. With central access to all systems to be managed and the option to manage periodic and ad hoc administrative tasks automatically, you can realize major savings in terms of both time and costs.

Functions

8.1.1   Local and Central System Administration

When dealing with system administration, a distinction is made between local and central administration:

▶ Local administration relates to an activity in just one managed system. This includes, for instance, managing users and their authorizations in this system.

Local system administration

▶ Central administration is initiated in a central system, for example, SAP Solution Manager, and results in administrative changes in one or more connected systems. An equivalent example here would be the task of centrally managing users across several systems (Central User Administration [CUA]).

Central system administration

Both types of administration are used in SAP system operations. SAP recommends the use of central administration because a central working environment reduces the workload and thereby brings down operating costs, especially in large landscapes.

In the System Administration work center, SAP Solution Manager offers you access to both local and central system administration. The work centers in SAP Solution Manager, above all, System Administration, also enable you to call up local tools in managed systems. The major advantage of this concept is that you can incorporate tools that are provided in the latest SAP releases but are not available in SAP Solution Manager. For example, you can integrate SAP NetWeaver Administrator 7.1 despite the fact that SAP Solution Manager runs on SAP NetWeaver 7.0. In addition to providing central access to daily tasks, therefore, work centers also guarantee that you can integrate and use tools from newer SAP NetWeaver systems in the future.

Access to new tools

The System Administration work center gives you access to a range of functions in the following views:

- Overview
- Task Management
- User Management
- Administration Tools

Overview The OVERVIEW view in the work center lists all of the tasks and activities you perform regularly when managing SAP solutions. You can see at a glance which systems are available and which tasks are open for a given system. To execute a task, you can navigate directly from the display to the corresponding administration tool.

System availability data is based on CCMS PING and shows which systems are currently available in the overview (see Figure 8.1).

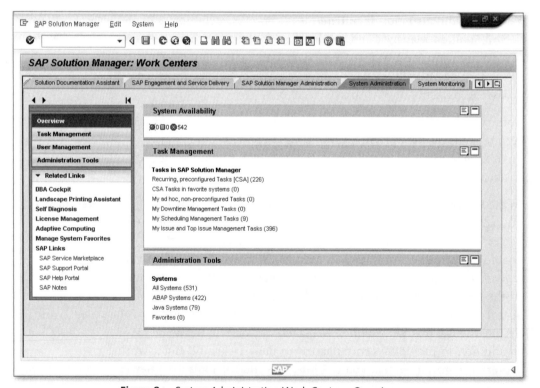

Figure 8.1 System Administration Work Center – Overview

You create tasks in different SAP Solution Manager applications, for example, Central System Administration (CSA), Downtime Management, Job Scheduling Management, and Issue Management (see Sections 8.3, 8.4, and 8.5).

Task Management

In the TASK MANAGEMENT view in the System Administration work center (see Figure 8.2), you can gain easy, standardized access to the different tasks and the tools used to manage them. You can also create tasks here that are not assigned to a particular SAP Solution Manager application so that you can immediately map and document application-independent, nonstandardized system administration work steps.

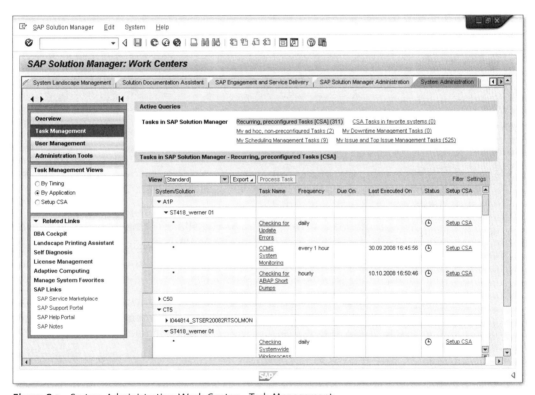

Figure 8.2 System Administration Work Center – Task Management

You can obtain an overview of all of the tasks entered in central task management in a calendar (see Figure 8.3).

Calendar function

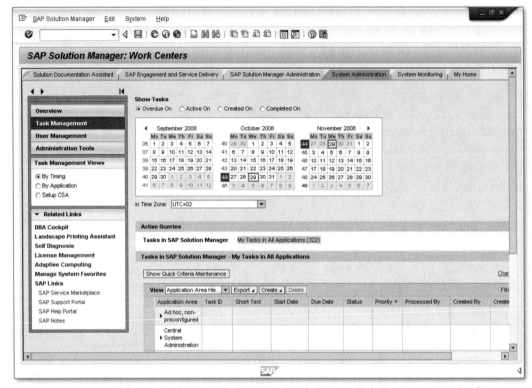

Figure 8.3 System Administration Work Center – Task Management: Calendar

With central task management, SAP facilitates initial knowledge transfer and offers a tool for standardizing SAP solution maintenance. This knowledge transfer is especially practical with new solutions, for which minimal knowledge has been established in your company. Central system management also allows you to create your own tasks, to which you can append comments, documentation, and documents. These documents can be external to the session but be displayed in it via a URL or a link to your document server. This captures internal knowledge and therefore ensures that standard maintenance can be carried out while you are on vacation or sick leave, or in the event of organizational changes within your company. Task completion along with the respective comments is logged automatically and can be summarized and accessed in report form at regular intervals.

When you create a solution and assign systems to it, a range of frequently used administrative tasks are presented, and you can assign these to the respective systems. If open tasks exist, the number is shown in brackets in the overview. You can display details of them by solution, system, or task type (see Figure 8.2).

When you select a component, its open tasks are displayed in a table arranged according to solutions. You can access the CSA session by clicking on a task (see Figure 8.4). *Infrastructure Service Sessions*, also known as *Service Sessions*, were originally developed for SAP Active Global Support and provide access to information and tasks for standardized system analysis. Here, tasks and information are saved in *checks* and *check groups*, which can be systematically processed from top to bottom. Service Sessions form the basis of the SAP EarlyWatch Alert, Service Level Reporting, System Monitoring, and Business Process Monitoring *self-services*, and of SAP Active Global Support remote and onsite services including SAP EarlyWatch Health Check and SAP GoingLive Check.

CSA session

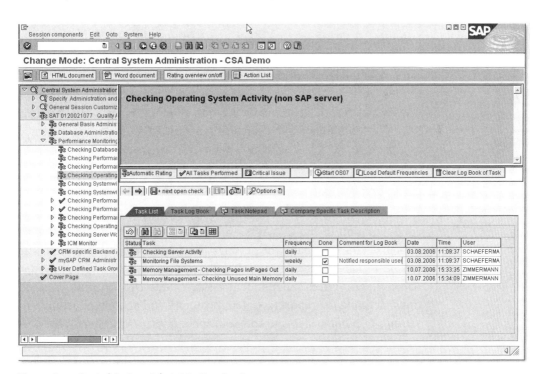

Figure 8.4 Central System Administration Session

The central system administration session allows you to process uncompleted tasks such as checking lock entries in Transaction SM12. Here, you confirm that a task has been completed, and, if necessary, add a comment. SAP Solution Manager helps you process tasks by:

- Enabling you to access the relevant transactions and expert monitors in the managed system

- Giving you direct access to the managed system without having to log on[1]

- Providing you with standard SAP documentation in the *task description* or your company-internal documentation on the same entry screen

- Making your comments or comments from colleagues available for processing the task (*task log history*)

- Automating recording of the user ID and time in the *task log book* after the task has been completed (selecting the DONE checkbox)

CSA reports
Once you have completed a task, you can process the next open tasks directly in the task structure without having to return to the task list or task display. When you have processed all of your tasks, you can create an HTML or Microsoft Word report to list your tasks and comments. You can define the layout of the cover sheet and content of this report yourself. For example, you can choose to list all completed tasks or only the tasks with appended comments. As with all other reporting functions in SAP Solution Manager, you can also schedule CSA reports to be created as a background job. This allows reports to be created automatically at regular intervals, such as on a daily, weekly, or monthly basis (see also Section 8.9).

Processing frequencies
You can also make the Customizing settings used for central system administration in the CSA session. The session is structured in such a way that you first make the settings independently of the system and task. Component-specific administrative tasks then follow with a system name check. System-independent tasks include checking RFC connections, defining the report layout and content, and applying Customizing settings of other systems to this solution landscape or others. These are

---

1 This requires use of the trusting-trusted RFC connection recommended by SAP.

accompanied by system-specific tasks, which are logically grouped into check groups. As a result, processing the tasks is easier and faster.

In SAP Solution Manager, you can use the processing frequencies recommended by SAP for your tasks by choosing LOAD DEFAULT FREQUENCIES. If you do not want to select individual tasks or their processing frequencies, deactivate the task or select a new processing frequency. You can choose from a large selection of processing frequencies, ranging from hours and days to monthly intervals. In addition, you can select irregular processing frequencies that are then always displayed as open tasks.

SAP Solution Manager helps you set up central system administration by:

▶ Preselecting the most important tasks

▶ Allowing you to select settings from one system or another (even if different landscapes are involved)

▶ Preselecting the frequency at which tasks are to be completed

The USER MANAGEMENT view in the System Administration work center gives you access to all of the tools you need to manage users locally for both ABAP and Java components.

User Management

You can manage users and roles here. For example, you can create, delete, or lock users. The systems are arranged clearly according to system component type or system type, for example, development, test, or production system. You can filter the systems and add them to your favorites.

All important tools and transactions, for instance, PFCG, SU01, and SU10, are incorporated here. The main administrative functions for managing users in Java, familiar from SAP NetWeaver Administrator, are integrated (see Figure 8.5).

The ADMINISTRATION TOOLS view in the SYSTEM ADMINISTRATION tab page groups the most important local administrative functions for both ABAP and Java components. Tasks that fall into this category include managing instances, managing databases, archiving, and managing output devices (for example, printers). The tools that enable you to complete these tasks can be found on the APPLICATION SERVER tab page. The functions familiar from SAP NetWeaver Administrator are also embedded here.

Administration Tools

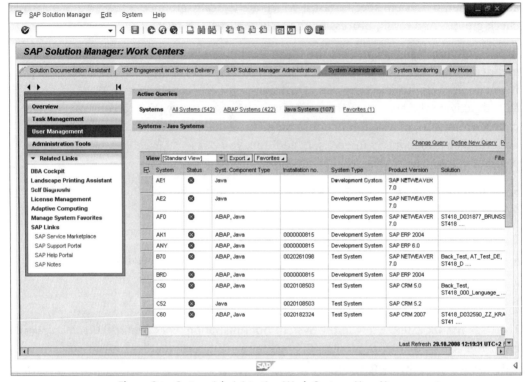

Figure 8.5 System Administration Work Center – User Management

In addition, you can access product-specific tools by choosing the MAIN INSTANCES tab page, for example tools for master data management (MDM). You can also add your own tools here.

SAP NetWeaver Administrator

In addition to task-oriented system administration as provided in the work center of the same name in SAP Solution Manager, you can use other tools to manage your systems, for example, *SAP NetWeaver Administrator*, which was first shipped in 2004 to facilitate the administration of Java-based software components. It is capable of handling cross-system or local administration tasks.

Central SAP NetWeaver Administrator focuses on activities that reach across systems and solution landscapes, for example:

▸ Displaying configurations of different systems
▸ Displaying log information from different systems

SAP NetWeaver Administrator has long been a component of SAP NetWeaver Application Server Java. It does not have to be installed or configured, but represents a useful tool to manage the local SAP NetWeaver Application Server Java that can be used straight away.

SAP NetWeaver Administrator undergoes constant development by SAP. As of Version 7.1, it completely replaces SAP Visual Administrator as the standard tool for daily operations. Furthermore, it is open to *usage-type*-specific enhancements: When SAP NetWeaver Composition Environment (SAP NetWeaver CE) is used, SAP NetWeaver Administrator receives important functions for managing service-based applications. The same applies to managing service-oriented architectures in the latest version of SAP NetWeaver Process Integration.

Cross-system SAP NetWeaver Administrator functions, on the other hand, enhance and bolster SAP Solution Manager in its role as the central operating platform for SAP NetWeaver system landscapes. Its functions have been fully integrated into the SAP Solution Manager System Administration and System Monitoring work centers.

Integration in SAP Solution Manager

8.1.2 Self-Diagnosis

SAP Solution Manager is an application that supports you in all aspects of system operations, in particular, monitoring your SAP solution landscape. This places certain demands on SAP Solution Manager with regard to stability and its ability to be installed, configured, and handled with ease. The overhead costs of an application whose goal it is to reduce your total cost of ownership should be as low as possible.

Self-Diagnosis helps you minimize the operating costs associated with SAP Solution Manager. It is an easy-to-use tool that verifies a range of indicators that allow you to assess the condition of SAP Solution Manager.

Minimizing operating costs

These indicators are structured as follows:

The lowest level of the hierarchy consists of *alert types*. These are basis indicators, of which there are currently about 100. You can view the complete list together with descriptions in Transaction SOLUTION_ MANAGER under SETTINGS • SELF DIAGNOSIS • ALERT TYPES, where you can find the following:

Alert types

- ▶ The *description* explaining the alert type

- ▶ The *procedure* you must follow to change an alert with CRITICAL or VERY CRITICAL status to UNCRITICAL

- ▶ The *context*, which can currently only be either SOLUTION-SPECIFIC or CROSS-SOLUTION

- ▶ The *metric* that is used to rate the alert type and the threshold values used to calculate the status of an alert (possible status values: uncritical = green LED, critical = yellow LED, very critical = red LED; shown in the Self-Diagnosis results)

- ▶ The semantic classification in *alert groups*, for example, infrastructure, to specify the type of alert

- ▶ SAP Solution Manager functions whose rating is affected by this alert type and the *rating strategy*, which specifies how the rating of the alert type affects the rating of the higher-level functionality

SAP Solution Manager functionalities

Accordingly, alert types can be grouped according to SAP Solution Manager *functionalities* whose rating depends on precisely these alert types. An alert type generally contributes to the rating of several functionalities. You can obtain the list of all SAP Solution Manager functionalities that have been verified at this time in Transaction SOLUTION_MANAGER under SETTINGS • SELF DIAGNOSIS • ALERT TYPES BY FUNCTIONALITY. As previously described, the rating strategy of the contributory individual alert types determines the overall rating of the functionalities, which, in turn, can take on status values UNCRITICAL, CRITICAL, and VERY CRITICAL.

Using SAP Solution Manager Self-Diagnosis

Settings

The Self-Diagnosis settings are not only a source of information about the content and structure of the Self-Diagnosis; they also enable you to manage the way in which the Self-Diagnosis is carried out. By selecting the ACTIVE checkbox on the ALERT TYPES, ALERT TYPES BY FUNCTIONALITY, and SOLUTION-SPECIFIC ALERT TYPES BY SOLUTION tab pages, you can restrict the objects to be checked. This is useful, for example, if there are certain SAP Solution Manager functionalities that you do not use at all, meaning you do not need to check their ability to run. Another potential scenario would be deactivating solution-specific alert types for solutions that are irrelevant, for example, demo and test solutions that are not used in production. The default setting shipped by SAP covers the maximum possible; that is, checks on all alert types, functionalities, and solutions are active. An overview of the activation status of the Self-Diagnosis is also located on the initial screen in the Self-Diagnosis settings (see Figure 8.6).

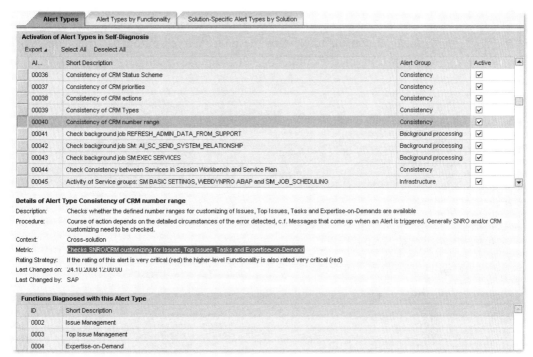

Figure 8.6 Self-Diagnosis Settings

Once you have made the Self-Diagnosis settings, you can either trigger the Self-Diagnosis interactively or wait while it is processed automatically over a 24-hour period (overnight) and then view the results.

You can interactively trigger Self-Diagnosis to be performed immediately either for each individual solution (Transaction SOLUTION_MANAGER • SELECT A SPECIFIC SOLUTION • SELF DIAGNOSIS • EXECUTE) or for all solutions (Transaction SOLUTION_MANAGER • SOLUTION OVERVIEW • SELF DIAGNOSIS • EXECUTE). Depending on the configuration settings made for Self-Diagnosis and the number of solutions, the latter variant may take considerable time. While the Self-Diagnosis is being performed, the CUR-

RENT PROCESSING STATUS shows whether a Self-Diagnosis run is currently being performed. You can check whether processing is complete during an interactive run by clicking REFRESH.

Summary of the results

The summary of results from the last time Self-Diagnosis ran can be found in the top half of the Self-Diagnosis initial screen and reveals the number of uncritical, critical, and very critical alerts, functionalities, and so on. The exact times at which the relevant run started and finished are also shown together with the next planned automatic run. Figure 8.7 shows a typical example of Self-Diagnosis results.

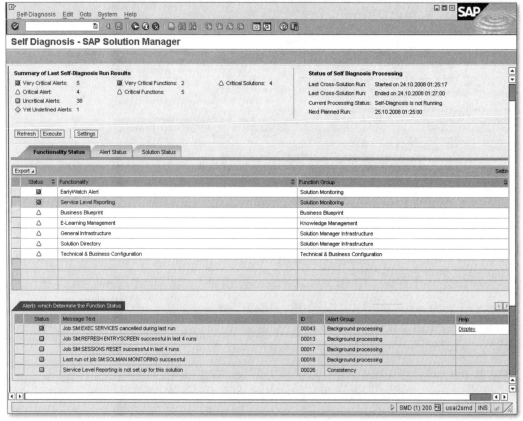

Figure 8.7 Self-Diagnosis Results

Below the summary, you can view the details of the Self-Diagnosis results, analyze them if required, and take corrective measures in accordance with the solution guides provided.

Reflecting the structure of the application, the results are arranged on tab pages entitled FUNCTIONALITY STATUS, ALERT STATUS, and SOLUTION STATUS:

Structure of the results

▶ Details of the functionality status are presented in a table showing an overview of the status values of the underlying (critical) alerts (lower table). You can click the DISPLAY link in the HELP column to obtain details of how to remedy alerts with critical status.

▶ Details of the alert status (including uncritical alerts) are provided in the form of a linear list of results from rating all active alert types. The instructions for measures to remove critical alerts are provided on the DETAILS tab page, and the impact they have on functionalities is shown on the IMPAIRED FUNCTIONALITIES tab page.

▶ The SOLUTION STATUS tab page contains a list of critical solutions and allows you to navigate to the Self-Diagnosis for each solution, where you can work just as you would on the ALERT STATUS tab page. Alternatively, you can access solution-specific information and results data by clicking the SELF DIAGNOSIS button within a given solution. You can also completely avoid navigating from cross-solution Self-Diagnosis to a specific solution by selecting an entry in the table IMPAIRED SOLUTIONS and then processing the individual critical links shown in the list that appears below this table using the DISPLAY link.

If the SELF DIAGNOSIS button is displayed with a gray diamond on it in either the solution-specific or cross-solution version of the Self-Diagnosis, this means that the respective Self-Diagnosis of all active alerts has not resulted in critical or very critical results. A green LED is not shown here because the lack of critical alerts is a necessary but not sufficient criterion for operational reliability. If the SELF DIAGNOSIS button is not shown at all in a solution, this indicates that Self-Diagnosis for this solution has been deactivated in the settings, that is, no data is available for the overall rating.

Self-Diagnosis Content

The contents of the Self-Diagnosis function are defined and shipped by SAP alone and change with each relevant Support Package. Customers are currently unable to create their own contents.

To facilitate navigation, the Self-Diagnosis reflects the main contents of the current run (if one exists) of the SAP EarlyWatch Alert service for the SAP Solution Manager system by displaying its key indicators, for instance, system performance, system load distribution, database performance, database administration, and so on.

Integration with Solution Manager Diagnostics Self-Check

Self-Check — The *Solution Manager Diagnostics* application contains a function related to Self-Diagnosis, namely, the *Self-Check*. Its job is to check the Java components of the SAP Solution Manager system and the components required for the Solution Manager Diagnostics function in the systems connected to SAP Solution Manager.

The results of these checks are contained in the Self-Diagnosis, so you do not have to call up the Self-Check separately.

Further Information About Self-Diagnosis

In addition to further details and practical tips for handling alerts with CRITICAL status, SAP Note 1073382 contains a Microsoft PowerPoint presentation about Self-Diagnosis and a link to an SAP Tutor demonstration on this subject.

8.2   Solution Monitoring

When a solution is up and running, the most important task is to ensure that the software runs reliably. This basically translates into continuous availability and satisfactory performance for which administrators working in internal IT departments are responsible. To reduce operating costs, however, more companies are also opting for external IT service providers to maintain their hardware and systems.

These outward shifts of IT know-how and responsibility have resulted in written agreements becoming increasingly important. These binding *Service Level Agreements* (SLAs) control the level of availability and software performance required. Proof of the services provided is documented via regular Service Level Reporting (SLR). The parameters on which Service Level Reporting is based are known as *key performance indicators* (KPIs). Besides including performance-specific aspects, KPIs have many technical indicators that provide useful information regarding the stability of — as well as the changes made to — the software and hardware. Examples of KPIs include system availability expressed as a percentage, database and transaction response times, CPU load, database growth, system parameters, and so on.

Service Level Agreements

SAP Solution Manager's central presence in your system landscape offers many ways of automating the exchange of data between your systems. For example, SAP Solution Manager can monitor your systems, collect technical data, compile reports, and relate them to your documented business processes (Figure 8.8).

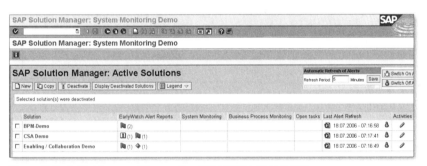

Figure 8.8 Initial Screen of Transaction SOLUTION_MANAGER

The purpose of the initial screen of Transaction SOLUTION_MANAGER is to centrally monitor all solution landscapes along with their most critical monitoring functions and ratings. By clicking on an alert, you can navigate directly to the respective detailed display in a landscape.

Solution Monitoring focuses on system monitoring, data collection, and data preparation in the form of preconfigured reports. *Solution Reporting*, on the other hand, brings together additional reporting options for a solution landscape, making it easier to flexibly compare and prepare

Solution Reporting

aggregated data. Solution Reporting is also a source for the detailed, graphic long-term analyses available in *SAP NetWeaver Business Intelligence Reporting* (BI reporting) (Figure 8.9). As the need for analyses and reports increases, SAP NetWeaver BI's function for gathering and processing data is becoming more and more crucial. Data from different sources such as SAP EarlyWatch Alert, Central Performance History, Business Process Monitoring data collectors, or *Solution Manager Diagnostics* constitute the foundation for further analyses. In SAP Solution Manager, the way BI data is gathered and presented is increasingly preconfigured, standardized, and incorporated into the work centers.

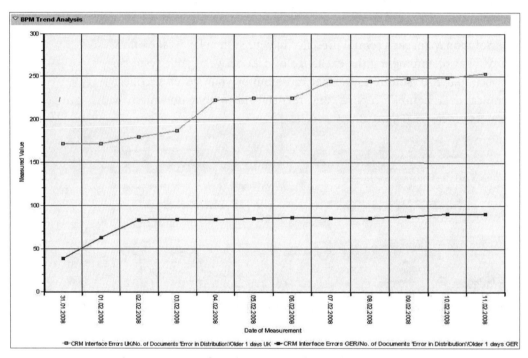

Figure 8.9 Preconfigured BI Reporting for Analyzing Trends in the Business Process Operations Work Center

The transition from monitoring to reporting is a seamless one ranging from automated, real-time monitoring in minutes (system monitoring and Business Process Monitoring) to long-term monitoring, as well as weekly and monthly KPI checks or trend analyses (SAP EarlyWatch Alert, Service Level Reporting, BI reporting).

Solution monitoring in the classic version of SAP Solution Manager includes all of the functions required for monitoring:

- ▸ Central System Administration
- ▸ System monitoring
- ▸ Business Process Monitoring
- ▸ SAP EarlyWatch Alert
- ▸ Service Level Reporting

The way these functions are divided up has changed with the introduction of the work center. They can no longer be called up from Transaction SOLUTION_MANAGER but instead have been spread out across the following work centers:

- ▸ System Monitoring
- ▸ Business Process Operations

Central System Administration is an exception and has been incorporated into the System Administration work center.

8.2.1   System Monitoring

The more productive software and hardware components you have running, the more important and cost-effective it is for you to centralize and automate monitoring.

If you only use one SAP system, you may be able to get by with one experienced administrator who monitors and manages the system manually. Such administrators are very familiar with SAP's expert monitors. In such a scenario, manually checking current values is a sufficient but very time-consuming process that requires a certain level of knowledge and, in large system landscapes, results in high operating and HR costs.

This is why companies are increasingly opting for central system monitoring; that is, a first-rate monitoring system, for example, SAP Solution Manager, centrally generates and automates warning messages (alerts) if disruptions are detected in a production component. If no warning messages have been issued, it can be assumed that systems are operating normally, thereby eliminating the need for time-consuming local activities.

In addition to central and automated monitoring, the current values for the most important KPIs are of interest — particularly in the event of a problem. You can view these values locally for each SAP system or centrally for several or all of your SAP systems. In other words, as with system administration, you can monitor your systems centrally or locally.

In local monitoring, you can see how many users are currently logged on to a system in Transactions SM04 or AL08. The same key figures are also made available to administrators centrally in SAP Solution Manager.

Both types of monitoring are used in SAP system operations. Local monitoring is used in particular when handling expert tools and data that would be generally unnecessary or too resource-intensive to display centrally. SAP recommends that you use central monitoring where possible because a central working environment reduces the workload and thereby brings down operating costs, especially in large landscapes.

System Monitoring work center
Exactly as in System Administration, the System Monitoring work center enables you to call up local tools in managed systems from a central location. Here also, the major advantage of this concept is that you can incorporate tools that are provided in the latest SAP releases but are not available in SAP Solution Manager.

SAP Solution Manager is therefore equally suitable as a platform for centrally monitoring heterogeneous SAP system landscapes.

SAP Solution Manager allows you to monitor all business-process-related system components in real time. System Monitoring is based on the *Computing Center Management System* (CCMS), a monitoring infrastructure that automatically gathers data in your local SAP systems and compares it with threshold values (see Figure 8.10).

Alerts
An alert is triggered centrally when a threshold value is exceeded or undershot. Autoreactions respond to alerts. These can automatically generate and send notifications. A range of channels can be used to provide notifications in the event of an error:

▶ Display in a *universal worklist* (UWL) or an alert inbox (Transaction ALRTINBOX)

▶ Notification by SMS, pager, email, or fax

▶ Service Desk message

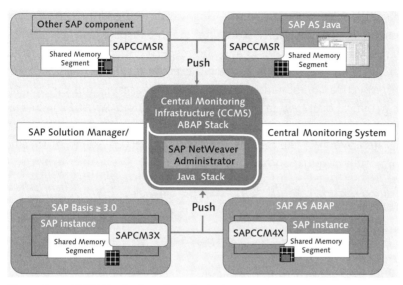

Figure 8.10 CCMS Monitoring – Data Gathering

In central Alert Management (ALM; see Figure 8.11), you can define rules used to control to whom and under what conditions you want to send alert information. You can also set up the Alert Management system in SAP Solution Manager.

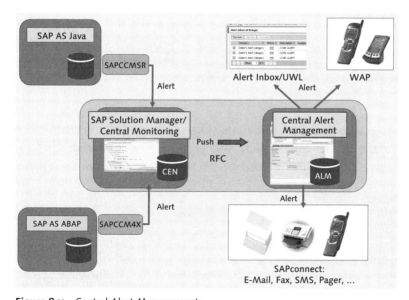

Figure 8.11 Central Alert Management

Alert overview One of the reasons System Monitoring was integrated into SAP Solution Manager is that the clearly structured graphic display provides a quick overview of system statuses and the respective interfaces. The major benefit of this approach is that the alerts are displayed together with the respective component(s) of a solution landscape. You can call up the graphical overview in Transaction SOLUTION_MANAGER. Alternatively, you can view all of the alerts for one or more landscapes as a list. This alert overview can then be sorted by red alerts, systems, or specific monitoring information (see Figure 8.12).

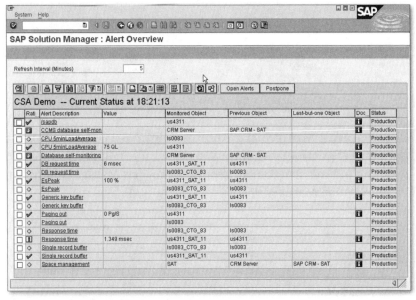

Figure 8.12 System Monitoring Alert List

The screen showing current alerts shows you the latest available alert information.[2] The current alerts are always overwritten with the most up-to-date information. If you want to process an alert, you can reset it

---

2 Please note that you can set up the graphic refresh times within a solution under OPERATIONS SETUP • SOLUTION SETTINGS • REFRESH RATE • MONITORING GRAPHIC. The refresh times of the solution overview can be stored directly in the solution overview under AUTOMATIC ALERT UPDATING. For performance reasons, it is recommended that you update only those solutions that are critical for monitoring your business processes.

for a defined time. The alert is not displayed during this time, thereby avoiding several administrators being notified simultaneously.

To correctly assess the relevance of an alert, it is important to know how frequently it has occurred in a given period of time. If, for example, you receive a performance alert for a core business process transaction that occurred only once within the space of a week, there is no need for you to take any action. If, however, this alert occurs 10 times in an hour, we recommend that you perform a Root Cause Analysis. The appropriate, alternative display option for an alert history can be found under HISTORY in the alert list and under OPEN ALERTS in the alert graphic. Even if an alert's current rating is green, past overshot threshold values will be displayed in this view. Once you have checked the alert and decided that it is no longer relevant, you can confirm it, at which point the alert will no longer be displayed. To start a detailed analysis of an alert, double-click its name. This takes you to the assigned analysis method for the monitored managed system (local CCMS) without having to explicitly log on. Analysis methods include calling up expert monitors (Transactions ST04, RZ20, and SM50), reports, function modules, and URLs (see Figure 8.13).[3]

Alert analysis

Configuring system monitoring in SAP Solution Manager is quick and intuitive. You can familiarize yourself with system monitoring by using SAP Solution Manager to provide an introduction to central system monitoring and working with the CCMS. Each solution landscape has its own *setup session* for system monitoring that you can process sequentially. First, select the systems you want to monitor. Next, check the RFC connections between the managed system and the central monitoring system. Settings can be copied from other systems in the solution landscape and alerts reactivated and configured. SAP Solution Manager already provides you with the most important component-specific alerts. All you have to do is select the alerts you need and enter the associated threshold values and parameters. The eight most important alerts are already activated (see Figure 8.14). You must, however, enter the parameters here as well because the most appropriate settings are too varied to be preconfigured by SAP.

Configuring system monitoring

---

3 This requires you to set up a trusting-trusted RFC connection as recommended by SAP.

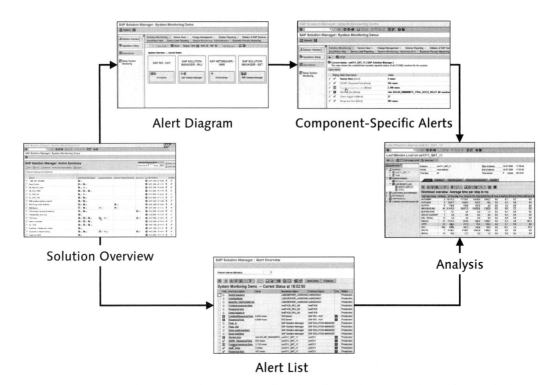

Figure 8.13 Alert Navigation from the Solution Overview to the Analysis Method

Performance Alerts of Instance		
	Dialog Alerts	
		Response time
		DB request time
	Memory Mngt and Buffer Alerts	
		ES Peak
		Single record buffer
		Generic key buffer
Setup Monitoring for Server		
		CPU 5MinLoadAverage
		Paging out
Database		
	Administrating DB	
		Space Management

Figure 8.14 Preselected and Activated System Monitoring Alerts

If the alerts you require are not listed in the setup session, you can add them under USER DEFINED ALERTS. To help you search for these alerts, the appropriate *counters* are provided in the input help. Parameters, threshold values, autoreactions, and alert analysis methods can be managed centrally from the *setup session*. Changes to values made centrally in SAP Solution Manager affect the respective local CCMS of the managed system.

In summary, using SAP Solution Manager as a central monitoring system has the following advantages:

Advantages of central monitoring

▶ Clarity (combination of graphic alert and component information, alert list with sort function)

▶ Additional information from other functions, facilitating problem analysis (system landscape context, SAP EarlyWatch Alert, reporting, Issue Management, and so on)

▶ Easy configuration (central management in setup, preselection of important alerts, and preactivated alerts)

Free monitoring system based on current SAP technology

SAP has enhanced the monitoring functions provided in SAP Solution Manager. The new System Monitoring work center is closely integrated with other work centers as a core operational component and offers the following functions:

New functions in the work center

▶ **System Monitoring – Overview**
The initial screen in the System Monitoring work center gives you a complete overview of the availability of all systems and corresponding solutions. This means you are provided with an overall picture of the status of systems, a list of systems and solutions, and an overview of instances and further detailed information.

▶ **Alert Inbox**
In contrast to the graphical display in Transaction SOLUTION_MANAGER, in the ALERT INBOX all technical alerts are listed in a table. They have been preconfigured accordingly and are based on CCMS data. You can view historical data for each alert.

In daily operations, a particularly useful feature is the ability to navigate locally from this screen directly to every managed system. If, however, you need an even more in-depth analysis of the alert, you can also create a Service Desk message from here directly.

▶ **Proactive Monitoring**
The Proactive Monitoring view is divided into ABAP, Java, and other systems. The CCMS OVERVIEW tab page shows all essential performance indicators based on CCMS. A historical rating accompanies each of these. The following tab pages give you access to monitoring tools for ABAP application servers, Java application servers, and main instances.

▶ **Connectivity Monitoring**
This view allows you to check the connections between the individual systems. You can check the status of RFC connections to ABAP destinations, HTTP destinations in ABAP systems, and TCP/IP destinations.

▶ **Job Monitoring**
The JOB MONITORING view gives you an initial overview of the status of the most important jobs in the system landscape. You can find further details in the separate Job Management work center, where you have a direct connection to SAP Central Process Scheduling by Redwood.

▶ **Setup**
The SETUP view contains the functions that you need to configure the work center. For example, this is where you define monitoring and select the relevant RFC connections.

▶ **Reports**
This view groups a range of historical reports: SAP EarlyWatch Alert, SAP EarlyWatch Alert for Solutions, Service Level Reporting, and Availability Reporting. The relevant data is gathered centrally and aggregated in SAP NetWeaver BI.

Therefore, over and above the established monitoring functions in SAP Solution Manager, central automated monitoring is accommodated fully in combination with central monitoring.

SAP NetWeaver Administrator

Finally, we come to *SAP NetWeaver* Administrator, which can be called up centrally for each Java component being monitored. SAP NetWeaver Administrator is particularly important when it comes to monitoring 7.1 systems:

▶ Integration of key Runtime Workbench monitors (SAP NetWeaver Process Integration)

▶ An application manager that groups all Java programs and services for an application

▶ Significant infrastructure and performance improvements in the area of Java logging

▶ A status monitor for the overall status of SAP NetWeaver Application Server Java

More information about Solution Monitoring can be found in *Conception and Installation of System Monitoring using SAP Solution Manager* by Corina Weidmann and Lars Teuber, 2nd ed., Bonn, SAP PRESS, 2009.

8.2.2 Business Process Monitoring

What is the impact on the solution landscape when a problem occurs? Due to the complexity of today's system landscapes and the associated business processes, it is becoming increasingly difficult to understand the overall picture and provide a correct and efficient response in the event of an error. This is where a holistic administration concept comes into play to ensure the smooth flow of core business processes. *Business Process Monitoring* is an integral part of this concept and includes the proactive and process-oriented monitoring of core business processes, with respect to all corresponding technical and application-specific functions. The goal is to guarantee the uninterrupted, reliable flow of these processes.

Holistic operations concept

SAP Solution Manager is a platform that can assist customers in implementing a Business Process Monitoring concept and conduct real-time monitoring.

Business Process Monitoring in SAP Solution Manager

SAP Solution Manager is capable of graphically depicting the flow of business processes and their corresponding process steps, interfaces, and technical components. Content-related and technical details can be defined and measured for each of these steps:

▶ How many application documents are created each day in the business process step and which of those are still open after several days have passed (for example, sales orders that have not been delivered or production orders that have not yet been released)?

▶ Which background job runs in this process step? When and how is this job scheduled and to what extent does its actual behavior vary from its planned behavior?

▶ Which dialog transactions are used and with what average response time?

Monitoring objects These details, as well as requirements from business departments, are used to define *monitoring objects*, which must be watched closely to safeguard the business process flow. When an error occurs, object alerts are triggered that are assigned to the respective process steps during the monitoring process. This approach ensures that problems can be assigned immediately to a specific business process step and that their relevance for the entire business process can be analyzed without delay, allowing the appropriate escalation measures to be implemented as required. A three-stage alert system (green, yellow, and red), for which individual threshold values can be defined, also allows the significance of a problem to be weighted accordingly.

A basic distinction can be made between two types of monitoring objects: application-specific monitors and cross-application, more technical monitors.

Application-Specific Monitors

Preconfigured key figures Since 2006, Business Process Monitoring has been continuously equipped with more application-specific monitors, with the result that you can now establish with ease how well the most common business processes supported by SAP Business Suite run. Are sales orders delivered as quickly as set out in Service Level Agreements, for example? Are planned orders converted into production orders on time, and are these production orders released on time and then technically completed? To answer these types of questions, Business Process Monitoring offers more than 200 preconfigured key figures for SAP ERP, SAP CRM, and SAP SCM that you can rapidly adapt to your needs by making restrictions according to document types and organizational units (for example, sales organization or plant).

Use in practice has revealed that precisely these application-specific monitors are capable of uncovering a broad range of problems, for instance:

▶ Lack of user training, which results in the system being used incorrectly

▶ Customizing errors causing unnecessary follow-up documents to be created

▶ Errors in process design with the result that processes are never completed conventionally

▶ Incomplete or nonexistent archiving strategies resulting in old documents remaining in the system

In addition to the monitors for SAP Business Suite, industry-specific monitors exist that cater in particular to the monitoring requirements of industries that rely on mass processing (such as energy providers or banks).

In SAP Solution Manager, it has been possible for many years now to use technical monitors as part of Business Process Monitoring, for example, to check the performance of background jobs and identify whether they are started too late or not completed on time from a business perspective. You can also analyze the average response times of dialog transactions and check for critical messages in the general application log. Interfaces can also be checked to detect any IDocs with a particular error status for a previously defined IDoc message type. Similar monitors also exist for other types of interfaces such as queued remote function calls (qRFCs), business documents (BDocs), workflows, XI messages, batch input sessions, and flat files.

Different technical monitors

Dedicated monitoring objects can be defined via user exits and integrated into Business Process Monitoring to configure the functions to meet your specific needs. Because SAP Solution Manager is based on the standard monitoring infrastructure (CCMS), you can also integrate CCMS monitoring objects into Business Process Monitoring.

Dedicated objects

Handling Business Process Monitoring in SAP Solution Manager

SAP Solution Manager's graphical monitoring interface is the single point of contact for Business Process Monitoring and provides an overview of the status of the systems in use and the business processes to be monitored on a single screen (see Figure 8.15).

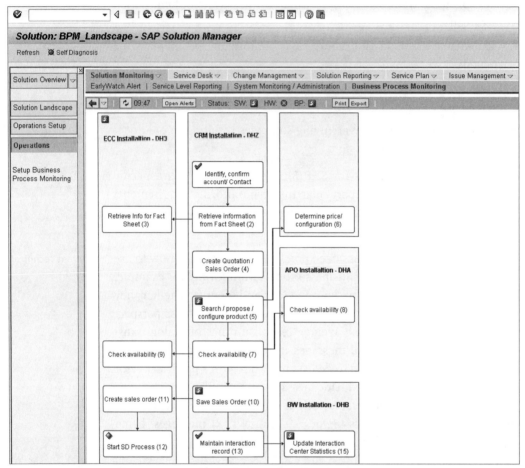

Figure 8.15 Graphical Monitoring Interface for Business Process Monitoring

Alerts   The business processes in the graphic are assigned an overall alert that corresponds to the highest single alert that occurred for the respective business process. Similarly, the highest single alert is displayed as the overall status for each process step. This allows the technical problem to be assigned to the business process step affected, making it clear which functional areas of the business process require attention and what effects the problem has on the overall process.

Monitoring tasks in the form of to-do lists, problem-solving procedures, and escalation paths can be defined in SAP Solution Manager for the end user. The employee responsible for monitoring can then access all of the information required in one central tool. For example, from SAP Solution Manager the employee can access the job log showing canceled background jobs or the list of open application documents and obtain information to resolve the alert situation. The employee also knows who to contact if the problem seriously threatens the overall business process flow. Furthermore, notifications can be sent to the employee via email or SMS.

Monitoring tasks

Once an alert has been successfully processed in SAP Solution Manager, it can be marked as COMPLETED. If the problem cannot be solved immediately, a message can be created in the Service Desk to allow the problem to be tracked and the message sent to SAP if necessary.

In addition, the values gathered in Business Process Monitoring can be extracted to a BI system (we recommend SAP NetWeaver BI 7.0, which runs on SAP Solution Manager 7.0). In the BI system, trends that have emerged in recent weeks and months can be analyzed so that problem situations can be tackled earlier. For example, it may be possible to identify a worsening in the runtimes of important background jobs before the critical threshold values are reached. You can also compare how many sales orders were not delivered on time, for example, in your sales organizations in Germany, the USA, and Japan. Finally, you can configure Service Level Reporting to automatically create a Microsoft Word document containing these business process trends over predefined periods (one week, one month, or six months) as graphics and tables.

Reporting

Additional Business Process Monitoring Offerings

SAP offers the following services to help create and configure a Business Process Monitoring concept using SAP Solution Manager:

▶ The Solution Management Optimization (SMO) service for business process management

▶ Course SM300, Business Process Management and Monitoring

▶ Course E2E300, Business Process Integration & Automation Management

You can find a guide to Business Process Monitoring and additional information on the SAP Service Marketplace at *http://www.service.sap.com/bpm* or in *Business Process Monitoring with SAP Solution Manager* by Thomas Schröder, Bonn, SAP PRESS, 2009.

8.2.3 SAP EarlyWatch Alert

SAP EarlyWatch Alert (EWA) is a preconfigured, automated service that collects the most important technical data in your SAP system and sends it to your SAP Solution Manager or SAP, where it is checked for critical system statuses. EWA collects only technical and administrative data by summarizing the values of a particular week and interpreting these values, therefore providing at-a-glance information about the system's current status. You can view and manage SAP EarlyWatch Alert reports by calling Transaction SOLUTION_MANAGER • OPERATIONS • SOLUTION MONITORING • EARLYWATCH ALERT. These reports are also integrated into the *System Monitoring* work center. The person responsible for the solution or the system receives the reports in the REPORTS view (see Figure 8.16).

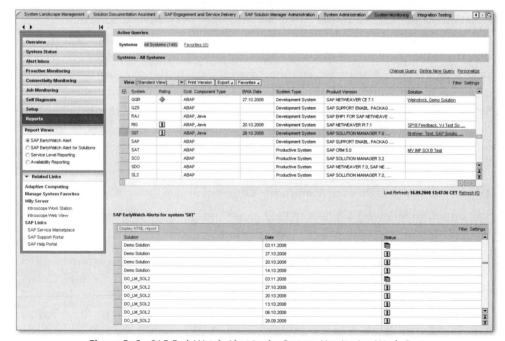

Figure 8.16 SAP EarlyWatch Alert in the System Monitoring Work Center

These assessments, called *ratings* or *alerts*, are presented as an easy-to-read, graphic analysis in the EWA reports and are used for key performance indicators (KPIs) and overall reporting functions. The rating for the overall report depends on how the individual KPIs are rated. If the KPIs are of secondary importance, for example, the report may have a green rating, despite the fact that a yellow rating is displayed for individual KPIs. The following ratings are used:

▸ **Red alert**
Critical problems were discovered that could jeopardize system operation.

▸ **Yellow alert**
Problems were discovered that require attention but have not yet reached system-critical status.

▸ **Green alert**
No problems were discovered.

▸ **Gray alert**
For technical reasons, no data could be acquired from the monitored system, and a rating could therefore not be assigned.

The ratings for the EWA reports are the same as those above, but with one additional rating:

▸ **Red flag**
SAP EarlyWatch Alert session data is overdue and has not yet been sent to SAP Solution Manager.

The data cannot be accessed until a week after it has been aggregated. EWA therefore serves as a diagnosis service that supports long-term Solution Monitoring for SAP and non-SAP systems[4] in SAP Solution Manager. EWAs can help you detect trends and bottlenecks that develop over a long period of time, for example, database growth and a gradual but constant increase in response times. EWAs allow you to react to deteriorating situations before problems occur. This characteristic fundamentally differentiates EWAs from the real-time-based system monitoring and Business Process Monitoring functions, which aim to detect

---

4 Limited to operating system data.

a problem immediately and notify the person in charge as quickly as possible.[5]

Functions SAP EarlyWatch Alert provides the following functions:

► Collects technical data and generates reports on the administrative system area for (internal) reporting

► Facilitates proactive system monitoring

► Lays the foundation for more specific (external) Service Level Reporting (see Sections 8.2.4 and 8.9)

► Establishes the data basis for efficient Service Delivery through SAP Active Global Support

The first versions of SAP EarlyWatch Alert were delivered to customers from 1993 to 2000 by SAP Active Global Support. EWAs were managed using Transaction SCUI. This version was replaced by the Service Data Control Center infrastructure. The latest trend is to gather and display data using the BI system. Some ABAP KPIs are already read from the BI system.

Non-SAP systems For non-ABAP systems, all performance-relevant data comes from the SAP Solution Manager BI system (see Figure 8.17), and all configuration data comes from the configuration and change database (CCDB) in SAP Solution Manager.

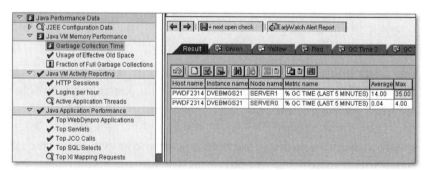

Figure 8.17 Non-ABAP Information in an EWA Service Session

All performance-data for non-ABAP systems is gathered using CA *Wily Introscope* (see Section 8.8), aggregated to hourly values, and written to

---

5 You can trigger an alarm using low threshold values before the problem occurs.

the SAP Solution Manager BI system. This ensures that the same data is used by Solution Manager Diagnostics tools, for instance, to analyze the workload, and the EWA.

For SAP Active Global Support, the EWA is still *the* data basis for fast but detailed system analyses. Fast system analyses can only be carried out and the resulting recommendations provided by SAP if the same criteria apply to all SAP customers. In other words, the analysis tool and its predefined standard parameters must be uniform across all SAP customers. This is why customers cannot influence content and EWA ratings.[6] Because almost every customer has different system requirements, EWA ratings cannot describe the severity of the system situation with 100% accuracy. A hospital, for example, uses an optical archive to store its X-rays. This archive is subject to very high data growth that would probably be viewed as critical by the EWA. The Service Level Reporting function was developed as a workaround for such discrepancies (see Section 8.2.4).

The results of monitoring activities, or KPIs, are output in EWA reports. KPIs not only provide information about system performance, but also predominantly comprise technical indicators that target defined situations or changes in system status.[7]

The information the EWA collects for ABAP and Java systems includes details of:

Available information

- General component status
- System configuration
- Hardware
- Performance development
- Average response times
- Current system load

6 One exception is the collection of additional transaction data, which can be triggered via Service Level Reporting.
7 Additional information can be found in Weidmann, Corina, and Teuber, Lars, *Conception and Installation of System Monitoring Using SAP Solution Manager*, 2nd ed. SAP PRESS, Bonn, 2009.

> ▶ Critical error messages and interrupted processes
>
> ▶ Database administration
>
> ▶ Trend analyses
>
> ▶ Solution landscape (*SAP EarlyWatch Alert for Solutions*)

Service Data
Control Center

You use the *Service Data Control Center* (Transaction SDCCN) to manage the way data is gathered and distributed. It runs in both the managed system and the SAP Solution Manager system. The Control Center allows you to use RFC connections to specify which systems receive the EWAs and other service data. Target systems can be one or more SAP Solution Manager or SAP service systems.

Service preparation
check

Before you start working with EWAs, you should ensure that all of the tools required for SAP Service Sessions are available. You can do this by carrying out a *service preparation check* (report RTCCTOOL). These tools must be used to ensure optimal data collection in your SAP system. Therefore, report RTCCTOOL verifies that you have the current versions of the ST-A/PI and ST-PI add-ons as well as all the current Notes. You must integrate Solution Manager Diagnostics including CA Wily Introscope for non-ABAP EWAs.

Task processor

The collection and distribution of (EWA) service data can now be automated by setting up the *task processor* in Transaction SDCCN in both the managed and SAP Solution Manager systems. This periodic background job should be performed when workload is low, for example, from Sunday night to Monday morning.[8]

Processing data

SAP Solution Manager processes data in the daily background job. The result, the EWA report, can be viewed as an HTML document. Alternatively, you can create a Microsoft Word document. You can also automate HTML reports and send them — depending on how they are rated — to the appropriate administrator, for example.

A report with a red rating is automatically sent to SAP Active Global Support. A service employee then checks the report and contacts you directly if a serious problem has arisen. If the ratings remain in the yel-

---

8 For detailed information about configuring Transaction SDCC, refer to SAP Note 91488.

low and green areas, however, a report is sent to SAP only once after the initial EWA activation and then every four weeks via the SAP Service Marketplace.

Session alerts also exist and can be sent to SAP individually or as a list if a red or yellow rating is set. The session alerts offer an automated, detailed description of the causes of errors that is based on special algorithms combined with additional attributes such as priority or category. This enables you to address and track problems directly. The amount of data exchanged is reduced considerably in comparison with sending entire reports. The *session alerts* can be reused in other services performed by SAP, and the time needed to analyze errors and handle issues is cut. The scope for taking proactive measures increases, and the risk to your solution operations is further reduced.

It is, however, advisable to check the status of your systems regularly yourself. The option to integrate all relevant systems into one solution landscape allows you to display, hide, archive, and automatically send all EWAs from a single overview screen.

Grouping EWAs

In the interests of clarity, EWA reports contain mainly critical data. Download data is processed as part of the individual EWA checks of the EWA Service Session and saved in check tables. These check tables can be accessed in Service Level Reporting and service reporting (see Sections 8.2.4 and 8.9.1). Ratings and data transfer for EWAs can be monitored centrally via SAP Solution Manager's *System Monitoring*[9] function.

In the EWA Service Session, you can use SAP Solution Manager to create the tasks listed in the EWA report. The EWA Service Session is the container for all download data on which the EWA report is based. It also offers other data, for example, Notes that have been implemented and system and operating system parameters.

SAP only processes service data from test and production systems. Your SAP Solution Manager can also be used to generate EWAs for development and training systems.

---

9 You can activate EWA monitoring in your solution under OPERATIONS SETUP • SOLUTION LANDSCAPE • SOLUTION SETTINGS • CCMS MONITORING EWA. This allows you to generate a support message via an autoreaction if a red EWA rating occurs.

As of SAP Solution Manager ST 7.0 SPS15 and ST-SER 700_2008_1, SAP EarlyWatch Alert has been enhanced with *SAP EarlyWatch Alert for Solutions*. This function does not focus ratings on individual software components, but rather displays technical data for an entire solution landscape and in the context of the core business process that this solution landscape supports. Some of the information provided by EarlyWatch Alert for Solution Landscapes includes:

- Aggregated KPIs for a solution landscape
- Performance of core business processes
- Action areas for improvements
- Important changes to the solution landscape
- Trends and wider context

To use SAP EarlyWatch Alert for Solutions, you must have activated at least SAP EarlyWatch Alert (see Figure 8.18).

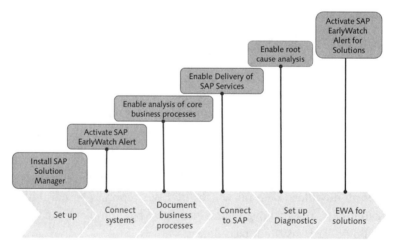

Figure 8.18   Requirements for SAP EarlyWatch Alert for Solutions

The following requirements must be met to make full use of the functions, including non-ABAP and business process information (see Figure 8.19):[10]

---

10 SAP Note 1040343 describes the SAP components for which the full version of SAP EarlyWatch Alert for Solutions is available.

▶ Solution Manager Diagnostics (with BI) is in place for the managed systems.

▶ The core business processes have been defined in SAP Solution Manager.

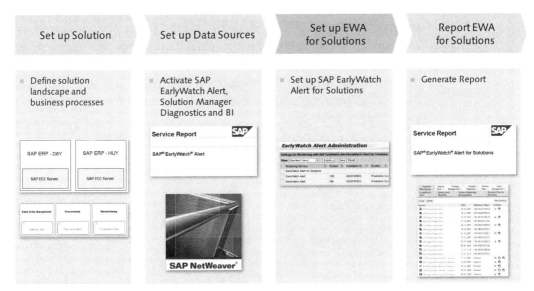

Figure 8.19 Setup for SAP EarlyWatch Alert for Solutions

8.2.4 Service Level Reporting

Service Level Reporting was originally based purely on *SAP EarlyWatch Alert* data and still uses the same standardized rating options. With Service Level Reporting, however, you can aggregate the raw EWA data to meet your specific needs and adapt ratings. You can combine EWA reports for several systems in one report. Like EWA, Service Level Reporting is largely preconfigured. By making just a few changes, you can create reports that contain only the relevant content and replace the standard interpretations of the EWA that result from the generally applicable rating settings with customer-specific ones. As with EWA reports, service level reports can be automated and sent to the appropriate or interested parties based on the rating. This makes Service Level Reporting ideally suited to internal or simple external Service Level Reporting. It is the interface between your IT department and the person responsible for a business process.

Functions In addition to providing content summaries, Service Level Reporting allows you to collect additional data and integrate ancillary data sources such as the CCMS or BI system by making just a few configuration changes (see Figure 8.20). It is also possible to adopt customer-specific business processes in the Service Level Reporting setup session. On this basis, you can trigger the collection of additional, transaction-specific data such as response times and display the Business Process Monitoring alerts in aggregated form.[11]

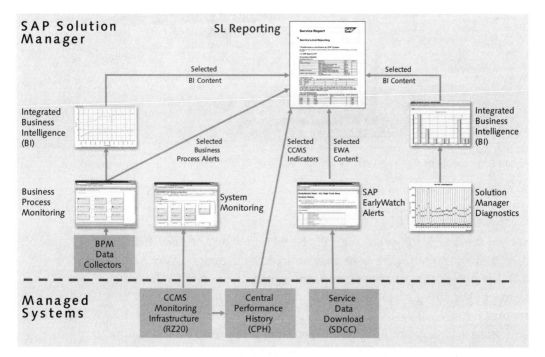

Figure 8.20 Structure of System Monitoring, Business Process Monitoring, EWA, Service Level Reporting, Service Reporting, and Availability Reporting Data Sources

---

11 You can also report on background jobs in Service Level Reporting in this way. To do so, create a business process step in Business Process Monitoring and monitor one or more jobs there. Then integrate this step into Service Level Reporting as described above.

Once you have set up Business Process Monitoring (see Section 8.2.2), you can integrate business process alerts into Service Level Reporting. This not only provides you with purely technical information; you can also identify performance, throughput, and backlog trends in your business processes. For each alert object, you can specify whether you want to perform the trend analysis for the last week, the last month, or the last six months. The data is output in the report in graphics and tables. To integrate Business Process Monitoring into Service Level Reporting, select the relevant business processes in the Service Level Reporting setup session using the input help and specify the time frame during which the trend is to be analyzed for the assigned alerts. From a technical perspective, this part of Service Level Reporting requires Business Process Monitoring to be integrated with an SAP NetWeaver BI system.

Integrating business process alerts

A major enhancement to the reporting options compared with the EWA is the integration of the *Central Performance History* (CPH) into Service Level Reporting as an additional data source (see Figure 8.21). This no longer binds you to the largely preconfigured EWA data, giving you the flexibility to incorporate CCMS data from real-time monitoring. Simply select the relevant elements from the CCMS, configure the data aggregation in the CPH, and select the required Service Level Reporting elements via the input help. Then decide whether you want to display values in graph or table form in the service level report. Define the upper and lower threshold values for the indicators selected and determine whether an extended, long-term history of three months is to be recorded automatically. You also have the option of grouping individual indicators and displaying them in graph or table form.

Central Performance History

The detailed system availability measurement in Service Level Reporting is based on the same technology. Here, too, the CPH forms the basis for this function, which goes far beyond the standard availability measurement associated with EWAs. While the extremely limited[12] system availability display in EWA is only suitable for use as a simplified availability overview, the CCMS-based measuring method in Service Level Reporting

System availability measurement

12 Only one measuring point per hour in the central instance.

285

opens up the following four options to monitor[13] and analyze system availability automatically:

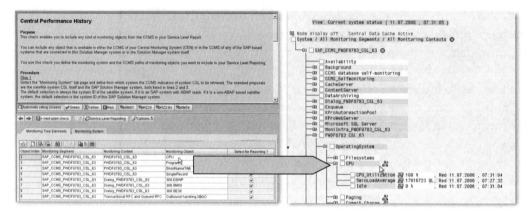

Figure 8.21 Integration of Central Performance History (CPH) into Service Level Reporting as an Additional Data Source, for Example, Selection of Monitoring Tree Element (MTE) CPU from Transaction RZ20

- Instance availability (availability of SAP Basis for every ABAP instance)

- Instance logon availability (logon availability of every ABAP instance)

- Logon group availability (availability of every logon group)

- System availability (ABAP and Java stack) measured based on the availability of the central instance (ABAP and Java Message Server)

Availability measurements are used to report on the 24-hour uptime (*24-h availability*[14]). Because Service Level Agreements can also be restricted to specific times of the day, and scheduled downtimes are typically not taken into account by the availability measurement, Service Level Reporting allows you to define these times. Availability can therefore be output for explicit time intervals (*critical uptime availability*) and adjusted for scheduled downtimes (*planned downtime-adjusted*).

---

13 For additional details of the CCMS-PING-based availability measurement in Service Level Reporting, refer to SAP Note 944496.

14 Service Sessions are only offered in English-, Chinese-, and Japanese-language versions.

The data source is *CCMS PING* and can be used to achieve very detailed measurements of availability, for example, by the minute. You can display the results of these measurements in the CCMS, trigger autoreactions, or store the results in the CPH.[15] You can then include the CPH results in the monthly service level report and send it automatically to the person responsible for the system and, after checking, to your customers.

CCMS PING

In the future, *Availability Reporting* in the service level report will be integrated with the Downtime Manager in SAP Solution Manager and allow system downtimes managed there to be adopted as planned downtime (see Section 8.3).

Another function that is supported in the Service Level Reporting setup is the ability to select and include KPIs from a BI-based data source, for instance, the SAP Solution Manager BI system or a customer BI system connected using an RFC connection. You do this in the same way as integrating CCMS-based data sources (see Section 8.2.4, "Service Level Reporting"). After you have defined the KPIs to be reported and the required BI queries, you can also configure output attributes such as display formats and long-term histories, and define customer-specific alert threshold values.

KPIs from BI data sources

In Customizing, you can select predefined standard KPIs that originate from the Solution Manager Diagnostics environment and that may contain response times for Java or TREX components, for example. Furthermore, you can to some extent integrate customer-specific KPIs into the report. As a technical requirement for this, you must configure the BI data source and the characteristics and value ranges required to create a suitable BI query (see Figure 8.22).

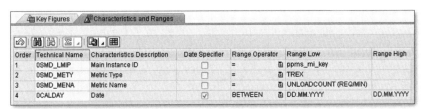

Figure 8.22 Selecting BI Characteristics and Value Ranges in Service Level Reporting

---

15 On the SAP Community Network at *http://www.sdn.sap.com/irj/sdn/netweaver* • Lifecycle Management • Operations, you can find detailed information and documentation about CCMS, CPH, CCMS PING, autoreaction methods, and so on.

SAP Solution Manager allows you to determine monthly values for the following KPIs and display *target values* that you have defined yourself. You can set whichever target values you like, regardless of whether weekly or monthly reporting is required. The histories for the past 12 months are also listed for monthly reporting. You can list a monthly history for the following KPIs:

- ▶ System performance
- ▶ Max. active users
- ▶ Average availability
- ▶ Average response time in dialog task
- ▶ Average response time at peak dialog hour
- ▶ Query performance
  - ▶ Average total runtime of the BW queries
  - ▶ Average DB runtime of the BW queries
- ▶ Database performance
  - ▶ Average DB request time in dialog task
  - ▶ Average DB request time in update task
- ▶ Database space management
  - ▶ DB size
  - ▶ DB growth
- ▶ Hardware capacity
  - ▶ Max. CPU utilization on DB server
  - ▶ Max. CPU utilization on Application Server

A green rating is assigned when self-defined target values are reached; a red rating is assigned when these values are not reached. History values are shown in tables and as graphics. Figure 8.23 is an example of an instance in which the target value of 440 ms was overshot once (in March).

KPI History: Avg. DB Request Time in Dialog Task

Month	ACTUAL	TARGET	RATING
Oct 2005	403 ms	444 ms	✔
Jan 2006	305 ms	444 ms	✔
Feb 2006	399 ms	444 ms	✔
Mar 2006	542 ms	444 ms	✖
Apr 2006	416 ms	444 ms	✔

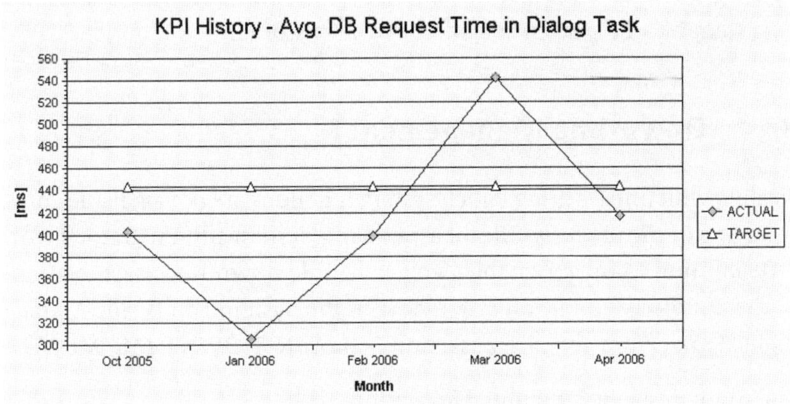

Figure 8.23 KPI History Values for Monthly Values of Average Database Response Time

The characteristics and functions of the service level report can be summarized as follows:

Characteristics and functions of the service level report

▶ Use of modified cover sheets

▶ EWA reports from several systems in a solution landscape combined in one report

▶ Self-defined reporting periods, for example, weekly, monthly, and quarterly reports

▶ History of important KPIs

▶ Specification of customer-specific target values for individual KPIs

▶ Restriction to target-group-specific information such as system availability and performance values

▶ Creation of multiple variants of a service level report based on the same data, but with different characteristics

▶ Transaction-specific response time analyses with customer-specific alert threshold values

- Integration of Business Process Monitoring data such as application alerts and their trend analyses

- Integration of Central Performance History (CPH)

- Technical system availability monitoring based on the CPH

- Integration of BI statistical data from the SAP Solution Manager BI system or a BI system specified by the customer

8.3   Downtime Management

Dealing with times during which system functions are not available constitutes one of the most significant aspects of a system administrator's work. SAP Solution Manager enables you to handle downtimes systematically in the DOWNTIME MANAGEMENT view in the System Landscape Management work center (or in Transaction SOLMAN_DOWNTIME_MGMT).

The following key functions are supported:

- Plan or, at the very least, record downtimes of system, instance, and logon group landscape components.

- Control how monitoring functions in SAP Solution Manager (for example, CCMS, Business Process Monitoring) respond during downtimes.

- Carry out downtimes, that is, stop or start systems, instances, and logon groups.

- Announce downtimes by SMS, email, or SAP system message.

The downtimes you can work with are split into the following types:

Planned downtimes *Planned downtimes* represent the ideal scenario in which downtimes are planned as part of a structured process long before they actually take place. This planning process is supported by an intuitive status profile. In general, the life cycle of a planned downtime starts with DRAFT status. If a planned downtime is to be reviewed before becoming official, its status can be set to IN REVIEW until a decision is made. If a decision is made in favor of the downtime, its status is changed to RELEASED; otherwise CANCELLED is used. As soon as the downtime start time arrives, the status changes to IN PROCESS. Once the downtime end time has passed, the status changes to COMPLETED.

It is only useful to create *modified planned downtimes* in association with a planned downtime with IN PROCESS status when it is apparent that its end time will have to be brought forward or put back. Because a modified planned downtime can only exist together with a planned downtime and after this planned downtime has been created, it is described as a phase of downtime and not only as a type.

Modified planned downtimes

Similar to modified planned downtimes, *real downtimes* are only used to supplement planned downtimes (once they have COMPLETED status). Their purpose is to record the period of time during which a system, for example, is actually unavailable compared with the planned downtime. The actual downtime can be recorded either manually or automatically (by accessing the Central Performance History database). As with modified planned downtimes, real downtimes are classified as phases of downtimes as opposed to a separate downtime type.

Real downtimes

Unplanned stops are required if a structured planning process is not possible due to unforeseen circumstances and downtime must be defined at short notice (but still in a controlled way).

Unplanned stops

Crashes are not controlled and can therefore only be recorded after they have occurred.

Crashes

Critical uptimes function as the counterpart to downtimes. A critical uptime generally indicates that downtimes should not be scheduled during this period. Settings enable you to make critical uptimes and downtimes mutually exclusive to stop them from being scheduled at the same time.

Critical uptimes

All phases and types have certain core attributes in common: Start and end times are self-explanatory. The title of the downtime helps you recognize it again more readily. Numeric IDs are also displayed. The category allows you to arrange downtimes according to their reasons, for example, maintenance. The textual descriptions provide details of the reason for a downtime or its impact on business processes. You can also link a downtime to documents.

The remaining attributes depend on the type or phase of the downtime.

8.3.1   Working with Downtimes

Long-Term Planning for Downtimes

Sequences

Over the course of your planning period, for example, six months, you can schedule planned downtimes and critical uptimes as either single events or a recurring sequence of downtime events.

You use the SAP NetWeaver appointment calendar for the time pattern of recurring downtimes. This allows you to make use of complex weekly and monthly patterns that you can refine with exceptions, for example, by using holiday and workday calendars.

After you have selected and saved a recurrence pattern once, a verbal expression of the pattern appears on the input screen, for example, EVERY TWO SATURDAYS IN THE PERIOD FROM 01.03.2009 TO 05.30.2009 FROM 10 P.M. TO 11 P.M., together with a complete list of the individual elements in the sequence, that is, all the days on which downtime is planned.

The principle of homogeneity applies to every individual component in a sequence of downtimes; that is, all attributes of the components in the sequence match each other — with the obvious exception of timing. The same applies for the status. In practical application, this means that when you select a downtime of this type, you are first asked whether you want to work with the entire sequence behind it or just that individual downtime. If you select the individual downtime and change it, before you save, you are advised of the fact that the downtime you have just edited will no longer belong to the superordinate sequence but will become independent.

You cannot alter the basic recurrence pattern of a sequence of downtimes once it has been defined. This means you cannot change a sequence from weekly to monthly, for example. However, it is possible to define exceptions for a sequence of downtimes after the sequence has been created; that is, you can delete individual components of a sequence or convert them to real, isolated downtimes.

The system automatically changes the status of downtimes. If a planned downtime still has DRAFT or IN REVIEW status when it is due to start, it is changed to AUTOMATICALLY CANCELLED when the downtime commences. If the planned downtime originally had RELEASED status, it changes to IN PROCESS and then COMPLETED at the start and end of the downtime. For the first planned downtime in a sequence of downtimes, automatic and manual status changes result in the downtime being removed from the sequence.

Status

As is the case when you plan downtimes in the long term, you can also schedule critical uptimes either individually or as a sequence.

Example

A typical scenario would be as follows:

A system administrator wants to schedule downtime every second Saturday for the next six months to carry out maintenance on the hardware of his production system.

First, the administrator contacts the people in charge of the business units that might be affected by the planned production system downtime and asks them to provide information about their business-critical uptimes.

The system administrator records these critical uptimes and the downtimes he would like to schedule in the DOWNTIME MANAGEMENT view in the System Landscape Management work center, categorizes the downtimes, for example, as HARDWARE MAINTENANCE: DATABASE SERVER, and enters a detailed account of the reasons for these measures and the impact they will have.

The administrator can export this information to Excel and forward it to his colleagues in the business units. The planned downtime retains IN REVIEW status for the time being.

Once checks have been completed, for example, with some requests for changes around times at which end-of-quarter closing is due to take place, and alterations have been included in downtime planning, the administrator sets the status of the planned downtime to RELEASED. At this point, he makes a number of settings, for instance, how CCMS monitoring should respond in relation to the production system during the downtime or who should be informed of downtimes in advance. These options are discussed in detail below.

Because the databases of the corresponding development, test, and demo systems must also be maintained, the system administrator can copy the downtimes initially planned for the production system to these other systems as well.

Finally, the administrator configures the details of the processes for executing the individual downtimes, for example, configuring tasks that then appear in the task inbox (see Section 8.1.1) and instruct him to take action as soon as a downtime is due. Alternatively, the administrator can make settings so that the production system stops and restarts automatically.

On the day of the first planned downtime, January 3, 2009, a task appears in the administrator's task inbox telling him to stop the production system at 10 p.m. and start it again at 11 p.m. The administrator performs this task by opening the upcoming downtime in the DOWNTIME MANAGEMENT view in the System Landscape Management work center in SAP Solution Manager. He then performs either a *hard* or a *soft* shutdown by choosing STOP SYSTEM NOW on the EXECUTION tab page. If the production system is running on an SAP NetWeaver release that includes the Adaptive Computing Controller (and this has been installed), you may opt to use this tool to shut down the system or otherwise use SAPControl. A soft shutdown does not cause the system to stop from a technical point of view; rather — in the ideal scenario — business processes are prevented from being executed on a number of instances without necessarily impairing the users.

At 10:45 p.m., the administrator realizes that the downtime is not going to be sufficient. Therefore, he goes to the DOWNTIME MANAGEMENT view in the System Landscape Management work center and schedules a modified planned downtime that starts at 10 p.m. and ends at 11.30 p.m. If necessary, he can then inform all relevant parties of the delay using the notification function, for example by email or SMS. Rather than simply extending the planning downtime, the administrator must add a new phase to the original downtime to ensure that the subsequent history reflects events accurately. By performing a statistical analysis, this history enables you to compare planned downtimes with modified planned downtimes. If planned downtimes are systematically too short or too long, you can identify and remedy this problem in future planning periods.

The administrator completes this maintenance work at 11:20 p.m. and uses the start function on the EXECUTION tab page for the opened modified planned downtime to restart the production system (or, again, using the Adaptive Computing Controller or SAPControl).

To conclude, the administrator creates a real downtime for the downtime originally planned from 10 p.m. to 11 p.m. by entering the data manually or accessing the CPH database in which the actual availability of the production system is stored.

Notification of Downtimes

First, you can click the NOTIFICATION SETTINGS button to define notification recipients for each system who may be interested in downtimes in that system. Possible recipients are divided into internal and external recipients. *Internal recipients* can be selected from the group of users working in the managed system (Transaction SU01) and from the business partners for the SAP Solution Manager system (Transaction BP). If any interested parties are not listed in these two sources, you can assign *external recipients* freely to the managed system. You must, however, explicitly enter their contact details.

Internal and external recipients

Once you have defined the notification recipients at the system level, you can edit the text templates for each notification mode (email, SMS, system message) that these recipients will receive in a genuine situation. The editor provided allows you to put together texts on the basis of a number of keywords that are set dynamically at runtime. For example, the keyword SURNAME is filled with the last name of the recipient when the notification is sent.

The editor also features a preview function that fills keywords with sample content to help you create suitable texts. Finally, you can define when you want notifications to be sent in relation to the core event — in this case at the start of the planned downtime. You are free to change the basic setting shipped by SAP (two SMS messages and three emails, the first of which are sent five days before the downtime, the last one hour beforehand) or just change the sending schedule for selected recipients.

Once you have defined the settings for possible notifications for every relevant system, you can elaborate on them further in the planned downtimes for these systems as required. When you open the downtime, you can — in the simplest scenario — go to the NOTIFICATION MANAGEMENT tab page and select RELEASE SCHEDULED NOTIFICATIONS to copy the notification settings made at the system level exactly as they are for this downtime. For this to be possible, the planned downtime must have RELEASED status. When you click the button, the contents of the NOTIFICATIONS RELEASED column changes from NO to YES, and the SAPconnect communication service (Transaction SOST) is triggered so that the emails and SMS messages are placed in the SAPconnect processing queue. If a

Managing notifications

recipient is deleted at a later point in time or a whole downtime canceled or removed, the content of the SAPconnect queue is adjusted to suit the new circumstances.

If you want to change the notifications pertaining to a specific downtime relative to the predefined notification settings, you can modify the recipient list as required on the NOTIFICATION MANAGEMENT tab page. In addition, notifications do not have to be sent according to the schedule in the notification settings; if the circumstances demand it, you can send notifications immediately by selecting SEND INSTANT NOTIFICATION. Before messages are sent immediately, you can adapt the text for each communication channel (email, SMS, system message). With system messages, you can also bypass the defined recipient list and instead contact all system users.

Handling Monitoring Functions During Downtime

With regard to monitoring in SAP Solution Manager, system administrators often complain that CCMS monitoring produces unwanted alerts during planned downtimes. The administrators then face the tedious task of removing them.

Phantom alerts
You can eliminate such phantom alerts in the DOWNTIME MANAGEMENT view in the System Landscape Management work center. To do so, you open a planned downtime, select the ALERTING PROPERTIES tab, and — depending on whether you use solely CCMS monitoring or both CCMS and Business Process Monitoring — define how you want monitoring to respond during a planned downtime. The following selection options exist for CCMS monitoring:

▶ FULL MONITORING: The CCMS continues to operate unchanged during downtime.

▶ MONITORING PAUSE: The CCMS stops all activities concerning the managed system, including the gathering of monitoring data.

▶ SUPPRESS ALERTS: The CCMS continues to gather data but does not analyze it, which means no alerts are triggered.

▶ SUPPRESS MALFUNCTION REPORTS: In the SAP Solution Manager ALERT INBOX, you can generate Service Desk messages from alerts (see Section 8.7). If you select the SUPPRESS MALFUNCTION REPORTS option, the CCMS still generates alerts that appear accordingly in the ALERT INBOX but cannot trigger Service Desk messages.

For Business Process Monitoring, you can only select the MONITORING PAUSE or FULL MONITORING options.

Scheduling Downtime at Short Notice

If there is insufficient time for a detailed planning process or this is not required, you can use an unplanned stop. Because this does not involve a complex process, the function is simpler than for long-term planning with planned downtimes. To be precise, you can only schedule one-time downtimes as *unplanned stops*; recurring sequences cannot be scheduled. Similarly, the status profile is much simpler because it is not necessary to map a planning process.

Unplanned stop

Other aspects that have already been described for planned downtimes remain the same, for example, options for describing an unplanned stop, determining how you want monitoring to respond, or actually triggering the system stop or restart.

With respect to notifications, emails and SMS are no longer sent well in advance of the stop. However, you can still send immediate notifications.

Entering System Crashes After They Have Occurred

If you use the CCMS, system crashes are saved in the CPH database, and, if required, you can easily transfer data saved there to the DOWNTIME MANAGEMENT view in the System Landscape Management work center.

If you do not use the CCMS, you can also enter a system crash manually.

In the DOWNTIME MANAGEMENT view in the System Landscape Management work center, you can document crashes to create a complete data source that not only offers you a quick and comprehensive overview of downtimes in your systems and other components, but also acts as a reference database for reporting.

8.3.2 Integration with Other SAP Solution Manager Functions – Particularly Service Level Reporting

The broad aim over time is for all SAP Solution Manager functions that are affected by downtimes to react to the downtimes defined in the System Landscape Management work center.

For some functions such as Change Request Management, Maintenance Optimizer, or Incident Management, integration has not yet been accomplished, whereas other functions such as the CCMS, Business Process Monitoring, and Task Manager have already been integrated. Although Service Level Reporting (see Section 8.2.4) within SAP Solution Manager still has its own input screen for planned downtimes, it nevertheless now relies primarily on data entered in the DOWNTIME MANAGEMENT view in the System Landscape Management work center.

8.3.3 Supported Applications

Logging

Downtime processes are logged by the application log in SAP NetWeaver (Transaction SLG1, object SOLAR, subobject DTM or object DTS, subobject API). Log entries are kept for seven days. You can also deactivate logging if required.

Task management

Alternatively or in addition to executing downtimes directly using SAP-Control or Adaptive Computing Controller, you can create tasks that integrate the person responsible for the downtime into the work process on the basis of corresponding tasks in the TASK MANAGEMENT view in the System Administration work center.

Reporting

The downtime data from the System Landscape Management work center is analyzed and included in the availability reports created by SAP NetWeaver Business Intelligence.

8.3.4 More Information

SAP Note 1129385 contains the latest news on this application and references to important technical background information, for example, requirements for using the function to deactivate CCMS alerts during downtimes.

8.4   Issue Management

Issues in SAP Solution Manager allow you to document problems threatening to compromise your business processes, organize how these problems are handled, and subsequently analyze the problem-solving process.

Unlike Service Desk messages (see Section 8.7), it is clear at the time an issue is created that finding its solution will exceed the level of support provided by your support organization or by SAP Active Global Support, for example, because *incidents* (see Section 8.7) of the same nature keep occurring without a plausible explanation.

Issues are a starting point, a tool, and a documentation medium for solving complex problems in a comprehensive and traceable manner. Issues cover the life cycle of a problem — from the time it is recorded right up to when it is resolved. An issue might, for example, have the title Recurring Performance Problems with the CRM Call Center at Peak Times. Using the Service Desk to handle a problem formulated in such a general way results in either secondary messages being created or no solution being provided because the required knowledge or solution instruments are lacking. Even in the best possible cases, it is difficult to document the link between secondary solution measures and the original Service Desk message. An issue in SAP Solution Manager, on the other hand, can fully integrate the measures undertaken for analysis and problem solving and record which SAP services and tasks as well as ordered consulting time (Expertise on Demand) were used with the support messages and change requests created for the issue.

Issues to handle complex problems

SAP recommends that you use issues in the following situations:

▶ If you need to solve problems that are not clearly outlined or record and analyze risks, that is, problems that have not yet occurred but are likely to do so

- ▸ For incidents that can be solved in isolated cases but recur frequently and therefore require more thorough analysis

- ▸ If you consider it important to fully document the life cycle of a problem so that it can be tracked and analyzed later

- ▸ If you do not operate Incident Management (for example, using the Service Desk in SAP Solution Manager) and want to use Issue Management as an easy-to-configure (but not very adaptable) alternative to Incident Management

- ▸ When the service provider (SAP Active Global Support, for example) that supplies your services (such as Solution Management Assessment) wants to systematically document the results and their recommendations (see Section 8.6)

Support messages for clearly definable problems

Individual Service Desk messages are appropriate if problems are well-defined and are not expected to complicate other problem messages or activities. You can assign an issue any number of Service Desk messages that shed light on the various aspects of the issue. Issues can, therefore, also be used to logically group Service Desk messages.

Issues are operative by nature. The concept primarily addresses users active in fields involving technical operations and service providers that supply services for your solution.

Top Issues for problems from a management perspective

A *Top Issue* describes the management view of a set of problems, the solution for which requires management to make decisions. In general, this is the type of problem that is viewed at the management level of your organization as being critical to the success of a project or a business process. The concept of a Top Issue therefore primarily focuses on non-technically-oriented project managers and includes a less specialized range of supporting solution instruments. However, Top Issues can also refer to issues and thereby, logically, group issues. Issues can arise from the action plan (tasks) derived from a Top Issue. Therefore, you can also access the (technical) issues that belong to a Top Issue from within that Top Issue. This helps you ensure that problems can be tracked easily and comprehensively.

Top Issues differ from issues in that the former can be forwarded to SAP for use to facilitate work between your management and management at SAP Active Global Support.

8.4.1 Working with Issues

Issues in SAP Solution Manager are usually created in the context of a project (see Sections 5.4 and 6.1) or a solution. Issues contain:

▶ A detailed *description and analysis* of the problem and a short descrip-   Content of issues
  tion. An issue can be documented in the long text using a template
  consisting of:

  ▶ Description

  ▶ The impact of the issue on your business processes

  ▶ Solution criteria that must be met upon closure of the issue

  You can supplement the description of an issue by attaching
  documents.

▶ *An analysis* in which you can record the steps that have been taken to
  analyze the issue.

▶ A standardized *subject matter* that can be selected from a predefined
  list containing values such as performance management, project management, system and data security, and so on.

▶ *A priority* with the default options very high, high, medium, or low.

▶ *A due date* by which a solution must have been found for the issue.

▶ *A status* of draft, open, in process, or completed.

▶ *A context* for specifying what an issue refers to. This context can be
  a system in your solution landscape, a business scenario, a business
  process, or a process step. Context elements can be freely combined.

▶ *Processing information* that describes the following:

  ▶ Who created the issue and when?

  ▶ Who is responsible for processing the issue?

  ▶ Who completed the issue and when?

> ▸ Personal processing notes that you can log here; important system events such as creating a new task within an issue are logged automatically.

> ▸ Information about the time that SAP Active Global Support invested in processing the issue

8.4.2   Working with Top Issues

The purpose of Top Issues is to support the problem-solving process. They are modeled in the same way as issues, and their attributes are essentially the same. However, business process steps are not available when selecting the context of Top Issues. The main attribute of Top Issues is that issues can be linked to them, which means Top Issues can be used to combine related issues. The tasks in a Top Issue can be taken as a basis for defining action plans and taking an integrated approach to related issues while keeping an overview of actions that have been carried out.

8.4.3   Cooperative Problem Solving with Issues and Top Issues

One of the key aspects of Issue Management in SAP Solution Manager is that customers and SAP Active Global Support work together to resolve issues and Top Issues.

Broadly defined, Top Issues, that is, problems relevant at the management level, can be the starting point for an SAP Active Global Support engagement. The related tasks represent the agreed upon action plan, which can be adapted or extended as time progresses. Any existing issues are linked to the Top Issue or its tasks, whereas new issues are assigned to it.

Operational issues involve all of the solution instruments listed below. Top Issues, which are geared toward the management level, are limited to the assignment of *tasks* to employees and the logical grouping of issues within a Top Issue.

Processing instruments

Tasks allow you to provide employees with instructions for resolving the issue. During the course of processing our example issue, Recurring

Performance Problems in the CRM Call Center, an SAP service recommends a CPU upgrade for the CRM system. You then define this upgrade as a task and assign it to an appropriate employee. You can also set up a notification mechanism to inform the employee, for example, by email, that he has been assigned a task (SAP Note 954034).

The following instruments can also be used to process issues:

▶ **Service Desk messages**
You can assign an issue any number of Service Desk messages to assist processing (see Section 8.7).

▶ **Expertise on Demand requirements**
An SAP expert can be requested directly from within the issue. SAP employs known experts in all functional areas; you can use these experts via the Expertise on Demand service. To use this service, you require an allotted amount of expert time. When you submit an Expertise on Demand request, SAP informs you of this time via a previously assigned contract number. This number is currently assigned to customers participating in the SAP MaxAttention program.

▶ **SAP services**
The SAP Service Portfolio encompasses known products such as the SAP GoingLive and SAP EarlyWatch services. As of January 1, 2006, SAP Solution Manager is required for the provision of SAP services.

▶ **Change requests**
SAP Solution Manager allows you to manage change requests (see Section 9.1). If a change request is required in the course of troubleshooting using an issue, you can assign the change request to the issue.

Figure 8.24 provides an overview of how issues and Top Issues relate to one another and other important objects when you use SAP Solution Manager as a platform for collaboration (between you and SAP Support). A Top Issue can contain tasks and issues. Issues, in turn, branch into a number of subobjects for issue processing. Service Sessions can be used to create a new generation of Top Issues and issues.

Relationship between issues and Top Issues

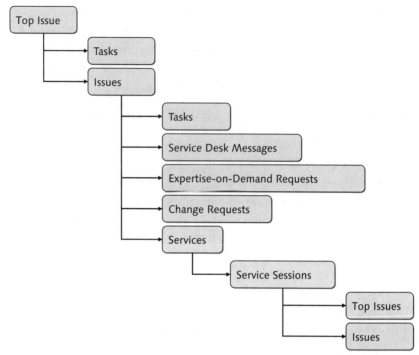

Figure 8.24 Relationships Between Objects in SAP Solution Manager: Top Issues, Issues, Tasks

8.4.4 Using Issues to Solve Problems Independently

You can also use Issue Management independently, without working with SAP Active Global Support, for example together with Incident Management in SAP Solution Manager. A typical (ITIL) scenario would be the recurrence of incidents that you can handle easily in isolation but whose frequency points to a more fundamental problem. In this case, you would create an issue, for example Recurring Performance Problems with the CRM Call Center at Peak Times, and on the MESSAGES tab page save the incidents that prompted you to create this issue and that contain information about the circumstances surrounding the problem.

Issue Management as an alternative to the Service Desk

Another example would be using Issue Management in SAP Solution Manager as a simple alternative to Incident Management with the Service Desk. While Issue Management is considerably less adaptable and contains fewer functions than the Service Desk, it can be deployed more rapidly.

Note that independent use of Top Issues is not supported at this time. They are closely interwoven with SAP Active Global Support customer service processes.

8.4.5 Practical Procedure and Handling

Creating, Processing, and Closing an Issue or Top Issue

You can create issues in the following ways:

▶ Directly from the core application, Transaction SOLMAN_ISSUE_ MGMT: Here, you can work with the complete list of issues and all Issue Management tools.

▶ In the SAP Engagement and Service Delivery work center: Here, however, you can only access issues that are linked to a solution because Service Delivery is performed using solutions only. Issues you create here always have the solution from which you create them as their context (ISSUES view, CONTEXT tab page in the issue details).

▶ In the Implementation/Upgrade work center: Follow the menu path PLAN • DEFINE BUSINESS BLUEPRINT • ISSUES/MESSAGES or PLAN • SHOW ROADMAPS • ISSUES/MESSAGES. The contents of the work center correspond to the familiar SAP Solution Manager Transactions SOLAR01/02 and RMMAIN. Issues you create here are always linked by their context to the relevant project.

▶ From the menu structure in Transaction SOLUTION_MANAGER, the original SAP Solution Manager transaction, by following the menu path OPERATIONS • ISSUE MANAGEMENT • ISSUES • CREATE.

▶ Within an SAP service

All of these options lead to the same entry screen (see Figure 8.25).

Variety of ways to create issues

305

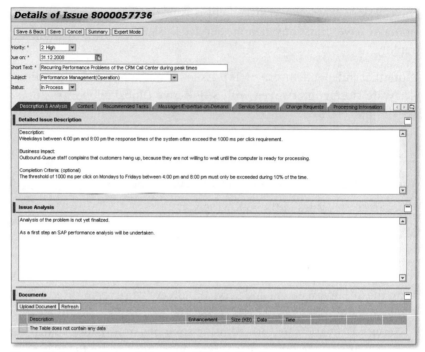

Figure 8.25 Entry Screen for Issues in SAP Solution Manager

Creating Top Issues Because Top Issues are strongly geared toward Service Delivery requirements, you can only create Top Issues in the SAP Engagement and Service Delivery work center or in Transaction SOLUTION_MANAGER • OPERATIONS • ISSUE MANAGEMENT • TOP ISSUES. The user interface for and the management of creating and processing issues and Top Issues differ only in that the tab page structure for Top Issues is simpler and that Top Issues can be forwarded to SAP.

You can obtain an overview of issues and Top Issues that have been created in Transaction SOLMAN_ISSUE_MGMT or in the SAP Engagement and Service Delivery work center.

Integrated Reporting Functions

In addition to standard reporting (see Section 8.9), Issue Management in Transaction SOLMAN_ISSUE_MGMT also contains a REPORTING VIEW option that gives you a full and clear overview of issues and their dependent objects (for example, tasks). By selecting SUMMARY, you can generate a clearly laid out compendium of the detailed contents of one or more issues in PDF or Microsoft Word format.

Logging Processing and Notifications for Processing

The PROCESSING LOG VIEW allows you to access *processing notes* directly from the issue list that you would otherwise have to call up in a rather indirect way by accessing the issue details on the PROCESSING INFORMATION tab page. The list not only reveals the latest entry in the processing log, but also enables you to change it easily by selecting EDIT PROCESSING LOG.

In addition to processing notes entered manually, entries are also made automatically. The triggers for such entries are summarized in SAP Note 914722 and include changes to the due date or the processor. The latter also causes an automatic notification email to be sent to the newly assigned processor if an email address has been stored for the relevant business partner (Transaction BP) or user (Transaction SU01) (SAP Note 954034).

Automatic entries

8.4.6 Overview of Processes for Troubleshooting with Issues and Top Issues

Figure 8.26 summarizes the most important processes that occur between the customer and SAP on the collaboration platform for issues and Top Issues, the individual steps of which are described as follows:

▶ Step 1: Issues and Top Issues can be created from Service Sessions.

Processes for tracking problems

▶ Step 1a: You create an issue in SAP Solution Manager and provide descriptions, priorities, due dates, processors, and so on.

▶ Step 1b: You create a Top Issue in SAP Solution Manager. Top Issues can have the same information as described in 1a.

▶ Step 2a: You specify objects related to the context of the issue and that can contribute to its solution, that is, tasks, Service Desk messages, Expertise on Demand requests, change requests, and SAP Services.

▶ Step 2b: You define tasks and any issues related to the context of the Top Issue and for which a solution must be found.

▸ Step 3: Top Issues can be transferred to SAP Active Global Support management via the SAP postbox system.

▸ Step 4: SAP is informed of the status of your Top Issues and of your solution's critical problems, at which point an action plan is agreed on with your management staff.

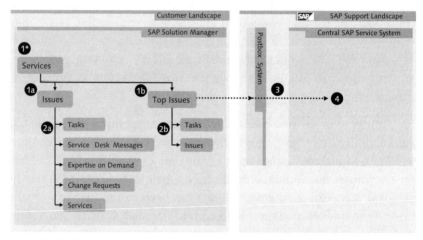

Figure 8.26 Overview of Underlying Processes of Problem Tracking in SAP Solution Manager

For more information about analyzing issues and Top Issues, refer to Section 8.9.5.

8.4.7 CRM Transaction Types and Customizing Issue Management in SAP Solution Manager

Issue Management in SAP Solution Manager is realized on the SAP CRM 5.0 platform using the following transaction types: SLFI (issues), SLFT (Top Issues), SLFE (Expertise on Demand), and TASK (tasks). You can access the standard CRM interface by clicking the EXPERT MODE button in the issue details. Note, however, that Issue Management does not support all of the functions in the SAP CRM application.

Limited Customizing Because the issue-related family of transactions is designed to facilitate collaboration between customers and SAP, you should not attempt to tailor these objects to your own requirements. Where possible, this restriction on Customizing has been implemented technically in the system as well. SAP Note 1019583 contains instructions relating to the few aspects of Issue Management that are adaptable. For issues and Top Issues, these comprise priority, status, subject, standard text in the description, and number ranges.

Additionally, the ISSUE SETTINGS button on the initial screen in Issue Management allows you to deactivate some of the tab pages shown in the issue details screen and activate the inclusion of the issue key of any non-SAP issue management application that you may have in use. This is useful if you want to link issues that you have recorded in SAP Solution Manager Issue Management with issues managed in a non-SAP issue management system.

Non-SAP Issue Management

8.5   Job Scheduling Management

The aim of *Job Scheduling Management* is to automate business processes fully or partially, taking into consideration the available hardware and any time restrictions. Job Scheduling Management is often seen as simply choosing the right tool for scheduling background jobs in one or more backend systems. This, however, is only one of many aspects. Generally speaking, the following three challenges must be overcome:

▶ Ensure that existing background jobs are documented in full and centrally to achieve a complete overview of the entire workload.

Challenges

▶ Distribute the background job processing load evenly and reach the required throughput for mass processing.

▶ Monitor background jobs efficiently and automatically and identify potential negative effects on existing business processes.

How can these challenges be tackled and a well-defined, standardized process be supported? You can use a process, for example, like the one shown in Figure 8.27.

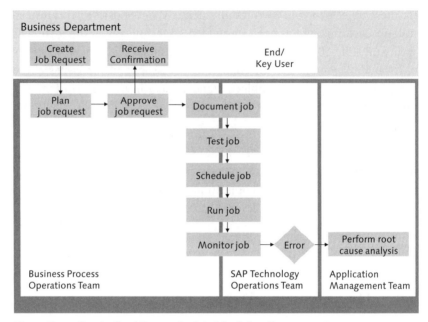

Figure 8.27 Standardized Process for Job Scheduling Management

This process is described in Section 8.5.2 on the basis of a concrete example. You will discover the extent to which such a process is supported when SAP Solution Manager and the SAP Central Process Scheduling application by Redwood are deployed together. For more information, see the white paper on the subject of Job Scheduling Management and the Job Scheduling Management best practice document at *https://service.sap.com/supportstandards* and *https://service.sap.com/solutionmanagerbp*.

8.5.1 The Challenges of Job Scheduling Management

This section begins by describing the challenges listed above in greater detail.

Complete,
centralized job
documentation

By achieving transparency across background processing jobs that run daily in your systems, you can tell exactly which jobs are running unnecessarily and are no longer needed, perhaps because the respective production plant no longer exists (in the system). To accomplish this, extensive job documentation is crucial. Until now, you may have been using Excel or Lotus Notes for this, for example. However, this type of documentation is rarely particularly transparent and usually only accessible to a limited group of people. Worst of all is the fact that the job documentation usually fails to cover all aspects that feature in complete documentation. For instance, documentation often only contains technical data (ABAP report and variant) and states in which system a job runs and when. Information about the business reasons behind a job and the business processes and business units it benefits is normally not provided. Details of contact persons, error handling methods, and scheduling restrictions are also generally overlooked.

This is where SAP Solution Manager comes in. It provides centralized, standardized job documentation directly as a tool and accounts for all of these aspects. This application can also be called up in a web browser and therefore made available centrally to multiple users, at least in display mode.

You can use Transactions SM36 and SM37 to schedule background jobs locally in your SAP backend systems or each individual system (if you have several networked SAP systems). However, along with certain other restrictions, Transaction SM36 notably does not support the scheduling of jobs with dependencies that cross system boundaries. To map such dependencies and better distribute the background job load, SAP provides *SAP Central Process Scheduling by Redwood*, which is associated with the SAP NetWeaver license. Using the standard XBP (eXternal Batch Processing) interface, this application also enables you to technically intercept background jobs scheduled by end users and reschedule them in a centralized and controlled fashion. In this way, you can minimize the danger of the SAP backend system being overloaded by jobs scheduled by end users with no control mechanisms in place. This application is not part of SAP Solution Manager but is integrated via an interface.

Improved load distribution and increased document throughput

Job monitoring is also a multifaceted subject. Some customers monitor nothing at all in practice, whereas many limit their monitoring activities to manual monitoring in Transaction SM37. This might involve checking sporadically throughout the day if jobs have been canceled and need to be restarted. Some customers have at least automated job monitoring to the extent that system monitoring tools are used to automatically check

Automated job monitoring in the business process context

if jobs are canceled or take longer than expected. Here too, many questions are left open and can only be answered by Business Process Monitoring in SAP Solution Manager. In addition to the functions that system monitoring tools present for job monitoring, Business Process Monitoring can also assess whether jobs have failed to start or end on time from a business perspective. Checks on content can also be performed by automatically verifying whether certain messages have been written to the job log. At the same time, jobs are linked to business processes and, in particular, business process steps. This means that if a job is canceled, you know straight away if it supports a sales or production process or belongs to the process for period-end closing.

8.5.2 Case Study: A Job Scheduling Management Process as Conceived in the SAP Standard System

This section uses a fictitious example to illustrate which functions SAP Solution Manager provides for Job Scheduling Management and how they interact with SAP Central Process Scheduling.

Step 1 – Job Request Submitted by User Department (or Project Team)

Our model company is due to open a new plant in the United States. The user department in the company wants to request a new background job to begin performing material requirements planning regularly for this new plant in the near future.

Web form for job request — In the past, you had to create your own Microsoft Word, Excel, or web forms for this purpose. Now, with SAP Solution Manager, you can use a standardized web form to submit a new job request or a change to an existing job. You can link this web form into SAP NetWeaver Portal or any other intranet. End users can save the form in their web browser favorites.

The form offers two views: a basic view that fits one screen page and a detailed view that is split over several tab pages. The detailed view can be used by project team members during an implementation project, whereas the basic view is intended more for departmental end users or key users who submit job requests as part of their daily activities. This example explains only the basic view. The user department enters details of the job name (in this case, S_DE_PP_MRP_1000_6H), system, and client for which the job is required. Scheduling information is also entered here (date, time, or free text descriptions of scheduling requirements, for example, every six hours).

In addition, you can save organizational information, for example, the region (AMERICAS), country (US), organization, and the business process for which the job is relevant. The user department must specify the business requirements in the mandatory field provided so that the IT department subsequently has a basis on which it can rate how important the job is and how best to fit it into the existing job scheduling arrangements.

Finally, you are required to enter Service Desk data because when you save the form, a Service Desk message is created in the background in SAP Solution Manager to create the integrated connection between the request form and job documentation. Accordingly, the reporter must be a *business partner* in SAP Solution Manager. However, it is not necessary for all end users to have a corresponding business partner in SAP Solution Manager. You can also use a generic business partner and enter the contact details of the reporter as free text. In this case, though, the generic business partner must be released for all relevant systems, or a business partner must be created for each system.

Step 2 – Notifying the IT Department and Evaluating the Request

So far, the user department has simply submitted a request that the IT department is unaware of. However, because a Service Desk message is created from the job request, the missing connection between the two departments can be established. The IT employee can navigate to the Job Requests view in the Job Management work center to see all new job requests that either he or his team have to process (Figure 8.28). By selecting a job request, the employee is taken directly to its details or the corresponding Service Desk message.

Job Management work center

313

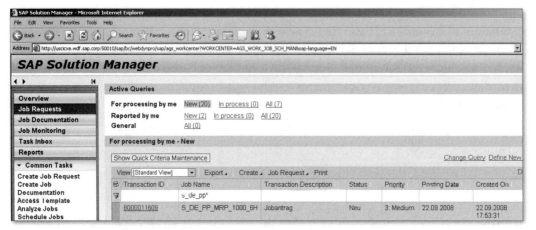

Figure 8.28 Job Requests – Overview

The IT employee then switches to change mode (if he is not already in it) and can select from a range of actions in the action profile. He can now view or process the job request.

Note that the same Service Desk messages for the job requests also appear in the Incident Management work center. This allows your Service Desk employees to handle job requests handled from there.

If you have the adapter for integrating SAP Central Process Scheduling with SAP Solution Manager, you can use the integration with Change Request Management, which also supports a formal approval process.

Step 3 – Creating a Corresponding Job Document

The IT employee has now looked at the job request and confirmed that the newly requested job can be included in existing job scheduling in its present form. The employee has also used the reporting functions in the Job Management work center to verify that corresponding job documentation does not yet exist. The job request will now be adopted together with the scheduling information and all other data provided by the user department. To do this, the employee selects the action to create a corresponding job document in the Service Desk message (see Figure 8.29).

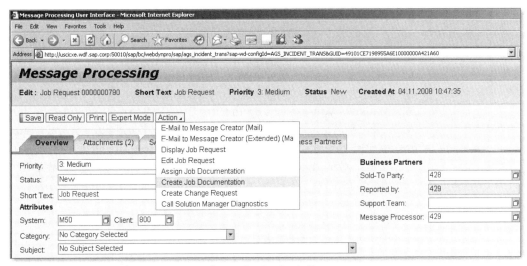

Figure 8.29 Creating Job Documentation from a Service Desk Message

The action is only performed when the Service Desk message is saved. Because no assignment to a logical component or business process has been made in the job request, the IT employee must specify in the popup that appears whether the job is to be assigned to a particular business process step (in which case the respective logical component is selected implicitly) or whether process assignment is not required and the job is only to be assigned to a logical component. The latter case would, for example, apply to an IT Basis job. Job S_DE_PP_MRP_1000_6H in this example is assigned to the ORDER TO CASH process and the RUN MRP process step.

Assignment to business processes

If the detailed view of the job request had been used in step 1, assignment to a logical component or a business process could have been made at that stage. Had this been the case, the popup would not have appeared when the Service Desk message was saved.

In our example, the job document has been successfully created and now contains all of the information saved in the job request by the user department employees. In other words, from the point at which the job request was created, all data has been passed on to job documentation automatically without external steps or any need for manual copying and pasting.

Step 4 – Completing the Job Document on the IT Side

The fourth step involves taking any necessary steps to complete the job document. First, it must be located. To do so, you can open either the Service Desk message again or the document flow. If you open the document flow, you can navigate to the job document by double-clicking it. Alternatively, you can call up the JOB DOCUMENTATION view in the Job Management work center, shown in Figure 8.30, and filter by job name, for example. If you call up the job document from the work center, you are shown individual tab pages that you can fill. Each of these tab pages represents aspects (best practices) of complete job documentation. This allows you to enter general technical data, business data, and organizational data in the same way. You can save different contacts and enter descriptions for error handling. You can also note restrictions in scheduling. The SYSTEMS tab page is of particular note. It enables you to configure scheduling itself as well as monitoring.

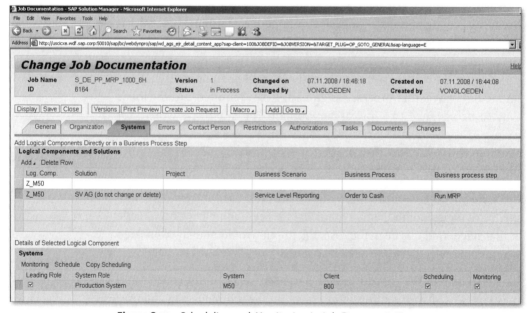

Figure 8.30 Scheduling and Monitoring in Job Documentation

Step 5 – Configuring Scheduling in SAP Solution Manager and Transferring Data to SAP Central Process Scheduling by Redwood

To configure scheduling, you navigate to the job document in the JOB DOCUMENTATION view in the Job Management work center and select the SYSTEMS tab page. First, you select a logical component or a solution with a business process and process step. Once you have done so, all of the systems belonging to the logical component are displayed in the lower screen area. You then select one of the lines containing a system. In our example, you select the production system. Clicking the SCHEDULE button takes you to a new window in which you can enter the job scheduling in detail. The user interface appearance changes depending on the selected scheduling tool. It either looks similar to the standard Transaction SM36 or contains basically the same fields that you see when you schedule jobs directly in SAP Central Process Scheduling by Redwood (as in this example).

You enter all of the important scheduling data and click the CREATE button. A job is now created in the background in the connected SAP Central Process Scheduling system. Depending on whether the SCHEDULE STOPPED checkbox has been selected in SAP Solution Manager, the job acquires either STOPPED or SCHEDULED status in SAP Central Process Scheduling. In the former case, the job must still be explicitly released in SAP Central Process Scheduling before it can run in the backend system. In the latter, the job is started as soon as the start conditions are met. Authorizations are used to verify whether SAP Solution Manager is permitted to create and even release jobs in SAP Central Process Scheduling.

Creating a job

If you want SAP Central Process Scheduling to send status data directly to Business Process Monitoring, you have to set the STATUS MESSAGE indicator.

Step 6 – Configuring Job Monitoring as Part of Business Process Monitoring

If you want to configure and activate monitoring, you must assign the job to a business process step. Assignment to a logical component alone is not sufficient. In our example, the job has been assigned to the RUN MRP step. On the SYSTEMS tab page, you now select the line that represents the assignment of solution, business scenario, business process, and step. A list of all system and client combinations covered by the assigned logical component is then shown in the lower screen area. You choose the line containing the system with the leading role (in most cases, this will be the production system, just as in our example).

When you click the MONITORING button, a new dialog box opens in which you can save information describing when you want the job to be monitored. You can enter whether you consider the job to be particularly critical; accordingly, a check is run every five minutes or once an hour to establish if there is a new status. Next, you enter the data source; you either receive the data directly from SAP Central Process Scheduling, or (if you are not using that application) SAP Solution Manager receives the data from the connected SAP backend system. The former case offers the advantage that SAP Central Process Scheduling can enable monitoring to be extended to non-SAP systems.

Monitoring data

Next, you enter the days on which you want to receive monitoring data because the job does not necessarily need to be monitored on every day that it is scheduled to run. For example, the job may only be (time-)critical on workdays and not on the weekend. On the ALERT CONFIGURATION tab page (Figure 8.31), you can enter the threshold values for the key figures yourself. Once you have saved all of the data, you activate monitoring directly from this application.

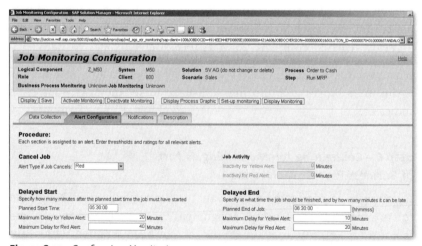

Figure 8.31 Configuring Monitoring

To ensure this is successful, you must first activate Business Process Mon- Summary
itoring for the respective process (in this case, ORDER TO CASH) and select
the CONSIDER JOB DEF. checkbox for the process in the general setup area
of Business Process Monitoring. You can close the dialog box now that
monitoring is active. SAP Solution Manager begins monitoring.

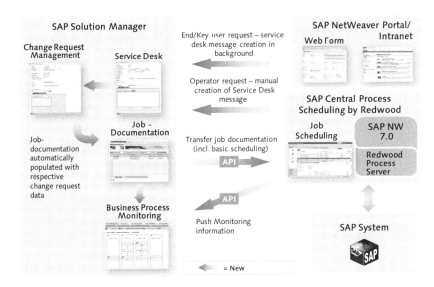

Figure 8.32 Integrating SAP Central Process Scheduling in SAP Solution Manager
Using Adapters

You can also use the SAP Solution Manager JOB REQUEST, JOB DOCU-
MENTATION, and BUSINESS PROCESS MONITORING functions together with
other scheduling tools. However, to do so you are required to transfer
the scheduling data from SAP Solution Manager to the planning tool
manually, as shown in Figure 8.33. This results in Business Process Monitoring being restricted to background jobs in the SAP environment.

To facilitate the process of implementing the SAP standard for Job Sched- Job Scheduling
uling Management as described here, a document about the implemen- Management
tation methodology has been created and forms part of the Run SAP
Roadmap (see Section 5.1.1).

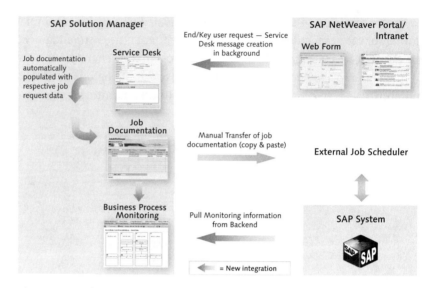

Figure 8.33 Job Request with External Scheduling Tool

8.6   Planning and Delivery of SAP Services

SAP Active Global Support presents SAP customers with several support offerings, for example, SAP Enterprise Support and SAP MaxAttention. Details of these offerings can be found on the SAP Service Marketplace (*www.service.sap.com/supportofferings*).

At the heart of all support offerings are services that have fixed contents and are delivered by experts. Together, the services on offer cover the entire software life cycle, from implementation to operations, optimization, and upgrading. You can view the list of available services on the SAP Service Marketplace (*www.service.sap.com/supportservices*).

Aim of services   The aim of all services is to proactively uncover and resolve critical technical issues before they cause damage to business operations. Technical issues are also documented while a service is being provided to assist any suitable follow-up services and the respective experts (see also Section 8.4).

The SAP Engagement and Service Delivery work center (see Figure 8.34) is the central access point for SAP support staff and the starting point for providing a service using the corresponding Service Session (automated checklists) on the basis of assigned issues. An overview of this work center can be found in Section 3.1.

Figure 8.34 SAP Engagement and Service Delivery Work Center

The outcome of an SAP service is a service report. It details the analyses performed and the issues identified. It also contains detailed, mainly technical recommendations (tasks) for resolving these issues. Together, the tasks defined for one or more issues or Top Issues form the action plan. This plan is used to prioritize the tasks, assign people or groups, and decide on deadlines. Tasks are stored as separate objects; that is, they do not only exist as part of a service report, but can also be distributed and monitored as they are completed. The REPORTS view in the SAP Engagement and Service Delivery work center offers you a range of ways to view the status of issues, Top Issues, and the enterprise service engagement.

Service report

8.6.1 SAP Services in SAP Solution Manager

An SAP service (for example, an SAP Technical Integration Check) in SAP Solution Manager is characterized by:

▶ A *status*

▶ A scheduled *processing date*

▶ A *context* that describes which solution, system, project, and milestone a service relates to within the project

▶ A *focus* or *comment* text that explains why a service is required, what must be noted in particular when carrying it out, and so on

▶ A *history* (processing information) that briefly documents the history of a service:

  ▶ The transaction number of the objects in the central SAP service management system for customer service plans

  ▶ The scheduled processing date for the service plan, that is, the service order

Service Delivery generally consists of four phases, which are described in the following section:

1. Send solution master data

2. Retrieve service or service plan

3. Plan service

4. Perform service

8.6.2 Sending Solution Master Data to SAP and Updating It

SAP Active Global Support can only provide services for the solutions it knows. If DATA TRANSFER CONFIGURATION has been set up to allow data to be transferred, you can send solution information from SAP Solution Manager to SAP in two ways (see Figure 8.35):

▶ Manually (in the work center or Transaction SOLUTION_MANAGER) by selecting UPDATE SOLUTION MASTER DATA AT SAP

▶ Automatically by scheduling a background job that sends solution master data to SAP once a day

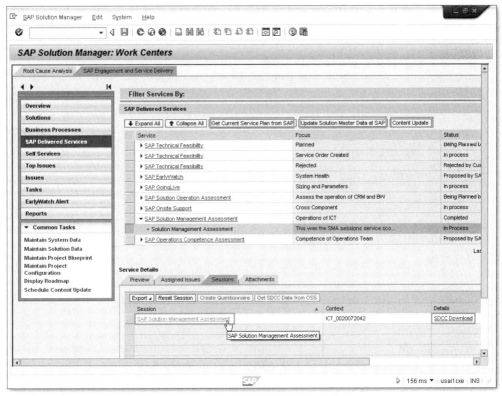

Figure 8.35 Updating Service Content – Access to a Session

The solution data that is sent includes only master data (systems, software versions, and business processes) from your solution, not transaction data. The data transfer is therefore not subject to special security measures. The data that is transferred is listed in detail in SAP Note 942403.

This data is then read by the SAP Active Global Support central service management system. Only when the master data of a solution is present in the *installed base* (IBase; see Section 8.7) can SAP create a service plan, link it with your solution, and make it available for collection.

Installed base: central solution master data for all customers

8.6.3 Collecting the Service Plan from SAP and Updating It

Here, too, you can either click the GET CURRENT SERVICE PLAN FROM SAP button (see Figure 8.35), or schedule a background job to obtain the latest service plan data from SAP. Background jobs are set by default to run once a day. When Service Delivery is urgent, SAP recommends that you update manually.

8.6.4 Planning an SAP Service

SAP Solution Manager covers the entire life cycle of a service, from planning to completion.

Central service plan management for all customers

The SAP-internal customer support system supports central service plan management. SAP Active Global Support can use this system, for example, to initially provide a nonbinding SAP GoingLive service for a particular system or solution. This service would then appear in the solution in SAP Solution Manager as a service with BEING PLANNED BY SAP status and a scheduled processing date.

At this time, the entry is only provided for information purposes, allowing the customer to respond by contacting SAP Active Global Support with regard to service planning and discuss any possible changes (for example, changes to dates) and the focus of the service. To ensure that the outcomes of such discussions are recorded, it is advisable to link the sessions of the service with issues.

8.6.5 Performing an SAP Service

When a service order is created, the status changes to IN PROCESS. Only service plan entries with this status give you access to the Session Workbench and Service Delivery.

Updating service content

Before you start the Session Workbench, you should check if new service content or corrections to the current content are available. By clicking the CONTENT UPDATE button, you can check if the upcoming service needs to be updated. Note that such updates only relate to the content of Service Sessions.

You access a Service Session by opening the subnode of a service, selecting the line, and selecting the text underlined in blue in the SERVICE DETAILS area on the SESSIONS tab page (see Figure 8.35).

SAP Active Global Support or an external service provider generally offers to run your Service Sessions. With the right certification, customers can also run Service Sessions.

The processing involved in most Service Sessions is largely automated; that is, the session analyzes data from the system being examined. This data is usually supplied by the Service Data Control Center (SDCC), an application that sends data to SAP or SAP Solution Manager on request. To ensure that the need for data is recognized, the field in the CONTEXT column must contain the system ID and installation number (see Figure 8.35).

Service Data Control Center

Service Data Control Center data is provided to SAP Solution Manager as follows:

▶ **For ABAP systems**
Every ABAP system linked to SAP Solution Manager includes a periodic background job that checks SAP Solution Manager for any sessions created with reference to this system. If this is the case, the SDCC module in the managed ABAP system creates a task that essentially triggers two processes: The collection of the required data in the managed system and its transfer to SAP Solution Manager.

▶ **For non-ABAP systems**
These systems currently do not have a mechanism like that of the SDCC modules in ABAP systems, which is why data from non-ABAP systems is actively retrieved. This data can be provided by *Solution Manager Diagnostics* (see Section 8.8).

The *Session Workbench* (see Figure 8.36) contains extensive checks for one or more systems or the entire solution. SAP offers training courses with certification for running Service Sessions.

Session Workbench and service report

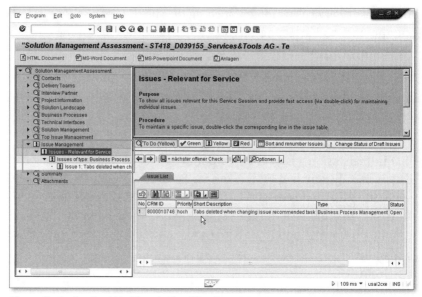

Figure 8.36 Session Workbench Checklist Containing Issues

The goal of a check is to analyze the status of a system, solution, or business process and present this information in a way that is easy to understand. Technical and process analyses can lead to the creation of issues and Top Issues, for which tasks can be recommended.

Quality assurance

Before you are provided with the final version of the report, experts at SAP Active Global Support check it (if the service was delivered by SAP).

Postprocessing

Issues and tasks in the form of a session report have been an integral part of the delivery of SAP services for years. Experience has shown, however, that you could not always fully track the implementation of these tasks. At times, this led to the same issues being identified again in a subsequent service or recommended tasks being insufficiently implemented, ultimately causing exactly what SAP's service offering seeks to prevent: losses in efficiency and, in extreme cases, escalations.

Consequently, issues are now always entered in *Issue Management* in SAP Solution Manager, even those from Service Sessions (see Section 8.4).

You can find the final version of a service report directly in the Service Session on the ATTACHMENTS tab page (see Figure 8.35). Alternatively, you can navigate to the SAP Service Marketplace message relating to the SAP service by selecting the service and the link to the Service Desk message on the SAP Service Marketplace on the PREVIEW tab page in the SERVICE DETAILS area (see Figure 8.37). In the Service Desk message, the customer's contact person can enter feedback on the service provided.

Feedback about the service

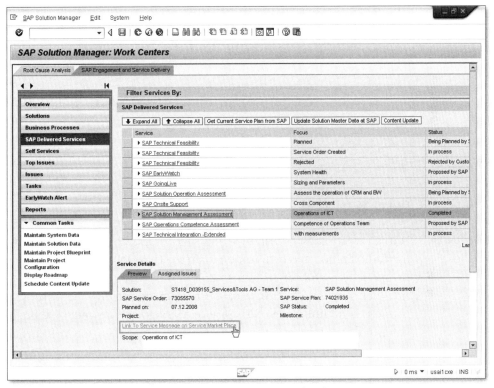

Figure 8.37 Link to Service Desk Message on SAP Service Marketplace

8.6.6 Performing a Self-Service

To create a self-service, that is, a service that does not originate from the SAP service planning system, click the CREATE button on the SELF SERVICES view (see Figure 8.38).

Creating a self-service

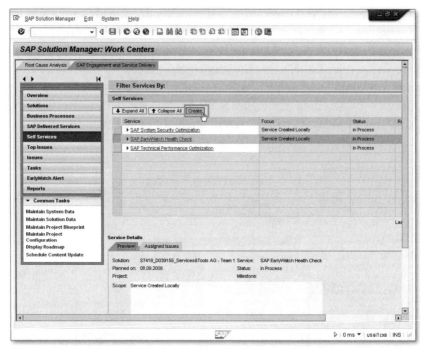

Figure 8.38 Creating a Self-Service Session

Certification key You can create and perform all services locally as self-services if you have the authorization and certification to do so. This type of Service Delivery is especially useful for customers that do not permit a connection outside their network. In this case, it is not possible to give feedback, that is, there is no link to the SAP Service Marketplace. In general though, you handle the service list and work your way to the Session Workbench just as you would for services delivered by SAP (see Section 8.6.5). Self-services simply do not require certification.

8.7 Incident Management

Research shows that 60% of today's IT budgets are used for operating the IT solution, with 30% reserved for consolidation. This leaves only 10% of the budget for innovation. The goal of SAP Solution Manager is to minimize administration costs to make more room for innovation.

The SAP Solution Manager *Service Desk* is a trouble ticket system that is integrated into all-important functions of SAP Solution Manager and its connected managed systems. Whenever problems arise during operations, end users or key users create problem messages. The Service Desk then automatically directs these messages to the right place within the customer's support organization. Here, or in close collaboration with SAP Active Global Support, the message is processed and resolved. The Service Desk provides everyone involved in the process with central access to the information relevant to them at all times. This also includes SAP system information. The SAP Solution Manager Service Desk therefore simplifies the process of handling error messages and considerably reduces processing times in Incident and Problem Management.

The following scenarios can be mapped using the Service Desk:

Scenarios

▶ A (global) group and a (global) support organization

▶ Multiple segments of a group with a common support organization

▶ A service provider that manages several companies

SAP Solution Manager 7.0 allows the Service Desk to be used for several parties or in a hosting operation, because support messages can be completely separated from each other. For more information, refer to SAP Note 920734.

8.7.1 Support Concept Basics

Developing an end-to-end support concept necessitates that internal support processes in your company be defined and transparently mapped. The SAP Solution Manager Service Desk provides a preconfigured solution for this that is optimized for SAP-specific support requests.

The concept for processing messages encompasses three or four levels. For customers without a Customer Center of Expertise (CCoE), three processing levels are proposed in the Service Desk, whereas for customers with a CCoE, SAP recommends four levels. This architecture is structured as follows:

Graded message processing concept

▶ **First-level support**
First-level support forms the *single point of contact* from the end user to the Service Desk and thus represents the customer's support orga-

nization. *Key users* are involved at this level or designated users in the managed system who also work in SAP Solution Manager. The following options, which can be combined with one another, are available for creating a message:

- ▶ End users can create support messages from managed systems.
- ▶ Key users can create support messages for end users from managed systems.
- ▶ Key users can create support messages for end users directly in the SAP Solution Manager Service Desk.

▶ **Second-level support**
Second-level support involves employees who are familiar with the details of a customer's own applications and business processes, and assume the role of system administrator. Second-level support therefore is composed of application and technology experts.

▶ **Third-level support (CCoE level)**
Typical activities at this support level include:

- ▶ Searching for Notes
- ▶ Managing and using the solution database in the Service Desk

Those responsible for third-level support typically are a function of the company's size. For smaller companies and customers that do not have a Customer Center of Expertise (CCoE), this level corresponds to fourth-level support. In this case, the tasks associated with the CCoE level are assumed by the customer in second-level support.

▶ **Fourth-level support (SAP Active Global Support)**
Fourth-level support represents SAP Active Global Support. This is the final message processing level for large customers and customers with a CCoE. This support level also includes certified partners that are involved in processing and resolving messages through the SAP global support backbone (see Chapter 11).

This structure allows problem messages to be handled and resolved efficiently with focus on the solution throughout the entire SAP ecosystem. If required, you can set up additional support levels in the Service Desk.

8.7.2 Master Data

To be able to use the Service Desk, you need to be familiar with your company's master data and authorizations, in addition to the support organization. SAP provides a preconfigured standard for just this purpose, which you can tailor to meet your needs.

Business Partners

Before you can create or process messages in the Service Desk, you must save certain master data. Business partners in SAP Solution Manager guarantee effective and easy communication among all employees involved in the Service Desk process. All relevant information on a business partner can be accessed from one central point.

Business partners are added to SAP Solution Manager once only in the Maintain Business Partner transaction (Transaction BP). Here, it does not matter in which part of a process the business partners are involved. For example, a single employee can function as a processor and a reporter. Therefore, you can use SAP Solution Manager to assign a business partner different roles and relationships to other business partners.

In the Service Desk configuration shipped by SAP, five partner functions have been defined. You can adapt these by making Customizing settings:[16]

Predefined partner functions

▶ **Sold-to Party**
Represents the role of the customer and answers the question, "Which customer will bear the costs of the inquiry?" The Sold-to Party partner function is mandatory and cannot be deleted.

▶ **Administrator**
Represents the administrator responsible for the system for which the message was created.

▶ **Reported by**
Answers the question, "Who created the message?"

---

16 For a detailed description of the configuration, refer to *SAP Solution Manager 4.0 Service Desk – Functionality and Implementation* by Matthias Friedrich and Torsten Sternberg, SAP PRESS, Bonn, 2008.

> ▸ **Support Team**
> Represents the support team in the customer's organization.

> ▸ **Message Processor**
> Represents the employee responsible for the message.

IBase (Installed Base)

To use the Service Desk and Change Request Management scenarios in SAP Solution Manager, you must first define the installation (IBase). An IBase component must be created for each component system used to send support messages to SAP Solution Manager. An IBase component therefore represents a managed system in your solution.

IBase components in SAP Solution Manager are managed in the IBase structure SOL_MAN_DATA_REP (installation 1) in the standard system and updated automatically with subsequent enhancements to the system landscape (Transaction SMSY).

8.7.3 Standard Process

Application scenarios

SAP Solution Manager offers three Service Desk application scenarios:

1. **Service Desk**
   This scenario includes all of the components needed to support SAP landscapes.

2. **Connecting an external help desk**
   If you operate a help desk from a third party and want to connect it to the Service Desk, you can connect external help desk systems to SAP Solution Manager (see Section 8.7.5).

3. **Preconfiguration for service providers**
   Preconfiguration for service providers covers all parts of the basic scenario and includes additional functions required for using a Customer Center of Expertise, for example. A differentiated authorization check can be defined with an authorization object.

Incident Management scenario steps

The SAP Solution Manager Incident Management scenario is composed of the following steps (see Figure 8.39):

1. Message creation and automatic distribution to the support employees

2. Message display, processing, and solution determination by searching in the solution database, by conducting a Notes search on the SAP Service Marketplace, or by collaborating with SAP Active Global Support

3. Delivery of solution

4. Evaluation and acknowledgement of solution by reporter; closing of the message and transfer of the solution to the customer-specific solution database

This process follows the Information Technology Infrastructure Library (ITIL) processes of Incident Management and Problem Management and allows for communication among everyone involved via message texts, email, fax, SMS, and so on.

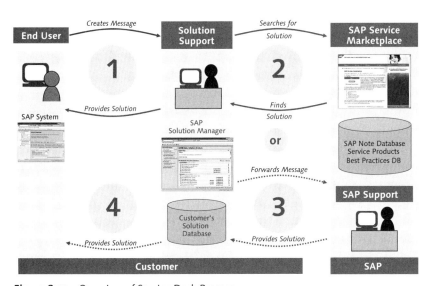

Figure 8.39 Overview of Service Desk Process

Creating Messages

As mentioned in previous chapters, all systems used for the solution are linked to SAP Solution Manager via remote function call (RFC) connections. One of the things that makes the Service Desk unique is its integration into the existing landscape and into other SAP Solution Manager functions, such as Root Cause Analysis and Change Request Management (see Sections 8.8 and 9.1).

You can create a message in several ways:

▶ As an end user, you can create a message directly from the transaction in which an error occurred. To do this, you simply select HELP • CREATE SUPPORT MESSAGE (see Figure 8.40). You can enter a short text, a priority, and a problem description (long text) in the dialog box that appears. The component in which the error occurred is automatically completed by the system.

This is not the only information that SAP Solution Manager automatically acquires to provide effective and targeted support for the SAP solution. Every message saves technical data such as the system ID, client, Support Package version, and transactions in the background to minimize questions sent to the reporter by the Service Desk employee and to accelerate the support process.

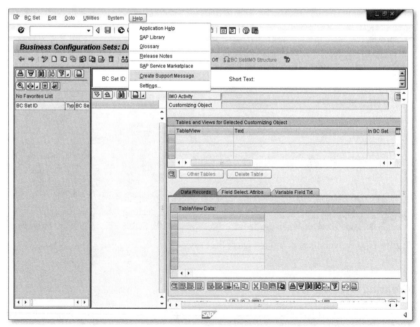

Figure 8.40 Creating a Support Message from the Transaction in which an Error Occurred

Sending the support message marks the end of message creation, and you are then notified that the message was created in SAP Solution Manager, along with the message number in the form of a system message.

▶ If you want to create a message outside of SAP Solution Manager, you can generate a URL with Transaction NOTIF_CREATE_BSP and create messages in a browser window. URLs provide the same entry screen as appears in a Business Server Page application. Creation of the message is completed when you save it.

Figure 8.41   The Incident Management Work Center in SAP Solution Manager

▶ A message can be created directly in SAP Solution Manager. This approach is recommended when end users are not authorized to create messages themselves. You may opt for this setup to keep the volume of messages sent to customer support organizations (a CCoE, for example) as low as possible. Rather than creating messages themselves in the event of an error or an information query, end users contact key users who are more knowledgeable and who can answer many questions before the need to create a message arises. For those questions that remain unanswered, key users use the Incident Management work center (Transaction SOLMAN_WORKCENTER • INCIDENT MANAGEMENT • COMMON TASKS • NEW MESSAGE) to create their own support messages in SAP Solution Manager. The technical background information for this creation variant therefore cannot be automatically saved (data can only be acquired from the managed system). Because preliminary clarification is provided by the key user here, however, this information is not essential.

File attachments The Service Desk in SAP Solution Manager allows you to add any file attachments to a support message. Attachments can include screenshots of an entry screen in which an error occurred, presentations, or other documents. If you want to reuse attachments during the processing stage to answer questions, for example, this can be done at any time and as often as desired.

Automatic Distribution to the Support Employees

The support message can now be accessed in your Service Desk. The system automatically assigns it to the correct support level on the basis of the SAP component, priority, and category, and automatically determines the corresponding business partners, such as the customer, reporter, and support team (for instance, the Basis support team for the BC component).

If you have configured SAP Solution Manager to do so, the system determines whether contracts have already been negotiated with the customer on the basis of the system installation number for which the message was created. Such a contract might include a service level agreement (SLA), in which the delivery of services has been agreed upon with the customer within a defined framework. In this case, you can select a specific contract item, such as support, consulting, or development.

Profiles for SLAs Two profiles are available for service level agreements in the Service Desk and can be adapted to meet the customer's needs. These profiles are known as on-call and reaction profiles, and are based on the service agreement. To be able to report on individual regions, it is necessary to define several service agreement products and profiles, whereby messages are also assigned to the relevant service agreements. *Follow-the-sun* support, for example, means you must define the *early support, day support*, and *night support* (8 hours) products and the respective profiles to ensure round-the-clock support.

Displaying and Processing Messages

The Incident Management work center enables you to monitor messages as they appear and are processed. The standard shipment offers filters, for example, FOR PROCESSING BY ME or REPORTED BY ME, but they do not have a delimiting effect in the sense of authorization objects. The filters simply provide a view to facilitate processing. You can define delimiting authorization objects using preconfiguration for service providers (see Section 8.7.6) The organizational model defines responsibilities accountable for queue monitoring.

Notification is another aspect of message processing. Those involved in message processing can be notified by email, fax, or SMS, for example. Messages are determined in background processing with condition checks. For more information, see SAP Note 691303. It is also possible to trigger an SAP workflow via actions using SAP standard functions. The interaction between workflow and approval allows messages to be selectively stopped or sent to SAP.

Notification

Solution Database

A member of the customer's support organization takes on responsibility for processing the support message and searches for a solution to the problem described by the reporter. The customer's own solution database can be used for this (SOLUTION DATABASE tab page).

The solution database is initially empty and is filled with data by the customer's support organization. This database can be used to record known solutions. Searches can also be made across all known problems with corresponding solutions (SAP Notes, for example) and Service Desk documents.

The solution database employs a classification method, but you can also search based on subject, solution type, symptoms, and attributes such as release information. It is currently not possible to search by processor or reporter. When you implement the Service Desk, you can enhance the standard functions to suit your own purposes by making Customizing settings.[17]

Search function

---

17 For detailed information about the solution database, refer to *SAP Solution Manager 4.0 Service Desk – Functionality and Implementation* by Matthias Friedrich and Torsten Sternberg, SAP PRESS, Bonn, 2008.

Searching for Notes on the SAP Service Marketplace

If the problem has not previously occurred and is not documented in the solution database, the Service Desk employee can search for SAP Notes directly from the message. Performing a Notes search via the Service Desk is considerably more effective than a manual search on the SAP Service Marketplace because the search criteria are filled in automatically using data from the support message (see Figure 8.42). To search for an SAP Note, click on the FIND SAP NOTES button on the SAP NOTES tab page.

SAP Note Assistant | Select the appropriate SAP Notes. You can attach the Notes to the support message by clicking the TRANSFER DATA button. SAP Notes with the applicable code corrections can be imported directly into your development or test system and tested using *SAP Note Assistant* (Transaction SNOTE). You transport tested changes into your quality assurance or production system. You can discard unwanted changes using SAP Note Assistant.

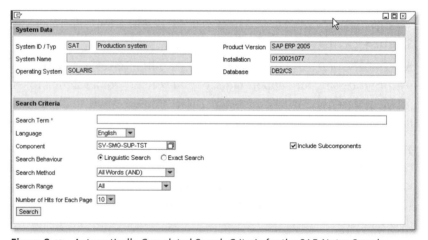

Figure 8.42 Automatically Completed Search Criteria for the SAP Notes Search

Forwarding Messages Internally

If you cannot find a suitable SAP Note on the SAP Service Marketplace, create an internal note in the message describing which measures were taken previously to find a solution and forward the problem message to the downstream support units.

A support message can be processed effectively and promptly on the Forwarding basis of the attributes selected for it. Such messages can also be forwarded manually or automatically in the Service Desk. Every Service Desk employee can forward a message to another business partner (see above) in the standard system. Forwarding can be restricted to certain recipient groups offered by an input help. This restriction is placed using a *Business Application Programming Interface* (BAPI). Forwarding to SAP is controlled by an authorization object.

If a message can only be forwarded after an approval procedure, you can achieve this by setting status values. To do this, set the status of the message to TO BE APPROVED. An employee with the appropriate authorization can authorize forwarding by using APPROVED status. Processor determination rules can be defined for support scenarios such as follow-the-sun or very high processing.

Working with SAP Active Global Support

If the various support levels of the customer support organization cannot solve the problem, you send the support message along with an SAP information note (including attachments, if necessary) to SAP Active Global Support. You can decide which text modules of the message are to be sent to SAP.

As described above, one of the unique features of the Service Desk in Service connection SAP Solution Manager is the option of collaborating with SAP Active Global Support to achieve shorter solution times, as targeted information allows SAP Support to better process your message. *Service connections* are an important part of this collaboration because they give SAP Support the opportunity to access your system from a remote location to understand the nature of the problems occurring in your environment.

Access information is saved in what is known as the *secure area* for secure Secure area support. This area allows only authorized support employees to access your systems, thereby protecting your applications from unauthorized access. Previously, logon data had to be saved apart from the support message on the SAP Service Marketplace.

As of Release 7.0, the Service Desk integrates the secure area into SAP Solution Manager so the logon data for SAP Active Global Support can be saved to the secure area directly from the support message. To do this, choose MAINTAIN SAP LOGON DATA. This action does not involve any change on the part of your support employees. The user interface is the same as the previous one on SAP Service Marketplace; support message integration merely facilitates more efficient handling. Data is still saved in the secure area and protected using the basic, familiar safety concepts.

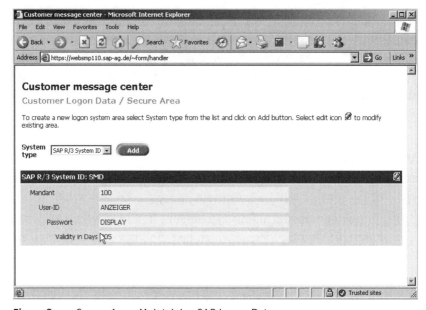

Figure 8.43   Secure Area: Maintaining SAP Logon Data

Working with the secure area
You can display your existing systems and add new systems on the following screen. Select EDIT (Figure 8.43) to call up an existing system and save the logon data or ADD to add a new system. You can include the system, client, user, and password, as well as the amount of access time assigned to the user. Save your entry by clicking SAVE. In the operation data of the support message, you can see that the action has successfully concluded on the ACTIONS tab page (see Figure 8.44).

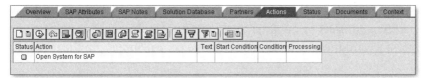

Figure 8.44 Successful "Maintain SAP Logon Data" Action in the Transaction Data of the Support Message

In the support message, you can inform the appropriate support employee that he or she now has access to the systems via the UPDATE SAP MESSAGE action.

Providing and Evaluating the Solution

SAP Active Global Support processes the message and returns it to you along with a proposed solution or a question and an updated status. You can track the status of the message at any time in your Service Desk on the SAP ATTRIBUTES tab page. If a partner's software is affected by the problem, the SAP global support backbone gives the partner access to all of the functions available to SAP Active Global Support, for instance, Root Cause Analysis or the ability to create Notes (see Chapter 11).

The responsible employee in the customer's support organization is informed in the Incident Management work center or by means of email notification that SAP has proposed a solution. The employee tests and evaluates this solution and notifies the reporter of the change of status, at which point the reporter tests the proposed solution and confirms it.

Closing the Message and Transferring the Solution to the Customer-Specific Solution Database

The Service Desk employee closes the message and prepares the solution for the internal solution database to give other support employees access.

8.7.4 Extended Use of the Service Desk (Service Desk XT)

As described in Section 8.7.1, the SAP Solution Manager Service Desk enables user support for your SAP solution landscape and SAP applications. It should be used to handle all SAP-related support queries submitted by end users to the internal support organization. If necessary, you can forward these queries to SAP Active Global Support in the course of message processing.

Service Desk XT is an SAP Solution Manager enhancement subject to a separate charge. It allows support messages that are not related to SAP to be handled using the SAP Solution Manager Service Desk. This enhancement covers service queries concerning IT infrastructure, non-SAP applications, IT hardware, and telecommunications. Service Desk XT therefore makes it possible for you to establish one central, integrated support channel for your entire IT infrastructure. This approach offers the following advantages:

▶ There are no extra hardware costs because you are already using SAP Solution Manager.

▶ You can build on experience gained so far.

▶ Your infrastructure is maintained without any difficulty by your experienced application team.

8.7.5 Integrating Help Desk Systems from Other Providers

Release 7.0 of SAP Solution Manager includes an open interface for exchanging messages with help desk systems from other providers. Customers requested this feature because, in addition to having an existing support infrastructure, they wanted to use the extended options of the Service Desk to provide support for SAP applications.

The purpose of the open interface is to act as a central access point for reporters and support employees. The official interface certified by SAP (see Figure 8.45) is accessible to all SAP partners and can be implemented in their tools. This means you can integrate the SAP Solution Manager Service Desk in your existing help desk systems. Messages are exchanged in SAP Solution Manager with Web services for simple, flexible, and platform-independent operation.

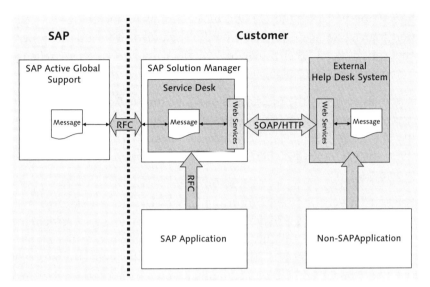

Figure 8.45 Architecture of the Service Desk Interface for External Help Desk Systems

This combined solution offers functions that allow you to fulfill the following tasks:

▶ Improve the quality of information

▶ Increase communication options

▶ Simplify message processing management

You are therefore able to identify and leverage the optimization potential of your existing SAP landscapes and non-SAP applications. Information such as priority, SAP category, and SAP component can also be sent to maximize synergies presented by the *Customer Solution • SAP Solution Manager Service Desk • External Help Desk* value chain. Unique IDs of the support messages from different tools are then taken into account and forwarded as well, because increasingly complex, business-critical SAP environments with additionally integrated non-SAP applications must be managed end-to-end. Monitoring the availability and performance of SAP applications is, in itself, only part of the solution. Non-SAP applications that form part of a business process also need to be monitored. This applies equally to the hardware and software infrastructure on which all of these applications are implemented. The platforms and tools provided by SAP for managing the SAP-specific environment, including SAP Solution Manager and CCMS, can now be expanded to include help desk applications from other providers. You can configure message exchange in the SAP Solution Manager IMG.

Distributing the workload
The architecture of the interface is designed for the Service Desk to process SAP-specific incidents and information queries, whereas the external help desk system handles all messages not affecting SAP applications, such as hardware queries and problems in applications from other providers.

You can forward messages from the Service Desk to an external help desk and vice versa (see Figure 8.46). The system creates a corresponding message that can be uniquely identified and is assigned to the original message in another system. The message can only be processed by one of the other connected help desks. In other words, either the Service Desk or the external help desk assumes the responsibility. Additional information such as message texts can be exchanged asynchronously.

A message can be exchanged several times between the SAP Solution Manager Service Desk and the external help desk application as the message is being processed. It is important to have the responsibilities of the respective help desk system clarified for this purpose. The following is a possible scenario:

Scenario
The external help desk assumes the role of general first-level support, where all messages are entered. Those messages not related to an SAP-specific problem are either resolved or forwarded to second-level support in the external help desk. The SAP Solution Manager Service Desk assumes the role of second-level support for SAP. In the event of an SAP problem, for example, the message is forwarded to the Service Desk used by SAP experts at the customer service organization. Collaboration with SAP Active Global Support is very easy at this point. As already mentioned, messages can also be returned to the external help desk. Communication is possible at any time, and central access ensures that no information is lost, because every processor can read all of the information contained in the message.

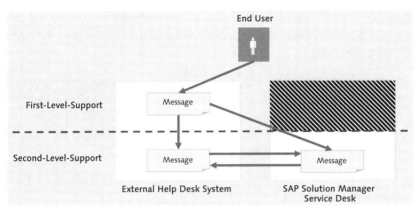

Figure 8.46 Message Processing with Integration between SAP Solution Manager and an External Help Desk

This does not mean that messages cannot be sent directly from the transaction in the SAP system as described in Section 8.7.3. This support channel is still valuable for message processing thanks to the background information it provides. When configuring the interface, you can alternatively specify that when a message is created in SAP Solution Manager, it automatically generates a corresponding message in the external help desk. This message then appears with SENT TO SAP SOLUTION MANAGER status and an overview of all messages can be viewed at any time from the leading help desk.

Overview of all messages

The second alternative is to generate messages only when a message is explicitly sent to the external help desk (*on demand*). Here, it is important to know that messages processed and resolved in the Service Desk will not appear in external help desk reports.

If a message is closed in the help desk responsible, the status of the message is automatically set to COMPLETED in the other help desk. Automatic synchronization also does not occur.

8.7.6 Preconfiguration for Service Providers

Service providers that manage their customers using SAP Solution Manager (an SAP Customer Center of Expertise or CCoE, for example) must place strict demands on a trouble ticket application to ensure optimal customer support at all times. As such, these requirements also became a point of discussion between user groups and SAP Solution Manager Development.

Contents The preconfiguration for service providers function offers the following content in addition to the Service Desk functions already described:

- ▶ Message processing
    - ▶ Automated confirmation of messages
    - ▶ Action log extension
- ▶ Message forwarding
    - ▶ Improved input help in forwarding to other processors
    - ▶ Automatic forwarding of messages with *very high* priority outside of office hours
- ▶ Interfaces between central SAP Solution Manager and multiple connected SAP Solution Manager systems
- ▶ Web-based access to the Service Desk enabling key users to create, change, and track messages
- ▶ Connection of SAP Solution Manager to SAP NetWeaver Business Intelligence to improve reporting options (see Sections 8.9.4 and 8.9.7)

Extending support messages The preconfiguration for service providers function is a support message extension (Transaction SLFN). If you are interested in any part of this preconfiguration, you can activate the respective functions by configuring settings in the SAP Solution Manager IMG.[18]

The preconfiguration for service providers function changes the following parts of the support message:

- ▶ Status profile
- ▶ Roles
- ▶ Text types

---

18 For detailed information about the configuration, refer to *SAP Solution Manager 4.0 Service Desk – Functionality and Implementation* by Matthias Friedrich and Torsten Sternberg, SAP PRESS, Bonn, 2008.

▶ Authorizations

▶ Preconfigured message monitors

The status profile is extended to include a number of statuses required by service providers (such as AUTHOR ACTION status) when a Service Desk employee has a question.

New roles map the additionally required activities. This allows support employees in the support organization of a CCoE, for example, to define their special areas or forward messages to other support employees.

Additional text types that facilitate support processes and increase their transparency are available.

Authorization checks can be made if a Service Desk is used by several support organizations. If more than one support unit is to receive authorization to use the Service Desk (for instance, in a hosting scenario), we recommend that you place message access restrictions in each organization. The B_NOTIF_IB authorization object includes two Business Add-Ins (BAdIs) for this purpose:

▶ CRM_ORDER_AUTH_CHECK (checks for message access and call-up)

▶ CRM_DNO_MONITOR

The B_NOTIF_IB authorization object is part of the SAP Solution Manager standard shipment. It checks the installation number of the managed systems in which the message was created. This allows reporters to view only the messages they created.

B_NOTIF_IB can be used for all messages at the following organizational levels:

▶ Region

▶ Support level

▶ SAP component

You can also use the CRM_TXT_ID authorization object to specify which texts users can change or create.

Refer to SAP Note 920734 for more information on authorization objects.

Preconfigured
message monitors
SAP supplies preconfigured monitors that answer common support questions to help you configure the Service Desk as efficiently as possible. You can access all monitors in the Incident Management work center:

- Reported by me
- For processing by me
- My special areas
- Author action
- Messages at SAP
- Completed today
- My team
- Open messages
- Open messages (priority 1)
- Escalated messages

8.8 End-to-End Root Cause Analysis

Heterogeneous systems and increasingly complex customer solutions require you to take a systematic approach to identify the precise cause of a fault. This standardized process must first broadly identify the components concerned and then analyze them more closely to arrive at the cause of the fault by process of elimination (top-down approach).

If, for example, a user notices a performance problem in a browser-based application, the problem might have to do with the user's PC, the server landscape made up of components based on different technologies, or the network. If the problem concerns the server, it may originate from a Java-based SAP NetWeaver Portal, an ABAP-based SAP ECC backend system connected by remote function call (RFC), or a database that retrieves data from a storage subsystem. A performance problem or functional fault can occur at any time in any of the components used by the end user, from the browser to the storage subsystem.

The aim of end-to-end Root Cause Analysis with Solution Manager Diagnostics is to provide the support organization with tools and methods that reliably identify the affected component while minimizing the time needed to solve the problem.

Solution Manager Diagnostics is part of SAP Solution Manager and constitutes a basis on which standardized support can be provided by SAP, customers, and SAP partners. Root Cause Analysis is composed of the following elements:

Standardized support

▶ A central, comprehensive console for all tools required to perform cross-component and component-specific problem analyses. All of the tools it contains offer a secure way of providing support, because it is not possible to make changes unless they are explicitly requested by the customer. In addition, you can open all tools in the web browser via an HTTP connection, eliminating the need for operating system access.

▶ Standardized, proven procedures for systematically analyzing problems in a top-down process.

▶ An open diagnostics infrastructure (Figure 8.47) with interfaces for different types of data relevant for diagnosing problems (workload, exceptions, technical configuration, traces, changes, client diagnosis). SAP is not only enhancing the SAP technologies supported in the past but continuously integrating components from independent software vendors (ISVs) for which SAP has a maintenance contract with customers (OEM).

The end-to-end Root Cause Analysis tools in SAP Solution Manager do not rely on the SAP system administration tools that were developed to manage and make changes to production landscapes. Changes to the production landscape are managed by the customer and made either centrally in the System Administration work center or locally with the SAP NetWeaver Administrator tool. In other words, you use the Root Cause Analysis tools to analyze problems and plan measures, and then the system administration tools to implement these measures.

No changes to production landscapes

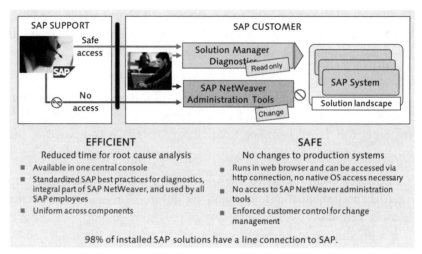

Figure 8.47 Solution Manager Diagnostics: Mode of Operation

With the Root Cause Analysis tools, SAP maps the different roles required to provide second-level support for an IT solution. The SAP NetWeaver Administrator is a tool used to manage daily system operations. Therefore, the Root Cause Analysis tools are used by customers in Customer Centers of Expertise (CCoEs), partners, or SAP, whereas the SAP NetWeaver Administrator is used in outsourcing or customer operations.

8.8.1 Process for Performing Root Cause Analysis in Solution Manager Diagnostics

If the Service Desk is unable to solve a problem that has occurred in the business units, the customer's application management team performs a Root Cause Analysis to isolate the component responsible for the performance problem or functional fault: client, network, different SAP systems (for instance, SAP NetWeaver Portal, SAP CRM, SAP ERP, and so on), database, or storage subsystems.

Cross-Component Root Cause Analysis

Systematic approach — The Root Cause Analysis in SAP Solution Manager helps you identify the component responsible for the fault. This approach helps you systematically determine the cause of the fault without involving countless experts, therefore allowing you to avoid an unfocused approach based purely on intuition.

Component-Specific Root Cause Analysis

Once the application management team has performed the Root Cause Analysis and identified the component responsible for the fault, you can use Incident Management to call on the required experts from development, business process operations, SAP operations, or the IT infrastructure to solve the problem.

SAP Solution Manager supports this component-specific Root Cause Analysis with a range of tools, which can be found in the different systems in the system landscape. The Root Cause Analysis represents a central console that offers all experts involved central access to the tools.

Central access to tools

Analysis Performed by the Software Provider (SAP or SAP Partner)

Even after performing a Root Cause Analysis on a fault, customers are not always in a position to solve the problem straightaway due to a lack of knowledge of the component concerned. In this case, they need to include SAP or the appropriate SAP partner in the analysis. The experts must be able to access the customer's IT landscape to perform the analysis efficiently. The root cause analysis grants SAP and SAP partners access to the required tools, while ensuring that no changes can be made to the customer's production environment. In addition, it also guarantees that the customer, SAP, and the SAP partner use the same tools and therefore also the same data basis to analyze the problem.

The Root Cause Analysis offers the following advantages:

Overview of advantages

▶ **Safeguard availability of critical business processes**
The greatest advantage of the Root Cause Analysis tools is that they speed up the process of solving the problem and therefore ensure higher availability of the critical elements of the customer solution.

▶ **Costs for support experts kept to a minimum**
By taking this standardized, focused approach to analyzing problems, you can identify the experts you need to solve the problem in just one

analysis step. This not only cuts the time required to come up with a solution, but it also minimizes the number of resources involved.

In addition, the method used to gather data across components and technological boundaries greatly reduces the knowledge required to isolate the problem.

▶ **Reduced license costs**
The license to use all tools provided in the Root Cause Analysis and the required third-party tools is included in SAP Solution Manager Enterprise Edition; no further license costs are incurred.

▶ **Necessary Root Cause Analysis tools are shipped as part of the solution**
Because the tools required to perform the Root Cause Analysis are included in the shipment, the customer does not need to invest time in bringing together the right tools. In addition, SAP ensures that all tools are preconfigured before being shipped and the necessary data extractors are provided. This means customers are not required to develop their own tools and infrastructures to analyze problems.

▶ **Data basis for monitoring and IT reporting**
Once the Root Cause Analysis has been implemented, you have the required data basis for the SAP technology and monitoring applications at your fingertips. The integrated SAP NetWeaver Business Intelligence system provides data for IT reporting supported by this data basis.

Work in the operate phase is simplified for you in the long term because you benefit from the newly developed tools. When SAP Active Global Support offers you assistance for problems relating to the Java environment, you do not have to give SAP support employees access to the operating system for them to perform a Root Cause Analysis. In this way, you can maintain the security of your solution and retain full control, and can ensure that any changes made are traceable.

8.8.2 Architecture

Structure of the Root Cause Analysis tools
The Root Cause Analysis in SAP Solution Manager (Figure 8.48) is based on the central diagnosis database, which is filled by diagnosis agents

installed on every managed system. These agents are preconfigured and shipped by SAP. It is their task to gather the data from the connected components that is required to analyze the problem. Data gathered continuously by these agents includes exceptions, for example, critical log entries, dumps, queue errors, configuration snapshots, and workload data relating to the operating system, host, and database of each managed system. This data is gathered in Solution Manager Diagnostics from all technologies and made available to the different tools.

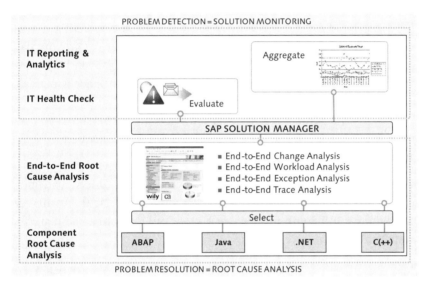

Figure 8.48 Architecture of the Root Cause Analysis

The data gathered is compressed, correlated with landscape data, and presented in aggregated form for extensive IT reporting.

Integrated third-party software

The third-party products used to gather data demonstrate the openness of the Root Cause Analysis as a transparent diagnosis platform for customers. The Root Cause Analysis includes a license for CA Wily Introscope (subsequently referred to as *Introscope*), which enables you to obtain special performance statistics for Java and .NET components without the need to access the application source code. To achieve this, Introscope uses its own byte code instrumentation technology (BCI), which can set and evaluate measuring points during the runtime of applications. The Introscope license included in SAP Solution Manager covers measuring techniques and dashboards, which are preconfigured by SAP before being shipped. On the basis of this technology, it is possible to integrate performance statistics for both ABAP and non-ABAP components in the Root Cause Analysis tools.

In addition to CA Wily Introscope, SAP Solution Manager Enterprise Edition contains a license for BMC Appsight for SAP Client Diagnostics (subsequently referred to as *Appsight*). Appsight is a tool for analyzing problems on users' PCs. It records not only all interactions between the user and the SAP application, but also all calls and actions executed in the background at the level of the application code and operating system. To do so, it uses a patented blackbox technology that records the data on a profile basis in the background. The recorded data can be used to analyze client-specific problems and performance bottlenecks or make cross-client comparisons to identify differences between two users' PCs. For example, by comparing registry entries or driver versions, you can investigate why the performance of one user's PC is adequate whereas another's is not.

Implementation sequence

When you install the Solution Manager Diagnostics tools, you must ensure that the required components are available in the right versions on the SAP Solution Manager system and the connected managed systems:

▶ Solution Manager Diagnostics requires SAP Solution Manager 7.0 as an SAP dual-stack system (SAP NetWeaver AS ABAP and SAP NetWeaver AS Java in an SAP system). SAP recommends that you install it in a Unicode environment (see also *http://service.sap.com/Unicode*). For new SAP Solution Manager installations, you are required to install it as a Unicode system. For customers upgrading from earlier versions to SAP Solution Manager 7.0, SAP recommends migrating from SAP NetWeaver AS ABAP to Unicode. Additionally, minimum versions are required for the SAP Solution Manager kernel and the ST-(A)PI component, as documented in SAP Note 1010428.

▶ Wily Introscope Enterprise Manager must be installed on either the SAP Solution Manager host or a separate host. You can find more information on the SAP Service Marketplace at *http://service.sap.com/diagnostics* • INSTALLATION AND CONFIGURATION • WILY INTROSCOPE INSTALLATION GUIDE.

▶ A diagnosis agent must be installed on every managed system. As of SAP NetWeaver AS 7.0 SR3, the diagnosis agent is installed automatically. The applications running in the diagnosis agent, such as the Wily host application, are used automatically by SAP Solution Manager during configuration. This is enabled by a two-layer agent infrastructure in which the agent consists of a core agent capable of referencing and executing other SAP Solution Manager applications at runtime.

▶ The ports required between SAP Solution Manager and the managed system must be released in the firewall.

Once you have logged on to SAP Solution Manager, you have access to all Root Cause Analysis functions and tools in the Root Cause Analysis work center (see Figure 8.49).

Logging on to SAP Solution Manager

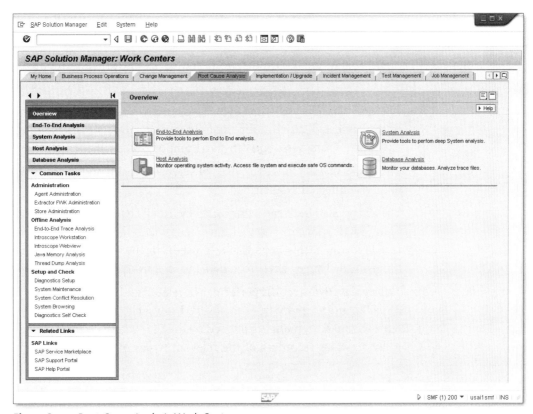

Figure 8.49 Root Cause Analysis Work Center

8.8.3 Tools in the Root Cause Analysis

Views The navigation area in the Root Cause Analysis work center consists of four tool groups that correspond to the top-town approach:

▶ END-TO-END ANALYSIS

▶ SYSTEM ANALYSIS

▶ HOST ANALYSIS

▶ DATABASE ANALYSIS

Each of these four views offers the tools you need to perform further-reaching analyses. When you choose the END-TO-END ANALYSIS view, you have access to freely definable queries that allow you to group the systems according to your needs. In doing so, you can use different filter criteria such as system ID, system type, solution, and so on.

Once you have selected the required systems, you can start the tools contained in the view on your selection.

End-to-end analysis The end-to-end analysis tools are designed to perform the following tasks:

▶ The *exception analysis* allows you to centrally analyze all exceptions from connected systems, for example, serious error messages in logs or dumps. From here, you can start component-specific tools.

▶ The *workload analysis* is composed of server-related workload statistics for the connected systems.

▶ The *change analysis* creates transparency for all changes (technical configuration, code, content) that have been made in the connected system landscape. This is particularly useful in the event of faults that occur once changes have been made to the production landscape.

▶ The *trace analysis* records performance-related and functional faults in a specific user activity from the user's browser to the storage subsystem. The measurement is triggered by the user interface and automatically activates recording of the relevant traces on every component processed by the user query.

System analysis The following tools are among the most important for system analysis:

- *CA Wily Introscope* provides historical and real-time data for analyzing system responses and resource consumption. The dashboards give you a quick status overview. A hierarchical search query in the component-specific dashboards and the detailed analysis in investigator mode provide detailed system-specific and component-specific data for expert analyses.

- The *change reporting tool* allows you to compare configurations from different points in time and thereby identify changes that may cause a fault to occur. It also gives you the option of comparing configurations from different landscapes if problems appear in the production landscape that you are unable to reproduce in the quality assurance landscape.

- The *Java memory analysis* allows you to analyze Java heap dumps so that when storage capacity is completely used up, you can identify which objects require the most storage space.

- The *thread dump analysis* is a tool that enables you to centrally trigger and schedule thread dumps for one particular or all J2EE nodes. You can also analyze thread dumps and the memory-clearing characteristics of your monitored system. The thread dump represents a snapshot of the current status of all Java threads and provides important information enabling you to spot problems such as performance bottlenecks.

The most important host analysis tools are as follows: **Host analysis**

- The *file system browser* gives you secure, central access to files for performing Root Cause Analysis. The restriction to preconfigured paths that lead to files relevant for the Root Cause Analysis ensures that access to business-relevant data is not granted.

- The *OS command console* provides you with central access to the managed system's operating system. This means you can use analysis tools that are specific to the network and operating system. For the sake of security, only read-only commands are permitted.

Finally, there is one other important tool for analyzing the database: **Database analysis**

▶ *Database monitoring* gives you central access to the database analysis and monitoring tools for the databases of all managed systems, regardless of the database manufacturer and version.

Other tools for component-specific root cause analysis are referred to in the sections below.

8.8.4 Root Cause Analysis: The Tools in Detail

End-to-End Exception Analysis

Variety of logs

In a landscape with different components based on different technologies, for instance, the ABAP stack and J2EE stack of an SAP NetWeaver Application Server, the task of analyzing exceptions is becoming increasingly complex. Each of the components writes different log files. A range of tools are needed to access and evaluate the log files. To analyze the actual fault in a business process that makes use of several components, you need to use all of the tools. The end-to-end exception analysis (subsequently referred to as *exception analysis*) offers a central access point to facilitate this task.

Procedures

The exception analysis supports two approaches:

1. An exception trend analysis in which the system is monitored over an extended period. This can be used to clarify, for example, which component in a system is responsible for an unusually high number of errors. You might also use the exception trend analysis to tell whether the number of errors has increased or a particular error has been eradicated after you make a change to a component, perhaps with a patch, a Support Package update, or a configuration change.

2. If you know the exact time at which an error occurred, you can use the exception analysis to identify the component responsible. In this case, it helps to analyze not only the exact time of the error, but also the periods immediately preceding and following the error.

When you start the exception analysis, an overview of all of the systems involved is shown. To the right of the graphic in the overview, the most important key performance indicators (KPIs) for all components are displayed (see Figure 8.50).

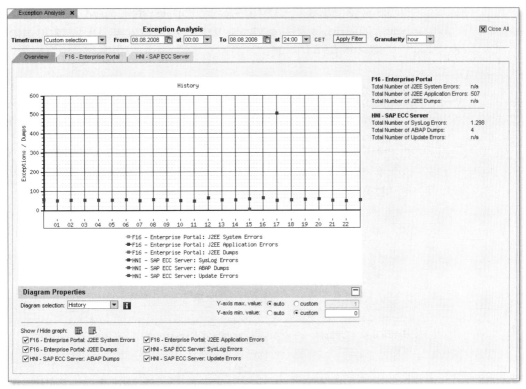

Figure 8.50   Graphical Display in the Exception Analysis

The graphic helps you select the component that you want to examine more closely. A separate tab page containing further details is provided for each component. Figure 8.51 shows an ECC system with the following views: ABAP SysLog Errors, ABAP Dumps, ABAP Update Errors, IDoc Errors, qRFC Inbound Exceptions, and qRFC Outbound Exceptions.

Error Text	Severity	Problem Class	Application Component	Number of errors
Communication error, CPIC return code 020, SAP return cod...	2	SAP Web AS Problem	BC-CST	1.245
Error 000104 : Connection reset by peer in Module rslgsen...	1	SAP Web AS Problem	BC-CCM-MON-SLG	29
Operating system call recv failed (error no. 104)	1	SAP Web AS Problem	BC-CST	8
Communication error, CPIC return code 020, SAP return cod...	2	SAP Web AS Problem	BC-CST	6
Run-time error "CALL_FUNCTION_NOT_FOUND" occurred	1	Transaction Problem	BC-ABA-LA	4
Transaction Canceled 15 100 ( )	1	SAP Web AS Problem	BC-ABA-SC	2
Validity of certificate from list with PSE type »SystemPS...	2	Warning	BC-SEC-SSF	2
Connection to user 15573 (BARTHOLDM), terminal 192 (P124...	1	SAP Web AS Problem	BC-CST	2

Figure 8.51   Detailed View of the Exception Analysis on an ABAP System

Figure 8.52 shows an SAP NetWeaver Portal system based on J2EE technology and the following views: J2EE SYSTEM ERRORS, J2EE APPLICATION ERRORS, and J2EE DUMPS.

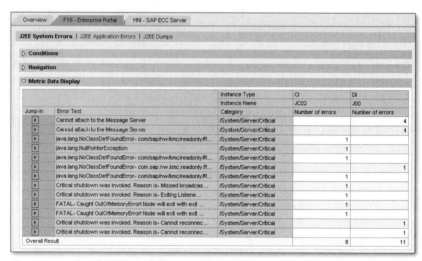

Figure 8.52 Detailed View of the Exception Analysis on an SAP NetWeaver Portal System

Hierarchical search query

Each view contains a table of the most important information on the selected error category. You can show additional table fields with a hierarchical search query. When you click the marker shown, a new window opens with further analysis options. For ABAP system log errors, you are taken directly to Transaction SM21 in the managed system, and the selected exception is shown for analysis.

Ideally, the exception analysis leads you to the point where you can trace an error in the system back to one component and one exception. If you want to analyze the exception in detail, component-specific tools are essential.

End-to-End Workload Analysis

Component-independent workload information

The end-to-end workload analysis (subsequently referred to as *workload analysis*) provides all workload information independently of components, enabling you to analyze general performance bottlenecks in complex landscapes. Different monitors and tools deliver all important KPIs for the different components. Initially, in most cases, the response times of all systems are verified.

For this purpose, the workload analysis offers an overview of all selected systems.

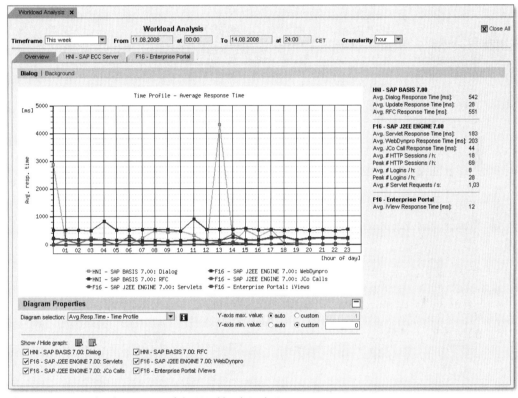

Figure 8.53 Graphical Overview of the Workload Analysis

The graphical view shown in Figure 8.53 maps the time profile of a given period. On the Y axis, the average response times are related to the respective hour on the X axis. This type of display enables you to identify peak workload times that usually occur during end users' typical working times. To analyze a performance problem in greater depth, you have to take into account not only the average but also the accumulated response time.

Accumulated
response time

To do so, you switch the view to Portfolio in the diagram selection. The graphic then shows the average response time on the Y axis. The size of the circle reflects the accumulated response time. Critical situations are represented by large, ascending circles (see Figure 8.54).

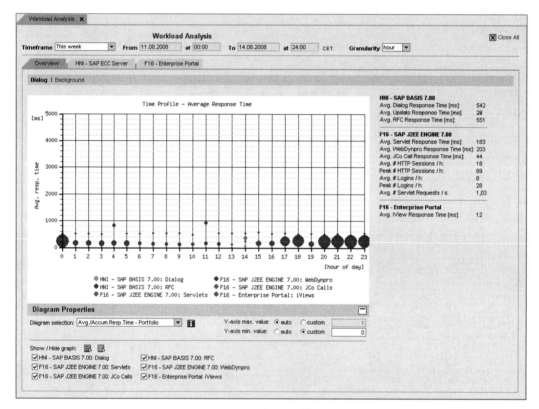

Figure 8.54 Portfolio View of the Workload Analysis

In addition to the overview displayed, analysis tab pages are provided for all connected systems showing application-specific workload data. Figure 8.55 shows the detailed data for an ECC system based on ABAP.

Overview   HNI - SAP ECC Server   F16 - Enterprise Portal

ABAP Basis   RFC   Host

Workload Summary | Top Dialog | Top Update | Top Batch | Top HTTP | User Load | ICM Load | Work Process Load | GW RegisteredTP

▷ **Conditions**

▷ **Navigation**

▽ **Metric Data Display**

Task Type	Tot. Resp. Time (s)	Avg. Resp. Time (ms)	Avg. CPU Time (ms)	Avg. DB Time (ms)	Avg. Wait Time (ms)	Avg. Roll Wait Time (ms)	# Dialog Steps
Overall Result	128.850	597	54	126	0	267	215.742
AutoABAP	1.146	1.165	894	69	0	0	984
AutoTH	9	9	1	0	8	0	1.005
Batch	42.531	884	61	480	0	0	48.106
DELAY	9	2	0	0	1	0	4.932
Dialog	1.152	542	101	205	1	157	2.124
HTTP	75	60	40	18	0	0	1.250
RFC	83.374	551	48	22	0	378	151.427
RPC	513	622	422	188	0	0	824
Spool	35	7	2	1	1	0	4.920
Update	5	28	9	7	1	0	168
Update2	2	861	45	792	1	0	2

Figure 8.55   Detailed Data for an ECC System

End-to-End Change Analysis

The parameters you can analyze with the end-to-end change analysis (subsequently referred to as *change analysis*) include:

▶ OS parameters

▶ DB parameters

▶ ABAP parameters

▶ Java parameters

▶ Transport requests

▶ Support Packages

The change analysis is the central access point to start a Root Cause Analysis. Arranged by system, category, and change date, it gives you access to all changes in a system landscape. You can establish here whether a given error has occurred due to changes to a connected system and which changes have been made. The change analysis provides an overview of the total number of changes to the managed systems in the landscape. The changes are grouped according to main instances. Figure 8.56, for example, depicts a solution with the main instances SAP CRM server and SAP ECC server.

Central access to Root Cause Analysis

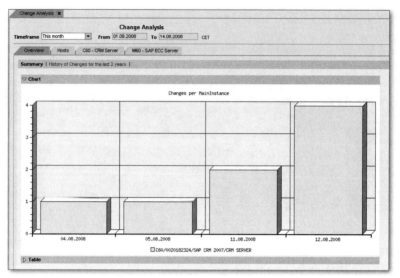

Figure 8.56 Change Analysis Overview

By selecting the system details, you can analyze changes per category in a selected period.

Figure 8.57 shows changes to the SAP CRM server grouped by days. The legend below the graphic reveals the types of changes that have been made. A further hierarchical search query in the respective category shows the actual details of the change.

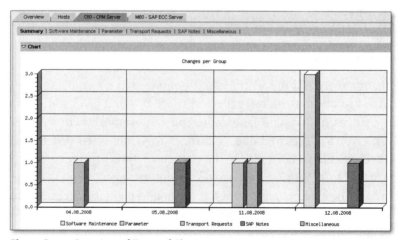

Figure 8.57 Overview of Types of Changes

End-to-End Trace Analysis

End-to-end trace analysis (subsequently referred to as *trace analysis*) is used mainly to identify why certain user requests take so long in complex landscapes. You can use it to isolate a single user action and identify the component causing the problem. It records the response times of the components involved in the request and the path the request takes and makes this data available for detailed analysis.

The trace analysis is split into two phases. In the first phase, the trace is performed and recorded. In the second phase, the recorded traces are then evaluated. Before you start recording, you must ensure that you are able to reproduce the problem.

Trace analysis phases

To record a new trace on web applications, a plug-in must be added to the end user's browser. Its purpose is to instrument the browser's queries so that the components used to execute them can activate particular trace functions.

In the final quarter of 2008, the SAP Solution Manager trace functions are expected to become available for the SAP GUI also. To record a trace, you have to start Report /SDF/E2E_TRACE before you start the actual program. You then trigger the transaction using this report (see Figure 8.58).

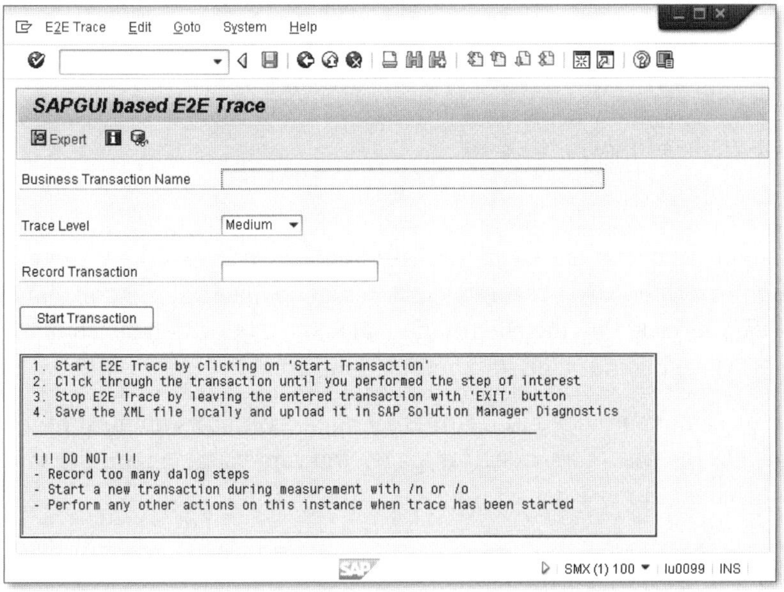

Figure 8.58 Trace Analysis for the SAP GUI (Planned for Final Quarter of 2008)

Once you have successfully performed the trace and uploaded it to SAP Solution Manager, you can use it for further analysis. Figure 8.59 shows an overview of the detailed information about the recorded trace.

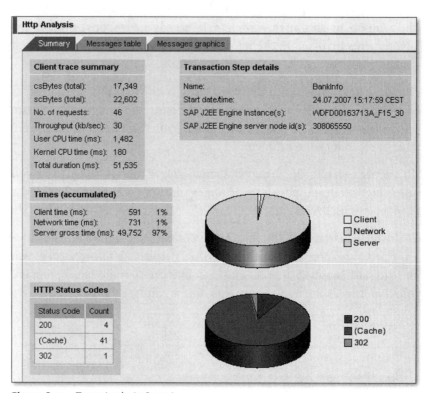

Figure 8.59 Trace Analysis Overview

Analysis   The data shown under TIMES (ACCUMULATED) lets you quickly identify the component that has taken the most time (client, network, or server). In addition, the CLIENT TRACE SUMMARY area provides information about the data recorded by the client. The HTTP STATUS CODES table contains the HTTP status codes for all requests in the trace.

In the example provided in Figure 8.59, the server takes up most of the time. On the MESSAGES TABLE tab page, you can examine requests sent by the client in more detail.

In the REQUESTS TREE view (see Figure 8.60), you can trace the request through all components involved and, after identifying the problematic components, navigate to the respective analysis tools. In the selected example, the HRXSS_PER_INIT_PERNR function module is the cause of the lengthy response time.

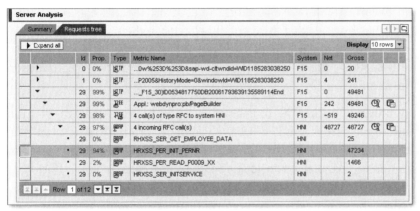

Figure 8.60 Requests Tree Display

8.8.5 Quality Assurance with the Root Cause Analysis Tools

The methods and tools for the Root Cause Analysis can be used not only reactively in the Problem and Incident Management process, but also in the quality management process. The aim of a quality process supported by analysis is to implement changes discretely in the production for the business unit. It should be possible to implement changes without affecting ongoing business. This goal should be achievable with a reasonable level of testing effort.

As part of the stabilization activities undertaken in the test phase of a project, the quality manager needs ways to monitor development activities at the customer's location, particularly a development stop or *code freeze*. In this phase, no changes may be imported to the quality assurance system unless they have been agreed upon by the quality manager. The change analysis enables the quality manager to check the entire customer solution for uncontrolled imports to establish if the code freeze has been flouted.

Code freeze

Critical process
steps

After you have performed functional quality assurance, SAP recommends that you trace the critical core business process steps, such as creating a sales order, in single user mode. This helps you detect problems with performance, data consistency, and technical correctness before they occur in the load test or production operations. By analyzing the end-to-end trace effectively, you can anticipate performance problems that will occur during multiuser operations. You can also identify data consistency problems by analyzing the commit behavior in the trace (SQL behavior) and technical exceptions that are not visible on the interface but nevertheless have the potential to cause significant problems in production operations.

Fewer load tests

By precisely tracing the program flow with the trace analysis, you can reduce the need for and effort involved in performing load tests and significantly improve the continuity of the business processes after changes. Simulating parallelism in load tests requires considerable effort with regard to script management and providing test data. Each time you reduce the effort needed to perform load tests, you make a major contribution to lowering total cost of ownership (TCO). The load test itself can be efficiently monitored and statistically analyzed with the workload and exception analyses. Rather than logging on to the individual systems manually, you can monitor and analyze the load test centrally in SAP Solution Manager.

Integration
validation

The process associated with the functional integration test for systematically analyzing performance, data consistency, and technical correctness is referred to by SAP as *integration validation*. In this process, SAP is enhancing traditional quality management with best practices and the validation of integrated, cross-technology, cross-component solutions — something that must be given special attention in distributed, heterogeneous landscapes.

8.9   Solution Reporting

Link to IT service
management

Solution Reporting enhances the existing tools in SAP Solution Manager for Service and Application Management and is an important link in ITIL-compliant IT Service Management. It is especially used for Service Level Management to monitor service level agreements. Solution Reporting can also be very helpful in Problem Management when, for example, an overview of the current Support Package status or changes to system parameters is required.

With SAP Solution Manager Enterprise Edition, relevant reporting options are provided for each individual work center. Not a single work center is dedicated solely to reporting. Most work centers contain a REPORTS view, in which not only reporting tools, but also documents you have created, are usually stored. The difference between this and Solution Reporting in Transaction SOLUTION_MANAGER is the option to perform cross-solution reporting. The solutions available for reporting depend on various factors, including the authorizations assigned to the user. Additionally, the *Business Process Operations* area, for example, allows you to include links to your own dashboards in an analysis list so you can gain fast access to information for a particular period or key performance indicator. A further benefit of using your own dashboards is that they can also be used in other applications (for example, SAP NetWeaver Portal) and adapted to include your own company logo.

You can access Solution Reporting for an individual solution in Transaction SOLUTION_MANAGER under OPERATIONS • SOLUTION REPORTING. Reporting tools are available for the following areas:

Reporting areas

- ▶ Services
- ▶ Administration
- ▶ Service Desk
- ▶ Change Management
- ▶ Issues and Top Issues
- ▶ Expertise on Demand
- ▶ SAP NetWeaver Business Intelligence (BI): Gathering data for SAP-EarlyWatch Alert data

Figure 8.61 gives an overview of the reporting structure in SAP Solution Manager. Each area design is very similar with respect to layout and functionality. On the selection screen, you can make different selections with respect to time periods, specific parameters, and systems to be analyzed and save this information as a variant. The results are displayed as a list in the *ABAP List Viewer* (ALV), and the same layout is used for all

Reporting structure

tools. The *comma-separated value* (CSV) files created with the tools can be opened in Microsoft Excel or another spreadsheet program at any time. Due to the generic output of numeric values, however, it is necessary to separate these values from each other using a semicolon (;), thereby deviating from CSV format. Otherwise, having many numeric values including a comma (,) in place of a decimal point (.) could lead to display problems. You should therefore check your spreadsheet's settings before opening such documents to ensure that columns separated by a semicolon are correctly displayed. If you do not do this, a comma used in place of a decimal point could be interpreted as a column separator and distort the display of data.

Additional functions
You can use additional functions for managing documents in every reporting area. For example, you can upload your own documents, which can be subsequently edited and updated. This function is displayed by an additional icon next to the activities. You can also archive documents. The archival process is the same as for archiving service documents and can be configured according to SAP Note 546685. The ARCHIVE button is displayed above the document list when configuration is complete.

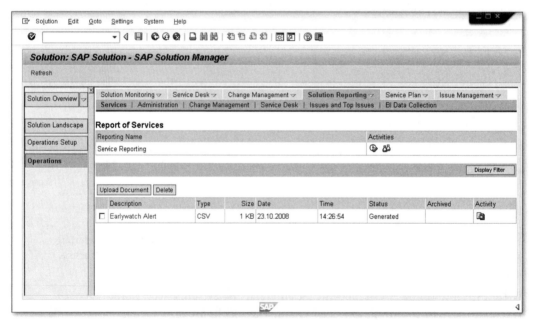

Figure 8.61 Solution Reporting in SAP Solution Manager – Overview

To ensure that the number of current documents remains neatly arranged, simply click the column headings to sort the documents. Sorting automatically occurs by date (default setting) so that the most recently created documents always appear at the top of the list. You can also use filters to generate views by file type, description, date, or status, for example. This reduces the size of the output list and makes it easier to read. If no filters are used or a standard filter has already been set, you can further minimize the filter area to make more room for displaying the documents on screen. These settings are user specific and are saved as such. In other words, the settings are applied the next time Transaction SOLUTION_MANAGER is called up.

Sorting and filters

When you use one of the report variants defined for a solution, you can start jobs periodically in the background that create reporting documents at regular intervals and automatically save these reports in the corresponding area (such as Services, Administration, Service Desk, and so on) in SAP Solution Manager. The report for reporting tool planning indicates the name of the solution and the settings for reporting and job scheduling below. An input help displays every variant of this solution that can be selected for the report. The default prefix for all jobs is \SM_REP:\. The name of the report follows, and below it is information about the previous, most recent report run along with the following status:

Scheduling reporting as a job

▶ Yellow icon: No scheduling as of yet

▶ Green icon: Scheduled job successfully completed

▶ Red icon: Job processing canceled

Clicking the SCHEDULING and DISPLAY buttons takes you to the job management section (Transactions SM36 and SM37), in which the information you specified on the initial screen of the scheduling tool is already filled in.

To ensure that the analysis functions cannot be accessed to the same extent by all users, authorization object D_SOL_REP in role SAP_SV_SOLUTION_MANAGER can be used to assign activities to individual users. These activities include:

Authorizations

▶ Display results

▶ Start reporting tool

▶ Reporting: Define selection variants

▶ Delete documents

Selection variants allow you to define selection parameters in service reporting, for example. More information on selection variants can be found in the following section.

Browser-based reporting

Every function described in this section can be used for Transaction SOLUTION_MANAGER_BSP. This allows you to work independently of the SAP GUI in a browser, such as Internet Explorer. Result lists and selection variant definitions via an ABAP List Viewer (ALV) Grid are also supported by browsers.

With SAP Solution Manager Enterprise Edition, the reporting tools are provided in a number of work centers. Most Solution Reporting functions are contained in the SAP Engagement and Service Delivery work center. Figure 8.62 shows a list of the tools that exist for each solution.

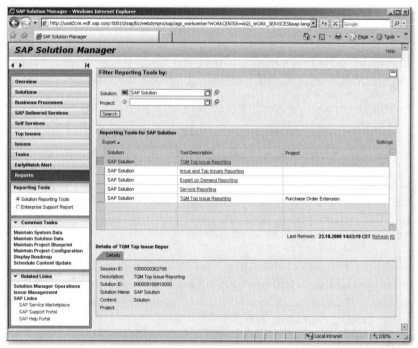

Figure 8.62 Service Reporting

8.9.1 Service Reporting

Service Reporting was developed especially for the SAP EarlyWatch Alert service, because the latter includes a wealth of data not found in the SAP EarlyWatch Alert report but in the session, which can be opened in display mode after the report has expired. The focus of analysis is on meeting special requirements with respect to system settings and system or profile parameters, as well as key server, database, and application figures.

SAP services form the general basis for Service Reporting, whereby only the SAP EarlyWatch Alert and Service Level Reporting services will be regularly scheduled for a solution. In addition, you can include information about the product, database, and installed components in your reporting from the Solution Manager System Landscape transaction (SMSY). You can also add system attributes to your reporting that are predefined (a support package stack, for example) or that you individually define in Transaction SMSY, such as the location or contact for a system. A detailed input help assists you in integrating these parameters.

Figure 8.63 shows the initial screen in Service Reporting. Below the solution, the SAP EarlyWatch Alert service is set by default. You can now analyze all systems or selected systems of a solution. When defining the analysis period, you can select the current week, last week, or any period; however, only the current service for the selected period will be considered. The checkboxes for the basic data (data source: SMSY) and the service data are set, but you can deactivate them, for example, if you are not interested in the basic data.

Any information from the tables of the individual SAP services can be included in reporting within the service data. The SAP EarlyWatch Alert service encompasses a standard variant for which a number of checks have already been completed and can be activated for reporting. To do so, select the checkbox in the ACTIVE column. Once you have configured all settings, you can save this configuration as a selection variant, which will then be available as a selection parameter variant on the initial input help screen. This is important, because variants can be saved to the initial Service Reporting screen for scheduling and starting jobs. Therefore,

SAP EarlyWatch
Alert

Service Reporting includes not only standard report variants, but also selection variants for use in controlling output.

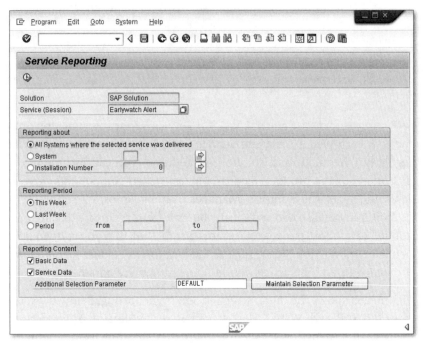

Figure 8.63   Service Reporting – Initial Screen

Including data   To include data in reporting that is not part of the delivered section variant, you need to open a service (SAP EarlyWatch Alert, for example) in display mode. A list of checks is created in the Service Session Workbench. In this tree structure, you can navigate to checks whose content you want to include in reporting. The menu path GOTO • TECHNICAL INFORMATION provides you with check information, such as the check group, check ID, and context (SESSION, SERVER, INSTANCE, or DATABASE, for example). This information is required to define the reporting content. You enter this data in the ALV list (see Figure 8.64). Typically, you do not need to complete the context instance unless you are dealing with a large system with several instances or servers, and only the data from a specific server or instance is included in reporting. If the CONTEXT INSTANCE column is empty, the content of all instances or servers is automatically included in reporting.

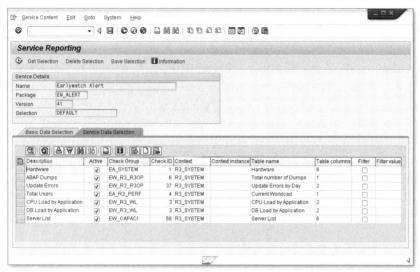

Figure 8.64 Service Reporting – Adding Service Checks

You can define the table content to be included in reporting in the TABLE
NAME and TABLE COLUMNS columns. The input helps you make a selection, especially for table columns whose names are listed next to the
ACTIVE checkbox. Only the number of table columns selected (six in the
last line of Figure 8.64, for example) are then added to the display. At
the end of the list are two additional columns with a checkbox for the
filter and an input field for the filter value. In these columns, you can
select the lines of a service table to include specific information in the
report. The main area of application is filter values for profile parameters
or OS parameters. The settings for the same check can be copied with
another description several times, whereby different entries can only be
included in reporting via the filter value. Once you have assembled the
data, the selection can be saved. You can make your output selection on
the initial screen.

8.9.2 Administration Reporting

Administration Reporting was developed for system administrators to
provide an overview of the tasks to be completed or monitored as part
of central system administration (see Section 8.1.1) in SAP Solution Manager and to provide a general overview of all systems for a solution.

Administration Reporting is an easy tool to use not only for setting the systems to be analyzed (as with Service Reporting) and for defining the analysis period, but also for adding tasks from central system administration to the analysis either with or without a comment. These tasks are defined in central system administration and must be completed on an hourly, daily, weekly, or monthly basis with respect to their set frequency. No overview is provided for tasks that have not been completed. Administration Reporting refers only to entries that have been added to central system administration, including for the generation of HTML or Microsoft Word reports. The checkbox for updating system management tasks should be set to update the report with the latest status. Figure 8.65 shows the selection screen for Administration Reporting.

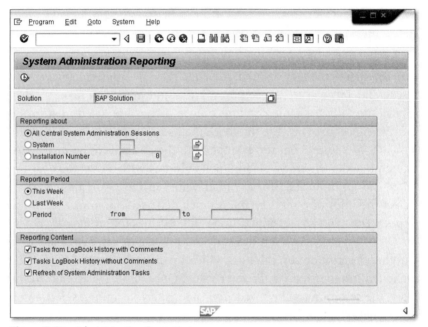

Figure 8.65 Administration Reporting

8.9.3 Change Management Reporting

Change Request Management is a central component of SAP Solution Manager. *Change Management Reporting* allows you to trace activities in the system landscapes managed by Change Request Management and perform detailed monitoring of these activities in the system. Change transactions are managed via SAP Solution Manager projects and service processes. Every change to a transportable object can be uniquely identified with a service process. Maintenance and development, as well as the supply of SAP Notes and support packages, can be mapped via Change Request Management (see also Section 9.1). Change transactions affect business processes, the controlled activity of which is made transparent by Change Management Reporting.

As is the case with all reporting tools, Change Management Reporting is accessed from a selection screen. This is shown in Figure 8.66. You can enter data in the following areas:

Accessing Change Management Reporting

▶ Transaction data

▶ Organizational units

▶ Project header

▶ System data

▶ Maintenance units

▶ Transport requests

▶ Transport objects

In the upper area of the selection screen, you can limit output to a specific number of entries. After you have selected which service processes you want to analyze, you can choose the selection list version next to the DISPLAY field. Several views are available, from the single document header display, to display of the project, transport, and transport object data.

The TOPICALITY OF THE DATA is shown in addition to the individual input areas listed above. Reporting data from all connected systems is updated on a regular basis, with the last successful update displayed along with the date and time. Systems whose data could not be updated are listed as deviating systems on the selection screen. The reporting data for these deviating systems can be updated manually at any time by clicking the corresponding button.

Updating data

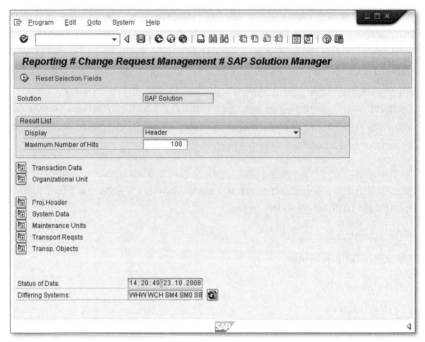

Figure 8.66 Change Management Reporting

Transaction types

Service transaction types that enjoy especially frequent use are *change requests* (SDCR), *urgent corrections* (SDHF), *Service Desk messages* (SLFN), *issues* (SLFI), *Top Issues* (SLFT), and *expert on demand requests* (SLFE). Other transaction types also exist, but they have no or almost no relevance here. Many additional fields — including POSTING DATE, DESCRIPTION, and LAST CHANGED BY — allow for even greater restriction and are also of interest when searching for specific change requests.

Organizational units

Under ORGANIZATIONAL UNIT, you can select the service and sales organizations set in SAP Solution Manager. The service organizations typically have first- or second-level support (see Section 8.7), and reporting is practical for both areas from a management point of view. Details of the reference object, such as *product* and *installation*, can also be selected. You can also enter the product name directly. When you want to restrict reporting to special measures or activities, you can complete the CATALOG, CODE GROUP, CODE, and EXTERNAL CODE fields in the CODE area.

You can limit the results list to typical project header data (PROJ.HEADER; see Figure 8.66) within the project data. Examples include the PROJECT ID, the PROJECT TYPE, and LOGICAL COMPONENT. You can also use the TRANSPORT TRACK to restrict an IMG PROJECT or CTS PROJECT. For more information about project data, see Section 5.2. The project status can also be selected with checkboxes in addition to the time stamp of a project, which generally has a creation date and an end date. You can set different statuses or select a self-defined status using the input help next to the OTHER STATUS field.

The SYSTEM DATA includes the LOGICAL SYSTEM (see also Section 5.2.5) and the SYSTEM ROLE (production system, for example). Selections can also be made regarding the system components and the kernel version.

Examples of maintenance units include SUPPORT PACKAGE STACKS, SUPPORT PACKAGES, and SAP NOTES. You can make settings here as well, not only for restricting the results list, but also for locating specific change documents. You can display all maintenance units in a system or all systems with a specific maintenance unit.

Specific transport orders can be entered under TRANSPORT REQSTS. Among the input fields is the transport order itself, as well as the order type, order category, owner, goal, and change date of the transport order. For each transport order, you display the respective export system and the systems in which the order was successfully imported. Checkboxes are used to select the status.

Within the TRANSP. OBJECTS, you can make restrictions according to objects or development classes. Change Management Reporting supports all ABAP object types, including DDIC, repository, and Customizing objects. For a table entry, you can select and display all transport orders and service processes that were used to approve, carry out, and transport the change. For subobjects such as a method, Change Management Reporting also selects all processes that include the main object (for example, the class belonging to the method). Similarly, when you specify a function group, all processes that were involved exclusively in transporting subobjects of the function group (function modules, for example) are selected.

Project data

System data

Maintenance units

Transport requests

Transport objects

8.9.4 Service Desk Reporting

Service Desk Reporting (Figure 8.67) allows you to perform various analyses using Service Desk messages. Here, the solution reference is especially important, because only in this case can the full functionality for saving documents be accessed for regularly scheduled reports.

When performing a standard analysis, you can use the selection parameters described below to limit a hit list of Service Desk messages. Each line represents a message and can be called up by double-clicking it.

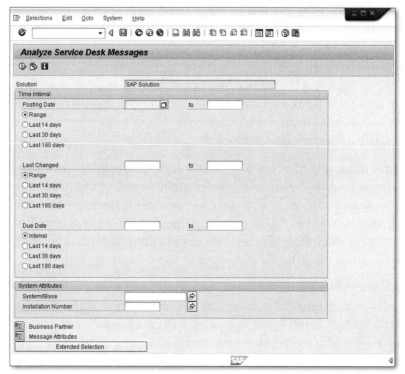

Figure 8.67 Service Desk Reporting

Extended analysis   In extended analysis (EXTENDED SELECTION button), one of three analysis types can be selected:

▶ **Business Partner**
Business partners must be assigned accordingly to carry out a business partner analysis.

▶ **Status Analysis**
A status analysis is probably the most commonly used analysis type, because all status messages over a specific period are included in the report (all solved messages, for example).

▶ **Solution Information**
You select a solution information analysis when you want to perform an analysis on messages that pertain to a solution in SAP Solution Manager.

Different approaches can be selected for the TIME INTERVAL. Here, you can make a selection based on the creation date, the date of the last change, or the due date. In addition to selecting a specific time interval, you can make settings to select messages from the past 14, 30, or 180 days.

Time interval

You set SYSTEM ATTRIBUTES when you want to make a selection based on particular systems. Note that you select the system ID, installation number, and client in the input help, while an IBase component corresponding to your selection is shown on the entry screen itself. If you do not select any attributes, the report is created using all IBase components.

In the BUSINESS PARTNER subarea, you can analyze the business partners assigned to the user or analyze a corresponding substitute. To do this, you must specify the partner number or partner function, both of which are defined in SAP Solution Manager. A multiple selection option is provided for this purpose. You can make restrictions according to reporting and processing user groups.

Business partner

MESSAGE ATTRIBUTES are divided into two areas. In the first area, you can configure basic settings such as priority, SAP component, category, and user status. Here, an input help with multiple selection options is available for all input fields. The second area allows you to make restrictions according to subject, catalog, code group, and code.

GROUPING is the most important area in extended analysis. By setting the attributes (time periods and checkboxes), you can control the output fields of the report. The posting date, monthly message total, and user status are selected by default. The result is a list of the messages that correspond to these settings. This list can be saved as a file in SAP Solution

Grouping

Manager or opened in a spreadsheet using the standard ALV list functions and saved locally.

8.9.5 Issue and Top Issue Reporting

In SAP Solution Manager Enterprise Edition, the most important reporting options for issues and Top Issues can be found in the SAP Engagement and Service Delivery work center. Here, the REPORTS view contains reporting services with their documents for the technical quality manager (TQM).

TQM Top Issue Reporting is structured like a Service Session in which a report can be generated in Microsoft Word format at the end. This report is saved in the attachments for the session. You can call it up any time and save it locally.

Issue and Top Issue Reporting are of special interest when it comes to reporting open and resolved issues within a specific time period. Analysis is first performed according to the transaction type. You can select either Top Issue or issue. Unlike Service Desk messages, in this case there is no time interval selection. Instead, a multiple selection option allows you to select your own time intervals for the creation date, the date of the last change, and the due date. Only the preconfigured system status values can be used for the status. As such, you can select the following status values:

▶ Open

▶ In Process

▶ Draft

▶ Completed

You can also make a multiple selection here in which you can restrict the process attributes according to any name.

Follow-up transactions

Follow-up transactions including tasks, Service Desk messages, Expert on Demand queries, change requests, and issues can be allocated from issues and Top Issues. In reporting, you can also incorporate these transactions into issue and Top Issue analysis. The transaction type (issue or Top Issue) determines which follow-up transactions are available for analysis. For more information, refer to Section 8.4.

Follow the menu path OPERATIONS • SOLUTION REPORTING • ISSUES AND TOP ISSUES in Transaction SOLUTION_MANAGER to create simple statistical analyses of issue and Top Issue reporting.

For a more detailed analysis of your Top Issues, follow the menu path OPERATIONS • CONTINUOUS IMPROVEMENT • TOP ISSUE REPORTS.

You can summarize an issue in printable PDF format (useful for meetings, for example) by going to Transaction SOLUTION_MANAGER OPERATIONS • CONTINUOUS IMPROVEMENT • ISSUES, and then opening an issue and clicking the SUMMARY button.

Summarizing an issue

8.9.6 Expert on Demand Reporting

Expert on Demand Reporting is especially of interest to customers who use the Expert on Demand service and want to monitor their quotas (see also Section 8.4.3). In SAP Solution Manager Enterprise Edition, this reporting option can be found in the REPORTS view in the SAP Engagement and Service Delivery work center. This kind of reporting option is provided for each solution.

The analysis is based on the time interval (creation date, change date, and due date) as well as on process attributes. Here, you can preassign the status, name, subject, transaction number, priority, and user who created the message. Input helps can be used for all of these fields except the name field. The result also includes the time expenditure, which must be entered for every Expert on Demand process.

Time interval and process attributes

8.9.7 Reporting with SAP NetWeaver Business Intelligence

The main advantage of the SAP NetWeaver Business Intelligence (BI) connection in SAP Solution Manager is that important key figures from operational systems can be accessed in a form suitable for detailed analysis. Of special interest here are time series analyses over an extended period of time. Another important argument for using

SAP NetWeaver BI is the ability to expand on a consistent dataset that is built through ongoing reporting. SAP NetWeaver BI offers other options for summarizing and preparing data in addition to flexibility. The SAP EarlyWatch Alert service constitutes the data basis for these reporting activities.

In SAP Solution Manager Enterprise Edition, you have extra reporting options at your disposal when you use the root cause analysis processes in Solution Manager Diagnostics. These processes enable a better breakdown of data to be loaded more flexibly to SAP NetWeaver BI. The SAP NetWeaver BI connection for SAP EarlyWatch Alert data, however, is still valuable as an overview.

Data collector

The data collector for BI Reporting presented here was developed to provide data from SAP EarlyWatch Alert and the Solution Manager System Landscape transaction (SMSY) for BI extraction. This data is selected in close cooperation with the German-Speaking SAP User Group (DSAG). The main focus of the specification here was on monitoring key performance indicators (KPIs) such as database growth and the average response times of the most important transactions, as well as installed SAP Notes and system or profile parameter settings. Service Level Management, in particular, can benefit from this data, which can be used to create Service Level Management reports.

Figure 8.68 shows the initial screen of the data collection tool.

Report

The data collection report is structured just like the other reporting tools and can be scheduled to be included in a batch job using a variant. It is important that only the last successfully completed SAP EarlyWatch Alert service be considered with respect to the period selected for the systems. This is how Service Reporting works. We recommend that you select the period in which reporting is scheduled a week after the SAP EarlyWatch Alert service has been successfully processed. In the settings for the BI data collection tool, you can delete data in the transfer table and display documentation on the success of the extraction by selecting the appropriate checkboxes. No checkboxes are selected in the standard configuration.

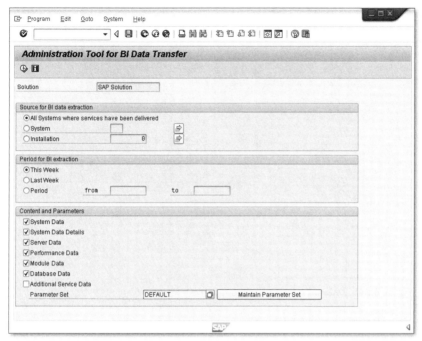

Figure 8.68 Initial Screen for BI Data Transfer

Initially, you should select the checkbox for documenting the content of the transfer table to document extraction to the transfer tables and to log whether the report is scheduled to be included in a batch job.

Upon successful completion, you should also select the checkbox to delete the existing data in the BI transfer tables to reduce the data quantity. If you do not delete this data, the transfer tables will grow much faster than they need to, and the data that has already been included in SAP NetWeaver BI will be transferred again. Because no aggregation occurs for any of the characteristics and key figures (only the last value is added), the value first transferred is retained for future transfer. If, however, an SAP EarlyWatch Alert is performed another time using different download data (typical for postprocessing), this data enters the BI system. If you have several solutions, we recommend that you schedule only the first batch job with the indicator to delete the transfer table.

Deleting transfer data

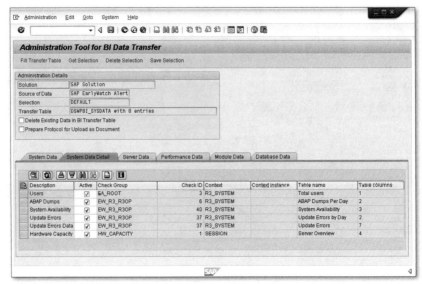

Figure 8.69 BI Data Collection – Settings

The content or parameters for data collection are defined (see Figure 8.69). All checkboxes in the ACTIVE column are selected. Parameters or settings that are not relevant for you do not need to be completed.

Arrangement of data collection

The subject areas are arranged on the following tabs:

▶ **System Data**
Product, database, components, and system attributes

▶ **System Data Detail**
System user(s), ABAP dumps, system availability, update errors, update error details, hardware configuration

▶ **Server Data**
Server list, CPU, memory utilization, paging, R/3 profile parameters, operating system parameters

▶ **Performance Data**
Logged on users by activity, selected ST03N statistics

▶ **Module Data**
CPU, DB, and application module load

▶ **Database Data**
Missing index, database size, available memory, additional information (as a function of the database)

▶ **Additional service data**
Ready-to-enter list as found in Service Reporting

All areas are preconfigured with the exception of additional service data. All you can change is the data that you do not want to extract. SAP recommends that you deactivate all parameters that your solution does not provide any data on for database extraction. For example, in a 100% Microsoft SQL Server environment, no Oracle parameters would be found, and vice versa. Seven databases are supported (Microsoft SQL Server, Oracle, MaxDB [previously Adabas], DB2, DB390, DB400, and Informix).

By selecting the bottom-most checkbox on the initial screen in the CONTENT AND PARAMETERS area, you can display an additional tab (ADDITIONAL SERVICE DATA) when displaying the parameter set. Here, you can include individual checks as in Service Reporting, and their data is imported into a transparent transfer table. To enable analysis in SAP NetWeaver BI, you need to create the InfoObjects (characteristics and key figures), transfer rules, update rules, and the InfoCube. In the process, it is critical that the sequence of entered checks cannot be subsequently changed. The fields for the transparent table used for extraction into SAP NetWeaver BI are generic.

Because SAP Solution Manager is based on SAP NetWeaver, it can also be used as a BI system, but must first be configured accordingly. All necessary steps have been summarized in the SAP Solution Manager Implementation Guide (IMG). You can access the relevant IMG activities from Transaction SPRO and the SAP Reference IMG for SAP Solution Manager. Every step up to the point of activation is described in detail. This function can only be used, however, if all objects in namespace 0SM have been activated.

SAP Solution Manager as BI system

Figure 8.70 shows what the InfoProviders in the modeling workbench must look like. There is a *data store object* (DSO) for every InfoCube. By expanding the subtree below the objects, you can access the update and transfer rules and InfoSources and DataSources marked ACTIVE. When activation is faulty, there are no icons with which to expand the subtree or the icons are grayed out. In this case, you have to repeat the steps for activating the content or reconfigure the steps in the IMG.

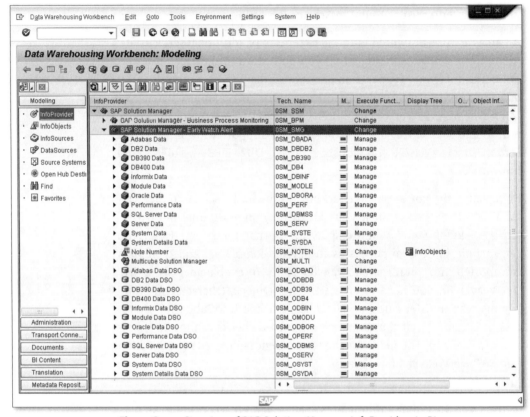

Figure 8.70 Overview of SAP Solution Manager InfoProviders in BI

After configuration, you can use the processes described for the loading process by referring to the numerous predefined process chains available in Transaction RSPC (context SAP SOLUTION MANAGER). Two process chains exist for each InfoCube: one for the initial loading process and one for all subsequent loading processes. You can use the following collective process chains to avoid having to start each process chain individually:

▸ SAP_SOLUTION_MANAGER_INIT

▸ SAP_SOLUTION_MANAGER_DELTA

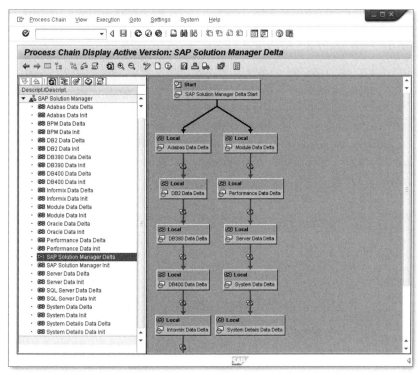

Figure 8.71 BI Process Chains for the Loading Processes

The SAP_SOLUTION_MANAGER_DELTA collective process chain is highlighted in Figure 8.71 and displayed in network form on the right of the figure. Both collective process chains include the individual process chains for each InfoCube. These process chains can be monitored using the logging function or Transaction RSPCM. Errors are displayed in color, and additional analyses can be performed by double-clicking the batch monitor or the BI analysis monitor.

Collective process chains

After the process chains have been successfully run and data has been updated to InfoCubes, analyses can be carried out using queries and workbooks. If you have assigned users to the SAP_BW_SOLUTION_MANAGER role, they can call up the workbooks shipped and defined for the SAP InfoCubes directly from the SAP Easy Access menu. You also have the option of defining your own queries and workbooks using Transaction RRMX.

Another SAP NetWeaver BI application is business process and interface alert reporting. It is structured in the same way as SAP NetWeaver
BI Reporting for SAP EarlyWatch Alert data. The data model is similar,
and there are process chains that load extracted data (extraction also
takes place using a report) to the SAP NetWeaver BI system. The results
can be displayed graphically with one or more dashboards. Figure 8.72
shows one such dashboard, accessed from the Business Process Operations work center. You can view the dashboard in a separate browser
window using a link simply by entering the name of the template, the
server, and any parameters you want to set.

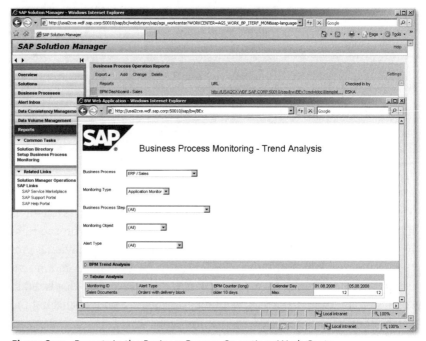

Figure 8.72 Reports in the Business Process Operations Work Center

During the optimize phase, you can act on key figures and data collected from the live solution to curb expenditure or boost performance. The important thing is that you can retrace any changes made in the solution. This chapter explains the functions of Change Request Management, the quality gate management of upgrade support, the concept of global rollouts, and the maintenance of SAP solutions.

9 Optimize Phase

The optimize phase is a time for ensuring that software changes are planned and implemented consistently once your software is in operation. SAP Solution Manager supports you in this task with its functions for managing change requests. Quality gate management provides an additional quality inspection for the projects and ensures that changes are transported correctly to the production systems. The Maintenance Optimizer supports the maintenance of your solution landscape. If you need to make radical changes, for instance, upgrading a software component in your solution, the tool lets you take a professional approach using tried and tested procedures. Another challenge you may face during the optimize phase is distributing a template defined at the head office to your organization's subsidiaries. SAP Solution Manager's answer to this challenge is the *global rollout* function.

9.1 Change Request Management

The ability to retrace changes is a key factor in ensuring quality and transparency in a software solution and observing IT standards. This is true for software changes and configuration changes. This section shows how SAP Solution Manager can help your organization make changes traceable through clearly defined procedures and comprehensive documentation. SAP Solution Manager features an approval workflow, which

Ability to retrace changes

you can tailor to meet your requirements, and documents any activities performed while a change is being implemented, from the initial request through to its technical realization. As a result, your organization can always trace where a request came from, who implemented it, and when the change was imported into a production environment. A key aspect of this approach is that all of the relevant information is available in a central location and can be accessed at any time.

Within a given project, you can plan any changes that are to be implemented over a certain period and monitor their implementation. You can also efficiently document and resolve changes that are not part of a project plan but call for swift attention (*urgent corrections*), for instance, if an error occurs that could jeopardize a production environment.

Project plan   Your organization can record and plan all of the changes that need to be implemented in a project in a *cProjects* project plan. You can plan resources and establish a connection to the backend, for example, to the *Cross-Application Time Sheet* (CATS) component for recording activities. Change requests that have undergone the approval procedure can be scheduled here. The project plan is integrated in the project in SAP Solution Manager, which passes through several phases in what is known as a *project cycle*. The phases are controlled centrally from SAP Solution Manager and set forth basic conditions that cannot be sidestepped. This approach is discussed further below (see also Section 9.1.7).

Integration of Change Request Management and transport requests   In this regard, SAP Solution Manager closes a gap that exists in many change management solutions: When databases or lists, for example, are used to depict change management processes and log change requests and approvals, manual intervention becomes absolutely necessary when a transport request needs to be created or imported. The transport request number has to be copied to the database by hand, which is a potential source of error. A typo or mistake when copying invalidates the entire process. With Change Request Management, transport requests are generated centrally from SAP Solution Manager, and a reference to the corresponding change request is created automatically (with the ID and description copied to the transport request's name), enabling a clear relationship to be identified at any time. The Change Request Management scenario lets you track all transports relating to a specific project, enabling you to check where they were created and in which systems they have been imported. From SAP Solution Manager, you can navigate to the transport logs and import queue, as well as to the SAP Solution Manager maintenance project, the project plan, and the connected systems.

Changes without transport link

You can also record changes in Change Request Management that do not require transporting. As with all other changes, you produce a change request that goes through all of the approval steps. You document the required steps in the change request itself. SAP Solution Manager therefore advances SAP's vision of application management and IT governance by providing enterprises with indispensable functions for implementing and running solutions transparently. Transparency lies at the heart of many statutory regulations. It supplies answers to the question of who did what when, and who checked and approved the measures.

For an organization to run a system landscape smoothly in the face of constantly changing requirements, it must take into account the following aspects:

▶ Change requests, whether resulting from error messages or from idea management processes, must be classified and approved centrally.

▶ When a request has been approved, reliable procedures must be followed to apply the change, transport it to follow-up systems (quality assurance and production), and conduct tests. These procedures should be complemented by meticulous documentation containing all change-related information and data on all persons involved in the process.

▶ The status of a change request must be traceable at all times.

Integrated teams

Equally important is the integration of people within the organization, whereby SAP Solution Manager's focus on processes is instrumental in enabling communication between business departments and IT administrators. Everyone involved in implementing a change can always access all of the relevant information, such as requirements, specifications, documentation, test cases, test results, and status analyses, which are organized using the structures in SAP Solution Manager and stored centrally.

ITIL This offering from SAP is designed in line with the processes in the *IT Infrastructure Library* (ITIL). The ITIL defines the objective of change management as ensuring that changes are made economically and promptly with minimum risk. The Change Request Management scenario is composed of the *change administration, project management,* and *change logistics* processes (see Figure 9.1).

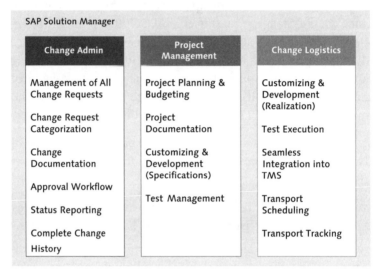

Figure 9.1 Overview of Change Request Management Processes

9.1.1 The Change Management Work Center

Work center The most important Change Request Management functions are available in the Change Management work center. Here, users are provided with a role-based view of all procedures assigned to them (such as change requests, regular and urgent corrections, and Maintenance Optimizer transactions). You can find an overview of the Change Management work center in Section 3.1.

9.1.2 Change Request Management

Scenario A user in a business department identifies potential for improvement in a specific transaction. The user can enter a Service Desk message directly from the transaction in question, describing the context and requesting a change. The message appears in the worklist of a Service Desk employee, who processes the message and generates a *change request*, if appropriate (see Section 8.7). Next, the system forwards the change request to the central person in the scenario, the *change manager*. The change manager is responsible for assessing and categorizing the request and approving or rejecting it. If the change request is approved, a *change document* is generated. If the request is approved, the system automatically creates a change document, which forms the functional basis in subsequent stages for developers, testers, and IT administrators. The Change Request Management process comes back into play once the processes described below have been completed and concludes the change request.

The change document appears in the worklist of a developer, who implements the change and releases it for testing so that it is forwarded to the tester. The change cannot be transported into the production system until it has been tested successfully.

What sets the Change Request Management scenario apart from other solutions is that it enables organizations not only to manage changes, but also to check them and trace their progression through the system landscape; this also applies to ABAP and Java objects. SAP Solution Manager offers support for planning the tasks of an IT administrator and enables automatic checks to be established for import sequences and transport tracking. The change logistics process therefore completes the Change Request Management scenario comprehensively and independently of technology.

Change logistics

9.1.3 Architecture

To understand the architecture of the Change Request Management scenario in SAP Solution Manager, you need to know how the individual entities interact. Figure 9.2 illustrates these interactions.

The central element in the Change Request Management scenario is the Solution Manager project in SAP Solution Manager (see Section 5.2). A project contains the following information:

Solution Manager project

▶ **Logical components**
   A logical component contains all systems that supply a production

system (for example, a production client). The assigned systems are usually connected to each other through transport routes.

▶ **IMG project**
From the project administration in SAP Solution Manager (Transaction SOLAR_PROJECT_ADMIN), you create an IMG project in managed systems to group settings made in the SAP Implementation Guide (IMG) for a Solution Manager project in one system.

▶ **CTS project**
A container in a logical system (system-client combination) that bundles transport requests that belong to one IMG project.

The Change Request Management scenario supports the following project types from SAP Solution Manager: implementation, upgrade, template, and maintenance projects.

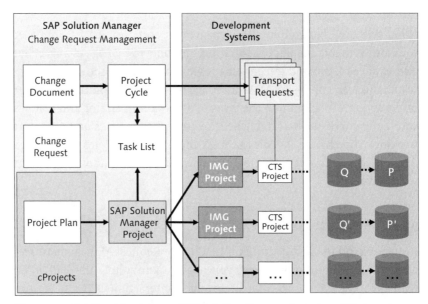

Figure 9.2 Relationships Between SAP Solution Manager Projects and Systems in Change Request Management

Depending on the settings made by the change manager in the change request before approval, two types of Change Request Management cycles are possible: project cycle and maintenance cycle. Designed to meet different requirements, the cycles differ in scope and are therefore explained in more detail below.

9.1.4 Project Cycle for Development Projects

To support implementation, upgrade, and template projects in the Change Request Management scenario, SAP Solution Manager offers the project cycle. The project cycle is a preconfigured service process (transaction type SDDV) that allows you to control the following activities over the course of a project (see Figure 9.3):

▸ Change requests and the resulting changes in systems used in your project

▸ Transport requests required to transport changes to follow-up systems

▸ Complete change logistics, that is, when certain transports can be imported into follow-up systems

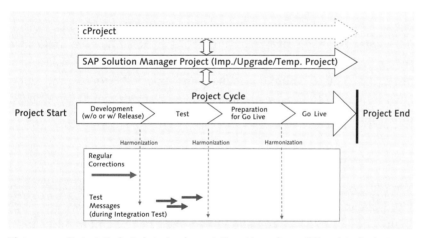

Figure 9.3 Project Cycle Role in Implementation, Upgrade, and Template Projects

Structured as a series of phases, the project cycle provides a functional supplement to the project plan. A single project cycle has the following phases:

Project cycle phases

- Development without release

- Development with release

- Test

- Preparation for go live (emergency correction)

- Go live

You close the project cycle after going live. The maintenance cycle is a special type of project cycle in which it is possible to run through the phases several times (see Section 9.1.8).

In the *development without release* phase, a transport request can be created but not released. It is not recommended that you use this phase with regular corrections (transaction type SDMJ), because it is not possible to generate test transports during this phase. Transport requests cannot be released until the *development with release* phase. It is initiated by a central body (*change advisory board* or *change manager*) and permits transports to be released and imported into the test environment for unit tests. Once project changes have been imported into the test environment, the *test* phase can be opened so that integration testing can begin. New change requests can no longer be created for this project; only bugs that are discovered during testing are fixed. The *preparation for go-live* phase enables users with appropriate authorization to make other necessary changes before the changes are imported into the production environment in the *go-live* phase. However, changes that have not been tested successfully in the *test* phase cannot be imported.

9.1.5   Change Request

You can assign any number of change requests to the cycle. Like a Service Desk message, a change request is a preconfigured service process (transaction type SDCR) containing all of the data relevant to the change. This includes:

- Sold-to party

- Requester

- Change manager

▶ Change advisory board

▶ System affected by the change (installed base or component)

▶ Priority

▶ Type of change (subject)

▶ Tests that safeguard communication (for example, description of change, reason for change, implications for business partners, implications for systems, and so on)

Depending on the change type selected in the SUBJECT field, the system automatically creates a follow-up transaction when the change request is approved. The Change Request Management scenario supports four types of change, enabling the change manager to classify change requests:

Types of change

▶ **Regular correction**
Requests for regular system maintenance activities, such as requests for Support Packages or SAP Notes to be imported.

▶ **Test message**
Reports errors discovered during testing to the development team. The developer can then also correct the error at a later date using the test message, because it is not possible to create a new regular correction during the test phase.

▶ **Administration message**
Concerns changes that do not require transporting, such as changes to number ranges.

▶ **Project request**
Concerns a major system landscape change, such as the implementation of a new solution or an upgrade for an existing one.

The Change Request Management scenario therefore covers the complete life cycle, from gathering requirements to implementing, testing, running, and continuously improving a solution. ÐÐIt is integrated in SAP Solution Manager's extensive range of functions, which include Incident Management, E-Learning Management, and upgrade support.

The Change Request Management scenario uses the IMPORT_PROJ-ECT_ALL method for transport control. Consequently, the IMPORT_

Transport control

ALL transport method must be replaced with IMPORT_SINGLE in the scenario configuration. The advantage of this is that you can work on specific projects and import the transport requests into the follow-up systems at the end of the cycle phases, harmonized and consolidated and in the sequence in which they were released. This approach minimizes the risk of *overshooters* in the transport system. At the end of the project, you can import all of the changes into the production systems and close the project.

9.1.6 Task List

Technical schedule

The task list in Change Request Management provides system administrators with an overview of implemented and scheduled actions. It summarizes all of the systems and necessary tasks and displays them in the correct sequence. Any tasks that you execute by performing actions on the corrections or project cycle user interfaces in SAP Solution Manager (such as system logon, create transport request, or import transport request) are defined in the task list.

For administrative purposes, the task list should only be used to trigger project imports, not to export requests for a regular correction. Because it is not possible to perform important checks here, inconsistencies could arise. Requests should therefore always be exported using the actions in the change document.

9.1.7 Types of Change in Development Projects

In development projects, various types of change, which differ in terms of status profile and transport, are available.

Regular Correction

A regular correction (transaction type SDMJ) represents the corrections made in a project and has the following status profile:

Status profile

▶ Created

▶ In development

- To be tested
- Consolidated
- Production
- Withdrawn

The workflow for a regular correction is explained in detail below.

A user detects missing functions in a system. The user can report the fault directly from the relevant transaction by sending a Service Desk message to SAP Solution Manager. The message contains all of the relevant system data and describes the request.

Process description

The Service Desk employee processing the support message finds that the request requires a change request. He then selects the CREATE CHANGE DOCUMENT action to create a change request in the Service Desk.

The change request appears in the change manager's worklist (in the Change Management work center). The change manager classifies the request, specifies how it is to be handled (regular correction), and finally approves or rejects it. The priority of the change request is an important factor here.

If the change request is approved as a regular correction, SAP Solution Manager automatically generates a change request of the regular correction type. The change request and the correction are linked by the document flow, and the relationship is always transparent.

The change transaction is the functional basis for developers, testers, and system administrators. First, the developer is notified that a new correction needs processing. The developer works on the correction and selects the appropriate action to set the status to IN DEVELOPMENT.

The developer creates a transport request in the development system, logs on to the development system directly and, when the correction is ready, releases the transport tasks in the development system (Transaction SE09). When development is completed, the developer generates a test transport by means of an action in the change request, which is then imported into the test system. The developer then tests the new development. If this test is successful, the developer sets the status to

DEVELOPMENT COMPLETED, prompting the request to be exported from the development system. All of the activities described can be executed directly from the change transaction using actions.

On the basis of a scheduled job (in the managed system), the newly developed function is imported into a test system during one of the regular imports of the project buffer. It undergoes unit testing or may be included directly in integration testing. A tester checks the change and can access all of the necessary functions in one place, such as system logon and the complete change history for the change transaction. The Change Request Management scenario supports the principle of dual control, enabling you to specify that the developer and tester must not be the same person.

After testing, a tester sets the status of the change transaction to CONSOLIDATED to indicate that the new function has been tested and can be imported into the production system. The regular correction ends with this step; from now on it only contains descriptive status values, but is handed over to the project cycle from a technical perspective and pursued further by it.

Importing changes   The following prerequisites must be met before changes can be imported into production systems:

▶ The system administrator cannot import a change into the production system unless the corresponding project cycle is in the go-live phase.

▶ The status cannot be set to PRODUCTION unless all regular corrections for the project have been imported successfully into the production systems. You can set this status for all imported regular corrections at the end of a project cycle by scheduling job CRM_SOCM_SERVICE_REPORT.

Regular corrections whose status is still IN DEVELOPMENT trigger a warning in the corresponding project cycle if the status is set during the test phase.

Figure 9.4 illustrates the various types of change in development projects.

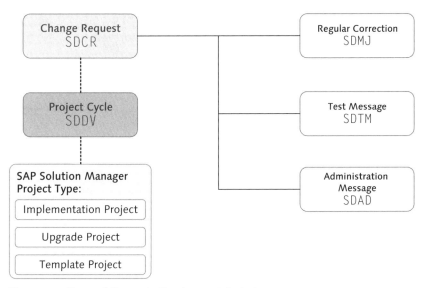

Figure 9.4 Types of Change in Development Projects

Test Message

The only phase in which you can create test messages (transaction type SDTM) is the test phase of the project cycle. Because a test message is used for integration testing, which applies to the entire project (all corrections), it does not refer to a single correction or change request. You use test messages to report errors found during testing to the development team so that the relevant developer can fix the problem by creating a transport request. Because the project scope has been approved on the basis of the change requests, a test message does not require any approval steps. It has the following status profile:

▸ Created

▸ In process

▸ To be retested

▸ Confirmed

▸ Withdrawn

Status profile

Test messages are vital because you cannot create new corrections in the test phase; doing so would distort the project's defined scope.

A tester creates a test message and describes the symptoms. A developer processes the message, creates one or more transport requests, and fixes the bug in the development system. To submit the change for retesting, the developer sets the status to TO BE RETESTED. Once the transport buffer has been imported into the test system again, the tester checks the functions, sets the status to CONFIRMED, and sets the status of the regular correction to SUCCESSFULLY TESTED.

Administration Message

An administration message (transaction type SDAD) lets you keep a complete change history for changes that do not require transporting, such as changes to number ranges or user data. It provides access to the task list and to activities such as system logon. It has the following status profile:

Status profile
- Created
- In process
- Completed
- Successfully tested
- Production
- Confirmed
- Completed
- Withdrawn

9.1.8 Working with Project Cycles

Project preparation
The project manager creates a project in SAP Solution Manager (implementation, upgrade, or template project) and generates IMG and CTS projects, as well as a project cycle for the project. The system administrator activates the cycle in the document (transaction type SDMN) using the corresponding action. You can now begin creating, classifying, and approving change requests. In this phase, therefore, you already define the scope of changes to be made in this project.

Once changes are approved, SAP Solution Manager assigns the resulting corrective measures to the project cycle. If you have several projects open at the same time, there will be more than one project cycle. In such cases, when you approve a change, the system asks you to confirm the cycle to which the correction is to be assigned.

The change manager sets the project cycle status to IN DEVELOPMENT WITHOUT RELEASE. With this status, developers can work on corrections in the system. They can create transport requests and tasks, but cannot release or export them. SAP does not recommend that you use this phase with regular corrections (transaction type SDMJ) because the developers do not have the option of importing corrections made to preliminary tests into the test system.

In development without release

When the change manager changes the project cycle status from IN DEVELOPMENT WITHOUT RELEASE to IN DEVELOPMENT WITH RELEASE, developers can generate transports of copies of the corrections they have made, which are imported into the test system for test purposes. Ideally, this import is performed by scheduled jobs or manually in the task list by the system administrator.

In development with release

Often, development systems do not contain the master or transaction data that would enable developers to test their corrections. Such data is often only available in test systems. This is why you have the option of scheduling unit tests in this phase of the project cycle, that is, before integration testing. This gives developers time to test their corrections once they have been imported to the test systems and to set their status to TO BE TESTED. This is followed by another transport of copies into the test system. The tester then sees the correction to be tested in the worklist in the work center and can perform the test. If the test was successful, the tester sets the status of the correction to CONSOLIDATED, triggering the correction to be exported from the development system in the background.

After switching to the test phase, transport requests for all corrections that have a status below TO BE TESTED can no longer be exported. The user is warned of this when he switches phases in the document (transaction type SDMN), as recommended by SAP. This freezes the code from

Test

405

the beginning of the test phase. Urgent corrections are not affected by this behavior and can still be used.

During the test phase, testers can check that corrections are acceptable in terms of functionality and business relevance. If they uncover a mistake, they can document it in a test message and notify the relevant developer. After receiving a test message, the developer can create a new transport request in the development system and fix the bug. The test phase is deemed complete when all corrections and test messages have SUCCESSFULLY TESTED status. Corrections (with a higher status than CONSOLIDATED) cannot be excluded from testing; they must be either tested successfully or withdrawn.

Emergency correction (preparation for go live)

If you need to make other changes once the test phase is complete, you can create, release, and move transport requests and tasks during the emergency correction phase, but only via the task list for the project cycle and with the appropriate authorizations. Urgent corrections are not affected by this and can still be used.

Go live

In the go-live phase, the entire transport buffer for the CTS project is imported into the production systems in the order of the releases. Transport requests cannot be created or released during this phase; it is not possible to use urgent corrections either. Following the import to the production system environment, no open transport requests remain, and the transport buffer is empty. You can now close the project cycle by setting the status to CONFIRMED. The project is then considered to be complete.

The project phase should be moved on only using the appropriate action in the document (transaction type SDMN). In a three-system landscape, for example, you will find all transport requests for urgent corrections with the TO BE TESTED status in the import buffer of the production system. If the phase cannot be switched using the SDMN document, but only using the task list, the user is not warned of this; urgent corrections are imported untested. When the phase is switched using the SDMN document, tests are performed so that the user is warned and can react accordingly.

9.1.9 Differences Between Maintenance Cycles and Project Cycles

Consistent with the life cycle model, you use an implementation project in SAP Solution Manager to implement a solution. You conclude the implementation project successfully, and the solution goes live. During this process, you copy the project data into a solution (see Section 7.1). To keep the solution current, you assign it a maintenance project with a maintenance cycle.

A maintenance cycle (Figure 9.5) is a project cycle that has been adapted to meet the special requirements of maintenance projects. A maintenance project does have a defined start time, but, unlike a development project, is a continuous, ongoing process; the individual phases of the maintenance cycle will continue to run.

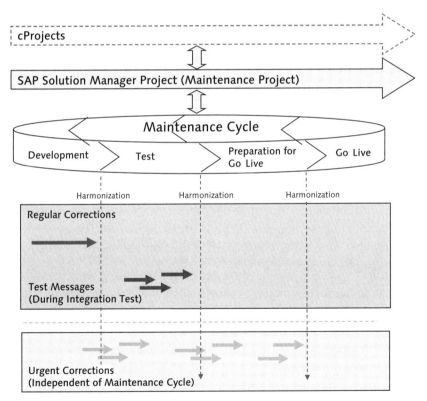

Figure 9.5 Maintenance Cycle Role in Maintenance Projects

Phase model   The maintenance cycle has the same phases as the project cycle, but with certain additional features. First, the maintenance cycle has an extra correction type, urgent correction, which gives you the flexibility to make corrections on short notice (see Section 9.1.10). Second, if you work with maintenance cycles, we advise adopting a different approach that meets the requirements posed by maintaining a solution.

We recommend that you assign a maintenance project to a solution, lasting for the same amount of time as you intend to run the solution. Within the maintenance project, any necessary corrections are effected in a series of maintenance cycles. The change manager defines the duration of a maintenance cycle, for example, one month. During this period, the project runs through all of the phases in the cycle, from IN DEVELOPMENT WITHOUT RELEASE to GO LIVE. At the end of the go-live phase, you do not close the cycle; it is checked for open and incomplete business transactions and transport requests. Documents that have not been closed are then carried over when a new maintenance cycle is created.

From a technical point of view, it is possible to not close the maintenance cycle but to reset its phase to IN DEVELOPMENT WITHOUT RELEASE and to run through the same cycle again. However, closing and re-creating the maintenance cycle facilitates and guarantees clearer and more traceable reporting, which is why it is recommended by SAP.

Example   The following example shows the benefits of this approach. You have defined the scope of your maintenance cycle by assessing and approving submitted change requests. Ten regular corrections have been approved for the current maintenance cycle (for example, OCTOBER 2008). During the development phase, you find that one of the regular corrections, correction number nine, cannot be realized in the time allotted to the phase.

As project manager, you have two options for dealing with the delay: You can increase the amount of time available for this correction so that it can be realized in the current maintenance cycle, or, if the change is not critical and has no dependencies with the other corrections, you can decide to complete it in the next maintenance cycle, NOVEMBER 2008. In this case, the status of the correction remains IN DEVELOPMENT. The other nine corrections go through the test and go-live phases and are imported into the production systems. Now you close the October 2008 cycle, and the open correction is ready to be carried over into the new cycle. When the NOVEMBER 2008 cycle is created, the correction is automatically carried over to this cycle and processed together with the new corrections in this cycle.

In this regard, this approach differs from that of the project cycle. If regular corrections with a status other than DEVELOPMENT COMPLETED still exist when you move from the IN DEVELOPMENT WITH RELEASE phase of the maintenance cycle to the test phase, the system issues a warning message only. These corrections are excluded from integration tests and cannot be released.

During maintenance, errors that demand a swift resolution can be reported at any time, for example, if production systems are likely to be jeopardized. A regular correction does not allow you to respond to such problems quickly enough, because it is dependent on the maintenance cycle phase. If the maintenance cycle is in the test phase, you cannot enter new corrections for the current cycle. This is why the Change Request Management scenario includes the option of urgent corrections.

Figure 9.6 shows the types of change in maintenance projects.

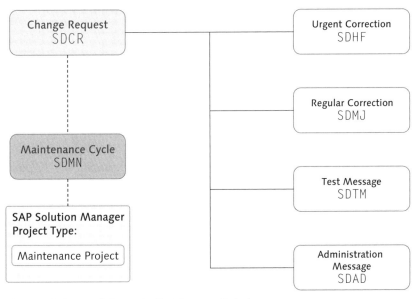

Figure 9.6 Types of Change in Maintenance Projects

9.1.10   Urgent Correction

Urgent correction

Urgent corrections have their own task list; they can be transported regardless of the phase of the assigned maintenance cycle. This enables you to import changes from urgent corrections into production systems before importing the regular corrections in the go-live phase of the maintenance cycle.

Transport control

Use the IMPORT_SUBSET transport method in this case; transport requests generated from an urgent correction are written to the transport buffer and imported into the follow-up systems. They remain in the buffer after the import. With regular imports based on the task list for the maintenance cycle, the entire transport buffer for the project is consolidated and imported using the IMPORT_PROJECT_ALL method; that is, the urgent corrections are imported a second time (see Section 9.1.10). This ensures data consistency.

Status profile

Urgent corrections have the following status profile:

▶ Created

▶ In development

▶ To be tested

▶ Successfully tested

▶ Authorized for import

▶ Production

▶ Confirmed

▶ Completed

▶ Withdrawn

In the standard release, SAP Solution Manager automatically imports transport requests relating to an urgent correction into the test system when you set the status to To be tested. This setting is intended to accelerate the process further, but you can change it in Customizing if necessary.

9.1.11 Retrofitting Transport Requests

In system landscapes in which it is possible to work on several releases at the same time, changes can be made in different development systems. New features can therefore be created in the development system and, at the same time, errors can be corrected or improvements made in a maintenance system for the production system landscape. In this scenario, it is very important that the release level of the system is synchronized regularly. Because work is carried out in parallel, it is not possible to make changes by simply transporting requests to the respective system, because of the danger that current software levels might be overwritten, resulting in inconsistencies. To avoid this, a controlled import into the target system can be performed. This procedure is called *post-processing* or *retrofitting*.

Retrofitting

If retrofitting is started in the task list (START RETROFIT), the user must first define the transport request that is to be imported into the retrofit system and select the appropriate retrofit tasks for it in this system. After an (optional) consistency check, retrofitting can be carried out. This can also be done for several transport requests at the same time.

Finally, retrofitting steps (importing unavailable objects, adopting existing objects, or manually implementing objects) may be possible before the status of the retrofit procedure is set. If it is set to SUCCESSFULLY COMPLETED, the transport request originally selected no longer appears in the overview of possible transport requests for retrofitting. The controlled transport from the maintenance system to the development system is now complete.

9.1.12 Correcting Import Errors Manually

If errors occur when importing a change, they must be corrected manually.

Correcting import errors manually

To obtain an overview of failed imports, you can view their import logs in the task list. Here, you can see which import has to be corrected or repeated. The administrator must do this manually, for example, by importing a transport request (to create the conditions for executing the original import again without errors) or restarting a canceled import.

The status of the import can then be set to ERROR CORRECTED in the task list. SAP Solution Manager then overwrites the incorrect status of the task with the manually set ERROR CORRECTED STATUS. This is especially important to enable accurate reporting that includes the subsequent manual corrections and to be able to process a document after an import error.

Note that the system does not correct the status of the underlying import in the log, because log files cannot be changed. This means the log of the import continues to show the status as incorrect. It is also not possible to repair faulty exports using this function.

9.1.13 Maintenance Processes

To enable you to manage maintenance processes effectively and, in particular, to help you download and distribute Support Packages, SAP Solution Manager provides the Maintenance Optimizer functions. For a detailed description of the Maintenance Optimizer, see Section 9.3.

SAP HotNews

SAP HotNews refers to SAP Notes with priority 1 (very high). These SAP Notes explain how you can avoid or solve problems that could cause loss of data or an SAP system crash. In the Change Management work center under HOTNEWS, the system proactively displays SAP HotNews relevant to the systems in your solution. You can:

▶ Display information about SAP HotNews on the SAP Service Marketplace

▶ Postpone a decision about SAP HotNews if you need more time to agree on proceedings

▶ Indicate SAP HotNews as being not relevant

▶ Create a change request for importing SAP HotNews

9.2 Quality Gate Management

For end-to-end solution landscapes, quality gate management ensures that the areas of design and development, as well as the implementation of a new service, are efficiently and effectively embedded in projects.

The aim is to establish an integrated and consistent quality process in the company and to involve all relevant departments.

The Change Management work center in SAP Solution Manager represents the central entry point for administering projects for quality gate management (see Section 3.1). This gives the user the opportunity to obtain a quick overview of the different software development projects and their statuses. In the OVERVIEW view, you can see projects that you are involved in, sorted by project phase. From there, you can go directly to the PROJECTS view, where you can process the projects. Various tabs are provided in the PROJECTS view, allowing you to access a lot of information.

Change Management work center

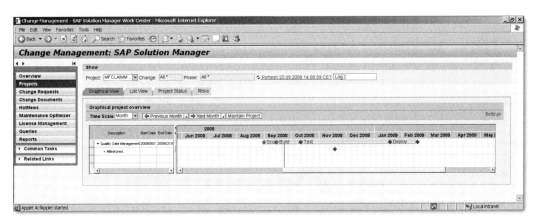

Figure 9.7 Graphical Project Overview

Using the GRAPHICAL VIEW tab page (Figure 9.7), you can display the status of a project and its phases. The quality gates (subsequently referred to as *Q-Gates*) and the milestones are also displayed in graphical form.

To use a project in quality gate management, certain requirements must be met. You have to create a Solution Manager project (Transaction SOLAR_PROJECT_ADMIN) and enter the system landscape in the Solution Manager System Landscape transaction (SMSY) (see Section 5.2). Only then can the project be selected. Once you have selected the required project, you can make the remaining configuration settings using the MAINTAIN PROJECT button. When you click the button, an assistant opens in which you have to define the dates of the individual Q-Gates in the first step.

413

The following four phases are defined with corresponding Q-Gates in the standard shipment:

- ▶ Scope
- ▶ Build
- ▶ Test
- ▶ Deploy

Quality gate   A Q-Gate is a special milestone in a project. Q-Gates come between the phases in the project that are especially dependent on the results of the preceding phase or in which special attention must be paid to technical dependencies. A Q-Gate involves checking the results of the preceding phase (Figure 9.8). You can upload the necessary result types and requirements placed on these phases in the form of checklists for a Q-Gate. The check is performed by those responsible for the project and experts on the particular phases during a session. Depending on the outcome, the project may continue as planned or be canceled or delayed. After a successful Q-Gate check, the import block on the subsequent system is lifted.

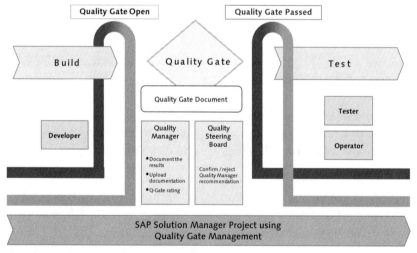

Figure 9.8 Overview of Q-Gate Process

Milestones   In addition to the Q-Gates supplied, you can create *milestones* that represent particular times in your project. A milestone is an event with special significance. In project management, these events are mostly interim objectives for a project that play a part in producing a significant project result. To highlight the importance of a milestone, you can assign a Q-Gate check to it and thereby impose an import block for subsequent systems.

The same step defines the *quality manager* and the *quality advisory board*. This establishes a principle of dual control in the project and the process (segregation of duties). The import block for the system assigned to the Q-Gate is only lifted if both persons or groups confirm that the Q-Gate has been successful; it is then possible to import transports to subsequent systems using the transport management system (TMS).

Quality manager and quality advisory board

In the second step, the logical components and their defined systems assigned to the project are displayed and verified against the transport route configuration.

In the third step, the individual Q-Gates are assigned to the system roles and therefore to the project phases.

Once the configuration is finished, the assistant displays the project landscape with the individual phases, systems, and Q-Gates (see Figure 9.9).

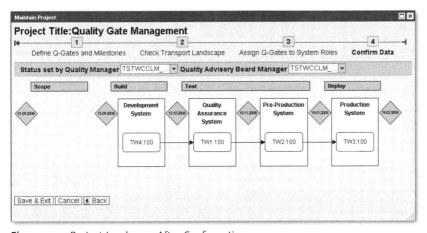

Figure 9.9 Project Landscape After Configuration

Once the configuration has been saved, the milestones and Q-Gates are displayed to the user in a graphical project overview (see Figure 9.7). When you select a processed Q-Gate, the results and requirements that you have already logged are displayed (see Figure 9.10).

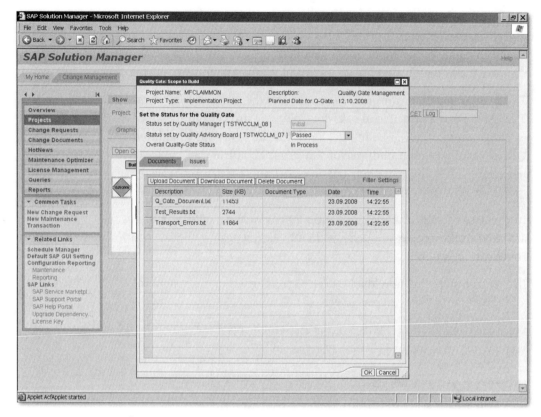

Figure 9.10 Q-Gate Documentation

The quality manager is responsible for the transition between the individual project phases (scope, build, test, and deploy). The check is performed by those responsible for the project and experts on the particular phases during a session. Users also have a variety of information and views at their disposal for their software development projects. They are always able to keep an overview from the tab pages in the work center.

The LIST VIEW tab page (see Figure 9.11) enables the quality manager to obtain information about current projects. By selecting a project, the quality manager has access to general and detailed information, such as defined project phases, number of changes and transport requests belonging to the project, and information about the division of responsibilities within the project (see Figure 9.12).

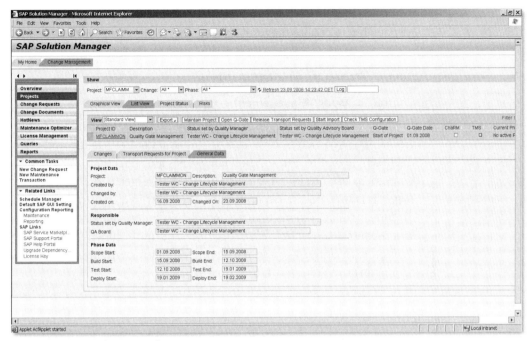

Figure 9.11 General Project Information

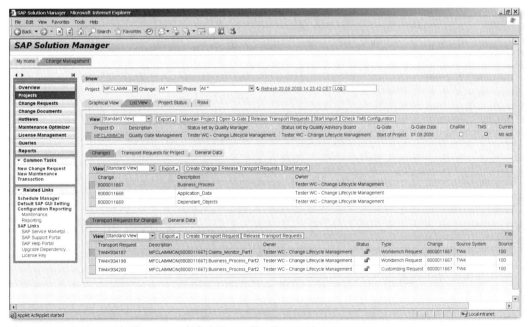

Figure 9.12 Project with Changes and Their Respective Transports

All activities are recorded in an action log with a time stamp and the user responsible to ensure they can be tracked.

9.2.1 Transport Management

Central Transport Management

Dependencies of objects

In today's heterogeneous, distributed customer solutions, it is necessary to ensure that a new service can be implemented efficiently and effectively where end-to-end solution landscapes are concerned. Whereas the main focus used to be on the dependencies of objects in a system landscape, it is now on the dependencies of objects in a solution landscape. This means that systems that are completely independent of each other in a technical sense are becoming more and more functionally dependent on each other. The aim must be to establish central transport management for the entire solution landscape.

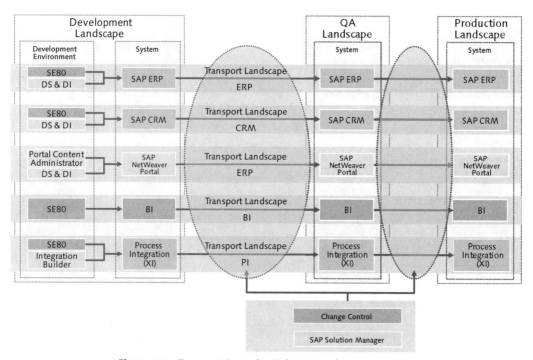

Figure 9.13 Transport Control in Solution Landscapes

With quality gate management, SAP Solution Manager provides the administration interface for central transport management in the Change Management work center.

The person responsible for transports can view the solution landscape defined in the project as a detailed graphic on the PROJECT STATUS tab (Figure 9.14). The solution landscape mirrors the customer-specific transport configuration and its transport routes. An assistant enables you to set up the solution landscape for a project quickly and easily. It is based on Solution Manager projects (see Section 5.2). The colored highlighting shows the phase of the project that is currently active and the Q-Gates that have taken place and those that are still pending.

Transport configuration and routes

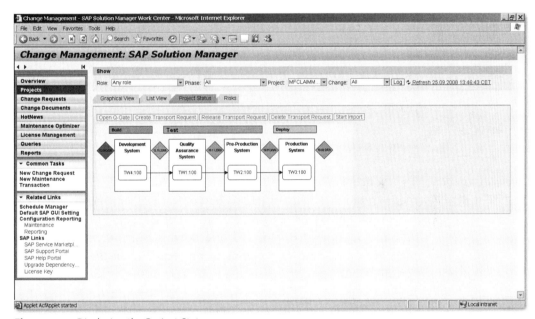

Figure 9.14 Displaying the Project Status

Once you have selected a project, the LIST VIEW tab (Figure 9.15) shows the number of changes that belong to this project. Any number of changes can be created for a project. The individual changes can be created by clicking the CREATE CHANGE button and assigned to the relevant projects (see Figure 9.12). You can assign any number of transport requests to a change. Changes form a logical reference for the transport requests that are assigned to them.

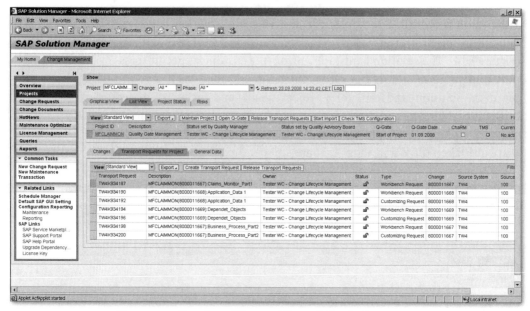

Figure 9.15 Overview of Transport Requests in a Project

Grouping transport requests logically

This concept makes it possible to group logically related transport requests and those that are dependent on each other specific to the system or solution. Depending on the current phase, entire projects or individual changes can be imported into downstream systems. In the *test* phase of the software development project, the quality manager can consolidate the project before the last phase of the project is activated. In the *deploy* phase, whole projects can be imported, but not individual changes. This ensures that all transport requests in a project are imported into the production systems fully and in the right order at a defined time. With this function, universal changes can be made synchronously to business processes in ABAP and non-ABAP components throughout solution landscapes.

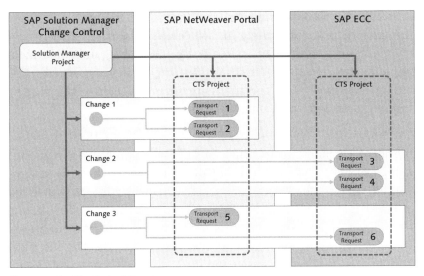

Figure 9.16 The Project Structure

Change and Transport System

In the quality management process, SAP provides complete control of all software changes. For this purpose, a consistent and highly integrated process is available, which optimally supports various task areas in a project with a variety of tools. SAP refers to the tools for managing changes as the *Change and Transport System* (CTS).

CTS is the central tool for managing changes made to Customizing and repository data in the Implementation Guide (IMG) and the ABAP Workbench. All changes are collected automatically by CTS and recorded in change requests. Logically related and interdependent changes can be recorded in the same change request. Members of a team can use one common change request. In the documentation for the change request, the recorded changes can be described in greater detail. This makes it possible to trace what data has been changed by which user for which purpose.

Central tool

You release the change request once work in the Implementation Guide or ABAP Workbench has been completed or an interim status has been reached. The change request is now used to copy the changes from the clients where they were implemented to other clients or systems auto-

Transport

matically. This automatic transfer is referred to as a transport. CTS therefore provides the opportunity to make changes in a separate development environment, test them in a test environment, and adopt them in production operations once they have been tested successfully. This ensures that production operations are not endangered at any time by incorrect settings or programming errors.

Enhanced CTS

SAP NetWeaver 7.0 SPS 14 has enhanced the existing CTS and now also provides the opportunity to manage and transport non-ABAP components. This enhancement was motivated by the request to provide central transport management for SAP environments and thereby utilize an established standard for non-ABAP components. Furthermore, it enables existing strategies and knowledge to be reused. This provides investment security and lower operating costs. This enhancement makes the transport functions of the Transport Organizer and the Transport Management System available for non-ABAP objects also. This means, for example, that you can transport the following SAP NetWeaver usage type objects in CTS:

▶ Enterprise Portal (EP) (Enterprise Portal Archive, EPAs)

▶ Process Integration (PI) (XI/PI transport files, TPZs)

▶ Development Infrastructure (DI) (software component archive, SCAs and development component archives, DCAs)

▶ System Landscape Directory (SLD) (SLD objects, ZIPs)

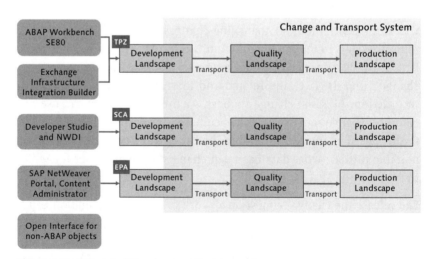

Figure 9.17 Connected Development Environments

To make your company's development process as integrated as possible, SAP-specific development environments (for example, SAP NetWeaver Development Infrastructure, Portal Content Administrator, PI Integration Builder, SLD) are connected to CTS. After being developed, the completed objects are automatically added to the transport request provided for this. In the future, SAP's aim is to connect all SAP development environments and SAP applications to CTS and integrate them in the best possible way.

Changes are transported between clients and systems according to traceable rules that are defined in the CTS configuration in a system landscape. For example, a rule might state that changes are first transported to the test environment before they can be copied to the production environment. All transports are also logged so that it is possible to trace when a change request was transported in a client or a system and whether any errors occurred.

Rules and logs

As a result, CTS is composed of all tools required to support SAP change and transport management for ABAP and non-ABAP-based products.

9.2.2   CTS Projects

Based on the CTS infrastructure, transport management offers you the chance to plan and transport your development and Customizing activities in project structures using CTS projects. Changes that are independent of each other can be split into different projects and imported separately into follow-up systems. This is recommended, for example, if various projects are to be used at different times in production operations or to form content assignments.

The assignment of a change request to a project is displayed in the import queue so that imports to the follow-up systems can also take place for each project. It is important to ensure that projects are as independent as possible even during planning.

9.3   Maintaining an SAP Solution Landscape

As SAP software is continuously enhanced, you are constantly presented with new functions and flexible ways to integrate services on the basis of open architecture. The new possibilities offered by the introduction of new SAP technologies have been accompanied by an increase in the number of software components in your system landscape. SAP has introduced the Maintenance Optimizer so that you can perform maintenance transactions efficiently and leverage innovations as easily as possible. It provides you with support for planning, downloading, and implementing enhancements and new functions.

Three-system landscape

A typical customer landscape consists of a development, consolidation, and production environment (three-system landscape). All changes from the development environment are transferred to the consolidation environment. As soon as the system is error-free, all changes are transferred to the production environment and can be used in the company.

The changes in an SAP landscape include:

- Patches for the operating system, databases, and SAP kernel
- Support Packages
- New developments, changes to customer-specific settings, and corrections contained in SAP Notes

All of the above-mentioned changes must be distributed and imported in the system landscapes in different ways. In the ABAP stack, you can use the Transport Management System (TMS) for this, and in this way distribute the changes (customer developments, customer-specific settings, or changes to the code from SAP Notes). Changes outside of the ABAP stack, Support Packages, and kernel updates previously had to be distributed manually in the landscape and imported into the individual systems. These activities were executed independently of each other without centralized control. The completeness and correct order of the import into the system could not be ensured in this way. The Maintenance Optimizer is SAP's answer to the above-mentioned challenges associated with maintaining a solution landscape.

To import the Support Packages into the individual systems, you require a valid maintenance certificate (see Section 9.3.4). These maintenance certificates can be distributed manually or automatically by SAP Solution Manager.

9.3.1 The Maintenance Optimizer

With the Maintenance Optimizer, SAP addresses the challenges associated with maintaining a solution landscape described above:

▶ The Maintenance Optimizer enables you to centrally manage all maintenance activities in your customer landscape.

▶ It determines which Support Packages are relevant and available for each software component in your solution and guides you through the necessary implementation steps using a guided procedure.

▶ The Software Life Cycle Manager service (SLM service) is available in the Maintenance Optimizer to automate the process of downloading selected Support Packages. This service is used to automatically save the Support Packages you require in a central directory. At the same time, existing Support Packages are recognized and not requested again for download from the SAP global support backbone. With the latest enhancements in SAP Solution Manager, it is now possible to control the distribution and import of Support Packages on the servers centrally using the Maintenance Optimizer. To import the Support Packages, the Maintenance Optimizer calls up the existing import programs, such as Support Package Manager (SPAM), Java Support Package Manager (JSPM), SAP Add-On Installation Tool (SAINT), and SAP Enhancement Package Installer.

▶ In the Transport Management System (TMS; part of CTS), it is possible to distribute changes, for instance, SAP Notes corrections, modifications, and configuration changes, in the system landscapes. In the past, this function was only available for the ABAP stack; the functions needed to support it were not available in the non-ABAP environment, for example, the ability to distribute an iView (application in SAP NetWeaver Portal). SP14 of SAP NetWeaver 7.0 has enhanced the TMS. These enhancements allow you to use the TMS for any enhancements outside of the ABAP stack (see also Section 9.2.1). The Maintenance Optimizer can now be used to control the TMS thanks to the latest enhancements.[1]

---

1   This function is currently being piloted.

Figure 9.18 shows an overview of the maintenance processes in the system landscape.

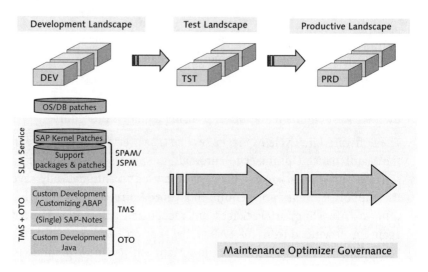

Figure 9.18 Overview of Maintenance Processes in the System Landscape

Aims and Advantages of the Maintenance Optimizer

To summarize, the Maintenance Optimizer facilitates the following improvements in the maintenance process:

▶ **Transparency**
The Maintenance Optimizer provides an overview of all maintenance activities in your system landscape.

▶ **Control**
The entire maintenance process is controlled using the Maintenance Optimizer.

▶ **Efficiency through standardization**
The Maintenance Optimizer is the central entry point for planning and implementing your maintenance activities. It guides you through the necessary steps, simplifies maintenance, and helps you lower your operating costs.

The Maintenance Optimizer in Detail

The Maintenance Optimizer supports you in managing and implement- **The basic concept**
ing maintenance activities in your system landscape.

The system and solution information in SAP Solution Manager accessible in the *Solution Manager System Landscape* transaction (SMSY) serves
as a basis and reference for maintenance transactions. You can assign a
solution or one or more systems to your maintenance transaction for the
greatest possible flexibility. The Maintenance Optimizer interacts with
the SAP global support backbone to download the Support Package you
have selected from there. To make this possible, s-users for SAP Service
Marketplace must be created and assigned to the SAP Solution Manager
end users.

Figure 9.19 provides an example of how SAP Solution Manager and the
SAP global support backbone interact.

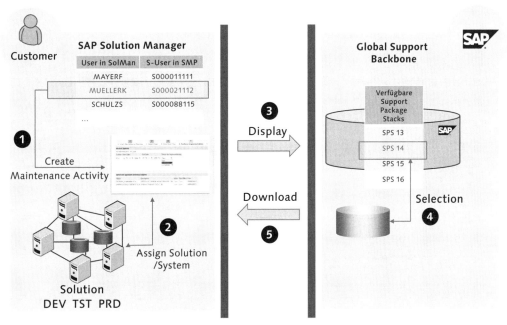

Figure 9.19 Interaction Between the Maintenance Optimizer and the SAP Global
Support Backbone

Process   The end user MUELLERK creates a maintenance transaction (1) and assigns a solution or system to it (2). SAP Solution Manager establishes a connection to the SAP global support backbone, and all currently available Support Packages (3) are displayed. The Support Packages selected by the user are stored in the download basket of end user S000021112 (4) and downloaded from there (5).

The Maintenance Optimizer (Figure 9.20) leads you through the following steps intended for the maintenance transaction:

1. Planning maintenance

2. Selecting the required Support Packages

3. Downloading the selected Support Packages

4. Implementation:

   ▶ Distributing and importing the Support Packages in the system landscape

   ▶ Controlling transports and distribution in the system landscape

5. Closing the maintenance transaction

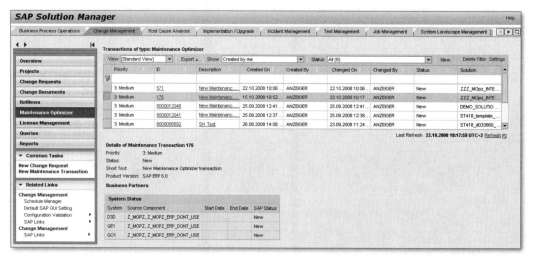

Figure 9.20   Maintenance Optimizer in the Change Management Work Center

You can call up the Maintenance Optimizer in SAP Solution Manager directly from the Change Management work center.

There, you first see an overview of all of the maintenance activities you have created. Then you create a new maintenance transaction in the Change Management work center.

You enter a priority and a short text for your maintenance transaction in the PLAN MAINTENANCE function step. You also assign it a solution or the systems that you want to maintain. You have the option of assigning documents, containing project information for example, to your maintenance transaction, as well as persons, to whom you can assign release authorization. When you implement a corresponding authorization concept, you can ensure that only selected persons can perform a release for your maintenance transaction.

Planning maintenance

SAP Solution Manager now establishes a connection to the SAP global support backbone and offers you the options described below. First, you receive an overview of all the Support Package stacks available for your product. After selecting the target stack you want, the Maintenance Optimizer calculates all Support Packages required. The calculation is based on the software status of the systems you have referenced in the maintenance transaction.

Selecting the Support Packages

After you have selected the Support Packages you want, you go to step 3, downloading the relevant Support Packages.

The Support Packages you have selected are now in the SAP Service Marketplace download basket and can be downloaded from there.

To download the selected Support Packages, you have the following options: You can continue to use the SAP Download Manager preinstalled on your PC, which connects to the SAP Service Marketplace and downloads all Support Packages in the download basket to your local PC. A significantly easier option is to use the Maintenance Optimizer available as of SPS 15. It now controls the Software Life Cycle Manager service (SLM service), which saves the selected Support Packages automatically in a central download directory. Available Support Packages are not downloaded again. The SLM service is optional and requires preconfiguration.

Downloading the selected Support Packages

All selected Support Packages are referenced in the maintenance transaction so that you can always see which Support Packages are being imported. You can also request a report on the side effects from SAP Notes. It contains a list of SAP Notes that correct errors that can occur when Support Packages are imported.

Implementation

Once the Support Packages have been successfully downloaded, they have to be distributed to the particular systems and imported there. Previously, the Maintenance Optimizer offered the option of managing the status of implementation in each system. This provided a quick overview of the status of maintenance activities, but meant that the statuses had to be saved reliably. Activities such as distributing and importing Support Packages into the systems and distributing transport requests previously had to be performed independently of the Maintenance Optimizer with the existing tools.

With the latest enhancements, these functions have now been integrated into the Maintenance Optimizer. The Maintenance Optimizer controls the processes of distributing and importing Support Packages[2] and distributing transport requests in the system tracks. It also calls up the appropriate SAP tools, ensures that the individual steps are called up in the correct order, and takes you through the maintenance transaction step by step. If you use this preconfigured function, you benefit from enhanced navigation for the implementation step, which provides the functions and tools you require.

Scenarios for the maintenance transaction

The Maintenance Optimizer essentially offers you two scenarios for the maintenance transaction: the single system update and the track update.[3]

Single system update

Single system update assumes that you want to install a new system on a system release defined by you, for example, when creating a development system for a new system landscape. In this case, the initially installed system is provided with the latest Support Packages.

The Maintenance Optimizer finds the Support Packages required for the system and, with confirmation from the end user, downloads them into the download directory. The Maintenance Optimizer helps to ensure that

---

2   In the current version of the SLM service, the distribution of SAP kernel patches is not yet supported.
3   This function is currently being piloted.

the import tools are available and started in the current version. The Support Packages are imported into the target system, and the Maintenance Optimizer displays the current status for each step in the procedure.

Track update allows you to bring a system group (development, test, and production system) to a standardized, up-to-date status. In addition to the Support Packages, it is usually necessary to import further changes into the entire landscape using transport requests. This might result in a need to adopt customer developments, because the SAP objects on which they are based have changed. It is also possible that any errors in Support Packages are corrected using SAP Notes or that changes occur in the settings you have adapted to your own requirements, although no customer developments are present in your system. These changes are imported into the system landscape by transport requests. You can create the transport requests from the Maintenance Optimizer and distribute them in the system landscape. The Maintenance Optimizer ensures that the activities are performed in the proper order by using additional interfaces that guide the end user through all of the required steps.

Track update

The enhanced implementation process includes the following steps:

Enhanced implementation process

1. **Planning**
   In the first step, planning, the Maintenance Optimizer checks the import tools and, if necessary, updates them to the current status. It also checks if all required Support Packages are available.

2. **Development**
   In the development step, the required Support Packages are first imported into the development system. The development system is now at the required status.

   You can now create a transport request and release it. It contains all changes that need to be transported into the production system. It is possible to use the enhanced Transport Management System (TMS; from SAP NetWeaver 7.0 SP 14 onward) for enhancements outside of the ABAP stack (see Section 9.2.1).

   After the final release of the transport request, it is ready to be imported into the test system along with all further changes.

3. **Test**

The required Support Packages are now imported into the test system, followed by the transport request. The test system now has the required status, and you can begin the tests.

If errors are detected during the tests, you correct them in the development system and transport them into the test system to perform the tests again. As soon as the test system is working free of errors, you can skip to the next phase, go live.

4. **Go live**

In this phase, the Support Packages and transports are imported into the production system. Your production system now has the required status, and you can close the maintenance transaction.

Closing the
maintenance
transaction

This takes you to the last maintenance step, and you can close the maintenance transaction so that it can no longer be changed.

The Maintenance Optimizer in SAP Solution Manager offers you all of the support you need to plan and maintain your systems and solutions. It guides you through the individual steps using tried and tested SAP tools to import Support Packages and transports. The tools are started directly from the Maintenance Optimizer. The Maintenance Optimizer is therefore the central application for carrying out comprehensive maintenance activities in your system landscape.

9.3.2 Maintenance Optimizer for SAP ERP

Enhancement
Packages

SAP's release strategy is to make all new functions of the SAP ERP standard software available as a series of optional enhancements (*SAP enhancement packages*). This allows you to enhance your business applications with new technology and processes using a flexible, modular approach without having to upgrade your current SAP ERP system. As an SAP ERP customer, you therefore avoid the effort associated with complex upgrades and can implement new product-specific or industry-specific functions and enterprise services with greater speed and ease.

You can find details of the SAP enhancement packages for SAP ERP on the SAP Service Marketplace at *http://service.sap.com/erp-ehp*.

The Maintenance Optimizer provides you with support for using SAP enhancement packages. When performing maintenance for SAP ERP, the Maintenance Optimizer offers you two options:

▶ Maintenance

▶ Installation of SAP enhancement packages

For maintenance, you import the new Support Packages for your SAP ERP system without using a new function. This involves importing Support Packages for SAP products that do not support any SAP enhancement packages. You therefore benefit from technical improvements or changes in the law or taxes but do not use any new business functions.

Maintenance

An important advantage of using SAP enhancement packages is that no release update is required; Support Packages are imported instead. The Maintenance Optimizer offers the following options for this:

Installing SAP enhancement packages

▶ Employ an additional *technical usage* of the SAP enhancement package already installed.

▶ Install a more recent version of SAP enhancement packages and an additional technical usage.

You currently have the option of installing SAP enhancement packages for SAP ERP version 6.0. On the basis of the referenced systems in the maintenance transaction, the Maintenance Optimizer recognizes that you want to maintain a product that supports SAP enhancement packages. In the SELECT FILES step, select the ENHANCEMENT PACKAGE INSTALLATION option. The Maintenance Optimizer then connects to the SAP global support backbone and provides you with the following options:

▶ Install another technical usage.

▶ Install a new SAP enhancement package with the option of selecting another technical usage.

It also determines the files you require. During the guided selection, the Maintenance Optimizer creates a configuration file (XML format) that contains details of the files to be selected. When this configuration file is being imported, the SAP Add-On Installation Tool (SAINT) or the SAP Enhancement Package Installer use it. This ensures that all files are imported into the systems in the correct order, thereby preventing possible errors and simplifying the import process. You can find out which SAP products are used by SAP enhancement packages in the current SAP release strategy at *http://service.sap.com/releasestrategy*. Using SAP enhancement packages makes it much easier for you to use new business functions for SAP ERP.

Upgrade to SAP ERP 6.0

To be able to benefit from simplified use of additional business functions in SAP enhancement packages, you first have to upgrade to SAP ERP 6.0. The Maintenance Optimizer provides support for this. All SAP releases (from Release 4.0B) can upgrade to SAP ERP 6.0.

If an upgrade to SAP ERP 6.0 is possible for the product version selected in the Maintenance transaction, the UPGRADE option is automatically available.

As well as a simple upgrade to SAP ERP 6.0, it is also possible to combine the upgrade to SAP ERP 6.0 with the installation of an SAP enhancement package.

Support from the Maintenance Optimizer

The Maintenance Optimizer provides you with support for determining and implementing the corresponding SAP enhancement package and calculates all files that you have to download in addition to the files on the upgrade DVD provided by the SAP global support backbone. It also guides you through the implementation of these files. The files you select are saved in a configuration file that is then used by the installation tools to import all necessary files in the correct order.

9.3.3   Authorizations and Reports in the Maintenance Optimizer

Authorizations

The Maintenance Optimizer specifies the individual process steps for planning and implementing your maintenance transaction. The process steps adapt themselves to the particular scenario, but cannot be changed.

Authorizations can be flexibly and easily granted to individuals so that you can implement your company-specific requirements.

Predefined roles are already available to you on delivery, which allow you to create, change, or just display maintenance transactions. You can use these roles as the basis for your maintenance transaction.

You can assign the authorizations you require for each step in the maintenance transaction and distribute them to the relevant people, so it is easy to separate substeps such as planning, requesting, or implementation, and distribute them to different people.

You obtain a list of all maintenance activities and their statuses from Transaction /TMWFLOW/MAINTENANCE. You can limit the search according to various criteria, for example, status, referenced solution or system, or priority to obtain a quick overview of the maintenance transactions.

Analyses

9.3.4 Maintenance Certificate and License Management

A *maintenance certificate* is required to import Support Packages. This applies to all SAP products that are based on SAP NetWeaver 7.0 and higher versions. The maintenance certificate makes it possible for the software logistics tools to recognize the exact scope of the maintenance contract and render tailor-made services, and helps you increase the quality of your SAP solution. The maintenance certificate prevents Support Packages from being downloaded accidentally and distributed to the wrong systems.

Maintenance certificates

You can view your maintenance certificates in the SAP Support Portal using a self-service. However, to make it easier for you, you can also call it up automatically from SAP Solution Manager. Once it has been set up, SAP Solution Manager regularly receives maintenance certificates for managed systems and ensures that the certificates are distributed to them. You can find further information about maintenance certificates at *http://service.sap.com/maintenancecertificate*.

Figure 9.21 shows how maintenance certificates are automatically distributed with SAP Solution Manager. SAP Solution Manager requests a maintenance certificate for the managed systems[4] once a day in the SAP global support backbone (1). The maintenance certificates are then

License Management

4 SAP Solution Manager currently supports the distribution of maintenance certificates for ABAP systems only.

generated in the SAP global support backbone (2). The next time a connection to the SAP global support backbone is established, maintenance certificates are received and are available in SAP Solution Manager (3). As soon as the managed system communicates with SAP Solution Manager, the available certificate is received (4). SAP Solution Manager always requests a maintenance certificate from the SAP global support backbone if none is available for a managed system or the one that is valid for less then 30 days. This ensures that the whole process runs smoothly.

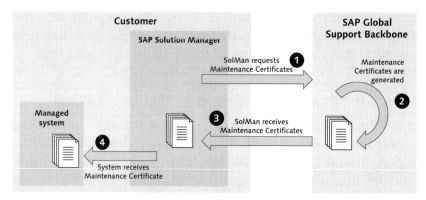

Figure 9.21 Automatically Distributing Maintenance Certificates

From the LICENSE MANAGEMENT view in the Change Management work center (see Figure 9.22), you can see the status of the maintenance certificates for all systems managed by SAP Solution Manager. This means you can see whether SAP Solution Manager has received a valid maintenance certificate for each system and whether it is on the managed system. You can activate automatic maintenance certificate distribution in License Management. You also have the option of downloading all maintenance certificates received together and distributing them to systems not connected to SAP Solution Manager. License Management also provides information about the license keys for your systems, for example, whether valid license keys are available for your systems or whether a license key might expire.

License Management in SAP Solution Manager has laid the foundation for integrating additional functions in the future, such as the ability to automatically call up license keys for SAP systems or perform license auditing using SAP Solution Manager.

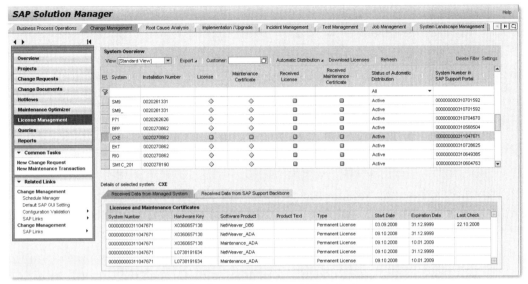

Figure 9.22 License Management in the Change Management Work Center

9.4 Support for Upgrade Projects

Upgrading to SAP ERP or another SAP solution or application poses many challenges for customers and their current SAP landscapes. Particularly where organizations already support projects with SAP Solution Manager, deploying this platform during upgrades can curb expenditures and significantly boost efficiency during planning and implementation. Complementary and integrated components for SAP Solution Manager, such as SAP Upgrade Roadmap and the SAP upgrade services, can also yield substantial benefits. They play a critical role in minimizing the costs and risks associated with upgrading to a newer release, while at the same time maximizing the value added.

SAP Solution Manager addresses a number of upgrade-specific cost drivers such as project management, test administration, implementation of new functions, and end user training. Organizations can draw on SAP's upgrade offerings available via SAP Solution Manager to tackle other known cost drivers, such as modification adjustments and the technical upgrade itself.

Cost drivers

437

Functions

SAP Solution Manager features the following functions and advantages for upgrades:

▸ An integrated test suite boosts efficiency, driving down the time and money invested in testing. SAP Solution Manager Enterprise Edition provides important enhancements to ensure effective and efficient testing (see Section 6.2).

▸ The ability to create training materials for specific processes and roles cuts the cost of compiling training materials and holding courses for end users (see Section 7.2).

▸ SAP Solution Manager enables you to integrate SAP Upgrade Roadmap to increase transparency and ensure the quality of your essential project tasks.

▸ SAP Solution Manager acts as the central collaboration platform for exploiting potential for optimization through the targeted use of SAP service offerings and SAP expertise.

Scenarios

SAP Solution Manager essentially supports two upgrade scenarios:

1. You have already carried out an implementation project in SAP Solution Manager that you can use as a basis for your upgrade project. In this case, you create an initial version of your upgrade project by copying the underlying implementation project.

2. You start your upgrade project from scratch. In this case, the functional support available for upgrade projects is comparable to that available for an implementation project. You can also select an implementation project as the project type for this scenario.

The following section provides a brief overview of the functions available in SAP Solution Manager for the different phases of an upgrade project, based on SAP Upgrade Roadmap. It focuses specifically on the upgrade scenario (1) and the additional functions available for upgrade projects that go beyond implementation projects.

SAP Upgrade
Roadmap

SAP Upgrade Roadmap provides methodical, phase-based guidelines to take you through your upgrade. It addresses aspects such as analyzing and defining objectives for existing business processes, the underlying IT infrastructure before and after the upgrade, the upgrade configuration, and testing for processes in the new release. *Accelerators* link you to transactions in SAP Solution Manager, SAP upgrade offerings, and other sources of SAP information, such as best-practices documents and project templates to accelerate your upgrade. During an upgrade, you can choose to display only Roadmap content that is relevant to your specific upgrade path, such as from SAP CRM 5.0 to SAP CRM 2007. The Roadmap guides you directly to the functions to be supported in SAP Solution Manager, such as central system management, documentation, and business process testing. You can monitor your project activities using the overview of documentation, statuses, and problem messages. In short, with SAP Upgrade Roadmap, you can always access all of the sources of documentation required for adapting the system's functions and technical settings.

Like all the other Roadmaps, SAP Upgrade Roadmap is available as a project-specific working version in SAP Solution Manager or as a self-contained HTML version. SAP is constantly adding to the list of content available for the Upgrade Roadmap. SAP Upgrade Roadmap currently provides product- and solution-specific information for over 60 upgrade paths.

Figure 9.23 illustrates which upgrade-specific activities SAP Solution Manager supports in the different phases of the SAP Upgrade Roadmap.

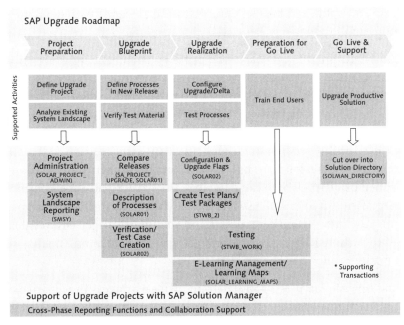

Figure 9.23 Upgrade Support from SAP Solution Manager

Run SAP Roadmap

For companies that are preparing for service-oriented architecture (SOA) and planning an upgrade, the Run SAP Roadmap (see Section 5.1.1) provides support to answer the question of which type of upgrade provide the best *return on investment*:

▶ **Technical upgrade**
The technical upgrade focuses purely on upgrading the technological base. Business functions used remain unchanged. Customer-specific enhancements and modifications are investigated and analyzed, and technical optimization is also performed, for example, in the areas of archiving and master data administration.

▶ **Functional upgrade**
A functional upgrade involves implementing new functions, customizing the user interface, replacing the modifications and functional enhancements with (new) standard functions, and generally reducing the complexity of systems. It is also possible to stabilize the basic functions, for example, by using SAP NetWeaver Master Data Management.

▶ **Strategic upgrade**
The strategic upgrade focuses on restricting competition by enabling new and optimized business processes and scenarios with new functions and introducing a service-oriented architecture.

Project Preparation

In the *project preparation* phase, you begin by defining an upgrade project as a container for your upgrade activities and results. This is also the stage at which you assess the present state of your system landscape. The options for *system landscape reporting* let you analyze your data using different parameters, for example, by software components and Support Packages for the product being upgraded, by associated SAP systems within the overall solution, by non-SAP products, or by database software and patch levels. You can download the system landscape information to Microsoft Excel and use it to define your ideal target IT landscape. Storing the information centrally in SAP Solution Manager ensures that all of the data remains accessible and gives a complete representation of your system landscape.

Upgrade Blueprint

In the *Upgrade Blueprint*, you determine which business processes and functions are new or different in the upgrade release. If your existing business processes were composed in the Business Process Repository (BPR), SAP Solution Manager can also detect such changes automatically using the comparison functions. Changes and new features include any business content predefined by SAP in the BPR for business scenarios, processes, and process steps as well as additional upgrade-specific documentation.

In this phase, you also define how modifications and interfaces are handled. The *Custom Development Management Cockpit* (CDMC) (see Section 5.5.1) can greatly help identify existing modifications and calculate the time required for the upgrade project. In this phase, you also decide whether existing test cases can be used in the upgrade project, or you create new ones. With SAP Solution Manager, you can easily upload test cases and save them centrally, regardless of their format; you can also incorporate non-SAP test tools. Training concepts also have to be created and training activities planned.

SAP Solution Manager is your central portal for accessing all of this information, allowing you to create new information or reuse existing resources. The project team and end users can therefore share their knowledge effortlessly. If you are using an existing Solution Manager project as a basis, you can tailor the information quickly and systematically to your upgrade project.

In the *upgrade realization* phase, SAP Solution Manager assists you with the upgrade and delta configuration. You no longer need to work through all of the activities in the SAP Implementation Guide (IMG) searching for the relevant configuration settings. SAP Solution Manager simplifies these steps. Using the release information about the SAP components, it automatically determines which IMG activities and documentation are relevant for your upgrade and proposes them in the SAP Solution Manager upgrade configuration transaction (*upgrade flag*). To ensure that you do not overlook an IMG activity that may be omitted from the list, SAP Solution Manager also lists the configuration activities that are not assigned to the upgrade project, thereby allowing you to check these activities as well. You can find this information in the *Solution Manager Analysis* (Transaction SOLAR_EVAL) in the *project view* reports.

Upgrade realization

Upgrade testing After configuration, you are ready to start testing the upgrade. You generate process-based test plans using SAP Solution Manager's integrated test suite and execute them. The test organizer has a single, central overview (see Section 6.2) in SAP Solution Manager, with test evaluation functions for monitoring the relevant test activities and status information.

Preparations for going live In the *final preparation* phase, you conclude the test series with system and integration testing to ensure that your business processes will run smoothly after the upgrade. To help promote end user buy-in, it is vital that you keep users informed of changes resulting from the upgrade. You can use the training concepts compiled in the Upgrade Blueprint phase to create training materials quickly and easily in the E-Learning Management environment, particularly if you use SAP Solution Manager's integrated *Learning Map Builder*. Training experts can create role-specific HTML-based Learning Maps: Lessons, PowerPoint presentations, and other documentation that were added to the project during the realization phase can be inserted into the Learning Map structure. Learning Maps compiled in this way can be sent centrally to the relevant end users by email (see Section 7.2).

Go live and Support The *go-live and support* phase is where you conduct all of the activities that pertain to upgrading the production solution and going live. You copy process and system information from the upgrade project to the directory of customer-specific solutions, the *Solution Directory*, and adapt existing information. Because this information is the basis for Solution Monitoring, this step results in an infrastructure you can use to monitor business processes proactively.

SAP Solution Manager cuts the duration and expense of upgrade projects. SAP's methodical upgrade expertise and predefined scenario content can reduce the total cost of ownership and significantly increase efficiency in many project tasks. Customers that already deploy SAP Solution Manager reap extra benefits when they upgrade: Information they stored in implementation projects can form the basis for an upgrade project; reporting functions supply upgrade-relevant information concerning the solutions, systems, and products in use.

Consistent use of SAP Solution Manager also leaves customers well equipped for future application management requirements. Upgrade projects, for instance, can be used for new implementation projects. All of the information can be copied in full or in part to new implementation projects. Business Process Monitoring lets you monitor updated and live business processes during production operations. SAP Solution Manager features a Change Request Management scenario for tackling changes that may become necessary over the course of an upgrade project (see Section 9.1).

9.5 Global Rollout

In recent years, global rollouts have become increasingly important in many organizations. The basic assumption is that certain business processes are identical or similar throughout the organization and thus lend themselves to standardization. The potential for standardization is particularly high in enterprises organized regionally or by business area. It therefore makes sense to harmonize and standardize procedures for implementing and tailoring such processes, so that the company need only design them once and can provide or reuse them in various solutions.

Identical processes company-wide

The concept's growth in significance can be attributed to a number of factors. One reason is increased internationalization and globalization coupled with the demand for, and thus expansion of, a company's business operations. This tendency goes hand in hand with the dynamics of technological and economic change, which are causing existing business models to be adapted at ever-shorter intervals. At the same time, group-wide process harmonization and standardization should improve the organization's efficiency and decrease overall operating costs. This leads them to elaborate on a standard, company-wide business process model for certain lines of business.

This is where SAP Solution Manager comes in: It makes it possible to create designed scenarios and processes as templates. In addition to process structures, templates contain process documentation, transactions, configuration settings and documents, developments such as test cases, and roll-out training materials. You can reuse templates straightaway in rollout projects (subsequently referred to as *rollouts*) without intensive preparatory work. The result is that you can go live faster and draw on

Templates

fewer resources in your rollouts because business processes only need tailoring and testing in line with local or business requirements.

Another way of reducing the amount of adjustment needed in rollouts if templates have been updated is to use a comparison tool, which automatically highlights changes and new features in a new template version and provides comparison functions.

9.5.1 Global Rollout: Overview

The scope of the example implementation project has been extended to include business processes from the Interaction Center. Following a successful pilot project to implement the Interaction Center at the head office, the management of the company plans to set up local Interaction Centers at various European, American, and Asian sales centers with the goal of making order processing procedures more flexible (see Figure 9.24).

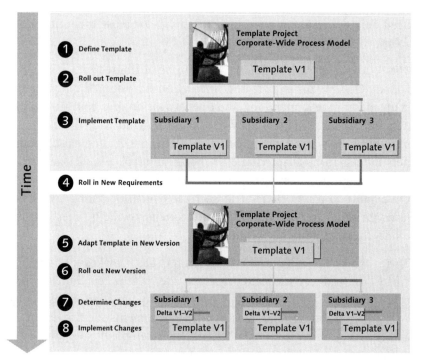

Figure 9.24 Global Rollout: Overview

A cross-functional team (a template team) is enlisted to create a global template (1). Based on the processes tested in the implementation project, the team creates a template project and defines the template, taking into account business and rollout-related issues. The template includes business processes and other content such as process documentation, cross-functional configuration structures, preconfiguration, and test documents — all of the materials that bring about faster implementations in rollout projects.

Defining a template

The template completed in the first rollout phase is made available to selected, local sites, for instance in Europe (2). Strictly speaking, this process is also a rollout. The application scenario dictates how this process is approached. If the template and implementation projects are in the same SAP Solution Manager system, you do not need to transport the template. In other cases, you need to transport the template to the relevant rollout target system of SAP Solution Manager. You also have to copy any content that was created locally in the reference systems, such as the preconfiguration, to the target systems.

Rolling out the template

Next, the rollout team responsible implements the template (3). The procedure is similar to the example implementation project described in Section 5.2. To implement the template, the team creates a rollout project of type *implementation*. In this case, however, the source for the implementation is the template that has been rolled out, not the BPR. The template's *global attributes*, in turn, can dictate the scope of the changes that can be made to a global template when actually implementing it.

Implementing the template

After piloting the template in Europe, the template team checks the change requests defined by the rollouts and gradually transfers them to a new template version (4).

Rolling in new requirements

In this step, the Interaction Center scenario is adapted, and CRM campaign management is set up to enable marketing campaigns to be planned, executed, and evaluated more systematically and cost-effectively (5). Part of the adjustment step entails considering local processes in terms of local requirements and making them known in the template project, because company policy is to store all processes centrally, both global and local. An alternative would be to define the local processes

Adapting the template and rolling it out again

in the rollout projects. In the second rollout phase, new versions of the templates are rolled out in America and Asia (6).

Identifying and implementing changes

The rollout team integrates new scenarios by selecting and implementing templates again. For existing scenarios, it uses a comparison tool that compares the old and new template versions and lists any changes that have been made to processes and the assigned objects. This enables the rollout team to identify changes as quickly as possible and to include and implement them in the rollout projects (7 and 8).

The next section explains the options provided by template and implementation projects for global rollouts.

9.5.2 Global Rollout: Details

Working with Templates

You create a template project in the Implementation/Upgrade work center or directly in the Project Administration transaction (SOLAR_PROJECT_ADMIN) by selecting the type TEMPLATE PROJECT. You define the actual template in the TEMPLATES tab page (see Figure 9.25). Here, you create the TEMPLATE SHELL in the customer namespace, for example, ZCAMPAIGN, to gather the corresponding processes and implementation-relevant assignments. You can customize templates on the basis of organizational, regional, component-related, or business criteria. Other potential criteria include the release dependency and the rollout phase. We recommend that you define separate templates for general organizational units, master data, or scenarios that are used in multiple rollouts. As a naming convention, you could include company codes, countries, and components in the template ID. You can create one or more templates for each project. If you want to roll out the template in a different SAP Solution Manager system, you must specify a transportable package when you define the template. We recommend that you enter this on the TRANSPORT REQUESTS tab page straightaway, so that the system offers the package you assign as the standard package for all subsequent templates that you create.

Visibility

A template's VISIBILITY is affected when it is rolled out. You can specify whether a template is still being edited and consequently not yet available (PRIVATE) or has been released for usage (PUBLIC). This is important as a means of preventing an unfinished template or new template version being used in a rollout project, particularly when the template and rollout projects are in the same SAP Solution Manager system.

In addition, you can selective the GLOBAL ROLLOUT FUNCTIONALITY IS ACTIVE checkbox to specify to what extent rollout projects can effect changes in delivered templates that are being implemented. The range of global attributes spans from GLOBAL, which does not permit changes to standard company-wide processes, across various other levels down to LOCAL, which lends rollouts the most flexibility.

Global attributes

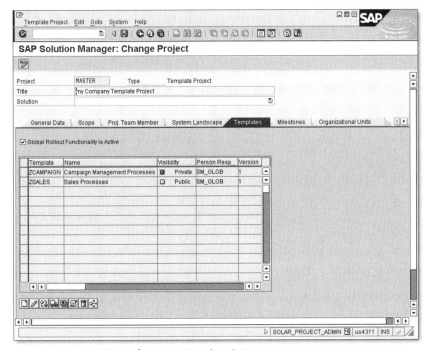

Figure 9.25 Template Definition in Template Project

You use your global rollout strategy to define project standards, which can take different forms, depending on whether you want to bundle only global processes or all of the processes used across the company centrally in one template. The general project data is similar to the data for implementation projects. The system landscape defines which systems should be used as a reference for creating and extracting the preconfiguration, test cases, and similar objects. In the managed systems, you set up IMG and change and transport system projects and assign transport requests to individual projects for grouping purposes.

Reference process
structure

Next, you create the reference process structure with all of the assign-ments relevant to the implementation — similar to an implementa-tion project — in the Business Blueprint (SOLAR01) and Configuration (SOLAR02 transactions. To make the processes available for a rollout, you assign individual scenarios to the templates with which the correspond-ing processes are to be delivered. For business scenarios and configura-tion structures, you use input help on the STRUCTURE tab page to assign the required template(s) in the TEMPLATES column. The GLOBAL ROLLOUT FUNCTIONALITY IS ACTIVE checkbox selected in the Project Administration transaction, along with the global attributes, lets you define the scope of changes that can be made in rollout projects. Initially, these settings apply only to the scenario, but you can transfer them to the lower-level processes and process steps by selecting PASS ON GLOBAL ATTRIBUTE.

Releasing the
template

When you have finished working on the template, you release it for usage in the Project Administration transaction (see Section 5.2). You must always set the visibility to PUBLIC by selecting CHANGE VISIBILITY. If you are transporting the template to a different SAP Solution Manager system, you need to click the template collector DELIVER icon to include it in a transport request. The wizard guides you step by step through all of the necessary activities until you have collected the template con-tent (process structure with implementation-relevant assignments) in a transport request, which you can transport directly to an SAP Solution Manager target system or to the consolidation system via a standard transport route.

Note that the objects created in the reference systems, such as separate reports or preconfigurations, have to be transported separately; the tem-plate contains only the references to these objects.

The procedure is different for template documentation created locally in SAP Solution Manager on the GEN. DOCUMENTATION, CONFIGURATION, DEVELOPMENT, and TEST CASES tab pages. This documentation is entered directly in the template collector and does not have to be transported separately. During the course of the rollout, you also need to ensure con-sistency between the template system landscape and the rollout system landscape, which means the components listed in the template actually have to be physically available. For example, if you extend a template to include the implementation of an SAP NetWeaver BI system, you must ensure that an SAP NetWeaver BI system has been added to the managed system landscape before you implement the template in the rollout. Otherwise, you will not be able to use certain content relevant for the implementation.

Special Features of Rollout Projects

You can now use the released templates for implementation in rollout projects. In the Project Administration transaction, the rollout team calls up the rollout project and selects the relevant templates on the SCOPE tab page. When the project is saved, the process structure is decoupled from the template and referenced, and the system creates copies and notes their origin (template). This reference relationship enables the rollout team to run comparisons against more recent template versions and copy changes at any time. Alternatively, the template documentation is not copied when a rollout project is created; it is only flagged for copying. The result is that the shipped documents are not copied until they are transferred to the project documentation area in the rollout project and actually changed.

Generating a rollout project

The global attribute, which controls the scope of the changes, comes into play during the rollout project. Globally defined scenarios, processes, and process steps offer few options for changing the process structure or implementation-relevant assignments. You can tailor local scenarios and processes to a specific rollout by using the BPR or by adding or deleting assigned objects, such as local programs, Customizing settings, or test cases. Between these two extremes, there is also the option of permitting enhancements but prohibiting deletions. For more detailed information, go to *http://help.sap.com*.

Because the functions that SAP Solution Manager provides for rollouts are based on those provided for implementation projects, you should also refer to the information in Section 5.2.

Comparing and Adapting Templates

Eventually, you may need to change a template in response to a wide range of factors. For example, new location-specific requirements, which you can manage in an organized rollback process, or forthcoming upgrades may trigger the next update cycle. The template team makes any necessary changes in the original template. For major changes, it uses the version counter on the TEMPLATES tab page in the Project Administration transaction and creates a backup copy. When the new version is complete, it has to be distributed to the target organizations again.

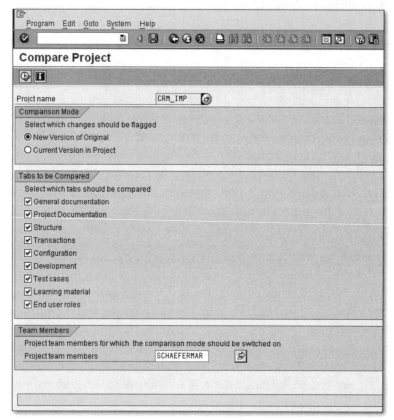

Figure 9.26 Transaction SA_PROJECT_UPGRADE Entry Screen

Comparison tool   This is where the comparison tool (Transaction SA_PROJECT_UPGRADE; see Figure 9.26) comes in. It enables the rollout team to quickly identify changes made to a specific template and copy them to the relevant rollout projects. The system compares the process structure implemented in a rollout project and its assignments against the source from which the structure items were initially copied. This means the comparison report automatically determines the origin and, by association, the relevant source of every structure item. Other possible sources include structure items from the BPR and structure items that were copied and possibly changed during the rollout project. The scope implemented in a rollout project can have a single source or a combination of sources. You can always access details about the origin of structure items on the STRUCTURE tab page in the SOURCE column.

Note that only one production version of a template exists per SAP Solution Manager system. This is the version last set to public or transported to a system. The system automatically uses this version as the source for comparison without you having to select it explicitly.

Besides the process structure, the tool also compares the following assignments that you made in the Business Blueprint (SOLAR01) and Configuration (SOLAR02) transactions:

▶ General documentation

▶ Transactions

▶ Configuration

▶ Development

▶ Test cases

▶ Learning materials

▶ End user roles

Note that the system compares only assignments. You cannot compare changes to the objects themselves. You can tackle these restrictions as follows:

Constraint	How to tackle it
Changes to implementation-relevant assignments not displayed for BC Sets, CATT or eCATT scripts, general documentation (with a few exceptions)	In the template project, create a new BC Set, CATT or eCATT script, or document by copying the existing objects, for instance. Assign this to the relevant structure item and remove the old assignment.
New scenarios not displayed	In the rollout project, copy new scenarios on the SCOPE tab page in the project administration transaction.

As you can see, the comparison tool is not only designed to identify differences between rollouts and their underlying templates, but can also be used earlier in the process. If you base your template on Business Process Repository (BPR) structure items, you can track down release-related changes and align your template with current processes if necessary. Furthermore, when you copy objects (such as a dominant process) within a project, you can use the comparison tool to update the copies with changes made to the master process.

Comparison results You can display the results of the comparison report (see Figure 9.27) in the Business Blueprint and Configuration transactions by clicking the yellow change icon (you must have selected the adjustment mode checkbox by following the menu path SETTINGS • USER-SPECIFIC, ADJUSTMENT MODE INDICATOR). The log for the SPROJECT_PROJECT_UPGRADE background job contains statistics for the changes detected by the tool. Changes are listed in the process structure and on the tab page where the change was found. For reasons of transparency, changes are only flagged for transfer and not copied to the existing project immediately. You can now run a detailed comparison. The ADJUST TO ORIGINAL function shows you details for the following:

▶ Changes (new features and deletions in original) detected by the comparison tool (NEW VERSION OF ORIGINAL)

▶ Changes not indicated by a yellow traffic light that were made in the rollout project after the template was copied (CURRENT VERSION FROM TAB)

If you look at the COMPARISON AND ADJUSTMENT dialog box in Figure 9.27, the area on the left shows you that a preconfiguration has been delivered in a BC Set with the new template version. On the right, you can see that a document has been deleted from the current project. First, the rollout team can copy changes resulting from the template to the rollout project and then implement them step-by-step. To confirm the scope of the changes adopted and close the comparison for the tab page in question, you select COMPLETE (not shown in the figure). This means you have verified all of the tabs indicated as changed for a given structure item. In subsequent comparison runs, the system displays only new changes made to the original, not ones that you have already accepted or ignored. Changes already made locally in the rollout project are never affected when you transfer current template content.

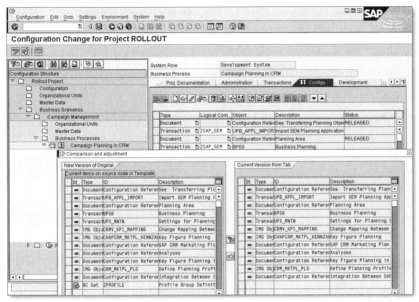

Figure 9.27 Detailed Comparison in Rollout Project

9.5.3 Methodical Support from the Global Template Roadmap

The Global Template Roadmap contains methodical guidelines for organizing projects aimed at compiling and delivering global templates. It is designed for complex implementation and harmonization projects, which generally span multiple solutions or applications, various locations, and, in some cases, various countries. Project managers, support managers, solution and technical consultants, and partners will find the Roadmap useful.

SAP recommends this Roadmap because it provides valuable information for all of the phases, from *global program setup* and *global blueprint and global realization* to *global maintenance and support*, and from planning a project of this kind to designing a rollback procedure. It centrally addresses all of the basic strategic issues relating to a global rollout, such as program management, creation and delivery of templates, system landscape aspects, CCC organization, support infrastructures, and procedures for global and local change requests. The ASAP Implementation Roadmap provides guidance for individual rollout projects. You can also

Phases

453

tailor the Roadmap's content to your organization's requirements and reuse it to define and implement templates (see Section 5.1.5).

Building on expertise validated over the course of many different projects, the Roadmap helps you achieve better results, coordinate a cross-functional team effectively, and simultaneously minimize the costs, risks, and time involved in implementing software across various sites.

9.5.4   Global Rollout – Tips and Tricks

In addition to the methodical instructions in the Global Template Roadmap, certain aspects need to be noted when using template and rollout projects in SAP Solution Manager itself.

Working with Authorizations

Particularly when you carry out template and rollout projects in an SAP Solution Manager system, it is important to assign authorizations at the project level to protect the template and rollout teams' work against unauthorized access. You can do this by adapting authorization object S_PROJECT, PROJECT MANAGEMENT: PROJECT AUTHORIZATION AND ASSIGNING THE RELEVANT PROJECT ID. We also recommend using different document contexts for SAP Solution Manager template and rollout projects to provide additional protection against unwanted or unauthorized changes.

Additionally, the RESTRICT CHANGES TO NODES IN PROJECT TO ASSIGNED TEAM MEMBERS checkbox in the Project Administration transaction enables you to specify that only users assigned to particular business scenarios or processes may edit those parts of the process structure. This can be useful if global and country-specific templates are being created as part of one template project but are edited by different template teams.

Project documentation

To enable members of the template team to create documentation, we recommend that you configure the Knowledge Warehouse authorization object S_IWB to give members authorization for the folder group with the same name as the project ID. You may also need to assign authorizations for editing (creating, changing, deleting) template documentation, general documentation, configuration documentation, test case and development documentation (folder group SOLAR00), and the document templates (folder group TEMPLATES). The rollout team, alternatively, usually needs display authorization only for document templates and general documentation delivered with the template. The same applies to project documentation, as for template projects.

In individual cases, you may need to change or delete global structure items. Only selected super users, such as project managers, should be authorized to do so. You need authorization for authorization object PROJECT MANAGEMENT: AUTHORIZATION FOR GENERAL PROJECT FUNCTIONS, S_PROJ_GEN, with the value GLOB in the PROJ_FUNC field, to delete structure elements from a template.

Working with Different Template Versions

You cannot display template versions that were created explicitly in the project administration transaction at a later date. However, if you want to reproduce the different versions and processing statuses and therefore display the versions, copy the relevant master project and indicate the versions in the project name and ID. If you still intend to deliver a template's predecessor version, you need to freeze the appropriate template state in a transport request, which you should create using the TEMPLATE COLLECTOR in the project administration transaction.

If the template and rollout projects are in the same SAP Solution Manager system, you need to consider the following points. The template documentation is referenced on a 1:1 basis in the rollout project. If documentation is changed in the template project, it becomes visible immediately in the rollout project, even if it cannot be changed there. Consequently, the documentation ceases to correlate with the business processes currently implemented. We therefore recommend that you change documents in the template project using copies by first copying the documents with a new name to indicate the version and then making your changes.

Working with Multilevel Templates

You can use multilevel templates in SAP Solution Manager. This means that you can use a given template, Template A, to enhance Template A', and use Template A' as the final basis for the rollout. This approach lets you create country-specific variants from an international master template. It also allows you to copy processes from the Business Process Repository (BPR) to a template project to be modified and rolled out in the template.

Transporting Templates and Template Projects

Always deliver templates from the original projects (the template projects in which they were created), not from copied projects. This is a basic condition for the comparison tool to function correctly; when you compare templates, the tool determines only the sources of the direct predecessor.

The following table clarifies which transport options are best suited to specific situations:

	Template Transport	Template Project Transport
Use	Recommended procedure for global rollouts if template is defined and rolled out in different SAP Solution Manager systems	Migrating a complete template project to a different SAP Solution Manager system
Scope of transport	All template data:	All template and project-related data:
	Project templates used in the template	All project standards (project templates, keywords, status values)
	Template documentation created locally (general documentation, configuration, test case, development documentation)	Template and project documentation created locally
		Process structure and configuration structure with implementation-relevant assignments
	Process structure and configuration structure with implementation-relevant assignments	Logical components with main instances and product versions
	Information about product versions and main instances (mapping to logical components in target system)	Header data (general data, scope, project team members)
	Structure in project language and translations (if translated and relevant option selected)	Data from the ADMINISTRATION tab page

Table 9.1 Recommendations for Transports

	Template Transport	Template Project Transport
Not considered	System landscape data for systems (Transaction SMSY)	System landscape data for systems (Transaction SMSY);
	Logical components	Manual checks required to ensure that system landscape data
	Data from ADMINISTRATION and PROJ. DOCUMENTATION tab pages	maintained with the project (logical components, RFCs) has been maintained in Transaction SMSY
Access to transport functions via transactions	Project Administration, TEMPLATES tab page, TRANSPORT icon	Project Administration, PROJECT • TRANSPORT

Table 9.1 Recommendations for Transports (Cont.)

Support for Rollback Processes

In terms of methodology, it would be practical to use the Global Template Roadmap with the Upgrade Template Version work package in this case. This basically entails setting up a process using change request mechanisms that takes into account local requirements the next time a template is changed. You also need to check which changes already made locally need to be rolled back into the central template to aid standardization.

The purpose is to define the scope of the rollback process in detail: Which elements from the process structure are to be transferred with which implementation-relevant assignments, for example, documentation, transactions, configuration, customer developments, and test cases. Other purely local objects, such as local documents, which are of no additional use to the template or other locations, and BC Sets with purely local Customizing values are not usually relevant for the rollback process.

Scope of the rollback

Although SAP Solution Manager does not provide explicit functions to support rollbacks, it does contain certain elements that help you identify what may need to be rolled back. For instance, you can use keywords or naming conventions for local objects so you can identify them directly and quickly by running a project analysis. This presupposes strict compliance with project standards defined earlier in the project.

The following approach offers another option:

1. Copy the rollout project immediately after you have selected the relevant templates but *before* you implement any local changes.

2. Compare the copy of the rollout project after the rollout project has been implemented against the last named project (Transaction SA_PROJECT_UPGRADE). This means the rollout acts as the source for the comparison, and the copy as the target.

The comparison tool identifies all changes that were made locally in the rollout project. You therefore have a list of all changes made to processes and assignments that you can use as a starting point for adapting the central template. This also reduces the risk of unnecessary duplicate developments.

In conclusion, SAP Solution Manager supports global rollout projects designed to standardize and harmonize your business processes by letting you adopt a systematic, structured approach. You can channel all of your process and preconfiguration know-how into templates for reuse in different locations. This allows you to keep resources and expenses associated with implementations to a minimum. You can compare different template versions to adapt and roll out projects quickly and supply them with the relevant changes. The Global Template and Implementation Roadmaps provide methodical support for this approach.

Success stories show how customers can optimize their application management processes using SAP Solution Manager.

10   Customer Success Stories

So far in this book, the concept of SAP Solution Manager and its individual functions have been described in theory. In this section, 12 customer success stories explain how these functions are used in practice. The stories describe how SAP Solution Manager is used in implementation projects (Sections 10.1 and 10.2), for test management purposes (Sections 10.3 and 10.4), in IT support (Sections 10.5 to 10.7), for Business Process Monitoring (Section 10.8), for system monitoring (Sections 10.9 and 10.10), and in Change Request Management (Sections 10.11 and 10.12). The overall effect is to highlight once again the fact that SAP Solution Manager covers the entire application management life cycle.

10.1   Telecom Argentina — Better Project Management and Communications with SAP Solution Manager

Summary

For the Argentinean telecommunications company Telecom Argentina S.A., SAP Solution Manager was crucial in successfully implementing SAP ERP. Contributing factors were the methodology provided, communication support, project documentation management, and the transparency created.

Telecom Argentina S.A. is a large company by anyone's standards — with around 15,000 staff and 10 million customers. So when it came to implementing new enterprise resource planning (ERP) software, the telco decided to team up with IBM and SAP Consulting. Together they introduced the SAP Solution Manager Application Management solution — optimizing the coordination of project participants and tasks and significantly improving documentation and communications.

Headquartered in Buenos Aires and with revenues of around US$2.4 billion in 2006, Telecom Argentina is one of the two largest telecommunications players in the Argentine market, offering a broad portfolio of fixed-line, cell phone, and Internet services. The company was one of the first in the region to deploy SAP Solution Manager and to reap its business benefits.

Shaping up for the future with SAP ERP

Not so long ago, Telecom Argentina was grappling with a complex array of legacy solutions. In late 2005 the company recognized that it was time for a sweeping change: It decided to replace its heterogeneous environment with a single, integrated application — SAP R/3 Enterprise software (functionality now found in the SAP ERP application). This delivered process standardization, greater efficiency, and greater adaptability. It also brought the company in line with the IT strategy of Telecom Italia, an established SAP customer and owner of 50% of Telecom Argentina's shares.

The project kicked off in February 2006, with go-live slated for January of the following year. It involved stakeholders at sites the length and breadth of the country, as well as a wide range of activities. So one thing was clear: Meeting the defined goals within the defined time frame was not going to be easy.

One powerful tool for the entire life cycle

Telecom Argentina needed a structured, proven approach to introducing the new software. The answer was SAP Solution Manager, a central platform for managing SAP software across the entire life cycle — from planning and implementation to customization and optimization. "SAP filled us in on the tool early in the sales process," says Alejandro Gozzo Bisso, project director at Telecom Argentina. "We particularly liked the ASAP methodology, which gave us a step-by-step approach to implementation. What's more," continues Gozzo Bisso, "we can use SAP Solution Manager in collaboration with any consulting partner — so we have flexibility in the future."

The perfect partner

In close cooperation with prime contractor IBM, Telecom Argentina worked together with SAP Consulting on the deployment of SAP Solution Manager. "SAP Consulting proved the ideal partner for the task," explains Guillermo Said, application technology manager at Telecom Argentina. "And not just because of their SAP Solution Manager expertise. We knew we could count on them to install the product with the correct configurations and aligned with SAP software strategies."

In addition to expert advice and assistance from SAP Consulting, Telecom Argentina received high-quality training from the SAP Education organization. Several workshops, developed by the SAP Solution Manager team, were provided to all customer key users, IT consultants, and partner consultants to establish a common understanding of the usage of SAP Solution Manager for each individual phase. These workshops were part of the ongoing support during the project.

Coordinating the sizeable team, with participants drawn from a number of companies, was a major challenge. "We had around 250 people working in diverse roles — so it was essential to manage activities and responsibilities as effectively as possible," explains Gozzo Bisso. "SAP Solution Manager helped organize the work using the defined methodology."

SAP experts keep the project on track

"SAP Consulting had a pivotal supporting role in the management of the project," Gozzo Bisso continues. "They worked closely with IBM and our in-house project team to coordinate consultants — and played an active part in project-team meetings."

Working hand in hand with SAP Consulting, Telecom Argentina put SAP Solution Manager through its paces — with positive results. "Each phase of the project was documented and all information stored in a single repository — making it easier to access and maintain," states Said. "As a result, we were able to efficiently manage and prioritize tasks such as testing and reporting and reduce the time needed to complete them. And employees joining the project at a later stage found the information they needed more quickly."

Big savings

But that's not all. The tool also enabled Telecom Argentina to streamline internal communications between team members. "We took advantage of the service-desk functionality of SAP Solution Manager to significantly cut the number of emails going back and forth," explains Said.

"Any questions were entered into the tool and automatically forwarded to the right person, so any issues could be resolved immediately. More than 5,000 messages were exchanged over the course of the project. Without SAP Solution Manager the figure would have been much higher. We made big savings in time and resources."

Great expectations, great results Telecom's SAP software went live, as scheduled, in January 2007. Within the scope of the initiative, the company also introduced the data warehousing functionality of the SAP NetWeaver Business Intelligence and SAP NetWeaver Portal components. As a result, the telco now enjoys greater integration, greater transparency, and greater agility — and is prepared for the challenges of the future.

Gozzo Bisso has no doubts that SAP Solution Manager played a major part in the success of the implementation: "SAP Solution Manager was a key factor in the project and met all our expectations, both in terms of timing and the quality of services delivered. Our people were quick to realize the value of the tool — and have really bought into it."

Total transparency Since go-live, Telecom Argentina has continued to reap the benefits of SAP Solution Manager. For example, Change Request Management functionality (ChaRM) has given the telecommunications giant 360-degree visibility into software modifications — based on a clearly defined process with complete documentation.

"The change request management functionalities of SAP Solution Manager have helped us establish a controlled environment where all modifications are reviewed and approved," explains Gozzo Bisso. "The whole process is transparent. And that means we can comply more easily with legislation such as Sarbanes-Oxley."

Just the beginning Telecom Argentina is now deploying the tool in other projects while supporting continuing production using the Change Request Management functionality. "At the moment, we are leveraging SAP Solution Manager to define and document processes within SAP NetWeaver Portal, and this will provide more user-friendly access to our ERP software," says Gozzo Bisso. "We're also using it to add new ERP functionality – for example, for human capital management, foreign trade, and real-estate management."

10.2   City of Vienna — SAP Solution Manager Streamlines Introduction of SAP Software for Vienna's Municipal Government

Summary

MA 14, the internal IT department of the City of Vienna, uses SAP Solution Manager to optimize SAP implementations. This high-performance tool facilitates efficient document management and quicker testing and provides a clearer overview of the status of projects.

When it comes to getting SAP software up and running quickly and effectively, project management is the key. That's why MA 14, the in-house IT unit of the City of Vienna, Austria, chose the SAP Solution Manager tool. This state-of-the-art tool includes proven methodologies to expedite SAP projects, and it also enhances visibility, accelerates testing, and provides a central repository for all project- and process-related documentation.

Vienna's municipal government is composed of 80 departments and agencies, each responsible for specific tasks or public services, such as refuse collection and water supply. The organization employs approximately 35,000 people to ensure that the Austrian capital runs smoothly. As part of its drive to streamline operations, the City of Vienna is implementing a number of SAP solutions with expert support delivered by MA 14. With a staff of around 450, MA 14 handles a wide range of tasks — from consulting to ongoing operations — and has a certified SAP Customer Competence Center location.

In-house SAP software expertise

Because SAP software plays a central role within Vienna's municipal government, MA 14 has built up a close relationship with the SAP Consulting organization over the years. "As our implementation partners, SAP consultants deliver expert advice and assistance across the entire solution life cycle, from planning to testing and go-live," explains Bernhard Stickler of the SAP Integration and Consulting Unit at the City of Vienna. "What's more, they provide direct links to SAP developers — a must when introducing new solutions."

To streamline management of SAP software implementations, MA 14 wanted to introduce a state-of-the-art tool. The new solution had to cen-

Multiple implementations with rapid introduction

trally store all relevant documentation, optimize implementation processes, and integrate tightly with SAP solutions. "We had vast numbers of documents stored on a variety of platforms, making it very difficult to find and organize information," says Stickler. "Moreover, we lacked insight into roles and responsibilities across our many projects."

SAP Consulting project managers suggested MA 14 check out SAP Solution Manager. Part of the SAP NetWeaver platform, this central application management platform is composed of integrated tools, content, and methodologies designed to ease implementation, operation, and ongoing enhancement of SAP solutions.

"SAP Consulting showed us SAP Solution Manager, and we liked what we saw," says Stickler. "The tool not only met our high expectations in terms of functionality; it's also included in the standard SAP maintenance fee."

With some tailor-made training developed with the SAP Education organization, plus coaching from SAP Consulting, MA 14 had the new tool up and running in next to no time. The implementation kicked off in August 2004 and was completed the following month — with MA 14 handling 80% of associated tasks itself.

"Obviously, our SAP software experience helped us get the software in place quickly and with little outside assistance," says Stickler. "But SAP Solution Manager was very easy to understand."

Streamlining document management

With a number of implementations already under way, it was important to transfer information on ongoing projects to SAP Solution Manager. "Because our existing documentation was already clearly structured, getting it into the tool was pretty straightforward," says Stickler. "In fact, it was often a matter of simply cutting and pasting."

MA 14 is currently handling 26 SAP projects, including 18 rollouts and 6 new implementations, using SAP Solution Manager. All documentation — from business process descriptions to customizing settings — is now stored centrally, making it considerably easier to track and retrieve.

360-degree visibility and reduced test times

SAP Solution Manager delivers greater insight into all aspects of implementations, including change management. "We can now quickly and easily call up the status of changes and identify associated responsibilities," explains Stickler. "That means we can spot where time lines are slipping and act accordingly."

The tool also helps plan, organize, and execute tests within the scope of implementation. As a result, MA 14 has a more structured approach, with clearly defined roles. "This really showed us what SAP Solution Manager has to offer," says Stickler. "Thanks to SAP Solution Manager, we've slashed the time needed to perform tests in the run-up to go-live by 75%. We can now do in days what used to take weeks." A reduction in the time required to perform tests has also resulted in lower testing costs.

MA 14 also benefits from the SAP Project Management service, delivered by SAP Consulting. This includes designated leaders for projects and sub-projects and dedicated tool kits. "SAP Consulting project managers work hand in hand with us to ensure effective coordination of the 50 or so external consultants involved in our implementations," says Stickler.

Expert Project Management Services

The City of Vienna now intends to enhance the functionalities of its SAP Solution Manager tool. "We're looking to move up to the latest release soon," says Stickler. "And we want to add a number of new features — including Learning Maps to enable end users to get to grips with new SAP functionality even faster."

Next steps

10.3   E.ON IS GmbH — IT Service Provider and Full-Service Provider Is Optimizing its Test Organization with SAP Solution Manager

Summary

IT service provider and full-service provider E.ON IS GmbH is optimizing its test organization with SAP Solution Manager. This is accelerating test scenario preparation and execution, improving and simplifying verification, and reducing the effort associated with testing.

E.ON IS is the IT service provider for the E.ON Group and one of the leading full-service providers for the power industry in Europe. With a team of over 1,800 employees, the company looks after around 100 customers at more than 30 locations across Germany. E.ON IS is represented

IT know-how geared toward the power industry

throughout Europe, with subsidiaries in Bulgaria, the United Kingdom, Italy, Romania, Sweden, Slovakia, the Czech Republic, and Hungary. In total, E.ON IS employs more than 3,000 people.

E.ON IS's strong position is the result of consistently gearing competencies and resources toward the power industry. The company offers the whole range of IT services for this industry, from consulting and design to implementation, operation, service, and support.

Goal: reduce test effort associated with release upgrades
One of the most significant activities currently linked with the SAP environment is the task of upgrading the SAP systems of companies operating in the power industry to the latest release version, SAP ERP 6.0. E.ON IS is using the Test Organizer tool provided in SAP Solution Manager to reduce the test effort associated with this upgrade.

As a central test management platform, the tool facilitates the structured administration of business processes and acts as a central location for storing test-related information, documentation, and results obtained in the course of testing. Missing documents, undocumented tests, and lost test results are things of the past. SAP Solution Manager speeds up test processes while making them more transparent and reducing the overall effort involved—all with minimal training requirements for the employees conducting the test. That is why project manager Bernd-Matthias Seele considers the introduction of SAP Solution Manager a success: "We were able to map our test process seamlessly, reduce the effort associated with testing, and create greater transparency throughout the entire testing cycle."

The goal of achieving such benefits was what motivated E.ON IS to seek out a replacement for the autonomous tools it had been using previously to support testing, which were deemed "too time-consuming and not well enough integrated." This situation prompted the company to improve the way it organized and conducted testing and to search for an alternative.

Workshop to set the course
One of the alternatives under consideration was SAP Solution Manager. The company obtained more detailed information about this application and, in particular, its functions for testing configured business processes in a workshop with SAP Consulting. A test management expert not only presented the relevant functions to the decision-makers, but

also provided information about the fundamental issues associated with implementing the application and adapting it to suit the specific needs of E.ON IS.

In project manager Bernd-Matthias Seele's judgment, "the added value of the consulting was unmistakable. We were expertly introduced to and guided through what was for us a new environment." After the workshop, it was clear that the SAP Solution Manager test functions could enable more effective test management for forthcoming upgrade projects. And because the cost aspect could be dealt with swiftly — no extra license costs are incurred through the use of SAP Solution Manager — nothing stood in the way of getting started. SAP Consulting helped with creating the implementation plan and conceptualizing how each of the SAP Solution Manager functions would be used. Mr. Seele described the activities performed by SAP Consulting as "thorough and methodical preparation for the implementation."

The test functions of the SAP tools proved themselves from a functional perspective in particular through their ability to be integrated with other SAP Solution Manager functions and, in turn, through its ability to be integrated into the SAP solution landscape. These features won the solution the most points when compared with competing products. "The structuring options offered across projects, processes, and systems and the ability to manage project-related documents along these structures significantly increase transparency," says Mr. Seele.

Integration strengths that speak for themselves

He identifies another key feature as being the end-to-end traceability of tests and test results throughout the entire test process thanks to accompanying monitoring measures. A predefined findings report that can be generated in a range of variants is a key contributor to this transparency. In this regard, E.ON IS concludes that "sophisticated reporting ensures traceability at all times." These reporting capabilities were also taken as the basis for communication between those organizing and those carrying out testing.

In the current upgrade project, the testing group numbers around 600 employees. Mr. Seele notes that "some of the group members and people responsible for IT were a bit skeptical at times." But this initial skepticism faded quickly, especially among testers when they saw how little train-

Short implementation times: a driver for high levels of acceptance

ing was required. With just one hour of training needed for each tester, this became a driver for widespread acceptance. Ensuring that access to the systems to be tested was kept as simple as possible also promoted this acceptance.

Test objects saved in the test case, for example, a transaction to be tested, pave the way for simplification: This information allows the tester to access the test object in the test system directly, without the need for a logon procedure. Because project activities are centralized, it is largely no longer necessary for testers to log on in different places. Each tester automatically gains access to the right system at the right time.

In addition, the task of documenting the actual test process is facilitated by using preprepared templates for test case descriptions and test notes. Master data and transaction data as well as key test findings are recorded in this documentation together with a full account of the tests performed.

Successful pilot implementation sparks interest In light of the persuasive findings, the initial skepticism of some IT colleagues also gave way to recognition of the fact that testing could be managed much more effectively with SAP Solution Manager. And with good reason: In addition to the reduction in effort, a leaner test process, and greater transparency, another notable benefit is the degree of standardization that can be achieved. A template project was created as part of the global rollout project with this goal in mind. This functional template already contains the business process structures to the level of the transactions and corresponding test cases. The result is an E.ON IS test standard that need only be adapted to accommodate local changes in consultation with the customers. "Now, we only need to adapt specific areas," says Bernd-Matthias Seele as he highlights the benefits. An authorization concept created concomitantly ensures that the different E.ON IS customers only have access to their own projects.

In Germany and the United Kingdom, this approach has already been taken to prepare SAP upgrades and accelerate their implementation. E.ON IS now wants to make use of further functions delivered as part of SAP Solution Manager. The spotlight is on the Service Desk function package to support error management in future upgrade projects. It represents a ticketing system that enables errors uncovered in test processes to be reported, checked, and tracked.

10.4 Panalpina — SAP Solution Manager Helps Logistics Service Provider Standardize and Centralize Processes

Summary

Using SAP Solution Manager, Panalpina Management Ltd. has completely standardized its implementation management strategy and can tap the full potential of these new software monitoring and analysis functions to increase the performance and availability of its IT infrastructure.

Logistics service providers realize that key to their success is the depth of knowledge of industry processes that keep the wheels of global freight management turning. With an increasing reliance on automation of supply chain processes, businesses are only as strong as their IT infrastructure. For Basel, Switzerland–based Panalpina Management Ltd., maintaining state-of-the-art SAP software is just as much a unique selling proposition for its portfolio of forwarding solutions as is its comprehensive industry know-how.

However, as any global company knows, no matter how sophisticated its software is, geographic and commercial expansion requires continuous improvements and upgrades to software. This, in turn, necessitates having the right tools and resources to ensure low costs of solution operations and maintenance. When Panalpina decided to update its tool for standardizing and centralizing its SAP software landscape efficiently, it knew immediately what the right choice would be: the SAP Solution Manager Application Management solution. By implementing this solution, the company now has a fully uniform implementation management strategy and can tap the full potential of new functionality for monitoring and analyzing software to ensure high performance and availability of its IT infrastructure. And by deciding to do all this with its own resources, Panalpina also managed to alleviate time and costs considerably.

Panalpina is one of the world's largest logistics service providers, with a network of approximately 500 offices in more than 80 countries and employing more than 14,000 people worldwide. In 60 more countries, the company cooperates with selected partners. To manage the entirety of its IT operations, Panalpina's IT infrastructure is highly centralized, with four software competence centers distributed across several continents. Because the company specializes in intercontinental air freight and ocean freight shipments and associated supply chain management solutions, its software needs to accommodate a whole range of internal requirements. Via the SAP ERP application, which Panalpina runs around the world, the company also needs unrestricted access to external networks — especially in conjunction with communication to customers or agents via its corporate portal, which is based on the SAP NetWeaver Portal component. For Gregor Bühler, SAP Basis manager at Panalpina, this means his team has to be on its toes constantly to ensure seamless operations.

In a global IT environment such as Panalpina's, implementing and improving solutions means constantly having to test and document configuration settings in line with implementation plans. Yet, with a geographically distributed infrastructure, this type of documentation is sometimes difficult to realize. "Before implementing SAP Solution Manager," Bühler explains, "our documentation was based on Microsoft Word, and test plans were on Excel sheets, which weren't interactive. We had to maintain several different sheets for planning implementations — one in each competence center."

Even though Panalpina stored test documentation, each competence center would run tests differently, with each center more or less free to manage its change requests and release changes independently. The challenge involved consolidating the SAP software landscape on the basis of a single, central platform management solution. Besides needing an environment for test planning, Bühler and his team also required a solution with diagnostics functionality that would enable them to monitor non-SAP applications on the corporate portal. On top of that, the implementation had to be fast and smooth to ensure seamless operation. In 2004 Panalpina implemented SAP Solution Manager, with functionality for documentation, testing, and customizing. In 2006 the upgrade to the latest release of SAP Solution Manager followed, with new monitoring functionality.

Besides meeting all of their requirements, SAP Solution Manager fit well with Panalpina's application management strategy, owing to the company's extensive experience with SAP software. In less than one month, Bühler and his team managed to implement the latest release of SAP Solution Manager all by themselves. As Gerd Rieger, competence center manager at Panalpina, explains, "We simply copied the earlier release to test the upgrade. Upgrading SAP Solution Manager went completely effortlessly. There were no interruptions to the productive application. And we only needed one test run. It was almost all out of the box." In terms of customizing, later corrections were minor and were resolved quickly and easily.

Out-of-the-box implementation

The advantages are best seen on a project basis, where SAP Solution Manager lets Panalpina monitor, analyze, and test all manner of transactions for various business processes. SAP Solution Manager offers a precise range of testing options, so that no transaction tests are excluded. This makes release changes more secure. Because the tests are more comprehensive and take less time, implementations are also a lot less costly. "We have definitely seen a great improvement in the quality and availability of solution operations," says Bühler. "We have managed to consolidate functionalities that were previously widely distributed. In doing so we have fulfilled all of the requirements we set for the SAP Solution Manager upgrade."

Expectations fulfilled

For test plan management, the response from key users involved in release change projects has been excellent. The test plans for the competence centers are now determined by IT headquarters. "We were able to give them guidelines on what needed to be tested, and we also have the option of evaluating centrally where problems have arisen," explains Bühler. "We have integrated the whole of Europe into this test plan. The feedback has been positive from all of our offices. This documentation is very valuable for our release management, as we can reuse configuration settings for all manner of new processes and implementations of support packages and so on." All Panalpina has to do is create tests plans once in SAP Solution Manager, and they can be generated again and again.

Excellent feedback

This reduction in the number of steps required to plan projects has alleviated the need for extra resources, allowing Panalpina to improve IT performance elsewhere and to prepare for release changes to its SAP software infrastructure. With a view to implementing functionality for change management, Panalpina recently started utilizing the help-desk functionality of SAP Solution Manager, which relays support messages to the SAP Active Global Support organization directly. "This method has led to 200% quicker processing than before. Now that we can document and monitor all of the new processes introduced at Panalpina and establish all of the test scenarios centrally, all of our initial expectations have been met, and we are definitely open to implementing further functionality," says Bühler.

10.5 Turners and Growers Ltd — SAP Solution Manager Saves Significant Costs over Outsourced Support Desk

Summary

Turners & Growers, a fruit and fresh produce distributor based in New Zealand, implemented SAP Solution Manager to avoid paying for an external Service Desk.

SAP customers have occasionally characterized the SAP Solution Manager tool as SAP's best-kept secret. Here is one example of the exceptional results achievable when a customer discovers just what's been bundled into their SAP enterprise software — and covered by their standard maintenance agreement with SAP.

Turners & Growers manages a domestic and worldwide produce distribution and marketing operation from their home base in Auckland, New Zealand. With revenues of approximately €295 million in 2004, the company employs a permanent staff of 1,400 domestically and internationally, with the actual number of employees varying by season. The present company is the result of a 2003 merger of the domestically focused Turners & Growers with ENZA, an international distributor of apples and pears.

Turners & Growers has been running SAP software for quite some time, with the export-logistics-oriented and financial functions being handled by SAP R/3 software, which is available today in the SAP ERP solution.

After the merger, the company began to review its outsourcing commitments. In particular, they were interested in bringing all support desk functions in-house. The company, which runs a thin-client network throughout New Zealand, had already begun to bring core systems management back in-house. In addition, the company was already supporting its SAP systems from a functional perspective, so it made sense to bring the support of the infrastructure back as well.

Outsourcing dilemma

However, that left company IT managers with a dilemma. As Turners & Growers moved away from its service provider, some functions were left behind. The service provider continued to host and operate the support desk function, for which it continued to charge the company.

"Cutting costs was an issue," says Michelle Lynch, IT support desk manager at Turners & Growers. "We had to pay for the external analysts that were working on the support desk as well as the application software and the hosting." Turners & Growers' response was to go out to bid for IT support desk software.

Fortunately, SAP Consulting got involved, and they reminded Turners & Growers that the company already owned support desk software. SAP Solution Manager, covered by the standard SAP maintenance agreement, includes support desk functionality as part of the complete solution management platform.

The SAP Solution Manager platform delivers the integrated content, tools, and methodologies required to implement, support, and operate an enterprise-wide SAP solution landscape. It provides support during project start-up, functional and technical implementation, and ongoing operation and optimization of SAP solutions. SAP Solution Manager offers seamless communication between SAP and its customers to complement SAP's extensive range of remote and on-site services.

A complete help desk solution

Furthermore, with its support desk functions, SAP Solution Manager offers a complete infrastructure for organizing and operating an on-site help desk — one that covers the entire solution landscape. Any user can post error messages quickly and easily. For serious problems, a direct connection forwards the message straight to SAP, where a team of experienced consultants, developers, and application specialists applies its skills to solve the problem immediately.

By the time SAP Consulting got involved, Turners & Growers had developed a requirements document. "We needed a system to log incoming calls," says Lynch. "When users have a problem, they call our help desk number or send an email, and an analyst takes the call and logs the job." The analyst determines the nature of the job, assigns it to someone in the IT department, and copies the IT support desk manager.

"We track all our jobs, so we have a list of open jobs at all times that we can refer to," says Lynch.

Four weeks to go-live An SAP consultant demonstrated the support desk functionality of SAP Solution Manager, which convinced Turners & Growers to bring SAP Consulting on board to configure the support desk software they already owned.

The SAP consultant, working with an in-house SAP development resource, performed the initial setup. "We had the system in development, so we could play with it," says Lynch. "You could almost call it a pilot. From the time we finished the requirements document and brought the SAP consultant in-house to the time SAP Solution Manager went live was about four weeks. It was built quickly so we could get all of our end users — our IT customers — loaded into the system. We also transferred all the historical data from the previous system — about 12,000 jobs that were logged in last year."

Turners & Growers' support desk logs an average of 1,000 jobs a month, and they cover the entire IT spectrum. "Setting up new users, changing a security setting, providing access to folders on the main server — there's quite a variety," says Lynch. "Having a quick system to log in a job or a request is quite important. SAP Solution Manager is certainly quick."

Payback in months Turners & Growers is already reaping the benefits of its in-house SAP Solution Manager support desk. "It's quite easy to use," notes Lynch. "If you know how to use SAP software, then you should find your way around this quite easily. Almost all our support desk people were already familiar with SAP software, so training and knowledge transfer requirements were minimal. In addition, at the other end of things, the users haven't noticed that we've changed systems at all. It's been a very straightforward transition, with no disruptions whatever to the users."

Furthermore, there are the cost savings that generated the interest in moving support functions in-house in the first place. The cost, of course, is unbeatable. Essentially, SAP Solution Manager comes free because it is covered by the standard maintenance agreement, and the implementation cost is minimal. "The savings we have achieved by replacing the outsourced support desk system with our own will pay for the development of SAP Solution Manager in a matter of months," observes Lynch. "It will also save us the support costs, as we already have people in-house who know SAP software."

Turners & Growers' plans for their support desk include expanding functions out to their customer base, at least on the domestic side. "Right now, if a customer wants to know whether an invoice has been paid, they have to call a different number," says Lynch. "They're using a different system and we want to get them into SAP Solution Manager. We're currently looking into that."

Further down the road, Turners & Growers is planning to expand its SAP system significantly. Customer service will be handled by the SAP customer relationship management solution. "The plan for the business is to have an enterprise-wide SAP system and to have it all aligned into one," says Lynch. "Our domestic users are looking forward to getting SAP software within the next two to three years, so there'll be a lot happening."

10.6 Carlsberg Polska — Renowned Beverage Company Leverages SAP Solution Manager to Improve Its IT Support Processes

Summary

Carlsberg Polska, the Polish subsidiary of Carlsberg Breweries, uses SAP Solution Manager to improve its IT support desk, change management, and Solution Monitoring, thus increasing the efficiency of the support organization.

Bringing people together and adding to the enjoyment of life is an honorable mission, one that is upheld by Carlsberg Polska, the Polish subsidiary of Carlsberg Breweries, with enthusiasm, determination, and hard work. Carlsberg Breweries — with 31,000 employees — is a dynamic, international provider of beer and beverage brands. In 2005 the company sold 121 million hectoliters of its products.

Carlsberg's three key markets are in Western Europe, Eastern Europe, and Asia. A strong portfolio of global, regional, and national beer brands appeals to a broad diversity of tastes, personalities, and lifestyles to ensure growth in all segments of the beer market.

To support this growth and uphold its commitment to quality, innovation, and continuous improvement, Carlsberg Polska sought to enhance the capabilities of its IT support processes. Carlsberg Polska had been using internally developed software — based on the mySAP Customer Relationship Management (SAP CRM) application — to support end users. The homegrown software, however, didn't offer the desired functionality. The company was looking for a new solution that would meet expectations and would support IT processes to improve IT service delivery. To meet the company's business needs, the new solution would integrate support and change processes and make them transparent.

As a result, the company chose to implement — with help from the SAP Active Global Support organization and a local consultant — the SAP Solution Manager Application Management platform.

IT home brew whets thirst for more — Based in Warsaw, Poland, IT Shared Services Center (SSC) provides support to approximately 600 users of SAP software. The users work in eight business entities that are located in four countries, use four different languages, and operate across two time zones. The companies process more than 4,000 sales orders a day.

To work more efficiently, the IT support group needed a solution that would channel end user messages to a central point of contact for processing and resolution, provide more timely information for resolving issues faster, and plan better to meet business needs. It also needed centralized, real-time monitoring of the IT landscape it supports and a more efficient system for managing system changes.

"It was our decision from the beginning to use SAP Solution Manager not only because of its strengths as a tool, but also because it offered the best level of integration of SAP and non-SAP software. We don't want our users to have to log on to different systems to register a support inquiry. With SAP Solution Manager, users can send support messages with a few mouse clicks from their desktops. The transaction is fully integrated," says Magdalena Cioch, IT director of SSC customer service. "We also are aware that SAP Solution Manager complies with the recommendations of the IT Infrastructure Library (ITIL) standards, the most widely accepted approach to IT service management in the world, which is another reason why we decided to implement it."

Carlsberg Polska decided to implement three scenarios in SAP Solution Manager to improve service desk efficiency, gain better control of change management processes, and enable better solution monitoring capabilities. SAP appointed technical experts in using the SAP Solution Manager and in customer relationship management (CRM) who worked with an SSC resource to define a prototype of the solution. The project team working with the SAP Solution Manager tested the software in four countries involved in the implementation project and, before making the switch to a productive system, ensured that the functionality worked properly.

Implementing improvements

"We deployed one central installation in Poland. The first area deployed was Solution Monitoring capabilities, then Service Desk and Change Request Management processes together, in one step," says Cioch.

The cooperation between the Carlsberg Polska project team, SAP Active Global Support, and the SAP development group helped streamline the implementation and ensure a successful go-live. As performance issues materialized, SAP Active Global Support called on SAP developers to quickly resolve them and reduce the technical risk of the implementation.

"After going live with SAP Solution Manager, we have all the information we need for managing incidents and change requests in all countries at the time they occur. This enables us to forecast our business needs immediately," Cioch adds.

Streamlining IT support desk

The Service Desk functionality included in SAP Solution Manager helps Carlsberg Polska support staff manage incidents more efficiently and eases the settlement of support costs. SAP Solution Manager provides information that improves problem resolution. Central handling of support messages makes the support organization more efficient. SAP Solution Manager integrated with Microsoft Outlook helps the company keep its end users informed about the status of their messages.

"Before the implementation, end users had several communications channels with which to inform the support team about problems with business applications. Thanks to SAP Solution Manager, when end users now have a problem, they can send us a message directly from the transaction they are working in," says Piotr Mazur, IT director of SSC Business Application. "Also important for the IT organization, the tool automatically sends some technical information for our IT consultants at the moment the user sends a message. So if the problem has to be escalated, all of the necessary information is automatically included."

Solution Monitoring Benefits

SAP Solution Manager performs central, real-time monitoring of systems, business processes, and interfaces, which reduces administrative effort. Furthermore, proactive monitoring using SAP Solution Manager helps Carlsberg Polska avoid critical situations. In addition, automatic notifications enable fast response to issues. If a critical situation occurs, an alert can be sent automatically so the system administrator can react quickly and decisively.

"SAP Solution Manager has reduced the workload for our service center," Mazur explains. "We now have an efficient support system with a central point of access to all monitoring information for critical situations to detect problems early and resolve past issues more easily."

Improving Change Request Management

SSC as a central support group is responsible for maintaining the SAP software to meet Carlsberg Polska's growing business expectations. To eliminate the risk from having one common SAP platform, it's essential that the group coordinates change requests coming from the locations in the four countries.

"Business and IT cooperation is a key factor of the implemented change management process. SAP Solution Manager enabled us to integrate all

IT and business steps — including change definition, change approval, testing, and results." Cioch says.

Cioch points out that planning and coordination of change requests is vital to maintain quality in the service delivery process. SAP Solution Manager harmonized — and made transparent — the change implementation.

"Thanks to SAP Solution Manager, both the business and the IT group keep track of support and change requests at every stage of resolution," adds Cioch. The highly automated Change Request Management process contributed to enhancing and optimizing administrative tasks.

"SAP Solution Manager is organized according to best practices. A change to the environment is managed more safely for our internal customers. We can control the whole process better from beginning to end," Mazur adds. "SAP Solution Manager provides greater transparency for our support services, enabling a clearer picture of the provided service, which is important for internal customers."

As a long-term benefit that will reduce total cost of ownership, SAP Solution Manager — a standard tool available to all SAP customers free of charge — will be supported and maintained by SAP. Carlsberg Polska receives new releases and patches as they are available. Should Carlsberg Polska have any issues or problems with the tool, they can report them to SAP for resolution.

Investment for the future

Looking ahead, Carlsberg Polska also wants — when the company is ready — to implement additional functionality and scenarios that SAP Solution Manager offers. In fact, the company already plans to incorporate management of service level agreements and to facilitate reporting requests by using SAP Solution Manager to help manage the implementation of the SAP NetWeaver Business Intelligence component.

"SAP Solution Manager is a sophisticated tool that has served us well. We are interested in developing the functionality in other key areas to support our business processes," says Przemek Duda, CIO at Carlsberg Polska. "Just as important though, we view it as an investment for the future."

10.7 Resource Informatik AG — SAP Solution Manager Helps SAP Service Partner Effectively Support Customers

Summary

Resource Informatik, a Swiss SAP Service Partner, wanted to provide its customers with both an extremely efficient and central Service Desk and proactive system monitoring and therefore decided to implement the SAP Solution Manager Application Management platform. It was then able to replace its old email-based system.

To enhance the quality and efficiency of support desk services for its customers, SAP partner Resource Informatik introduced the SAP Solution Manager Application Management platform. The powerful platform not only makes for faster, more effective handling and resolution of reported incidents, but also enables proactive monitoring of customer systems. Better yet, because it's included in the standard SAP maintenance charge, it involves no additional license costs.

One-stop SAP expertise | Based in Wollerau, Switzerland, Resource Informatik provides expert advice and assistance on SAP software across the entire solution lifecycle. The IT specialist serves large, small, and midsize businesses in a variety of industries, including retail, wholesale, utilities, and financial services. Resource Informatik is a qualified SAP service partner and a special expertise partner for the SAP NetWeaver platform. The company has a workforce of around 50 in Switzerland and supports international customers.

Limited visibility | In 2004 Resource Informatik decided to introduce new software to improve its support desk services. "One of the main problems with our email-based legacy system was lack of visibility," explains Reto Zwyer, consultant and head of the SAP Solution Manager project at Resource Informatik. "For example, we often had several customer emails on one incident, making it very difficult to track activities and status."

"We were looking for a solution that would enhance transparency and efficiency," continues Zwyer. "What's more, it had to integrate tightly with the SAP software we support, and include all the capabilities needed to deliver a wide range of additional services. And all this at an affordable cost." Moreover, the new tool had to support processes that comply with the recommendations of the IT Infrastructure Library (ITIL). ITIL is the most widely accepted approach to IT service management in the world and provides a cohesive set of best practices, drawn from the public and private sectors internationally.

After considering various alternatives, Resource Informatik opted for SAP Solution Manager, part of SAP NetWeaver. The central application management platform is composed of integrated tools, content, and methodologies designed to ease implementation, operation, and ongoing enhancement of SAP solutions. Furthermore, SAP Solution Manager provides a direct link to SAP, accelerating resolution of technical issues.

SAP Solution Manager – end-to-end Support

"SAP Solution Manager not only meets all our support desk requirements," says Zwyer, "but it also includes integrated functionality for a wide range of application management tasks in line with ITIL best practices. And because SAP Solution Manager is covered by the annual SAP maintenance fee, we had no additional software investment."

Resource Informatik set about implementing the new software in February 2005. Leveraging their own considerable SAP expertise, the IT specialists handled all aspects of the project t— from definition of in-house support desk processes to customizing and training — with a minimum of external assistance. Thanks to the skills of Resource Informatik's team, and close collaboration with SAP, the support desk functionality was up and running just two months later in April 2005.

Fast, effective implementation

Resource Informatik is now reaping the considerable benefits of its new solution. "SAP Solution Manager allows us to centrally store all incidents, statuses, and associated activities, making for greater transparency and efficiency and more straightforward tracking," states Zwyer. "Moreover, customers' SAP systems can be hooked up to our support desk with minimal modifications."

Enhanced insight and efficiency

Resolving problems is also a lot easier. "When we receive a customer message, it contains the technical details of their system, enabling us to pinpoint the right answer faster. For support desk problems that need further clarification, SAP Solution Manager allows us to forward them to SAP Active Global Support. And their response includes a direct link to the information we need. That's an efficient feature."

But it's not only Resource Informatik's specialists who are profiting. "With SAP Solution Manager, our customers have an exceptionally user-friendly, single point of contact for all support issues," states Zwyer. And to give customers greater visibility into the process, Resource Informatik has provided them with quick and easy, browser-based access to incident status via the SAP NetWeaver Portal component.

In September 2005, 10 companies had already reported incidents through SAP Solution Manager, and the figure was set to rise significantly. In addition to support desk services, Resource Informatik delivers system monitoring via the Application Management platform. "About a month into the implementation, we decided to introduce the monitoring capabilities of SAP Solution Manager," says Zwyer. "This enables us to proactively screen customer systems and forward any errors directly to the support desk."

Resource Informatik is now looking ahead. "We've already upgraded to the latest SAP Solution Manager release," comments Zwyer, "and we're now gearing up to implement additional functionality — including change request and test plan management, as well as e-learning. SAP Solution Manager gives us a firm foundation for enhancing our service processes in line with the ITIL standard."

10.8 Airbus Cuts Problem Resolution Time 40% by Performing Business Process Monitoring with SAP Solution Manager

Summary

Airbus, based in Toulouse, France, chose SAP Solution Manager to monitor its business processes. The SAP Solution Manager application management platform enables the company to proactively monitor its core business processes run in SAP and external systems using a central console.

"SAP Solution Manager addresses our entire infrastructure management needs, reduces risk, lowers the cost of ownership, and speeds the return on investment for our online buying solution," says Guillaume Legros, project leader at Airbus France SAS. Legros, who is also a member of the company's SAP Customer Competence Center, is talking specifically about the Business Process Monitoring functionality available in the SAP Solution Manager Application Management platform.

During on-site delivery of the SAP Solution Management Optimization service for Business Process Management, Airbus took advantage of SAP Solution Manager to set up Business Process Monitoring for Buyside Shopping Cart, its online e-procurement solution.

Business Process Monitoring for procurement

Now, when problems do occur in the multistep, online procure-to-pay business process, Airbus can rely on SAP Solution Manager to ensure they are escalated and quickly resolved. Recent stats reveal that the escalation process is now 10 times faster and that issue resolution is between 20% and 40% quicker. In addition, the number of user-reported errors is down by 20%. Moreover, typical problems that occur during systems operations can be detected much more rapidly — in two minutes or less.

This is all good news for this world-renowned aircraft manufacturer. Established in 1970 as a European consortium of French, German, and, later, Spanish and British companies, Airbus consistently wins at least half the orders placed for airliners with more than 100 seats. It currently has over 3,500 aircraft in service, with some 53,000 staff members on the ground working hard to make sure the company continues on a path of success.

In return, Airbus makes a concerted effort to ensure its employees have exactly what they need for their day-to-day activities. Using Buyside Shopping Cart, which is based on the SAP E-Procurement application, staff members in France, Germany, Spain, and the United Kingdom can easily purchase office supplies, stationery, and desktop equipment at the click of a mouse. Today, the single, consolidated online purchasing tool helps some 2,000 users throughout Airbus maximize their purchasing power and get the best prices for frequently used goods and services.

Before implementing the Business Process Monitoring functionality in SAP Solution Manager, Airbus was having difficulty detecting and quickly resolving issues related to Buyside Shopping Cart. The IT department was sometimes unaware of a problem until it was reported by an end user. As a result, insignificant errors, which should have been

From reactive to proactive problem detection

resolved in seconds, often became major problems, impacting service level agreements with users. Without centrally held records regarding these issues, the IT department could not draw upon past experience to speed resolution and prevent similar errors in the future.

"It became clear that what we needed was a single management platform that would allow us to monitor Buyside Shopping Cart in all four countries — and alert us immediately if preset performance thresholds were in danger of being breached," says Legros.

Single tool for real-time Business Process Monitoring

Provided to all SAP customers as part of their licensing agreement, SAP Solution Manager helps maximize a company's SAP environment. It is designed to support management of highly sophisticated system and solution landscapes, targeting interrelated business processes, interfaces, and technical components. For example, if a defined threshold related to a specific Business Process Monitoring object has been exceeded, an alert will be automatically triggered and will appear on the SAP Solution Manager graphic display.

"We evaluated several monitoring options, but we chose SAP Solution Manager because it fulfilled almost all of our business process management and optimization needs," says Legros. "It could also interface with the IBM Tivoli security management solution that we were using for system monitoring. This would enable us to receive alerts — on the same console — about potential problems across our entire solution landscape that might impact the performance of Buyside Shopping Cart. In addition, SAP Solution Manager's ease of use and out-of-the-box functionality would minimize implementation overhead and total cost of ownership."

Legros then adds, "Sup@irworld Support Center, which manages the Airbus procurement information system and is led by Thierry Chaput, chose SAP Solution Manager and is now very happy with it."

Key steps

SAP Active Global Support implemented the SAP Solution Manager business process monitoring functionality over a three-day period at the Airbus Toulouse facility, which houses the centrally managed Buyside Shopping Cart. SAP Active Global Support team members worked with Airbus to identify the key steps involved in creating a business process management concept and to establish the roles and responsibilities within the support organization. They recorded the core business process of Buy-side Shopping Cart in SAP Solution Manager, and then implemented the relevant monitoring objects, establishing thresholds according to business requirements.

In addition, the team members defined error handling procedures and escalation paths. They also set up Service Level Reporting, enabling Airbus to easily identify problem areas based on automated weekly reports.

The consultants from SAP Active Global Support, a part of the SAP Services organization, helped identify steps that were critical to the optimum performance of Buyside Shopping Cart. They targeted the average response time for specific dialog transactions, data transfer via interfaces, and the behavior of specific background jobs as key monitoring objects.

Process-critical monitoring objects

Customers such as Airbus can easily adapt SAP Solution Manager to meet their specific requirements or changing business needs. For example, since the initial implementation, Airbus has established requisition approval as an additional monitoring object to ensure that the purchase of urgently needed goods and services is not held up by a manager who fails to authorize the request. If a requisition has not been converted into a purchase order within five working days, an email alert is sent to the staff member who initiated the request. Email queuing is also monitored to ensure that procurement is not delayed due to slow performance of the email system.

Legros comments, "SAP Active Global Support configured the business process monitoring functionality within SAP Solution Manager to ensure that our critical success factors were met. Thanks to thorough knowledge transfer, our IT team members gained the skills and tools required for day-to-day monitoring. Plus, they can now embed additional monitoring objects, as needed, without us having to incur additional consultancy costs."

SAP Active Global Support also integrated the corporate backend systems in France, Germany, Spain, and the United Kingdom into the business process monitoring functionality used for Buyside Shopping Cart. Functional and technical errors, poor performance, and other issues

Faster problem detection and resolution

485

arising in these backend systems can now be detected, escalated, and resolved from the single management console in Toulouse. This means users experience no degradation in service levels. The 20% reduction in reported malfunctions and the earlier detection of errors and faster resolution times are directly attributable to SAP Solution Manager.

Support for the entire solution landscape

The Business Process Monitoring functionality within SAP Solution Manager is based on the SAP Computing Center Management System, which enables integrated system monitoring over the whole landscape. Malfunctions are identified quickly and reliably when a preset threshold value is exceeded or not reached, or if a system component remains inactive for a specific time period. System monitoring alerts generated by IBM Tivoli are converted into log files and monitored by the SAP Computing Center Management System. They appear on the SAP Solution Manager graphic display alongside business process–related alerts for Buyside Shopping Cart.

In addition, weekly service level reports are generated in SAP Solution Manager, recording aggregated alerts for Buyside Shopping Cart. Airbus's IT staff uses this information to benchmark performance against service level agreements in each country and to make strategic decisions regarding system changes and future IT investments.

Leveraging technology investments

The company is also using SAP Solution Manager to monitor its non-SAP-based sourcing solution used for purchasing wings, turbines, and other parts. Data regarding system performance is collected automatically in the sourcing solution and fed into SAP Solution Manager via XML user interfaces to provide a complete management view. Airbus also plans to extend Business Process Monitoring to its mission-critical SAP-based manufacturing applications.

"SAP Solution Manager provides us with a central point of control for solution and system landscapes with multiple components," says Legros. "This is of great value to us, as it enables us to leverage all our technology investments."

10.9 IVOCLAR VIVADENT — SAP Solution Manager Streamlines System Monitoring at Leading Dental Company

Summary

Ivoclar Vivadent AG, a dental product manufacturer based in Schaan, Liechtenstein, implemented SAP Solution Manager to reduce the administrative outlay of its international SAP environment. The versatile Application Management platform creates transparency across all systems, increases availability, and optimizes central tasks.

To get the very best out of IT solutions, enterprises have to manage and monitor their system's landscape efficiently, but in large, complex environments, potential problems can all too easily go unnoticed — with disastrous consequences. Thanks to the SAP Solution Manager tool, international dental products manufacturer Ivoclar Vivadent AG, headquartered in Schaan, Liechtenstein, enjoys 360-degree visibility into its SAP systems. As a result, its IT professionals can pinpoint and resolve performance, security, and availability issues rapidly.

Ivoclar Vivadent is a leading international maker of high-quality materials for preventive, restorative, and prosthetic dentistry. Through a worldwide network of subsidiaries and representative offices, the company delivers products and services to dental laboratories and practices in over 100 countries. Ivoclar Vivadent employs a global workforce of 2,166 and posted consolidated sales of over CHF523 million (€338 million) in fiscal 2005.

A global leader in dental products

To keep pace with rapid growth and internationalization, Ivoclar Vivadent decided to migrate its subsidiaries to a single, standard software platform. In 2003 and 2004 the company went live with SAP R/3 software (functionality now found in the mySAP ERP application) in Austria, Canada, Germany, Italy, Liechtenstein, and the United States. The SAP software supports core enterprise resource planning tasks, human resources, and business warehouse management (through the SAP Business Information Warehouse component — functionality now found in the SAP NetWeaver Business Intelligence component).

Mastering a
complex IT
environment

Efficient monitoring and management are vital if Ivoclar Vivadent's SAP software is to deliver the high levels of performance required. "In the past, we tackled these tasks manually," explains Mike Buchmann, head of SAP Basis support at Ivoclar Vivadent's IT unit. "But as our environment grew, we realized it was impossible to provide 24-7 coverage this way. We needed a cutting-edge tool that would give us transparency across our entire landscape, proactively identify problems, and show us where performance could be improved."

The right support
at the right price

After considering a solution from another vendor, Ivoclar Vivadent opted for SAP Solution Manager. This central application management platform features a wide range of integrated tools, content, and methodologies.

"SAP Solution Manager was the logical choice," says Buchmann. "After all, no one knows SAP better than SAP. Plus, the platform is available to SAP customers free of charge, so there are no additional license costs."

Rapid, pain-free
implementation

Drawing on their own considerable SAP software skills, Ivoclar Vivadent's IT specialists implemented SAP Solution Manager in-house. "I configured the monitoring functionality myself," explains Buchmann. "Setting up SAP Solution Manager was very straightforward, and there was plenty of help available online at the SAP Service Marketplace extranet."

Comprehensive
coverage – central
administration

SAP Solution Manager went live at Ivoclar Vivadent in August 2004. At present, five test and four production systems are handled using the platform. The new software enables IT staff to timetable and track recurring activities more efficiently. "SAP Solution Manager includes dedicated task lists," explains Buchmann. "These provide an overview of scheduled work across our entire landscape. And automatically generated logs allow us to quickly and easily confirm it has been completed."

Improved
monitoring –
increased
availability

Real-time, proactive monitoring gives Ivoclar Vivadent greater visibility. "SAP Solution Manager provides at-a-glance insight across our entire environment, helping us increase availability," says Buchmann. "User-friendly traffic lights show the status of individual systems. And central access via the new platform eliminates the need for time-consuming multiple logins to individual systems." SAP Solution Manager is also used to deliver the SAP EarlyWatch Alert service. Performed weekly, it shows IT administrators where there is scope for improving performance and stability.

Since mid-2005 Ivoclar Vivadent has been using SAP Solution Manager to enhance security through the SAP Security Optimization service. "This is obviously a very important issue for us," says Buchmann. "The service performs remote checks on the SAP R/3 software and recommends changes to system settings — helping us identify and rectify any potential issues."

Tighter security – greater productivity

Last but not least, the high degree of automation has increased productivity at Ivoclar Vivadent's IT unit. "All in all, SAP Solution Manager saves us a lot of time, freeing up our staff for more important project-related work," concludes Buchmann.

Ivoclar Vivadent is now gearing up for a number of new projects involving SAP software. "Later this year, we'll be upgrading to mySAP ERP," says Buchmann. In addition, the company is currently piloting the SAP NetWeaver Exchange Infrastructure (SAP NetWeaver XI) component. "We have some 30 non-SAP systems interfaced to our SAP R/3 software," states Buchmann. "By introducing SAP NetWeaver XI, we aim to improve integration."

Next steps

Going forward, Ivoclar Vivadent will also move up to the latest SAP Solution Manager release. "We're planning to introduce the platform's diagnostics functionality. And in conjunction with SAP NetWeaver XI, this will enable us to enhance our monitoring capabilities even further."

10.10 BTC Business Technology Consulting AG — SAP Solution Manager Is Producing Lasting Cost Reductions for the Entire SAP Landscape

Summary

BTC Business Technology Consulting AG uses SAP Solution Manager to proactively monitor and manage 178 SAP systems.

Within the field of customer-focused outsourcing, BTC Business Technology Consulting AG is responsible for operating and adhering to service level agreements for all of the EWE Group's SAP systems as well as an additional 26 customers. Alongside other monitoring systems in the company, SAP Solution Manager plays a pivotal role in providing optimal technical and process-related support for alert and event management, incident management, change management, configuration management, and capacity management processes.

Early in 2007, the decision was made to look into the system monitoring tools available on the market for SAP systems to establish their suitability for BTC AG and reach an implementation decision on the basis of a cost-benefit analysis.

In addition to their technical attributes, the cost of procuring and operating the products was taken into account. SAP Solution Manger emerged as the clear winner.

In the next step, an implementation project was launched for the System Monitoring, Central System Administration, and Service Level Reporting scenarios.

Since October 1, 2007, SAP Solution Manager has been used to proactively monitor and manage all SAP systems (currently 178).

The project, which involved 197 person days and a return on investment (ROI) of 11 months, led to a permanent reduction of operating costs and further gains in terms of the quality of SAP system operations.

BTC AG   BTC is one of Germany's largest IT consultancies. With operations in Germany, Switzerland, Poland, Turkey, and Japan, it offers its customers regional proximity and permanent availability at all times. BTC can look back on long-standing partnerships with SAP AG and covers all aspects of consulting, system integration, and system administration.

BTC AG has several years' experience of using SAP tools and procedures for implementing and operating solutions. An evaluation was carried out early on to check all of the functions of SAP Solution Manager, test them in real solution environments, and fully implement individual scenarios, for instance, Solution Monitoring, in larger-scale projects. The strong links between BTC AG and SAP at different levels during the implementation of projects proved mutually beneficial.

One of SAP AG's most important strategies for the future is optimizing implementation and adaptation projects and significantly reducing the operating costs associated with SAP system and process landscapes. Success story

After SAP AG had implemented SAP Solution Manager 4.0 at BTC AG in 2006 and then taken further stabilizing measures in 2007, the software represented an optimal solution as a customer platform to support the tasks of planning, implementing, monitoring, optimizing, and operating SAP solutions.

SAP Solution Manager is strategically positioned by SAP AG to cover the complete application management life cycle and is one of the key resources to realize the strategy for the future, namely, enabling customers to adapt to changes more rapidly and at significantly lower operating costs. This significant positioning of SAP Solution Manager translates into long-term planning reliability and investment protection for solution developments.

BTC AG was quick to recognize the strategic importance of SAP Solution Manager, and as early as 2006 and 2007 positioned the Implementation and Incident Management SAP Solution Manager scenarios and implemented them in selected SAP projects.

With its focus on the integrative application management life cycle, in 2007 BTC AG was able to move forward the completion of Application Management by evaluating and implementing the SAP Solution Manager functions for solution operations.

Emphasis was placed on the following operational components:

▶ Central System Monitoring

▶ Central System Administration

▶ Central Performance History

▶ Solution Manager Diagnostics (end-to-end Root Cause Analysis)

▶ Business Process Monitoring

▶ System Landscape Maintenance

To ensure that these functions were evaluated fully, new Business Blue-prints were developed from scratch and existing ones were extended. In addition, prototype solutions were built and partial rollouts were carried out.

The following section highlights, in particular, the implementation of system monitoring functions and the central administration tool for monitoring all SAP systems that BTC looks after.

The initial situation — BTC AG monitors and manages the SAP systems of the corporate group and those of external customers in its data center. The strong annual growth rate of approximately 20% experienced by the SAP system landscape led to a situation in which the non-SAP monitoring and administration tools and methods being used were no longer sufficient to monitor and manage the SAP system landscape in the best possible way.

At the outset of the projects, individual SAP monitoring objects were monitored using non-SAP tools. BTC checklists containing about 400 separate check steps existed for each system to be monitored (approximately 150 in 2007). For the most part, the SAP systems were not monitored proactively. The lack of any extensive automation in the handling of standard tasks resulted in valuable staff resources being tied up.

The evaluation phase — Early in 2007, the decision was made to conduct an evaluation project that would begin by examining the tools and methods being used and the SAP system monitoring tools available on the market in terms of their technical and organizational capabilities.

After the initial assessment, three products were shortlisted to go through to the next stage of the evaluation. Alongside SAP Solution Manager, two non-SAP products were identified as being suitable for professional deployment.

In the second evaluation stage, the system monitoring features of these products were tested in a real environment. The knowledge gained from reference customers' experience using the tools was especially important for the project team. This allowed details of the individual tools to be gathered from practice. The project team completely disregarded any judgments made on the basis of "prejudices" and "hearsay" and assessed only the information it collected itself.

Customer and market success stories and smaller-scale tests of the products offered further impressions of the products' attributes.

This newly obtained information and knowledge was then used to populate an assessment matrix in greater detail. In addition to technical and professional evaluation criteria, the cost of procuring and operating the products was taken into account in this phase. On the basis of the unequivocal findings of the assessment matrix and the personal feelings of the project team, SAP Solution Manager with its Solution Monitoring scenario emerged victorious.

Commercial Considerations	Technical Considerations
Financing option	Management of manual activities
Product and license costs	System monitoring
Configuration and development costs	Business process monitoring
	Service level reports
Training costs for SAP Basis team	Integration of BTC operations help desk
Exit costs	
Sales Considerations	**Operational Considerations**
Image at service providers	Rollout and operational handoff effort
Image at SAP customers	Rollout and operational handoff effort
Selling the project	Rollout and operational handoff effort
Image within BTC/EWE	Rollout and operational handoff effort
	Rollout and operational handoff effort

Table 10.1 Excerpt from Assessment Matrix

In the third phase, the implementation project for system monitoring and Central System Administration was initiated.

The execution phase

Over the years, each data center had implemented tools and procedures to best safeguard system operations. In addition to non-SAP monitoring tools, BTC AG had used manual checklists (MCLs) to serve as a basis for monitoring and administrative tasks.

Seq. No.	Inspection Point as per Checklist	Replaceable with Standard CCMS Objects			
		Yes	Check	No	Check/ Delete
4	Job terminations	✔			
5	Update terminations	✔			
6	SAP MaxDB	✔			
7	Transport job control				✔
8	Intermediate document (IDoc) monitoring			✔	
9	SAP NetWeaver Exchange Infrastructure monitoring			✔	
13	Restart logs			✔	
14	Check lock entries				✔
15	ArchiveLink monitor			✔	
16	Short dumps	✔	✔		

Table 10.2 Excerpt of Inspection Points from the Manual Checklist

Replacing the manual checklist — The main objective was to replicate as many inspection points from the MCL as possible in the automatic and proactive monitoring functions in SAP Solution Manager. Any necessary inspection points that could not be automated were carried over to central system administration. Some inspection points could be removed from monitoring completely.

▸ **Replacing the MCL with standard CCMS objects**
Including inspection points in the SAP Solution Manager central monitoring environment enabled systems to be monitored automatically and proactively, evaluations to be incorporated into holistic Service Level Reporting, and resources freed up to be deployed for other tasks.

▸ **Replacing the MCL with Central System Administration**
Including inspection points in SAP Solution Manager Central System Administration allowed tasks to be stored clearly in the SAP context and open tasks to be displayed directly. It enabled tasks to

be performed from a single environment and reports to be created automatically.

▶ **Checking necessity of the MCL for solution operations**
A further evaluation was performed on some MCL tasks to establish their necessity as well as the necessity to replace them with enhanced solution monitoring objects.

To enable proactive system monitoring of the SAP landscape, it is necessary to identify all monitoring objects required for operations. For this purpose, service level agreements with customers, the objects already being monitored in system administration, and the expert knowledge of the BTC employees were drawn upon once again to define the individual monitoring objects for proactive and automatic monitoring in the SAP Solution Manager system monitoring environment. One of the key activities when defining monitoring tasks is establishing initial threshold values for monitoring and issuing notifications when incidents occur.

Proactive system monitoring of the SAP landscape

Since October 1, 2007, SAP Solution Manager has been used to proactively monitor and manage all SAP systems (currently 178).

The production phase

The go-live was followed by the *settling time*, during which the threshold values of the individual monitoring objects underwent further adjustments to be optimized for system monitoring.

The benefits of this solution are its ability to proactively and automatically monitor the SAP systems, the high degree of automation in administrative activities, and the savings made in terms of resources planned in the area of quality assurance. The high level of automation lightened the workload of the BTC employees concerned. Optimized system monitoring also contributed to increased customer satisfaction and employee motivation levels.

The project, which involved 197 person days to implement the SAP Solution Manager system monitoring and Central System Administration scenarios, as well as a return on investment (ROI) of 11 months, paid for itself very quickly. Furthermore, it achieved a permanent reduction in operating costs for the SAP landscape.

In addition to cost savings, BTC system management considers the further enhancement of quality in system operations as an extremely significant gain.

10.11 Colgate-Palmolive — SAP Solution Manager Optimizes Change Control Processes and Enables Strategic Deployment

Summary

Colgate-Palmolive Company, headquartered in New York, is a major player in the consumer goods industry. With Change Request Management in SAP Solution Manager, it was able to manage changes more efficiently. Transparency was increased through an automated approval workflow, documentation, and status reports.

To be a 200-year-old global supplier of consumer products serving millions of customers in over 200 countries requires ongoing innovation and transformation. Colgate-Palmolive Company has mastered this ability, as evidenced by its position as a market-leading provider of oral care, personal care, home care, and pet nutrition products.

Colgate-Palmolive has achieved its long history of success in part by consistently identifying opportunities for growth. The company's technology platform therefore must be adaptable to change and facilitate new business processes. Colgate-Palmolive has been using SAP software in this capacity since 1994 and runs 99% of its business processes through the software. When it was time to integrate and centralize IT support as part of an overall global IT initiative, Colgate-Palmolive turned to the SAP Solution Manager application management platform to help them establish an integrated change control process.

Consolidating shared service organizations

Colgate-Palmolive relies on three shared service organizations (SSOs) that manage a heavy volume of change requests to support IT operations in the Americas, Europe-Africa, and Asia-Pacific. As part of an initiative to optimize IT operations, the company has recently established a global SSO in India to handle day-to-day IT support calls so the three SSOs can focus on more value-added initiatives. Before the redeployment of capacity could take place, Colgate-Palmolive recognized that it would have to standardize its change control process across the entire IT organization and integrate it within a single platform.

"We needed one change control process in one integrated software system," said Warren Kaufman, IT associate director of governance and project management at Colgate-Palmolive. "Each SSO was working on its own legacy application and change control process. To be successful in migrating support, we needed a single, standardized support process on a single, integrated platform."

Colgate-Palmolive considered other solutions but ultimately opted for SAP Solution Manager and customization services from the SAP Services portfolio of service offerings. "SAP Solution Manager was in line with our strategic direction, and no one knows the tool like the experts from SAP Services," Kaufman explains. "We were one of the pilot customers for the change management functionality, and we had good experiences working with it and SAP Services. They have the best experts for their solutions, so we chose to work with them."

Selecting SAP Solution Manager

As the central application management platform provided by SAP for standard software support, SAP Solution Manager was utilized to activate and customize the change control functionality. Members of the SAP Active Global Support, SAP Consulting, and SAP Custom Development organizations participated in the project. Once the global business process was agreed upon by all of the SSOs and global development, the application and process would be piloted in the Asia-Pacific region, and, upon success, the application would be implemented globally, with application support being migrated to the India-based global SSO.

Mastering change, meeting regulations

"There was some customization performed in regards to workflow, electronic signatures, and regulatory compliance," says Kaufman. "We also established customized reporting to analyze whether we are achieving our service level agreements, which was also internalized within the application."

Experts from SAP Services trained the global development team responsible for the application development, who in turn trained the global SSO in India. Following the Colgate-Palmolive support model, the global development team gradually transitioned off the project while the global

SSO took on work until the team had full ownership of the entire application, including the successful pilot in Asia-Pacific.

Reaping the
rewards

SAP Solution Manager is enabling Colgate-Palmolive to implement its global IT strategy while ensuring a change control process that keeps its application platform harmonized and transparent — benefits that will have a profound impact on overall business operations. "SAP Solution Manager gives us full visibility into our entire change control process. We now have an integrated process that improves our workflow and enforces regulatory compliance," Kaufman explains. "One workflow incorporates the entire IT division and documents everything involved in the change request — from service request initiation to requirement gathering, approvals, resource assignment, design and development, testing, documentation, and implementation. We are automatically notified of changes, can track status, and create reports. It has changed the way we communicate and work."

Looking ahead

The next step for Colgate-Palmolive will be implementing the change control process into the Americas, Europe-Africa, and global development — all within six months. By having one platform managing the entire day-to-day change control process, Colgate-Palmolive can migrate 100% support to its global SSO in India and redeploy its regional SSO teams on global development initiatives and implementations. In keeping with the company's commitment for ongoing innovation and transformation, Colgate-Palmolive continually evaluates its solution landscape to find opportunities for greater efficiencies and effectiveness.

10.12 Feldschlösschen Getränke AG — SAP Solution Manager Tool Leads to Unparalleled Stability in Key 24-7 Operations

Summary

Feldschlösschen Getränke AG, the Swiss subsidiary of Carlsberg Breweries, was looking for a way to standardize change requests in line with the IT Infrastructure Library (ITIL) standards and maintain its competitive advantage. With SAP Solution Manager, Feldschlösschen significantly improved the efficiency of both its change request management process and its operational process flows.

"It is of the utmost importance that the system stays online 24 hours a day. As a consumer goods company in the beverages industry, whose customers place their orders via our Web shop at all times of day and night, Feldschlösschen Getränke simply cannot afford to be unavailable for any amount of time," explains Manfred Weiss, SAP Competence Center manager of Switzerland's leading brewer and drinks supplier, Feldschlösschen Getränke AG. It was this key requirement that led the company — a subsidiary of Carlsberg Breweries with a firm foothold on 44% of the Swiss beverages market — to oust its legacy system and implement the SAP Solution Manager tool, the SAP platform for application management and collaboration. Weiss confirms that the platform has fulfilled all expectations: "Since implementing SAP Solution Manager in 2005, we haven't had any downtime whatsoever."

Several factors contributed to the decision to go with a new tool for managing applications. In the first instance, the legacy system — based on Microsoft Excel — was proving to be too awkward for managing applications and changes efficiently. While the tool may have covered all of the required processes, it was far from being system-defined to suit Feldschlösschen's business needs.

From manual processing to integrated software

In the area of change request management, these needs primarily included being able to track and show which changes were made when and by whom. In short, the application management processes had to be traceable enough to provide data effectively, both to Feldschlösschen and to its external auditors.

Moreover, the new tool had to comply with the recommendations of the IT Infrastructure Library (ITIL), the most widely accepted approach to IT service management in the world. What was clearly lacking was an efficient form of automating processes that incorporated best practices. Whereas Microsoft Excel previously split processes into several cumbersome and manual steps, which sometimes spanned several days before completion, SAP Solution Manager proved to be the better option. It was clear to Weiss during the decision-making process that SAP could provide what the company needed. "SAP applications provide an unparalleled level of integration. Anyone working with the SAP software can send a feedback message or a change request in two mouse clicks," he says. "It's very clean."

The initial transition from the legacy system to SAP Solution Manager took place at the beginning of 2005, with implementation of the Service Desk functionality. Building on that success, Feldschlösschen then went live with the Change Request Management functionality in the fall of 2005 after a rapid 1½-month implementation phase that was carried out by an SAP service partner, Resource Informatik AG. That things didn't go even faster was due mainly to Weiss's decision to concentrate resources on the main concerns of stability, standardization, and cost effectiveness.

By completely replacing a whole series of steps with a single process, the Change Request Management functionality of SAP Solution Manager contributed greatly to enhancing and optimizing administrative tasks. That isn't simply beneficial, but is a must for a company with a competitive lead as wide as Feldschlösschen's. "When the change request is entered, we now have a much more stable operation. This is vital with our current volume of up to 4,000 customer orders per day. If a customer cannot place an order, the bottom line is that we lose revenue. It's as simple as that," says Weiss.

Currently, the average volume of change requests is approximately 3,000 a year — fewer than 10 a day. Although SAP Solution Manager cannot contribute to lessening the actual number of change requests, it can process changes more quickly and in a far more structured manner than before. Being able to view how much was done, where, when, how, and by whom on a central display makes handling a lot easier. And, as Weiss likes to explain, "Because our maintenance operations are quicker overall, we can cut down on time and cost expenditure significantly."

However, to cut down even more on time needed to enter change requests, Feldschlösschen conducted its own analysis following implementation. Although Weiss and his team found they had reduced the time to place a transport order in the system from days to 15 minutes, they felt they could improve on that even more. With the help of the SAP Active Global Support organization, they managed to reduce the number of steps between the initial Service Desk message and the change request to 25 mouse clicks and reduce the time needed to just five minutes. "By reducing the change request management process to five minutes, we have actually introduced a lean change request into the system. With an average of fewer than 10 change requests per day, we need less than an hour now. Before, we needed almost double that," explains Weiss.

Now that the Change Request Management functionality of SAP Solution Manager has proved its worth for the company's key process of application management, plans are in the pipeline to implement further functionality, including testing and upgrade support. And, with the success of the tool, Feldschlösschen also led the way within Carlsberg's corporate structure. Weiss has already held presentations abroad and expects implementation of SAP Solution Manager to follow on a corporate level.

Weiss is certain of one thing, however: Feldschlösschen's long-term commitment to SAP has the full support and backing not only of the company's executives, but also of staff at all levels of the company hierarchy. One of the best effects he notes, after all, is the effect that the implementation of the Change Request Management functionality has had on key development personnel. Despite some questions being raised prior to implementation — with different developers championing their own methods — Weiss is happy to point out how things have changed. "The tool has distinctly succeeded in standardizing the way change requests are managed at Feldschlösschen Getränke," he says. "Now, if you tried to take SAP Solution Manager away from any of our developers, not one of them would let go of it."

Paving the way to the future with SAP applications

Partners play an important part in the SAP ecosystem. The quality and added value of support processes is increased by integrating partners.

11 Integrating Partners in the SAP Global Support Backbone

Globalization and increasing IT complexity are only two of the challenges that companies face today and that demand accelerated business process innovation. Customers are becoming more aware of the need to establish relationships within a network, access a broad range of expertise, and cooperate to achieve better business processes.

As part of its platform strategy, SAP has created an open customer and partner network, which it is continuously developing to drive the changeover to service-oriented architecture for business applications, promote joint innovation at SAP, customers, and partners, and thereby boost the added value for all parties. SAP and the SAP customer and partner network benefit from the sound industry knowledge possessed by a diverse community of partners, and use SAP NetWeaver as a platform for product and service innovation. This brings a new dimension to such collaborative efforts, allowing groundbreaking ideas to be turned into innovative solutions for customers.

Customer and partner network

SAP has also established a support network. It consists of support centers located in over 40 countries around the world, with 3,000 employees. The support centers look after 30,000 customers, over 84,000 installations, and 12,000,000 SAP users. They deliver 100,000 services every year. The range of support services provided are characterized by fast response times and high quality.

Support network

The role played by SAP partners in delivering support services has grown in significance. A number of different types of partners provide a very diverse range of services for SAP solutions, from sales and support of SAP software and own-brand software products to implementing and managing SAP solutions and providing SAP services. Partners must have access to the SAP global support backbone to enable them to be incorporated into SAP support processes. Furthermore, the requirements that the different partner types place on the SAP infrastructure must be accommodated.

11.1   SAP Solution Manager As Part of the SAP Global Support Backbone

The SAP global support backbone consists of the SAP Service Marketplace, which is operated by SAP, and SAP Solution Manager, which is integrated into the customer's system landscape.

SAP Service Marketplace *SAP Service Marketplace* is SAP's globally accessible Internet platform for calling up SAP knowledge. It is composed of numerous Internet portals that offer content aimed at specific target groups and enable SAP, its customers, and its partners to collaborate.

SAP Solution Manager is each customer's own point of entry to SAP's service and support organization. Figure 11.1 shows an overview of the SAP Partner Network.

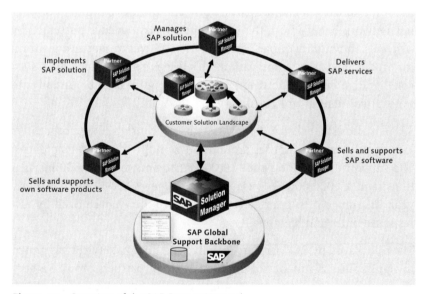

Figure 11.1 Overview of the SAP Partner Network

SAP partners are incorporated into the SAP global support backbone using SAP Solution Manager. This presents several advantages for SAP partners:

SAP Solution Manager is flexible and can be adapted to suit the partner's various support needs. Since SAP provides SAP Solution Manager for customers and partners, partners are not required to invest in their own support tools and processes. SAP Solution Manager also presents an easy way to exchange knowledge within the SAP global support backbone.

By including SAP partners in the SAP global support backbone, SAP and its partners can jointly support their customers, exploit valuable synergies, and increase the added value for themselves and their customers.

SAP Solution Manager helps partners perform the following tasks:

Support for partners

▶ Install and implement SAP solutions

▶ Process and resolve messages

▶ Establish remote connections to customer systems

▶ Change management (including Support Package administration, software logistics)

▶ Root Cause Analysis

▶ Service Delivery

▶ BI reporting

The processes for handling messages, establishing remote connections, change management, and Root Cause Analysis are explained later in more detail when the range of partner types is presented.

In addition to particular functions required to deliver services, partners must possess in-depth knowledge of the customer solution to solve problems quickly and competently, offer and deliver services tailored to the customer's needs, and implement any necessary changes in the customer solution. As long as the customer systems are connected directly to SAP Solution Manager, it provides access to the following customer information:

Accessing customer information

▶ Landscape description of the implemented solution including the core business processes

- Technical system data
- Software components in use (including Support Package level)
- Version of database and operating system

The information covers both SAP software and non-SAP software being used.

The range of services provided by software partners and value-added resellers is described in the following section, notably the particular requirements these partners have in terms of the SAP global support backbone and the instruments at their disposal to complete their tasks.

11.2 Software Partners

SAP software has always stood out from the crowd thanks to its technological openness. SAP software can be used on different operating system platforms and with different databases. In addition, SAP provides standardized interfaces, which ensures that the company solutions of SAP and other application systems are able to communicate smoothly.

Defined standard interfaces
SAP's software partner program puts defined standard interfaces at the disposal of software providers. These interfaces allow additional products to be integrated seamlessly with SAP solutions, enabling SAP software partners to develop complementary products that bolster the potential uses and benefits of SAP solutions. Partner solutions are certified by the SAP Integration and Certification Center (SAP ICC) to ensure that the entire solution is capable of operating.

In addition, partner products must be integrated into the customer's application management platform, SAP Solution Manager, to enable the customer to operate a business-critical solution encompassing both SAP and partner products. If a problem occurs, it is crucial that SAP can offer seamless support and a solution together with the partner. For this purpose, the software partner's support processes must be integrated into the SAP global support backbone.

11.2.1 Integrating Partner Products into the Customer's SAP Solution Manager System

SAP Solution Manager is used to manage a customer's entire system landscape. This applies to both SAP software and software from third parties and requires the processes in use — as well as the underlying infrastructure including software components and the versions installed — to be documented in SAP Solution Manager.

SAP Solution Manager collects this data from all managed systems and keeps it up to date. It is imperative that partner products are incorporated into this proven technology. For this reason, at the end of 2007 SAP made the SAP Solution Manager Ready Guideline an obligatory part of the certification carried out by the SAP Integration and Certification Center. This ensures that information about installed partner products is automatically available in the customer's SAP Solution Manager. Further information about the SAP Integration and Certification Center and SAP Solution Manager Ready can be found at *https://www.sdn.sap.com/ irj/sdn/icc.*

SAP Solution Manager Ready Guideline

The fact that partner products are certified also ensures that Solution Manager Diagnostics can be used to perform a Root Cause Analysis on them. The tools provided in Solution Manager Diagnostics enable problems that arise in a distributed customer solution with critical business processes to be systematically analyzed and resolved. Solution Manager Diagnostics has direct access to the error, log, and trace files for the partner product. This means the Root Cause Analysis for partner products takes place in a familiar environment in exactly the same way as for SAP products.

For partner products that are used in particularly business-critical processes, SAP and its partners are working on even more extensive integration with Solution Manager Diagnostics. For more information about Solution Manager Diagnostics, see Section 8.8.

The benefits for customers that use software from certified partners are as follows:

▶ Any partner software being used is automatically recognized in the customer's SAP Solution Manager. The information includes technical details, for example, release and version, and is provided without manual effort.

▶ If a problem occurs with the partner software, Solution Manager Diagnostics can be used to gain direct access to the error, log, and trace files for the partner product.

11.2.2 Support Processes – Overview

SAP provides customers with powerful tools so they can recognize and efficiently repair potential problems as early as possible, without impairing the business process concerned.

Knowledge network
In the event of a problem, your support organization can gain rapid access to an SAP knowledge network from a range of sources, for example, SAP Notes, online documentation, how-to guides, forums, wikis, and so on.

If necessary, you can then perform a Root Cause Analysis in Solution Manager Diagnostics to further analyze the problem.

If the analysis in your support organization is unsuccessful, you create a message and send it to SAP. SAP then takes on the problem. If required, after obtaining prior authorization from the customer, SAP can establish a remote connection to the customer system to analyze the problem there.

Troubleshooting by partners
If the problem relates to an error in the partner software, SAP transfers the message to the partner. The message is then received in the partner's SAP Solution Manager, which is connected to the SAP global support backbone and constantly checks if new messages have arrived. The customer can tell that a message has been forwarded to the partner from the message status. The partner can now start working on a solution to the problem and communicate directly with the customer. The partner can also log on to the customer system remotely if required. Figure 11.2 diagrams the support relationships between the customer, SAP, and the partner.

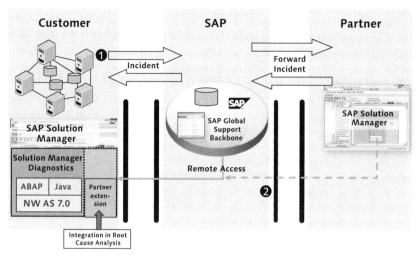

Figure 11.2 SAP Support Infrastructure: Customer, SAP, and Software Partner

11.2.3 The Message Process in Detail

Customers can send a message to SAP using the SAP Support Portal or the Service Desk in SAP Solution Manager. In addition to naming the system affected by the problem and providing details of how the problem manifests itself and its impact, the customer specifies the affected software area by selecting what is referred to as a component. Separate components have been created for partner enhancements:

▶ XX-PART-xxx* for OEM partners (original equipment manufacturers)

▶ XX-PART-EBS-xxx* for EBS partners (endorsed business solutions)

"xxx" stands for the respective partner.

The message is received in the SAP global support backbone, where it is processed. For messages relating to a partner solution, SAP may provide first- and second-level support, or, in certain cases, the partner may provide all of the support. Whether or not SAP provides support depends on the contractual relationship between the partner and SAP. For OEM partners, SAP generally provides first- and second-level support, whereas for EBS partners the message is usually transferred to the partner directly.

Message status The customer is always able to tell from the status of the message who is currently responsible for processing: SAP or the partner. All messages being worked on by a partner have status TO SAP PARTNER.

Messages for which a partner is responsible are made available to the partner. The partner's SAP Solution Manager regularly receives new or updated messages, which means messages are transferred without an integration gap.

A major advantage of SAP solutions and certified partner solutions being operated together is that they send all incidents to the SAP global support backbone, where they can then be forwarded automatically (Figure 11.3).

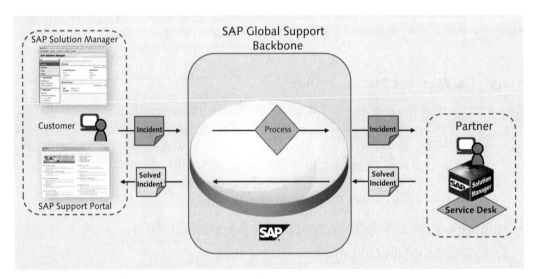

Figure 11.3 Message Processing with Partner Involvement – Process Flow

11.2.4 Remote Connections to Customer Systems

Standardized access To ensure that support services can be delivered in the right quality and scope for customer landscapes that include partner products, it is necessary to offer the partners standardized access to customer systems. This puts them in a position to provide customers with rapid, efficient support in the event of problems and also deliver services. In addition, the enlargement of the remote support infrastructure to incorporate partners presents the advantage that customers can use the established procedures without any need for new processes or infrastructure elements. The central log book provides information about partner accesses, logon data can be stored in the *secure area*, and, of course, access can only be gained with the customer's authorization.

The following benefits accompany the inclusion of partners in the existing infrastructure for remote connections:

▸ Customers use the existing procedures.

▸ Customers use the existing infrastructure.

▸ Established security procedures are deployed.

▸ Customers have a central overview of all connections made by partners and SAP.

To achieve this, the partner's SAP Solution Manager is connected to the SAP global support backbone using the SAProuter. As soon as the partner takes on processing of a message, the partner support experts can use a function to establish a remote connection from SAP Solution Manager. The SAP support colleague connects to the SAP global support backbone by obtaining authorization. The employee can then use the opened connection to dial in to the customer system and resolve the reported problem.

Comment: Remote Connection

A remote connection connects the customer network with SAP's support network and accelerates the process of solving problems and delivering services at a reduced cost. Remote connections are therefore fundamental to delivering fast and efficient support.

SAP customers establish a network connection once. This involves connecting the customer and SAP networks with SAProuters that manage network access. An SAProuter is a tool that represents an extra security layer in network communications. It is an additional physical access control for the network and thereby protects the network from unauthorized access.

Security Concept for Remote Connections from SAP to the Customer

One of the main reasons the remote connection concept became so well established was that emphasis was placed on the customer's security requirements from the outset. The following basic principles are always heeded:

- Numerous encryption mechanisms are in place, including software encryption using *secure network communication* (SNC) and hardware encryption by means of *virtual private network* (VPN).

- Every customer has full control of the configured connections and opens a connection at the request of SAP.

- Every remote connection to the customer network is logged. This information is accessible to all customers in the *log book*, which is available in the SAP Support Portal.

Secure area   In addition to a network connection, the SAP support employee requires a user ID and password to be able to log on to the target system. This information can be stored in what is known as the secure area. Customers can use authorizations to manage which particular employees have access to this data. Additionally, every time the customer or an SAP employee accesses the secure area, it is recorded in a log file. Logon data is also deleted automatically after a period defined by the customer. The secure area offers a controlled way to access logon data while preventing unauthorized access.

11.2.5   Note Creation for Partners

SAP Notes are accessible to all customers online. They describe known problems and their solutions. SAP Notes may also contain FAQs and tips and tricks on installing and configuring a solution.

Software partners are given access to the SAP Notes database and can create partner Notes for their enhancements that can be located using the Notes search and help customers solve problems efficiently.

Principle of dual control   To ensure that partner Notes display high levels of quality and comprehensibility, the established dual control principle was applied to them. This principle means that every SAP Note must be checked for correctness and comprehensibility by another person in addition to the author before it can be released for customers. A similar approach is taken for partner Notes: Two partner employees can create a Note that is checked and released by an SAP support expert before it becomes accessible to customers (Figure 11.4).

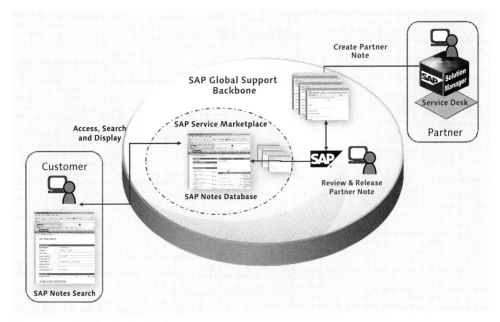

Figure 11.4 Creating Partner Notes

The inclusion of software partners in SAP's support processes enables SAP and software partners to work together in providing support to their customers to ensure that problems are solved efficiently. With SAP Solution Manager, software partners have a support platform that is integrated centrally into the SAP support infrastructure and supports a wide range of processes for providing partner support. SAP Solution Manager is constantly being developed further to accommodate the needs of software partners.

11.3   Value-Added Resellers

Value-added resellers sell SAP solutions tailored to the needs of small and midsize companies. These SAP solutions are cost-effective, fast to implement, and very flexible. Furthermore, the value-added resellers provide their customers with first- and second-level support.

Because value-added resellers sell the SAP solution directly to the customer, a contract is drawn up between the value-added reseller and the customer, not between SAP and the customer. The customer warranty therefore lies with the value-added reseller.

The number of small and midsize companies that use SAP solutions has risen sharply in recent years. In 2007, SAP experienced a growth of its customer base of 35% in the small business sector and of almost 20% in the midsize business sector. To ensure that these customers receive comprehensive and competent support, SAP has established a network of authorized value-added resale partners that is continuously expanding.

Central contact persons

Value-added resellers are central contact persons for their customers regarding questions about the SAP solution. They usually look after numerous customers. To deliver their support services, they must possess in-depth knowledge of the customer solution. They need a tool that makes the technical complexity of customer solutions transparent and supports the entire life cycle of SAP solutions. To respond to customer queries quickly and competently, value-added resellers must have access to central sources of information in the SAP global support backbone (Figure 11.5).

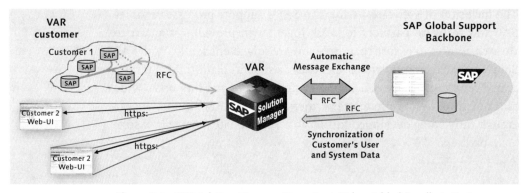

Figure 11.5 SAP Solution Manager Managing a Value-Added Reseller's Customers

SAP Solution Manager for value-added resellers

SAP Solution Manager meets all of these requirements for value-added resellers. A reseller only needs one SAP Solution Manager to take care of all its customers. This means that small and midsize companies that are looked after by a value-added reseller do not need their own SAP Solution Manager. All customer systems can be connected to the value-added reseller's SAP Solution Manager. When the customers' system data is changed, it is then updated in the value-added reseller's SAP Solution Manager automatically without manual intervention. SAP Solution Manager automatically forwards the data to the SAP global support backbone to ensure that SAP support employees can also access the same customer data if necessary.

Often, value-added reseller customers' systems are not yet connected to their value-added reseller's SAP Solution Manager as managed systems, usually because the customers' modest IT departments are concerned about the workload. This point was addressed by developing the Service Desks for value-added resellers. If its customers' systems are not connected directly to its SAP Solution Manager, the value-added reseller has no access to customer data, but because system data is essential when handling messages, in such cases the systems are regularly updated with data held by SAP.

Service Desk for value-added resellers

Every customer's solution landscape is described centrally in the value-added reseller's SAP Solution Manager so that the reseller has detailed knowledge of all of its customers and is therefore able to provide efficient support.

By connecting SAP Solution Manager to the SAP global support backbone, value-added resellers can gain access to the latest support information, for example, SAP Notes in the Notes database in the SAP Support Portal and expert forums.

11.3.1 SAP Solution Manager Processes for Value-Added Resellers

All value-added resellers can use the following processes supported by SAP Solution Manager to deliver contractually defined support services to their customers:

- ▶ Message processing using the Incident Management scenario in the Service Desk
- ▶ Remote connection to customer systems
- ▶ Maintenance optimizer and generating installation keys
- ▶ Root Cause Analysis

It is ensured throughout all of these processes that customer data is only accessible to the value-added reseller and cannot be viewed by other customers that the reseller looks after in SAP Solution Manager.

The following section describes the individual processes in more detail.

Message Processing Using the Incident Management Scenario in the Service Desk

The message-handling process in the SAP Solution Manager Service Desk is of central importance for value-added resellers. The Service Desk was specially developed in SAP Solution Manager in close cooperation with the value-added resellers. A tool for handling messages from several customer numbers belonging to the same corporate group had already been developed for companies with their own Customer Competence Center or Customer Center of Expertise (CCoE). A corporate group usually has all of the subsidiaries and branch offices that its CCoE takes care of connected directly to the CCoE's SAP Solution Manager. This represents an extension of the simple Service Desk. The scenario for value-added resellers was developed on this basis.

Incident Management work center

Switching to the new message process does not involve a great deal of effort on the part of the customer. Instead of using the message assistant at SAP to enter and respond to messages, customers now use their partner's Incident Management work center, which is also accessed via the Internet. A simplified version of the message assistant was developed for the Service Desk for this purpose. The interface for entering and responding to messages, selecting systems, and adding attachments is very clearly laid out, allowing users to get used to it quickly (Figure 11.6).

Once a value-added reseller is using its Service Desk in production, the customer's users also receive notification of the changed message process in the message assistant in the SAP Support Portal. A link to the customer's value-added reseller's support page is also shown. Customers can continue to use their SAP Service Marketplace user ID to enter messages in their value-added reseller's Service Desk.

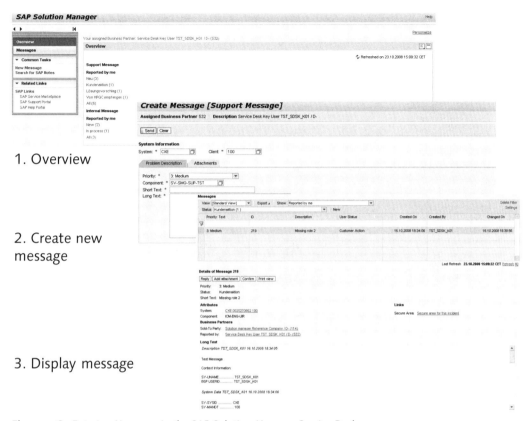

Figure 11.6 Entering Messages in the SAP Solution Manager Service Desk

Customer messages entered in the new way in the value-added reseller's work center can be distributed to different support teams immediately and automatically in the Service Desk if this is required. Criteria such as component, customer number, region, and so on can be used for this purpose. A message processor will only find a solution for a message by using tools such as the SAP Notes search or another solution directory that is only available to SAP and SAP partners.

In addition, value-added resellers can create an internal solution database in SAP Solution Manager to store solution Notes they have created themselves. Such Notes can be made available to both the value-added reseller's support employees and customers. If a proposed solution does not provide adequate assistance to the customer, the value-added reseller is free to forward this message to SAP Support just as before. After being

Internal solution database

processed by SAP, the message is then returned to the customer via the value-added reseller (Figure 11.7).

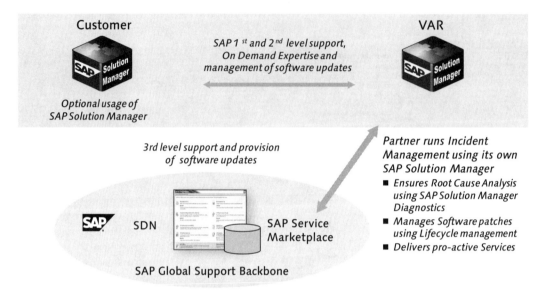

Figure 11.7 Message Handling Process for Customers of the Value-Added Reseller

Forwarding to SAP Support When a customer creates a message with very high priority outside its value-added reseller's hours of business, the message is automatically forwarded to SAP Support to prevent delays.

Integrated Service Level Management in the SAP Solution Manager Service Desk guarantees adherence to value-added reseller and customer-specific service level agreements.

All of these processes and functions were previously executed in a similar way for value-added resellers and their customers in an SAP-internal support system. The functions were relocated to SAP Solution Manager with the introduction of the Service Desk. For value-added resellers, this opens the door to the whole spectrum of options presented by SAP Solution Manager. The resellers manage SAP Solution Manager themselves and can make their own mark on it. This enables them to much better accommodate their customers' diverse needs.

Remote Connection to Customer Systems

Support specialists often find that they need to log on to customer systems using a remote service connection to analyze software problems more closely and resolve them quickly. Similar to the procedure for other SAP partners, value-added resellers gain access to customer systems using their SAP Solution Manager. A detailed description of the remote support infrastructure for partners is provided in Section 11.2.4.

Maintenance Optimizer and Generating Installation Keys

The Maintenance Optimizer is an SAP Solution Manager function that guides you through the process of planning, downloading, and implementing Support Packages and other patches as well as installing and incorporating SAP enhancement packages in an upgrade to SAP ERP 6.0. The maintenance optimizer is required for SAP products based on SAP NetWeaver 7.0 and subsequent versions. It can be used for all SAP products. The functions and benefits of the maintenance optimizer are described in detail in Section 9.3.

Customers of value-added resellers do not need their own SAP Solution Manager to download and implement Support Packages and other patches for SAP NetWeaver 7.0 and subsequent versions. They can use the Maintenance Optimizer by means of their value-added reseller's SAP Solution Manager.

Newer SAP solutions require an installation key to be generated in SAP Solution Manager before they are deployed for the first time. In this case also, customers of value-added resellers do not need their own SAP Solution Manager. Value-added resellers can generate the installation keys for their customers in their own SAP Solution Manager.

Root Cause Analysis

Value-added resellers can also perform Root Cause Analyses on their customers' systems using Solution Manager Diagnostics in their SAP Solution Manager. To do so, a network connection must exist between the customer systems and Solution Manager Diagnostics. For more information about Solution Manager Diagnostics, see Section 8.8.

11.3.2 Optional SAP Solution Manager Processes for Value-Added Resellers

Value-added resellers may extend the range of services they provide to their customers beyond contractually defined support services and use the following additional functions in SAP Solution Manager:

▶ Change Request Management (see Section 9.1)

▶ Enhanced monitoring and reporting (see Sections 8.2 and 8.9)

▶ Implementing and testing with SAP Solution Manager (see Chapter 6)

▶ Service Delivery (see Section 8.6)

The customer systems must be connected to the value-added reseller's SAP Solution Manager to use these functions.

SAP Solution Manager has proven its value as a support platform and is already used by numerous partners to support their customers. It is constantly being enhanced to accommodate the needs of customers and partners and keep up with the growing significance of SAP partners in providing support services.

Appendices

A   Additional Information

This book has presented SAP Solution Manager Enterprise Edition and its array of functions. This appendix summarizes additional information about SAP Solution Manager. It focuses initially on offerings for knowledge transfer, such as the Learning Maps on the SAP Service Marketplace and the training curriculum for SAP Solution Manager, which provides up-to-date information about individual functions.

It also contains information about SAP Solution Manager upgrades and the most common application scenarios, presented with an estimate of each scenario's complexity in a project context.

A.1   Offerings for Knowledge Transfer

A.1.1   SAP Solution Manager Online Knowledge Products

A wide range of E-Learning materials is available for SAP Solution Manager. You can access the *Online Knowledge Products* (OKPs) for SAP Solution Manager on the SAP Service Marketplace at *http://www.service.sap.com/rkt-solman*. There you can choose between SAP Solution Manager 7.0, SAP Solution Manager Enterprise Edition 7.0 EHP 1, and SAP Solution Manager Extensions.

OKPs tend to be used internally for transferring knowledge about new content and usually incur a surcharge. In this case, however, SAP has decided to make the content for SAP Solution Manager available to all customers free of charge. The fact that this offering for SAP Solution Manager is one of the most used OKPs and 96% of all evaluations rate its content as being *very good* validates this decision.

OKPs free of charge

The OKPs for SAP Solution Manager Enterprise Edition are composed of over 200 English-language learning objects (SAP Tutor sessions, presentations, and demonstrations), which are grouped into six, phase-based Learning Maps. The following phases are available:

Phase-based documents

▶ Overview and Setup of SAP Solution Manager

▶ Requirements and Design Phase with SAP Solution Manager

- ▶ Build, Test, and Deploy with SAP Solution Manager
- ▶ Operations with SAP Solution Manager
- ▶ Optimization with SAP Solution Manager
- ▶ Learning Map for Technical Quality Managers

A.1.2   SAP Solution Manager on the SAP Service Marketplace

The SAP Service Marketplace is a good source of up-to-date information. At *http://www.service.sap.com/solutionmanager*, information is grouped into the following categories:

Categories
- ▶ **SAP Solution Manager Enterprise Edition**
  Provides an overview of the content and value of SAP Solution Manager Enterprise Edition.

- ▶ **Value Proposition**
  Contains information about the SAP Solution Manager offerings and how they can boost the value of your IT solution.

- ▶ **Release Strategy**
  Provides information about release plans for SAP Solution Manager, such as maintenance strategies for individual releases and details of new developments.

- ▶ **Work Centers**
  Contains information about the new concept of role-based work centers.

- ▶ **Certification**
  Provides more information about SAP Solution Manager certification by TÜV Informationstechnik GmbH (TÜViT).

- ▶ **SAP Solution Manager in Detail**
  Contains detailed information about the individual functions in SAP Solution Manager. It is divided into:
  - ▶ Implementation
  - ▶ Upgrade of SAP Solutions
  - ▶ Service Desk
  - ▶ Solution Monitoring

- ▶ Change Request Management

- ▶ End-to-End Root Cause Analysis

- ▶ Delivery of Support Services

- ▶ End-to-End Integration Testing

▶ **SAP Solution Manager Extensions**
Contains information about available enhancements that enrich the functions of your SAP Solution Manager and establish interfaces to third-party products.

- ▶ Service Desk XT

- ▶ SAP Test Acceleration and Optimization

- ▶ SAP Quality Center by HP adapter for SAP Solution Manager

- ▶ SAP Central Process Scheduling by Redwood adapter for SAP Solution Manager

- ▶ SAP Productivity Pak by RWD adapter for SAP Solution Manager

▶ **Training**
Provides an overview of the training options offered for SAP Solution Manager.

▶ **SAP Solution Manager Services**
Contains information about available consulting and support services for SAP Solution Manager.

▶ **Media Library**
Contains current presentations, technical instructions, links to documentation, and success stories relating to SAP Solution Manager.

▶ **Information for Partners**
Contains information about deploying SAP Solution Manager for value-added resellers and software partners.

▶ **FAQ**
Gives answers to frequently asked questions concerning the SAP Solution Manager environment.

▶ **Downloads**
Contains links to pages where you can download Support Packages and other SAP Solution Manager content.

A.1.3 Training

SAP has drawn up a range of training courses covering many aspects of SAP Solution Manager. You can choose between classroom training courses and e-learning units.

Classroom Training

- SMI210 – Implementation Methodology Overview
- SMI310 – SAP Solution Manager: Implementation Tools in Detail
- SM100 – SAP Solution Manager for Operations of SAP Solutions
- SM150 – SAP Solution Manager 7.0: Service Desk
- SM200 – SAP Solution Manager 7.0: Change Request Management
- SM300 – Business Process Management and Monitoring
- E2E040 – Run SAP End-to-End Solution Operations
- E2E100 – E2E Root Cause Analysis
- E2E200 – E2E Change Control Management
- E2E300 – Solution Support – Business Process
- E2E400 – E2E Technical Upgrade Management
- CA611 – Test Management with eCATT
- TDMS10 – SAP Test Data Migration Server 3.0

E-Learning Offerings

- SM001 – SAP Solution Manager Overview
- SM510 – Global Roll-Out
- SM520 – Effective Knowledge Transfer with SAP Solution Manager
- SM530 – ITIL with SAP Solution Manager
- SM540 – Incident Management
- SM550 – Change Request Management
- E2E050 – E2E Solution Scope and Documentation
- OTDMS3 – OKP SAP Test Data Migration Server (TDMS)

A.2   SAP Solution Manager Roadmap

SAP Solution Manager is coming increasingly to the fore as a platform for implementing and running SAP software throughout its life cycle. Its array of coordinated functions makes it the ideal tool for dealing with tasks and problems that may arise and for supporting users in their work. The collaboration scenario provides a unique platform on which customers, partners, and SAP can work together.

Implementing SAP Solution Manager often raises many questions, such as how to map existing organizational structures, which functions to use, and how to apply or integrate tools from other providers concurrently or as alternatives.

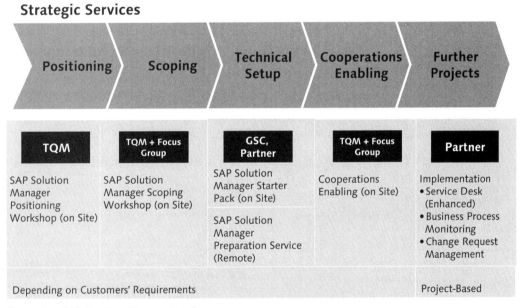

Figure A.1   SAP Solution Manager Roadmap

In response, SAP has drawn up the SAP Solution Manager Roadmap, which addresses such questions in a systematic, step-by-step manner (see Figure A.1).

SAP Solution Manager Roadmap

The first step, *positioning*, involves evaluating the different SAP Solution Manager options and matching their functions to your company's requirements. The collaboration scenario cannot be chosen freely because it contains the tools and methods required for frictionless collaboration between SAP and customers.

Scoping Workshop The next step is the *Scoping Workshop*, which provides an opportunity to define:

▶ How the organizations within an enterprise can be mapped in one or more systems running SAP Solution Manager

▶ The synergies and limitations of the functions selected, as determined by the customer situation

▶ The final shape of the solutions

▶ How third-party tools can be integrated

▶ Rough sizing for the required hardware

▶ A project plan with suitable milestones

The purpose of the technical setup phase is to ensure that SAP Solution Manager is ready to use.

The cooperation-enabling phase involves demonstrating the different options and handing them over to the customer. From this step on, you are ready to collaborate with SAP using SAP Solution Manager.

You can implement additional functions yourself or in collaboration with SAP and consulting partners.

B   Glossary

Action (Change Request Management and Service Desk):   A planned activity (follow-up action) or task that is determined and executed using the postprocessing framework (PPF) in response to a given situation. The action is recorded in the transaction document or determined for the transaction on the basis of a rule (action profile). Actions can be defined in the transaction header and apply to the entire transaction or for individual items. Actions can be scheduled (action type and start requirement), started (manually or automatically), and monitored.

Actions can be performed by persons, groups of people, organizational units, or in the background by the system.

Business Blueprint: A phase in the ASAP Implementation Roadmap and a transaction for mapping an organization's business processes in SAP Solution Manager, and its business and functional requirements as part of an SAP Solution Manager project (SOLAR01). These requirements are discussed at requirements workshops, and the results are summarized in a Business Blueprint document.

Business partner: A person, organization, group of persons, or group of organizations in which a company has a business interest. A business partner can also be a person, organization, or group within the same company.

Business process: The second level of the process-based structure in SAP Solution Manager. It consists of multiple process steps, represents part of a business scenario that a company can implement, and can span multiple components. A business process contains implementation-relevant assignments, such as process documentation, IMG activities, and transactions.

Business Process Change Analyzer (BPCA):   Tool used to precisely analyze the business processes that are affected by a change. You begin by creating a list of all SAP objects that are used when business processes are executed. This very detailed information is saved in the system as a technical bill of materials (TBOM). In the event of an intentional change, the SAP objects contained in the transport are compared with the SAP objects listed in the TBOMs to identify the affected business processes and areas. This allows you to schedule the required regression tests for precisely the affected areas and make well-directed use of your test resources.

Business Process Repository (BPR):   All of the SAP reference elements stored in SAP Solution Manager, which you can use in projects and the solution directory as a starting point for building solutions that your company wants to implement or monitor. Components include:

▶ **Structure items:** organizational units, master data, business scenarios, business processes, and process steps

▶ **Assignments to structure items, such as transactions and IMG activities**

▶ **Configuration structure:** for cross-scenario or technical configuration settings (not available in solution directory)

Business scenario: The first level of the process-based structure in SAP Solution Manager. It is composed of a number of related business processes, represents an end-to-end unit from an SAP solution or application that a company can implement, and is designed to achieve a specific business goal. A business scenario contains implementation-relevant assignments, such as a scenario description.

Change request: An electronic document containing a request for a software change. A problem message, for instance, can trigger a change request.

Change Request Management: A scenario in SAP Solution Manager that incorporates a workflow to support continuous changes to software and configuration settings.

Checklist: A list of items for completion.

Check rule: Check rules are automatically copied from the source (project, solution, or imported data) when an analysis project is created in the Solution Documentation Assistant. They can be edited or extended to increase the quality of the analysis. Check rules are divided into check sets and check steps.

Check set: In the analysis in the Solution Documentation Assistant, check sets enable nodes in the analysis structure to be rated. This rating is based on the results of check steps that have been assigned to the check sets. You are free to choose how many check steps you assign to each check set. In turn, you can assign as many check sets as you like to each structure node.

Check step: A check step is an object to be analyzed, for instance, a transaction, report, or SQL statement. The check step is the smallest unit in the check rules.

Clearing Analysis (CA): A function of the Custom Development Management Cockpit used to optimize custom developments. Clearing Analysis is used to identify and analyze obsolete repository objects. The results of a clearing analysis are the ideal starting point for clearing these custom developments.

Comparison tool: A report in SAP Solution Manager that enables you to check automatically for updates for the business processes implemented in a project and to adopt changes in projects in a controlled manner. It can be used to compare templates that have been implemented, for instance, as part of a global rollout, or to compare implementation projects to identify changes from the BPR.

Configuration: A part of the realization Roadmap phase and a transaction for customizing business processes in SAP Solution Manager (SOLAR02). Configuration entails working centrally in SAP

Solution Manager to implement and document the project scope defined in the Business Blueprint in the managed systems, make customer developments, and assign test cases and training materials to elements of the process structure.

Configuration guide: Microsoft Word printout generated using SAP Solution Manager, which contains documentation about IMG activities assigned in the configuration and other information that is relevant to configuration. It can be generated for the entire project structure or parts of it.

Configuration structure: A structure containing basic technical settings, such as settings for establishing communications links between different SAP systems and cross-scenario settings that apply to various scenarios or processes. Configuration structures are created for SAP applications and shipped as part of the Business Process Repository with SAP Solution Manager.

CTS project: A container in a logical system (client) that bundles transport requests that belong to an IMG project in one client. Change Request Management supports exactly one CTS project for each logical system.

DataSource: An object that makes data for a business unit available to SAP NetWeaver Business Intelligence (BI). A DataSource contains a number of logically related fields that are arranged in a flat structure and contain data to be transferred into BI.

Expert mode: In the issue tracking software in SAP Solution Manager, Top Issues, issues, tasks, and Expertise on

Demand objects are based on SAP CRM documents of types SLFT, SLFI, TASK, and SLFE. SAP developed new, intuitive user interfaces (UIs) that, compared to the standard CRM UIs, are much simpler and make the objects more user friendly. Expert mode enables users who prefer standard CRM UIs to call up the standardized interfaces.

Expertise on Demand: A type of request within an issue that enables you to call in named experts from SAP, from all functional areas, to resolve an issue.

IMG project: A project in a managed system that is created for performing customizing using the SAP Implementation Guide (IMG). An IMG project bundles in one managed system all changes that belong to an SAP Solution Manager project.

InfoCube: A type of InfoProvider. An InfoCube describes a self-contained dataset (from a reporting perspective), for example, for a business-oriented area. This dataset can be evaluated with the BEx query. An InfoCube is a set of relational tables that are created in accordance with the star schema: a large fact table in the center, with several dimension tables surrounding it.

InfoProvider: The superordinate term for BI objects into which data can be loaded or that represent a view of the data. As a rule, you can report on this data using BEx queries.

InfoSource: A unit of logically related information. InfoSources can include transaction data and master data (attributes, texts, and hierarchies).

Issue: A problem that threatens to impede business processes in your SAP solution landscape. The options for recording and managing issues in SAP Solution Manager enable you to document such problems in relation to your solution, to organize how they are processed, and to analyze the troubleshooting process later. The Issue Management facility in SAP Solution Manager offers a catalog of measures for resolving issues and is designed primarily for IT personnel.

Logical component: A logical reference for bundling different systems with the same (SAP) product release so they can be used consistently throughout the system landscape in a range of SAP Solution Manager application scenarios during implementation, operations, and continuous optimization. The combinations of systems and clients assigned to a logical component are usually linked by transport routes and have different roles, such as development system, quality assurance system, and production system. A logical component enables the abstract component level to be decoupled from the physical system level, allowing business processes to be defined that are not dependent on one system.

Logical system: A system in which applications sharing a common data basis run. Logical systems are defined in client table T000 and uniquely identify a client both within one system and across several systems. In SAP Solution Manager, logical systems have corresponding system-client combinations, which, in the context of a logical component, are assigned a system role in accordance with their purpose.

Main instance: An instance of a product (product version). A group of component versions that are technically dependent on one another and that are installed and run on a single (logical) server. As a group, these component versions provide business or technical functions. Main instances in SAP Solution Manager are used for defining systems and for logical components. Example for product SAP ECC: main instance SAP ECC server.

Maintenance cycle: A container for all of the tasks to be completed during a maintenance period. It is also the name used for a task list in the schedule manager.

Management of change requests: see Change Request Management.

Phase: A self-contained period in a project. A phase begins when it is released and ends when it is approved.

Product: A deliverable software unit for processing business-related tasks in an SAP system. It can be viewed, installed, and renewed by customers. A product can be implemented in one or more SAP solutions or applications. It consists of smaller units: main instances and software components. A product generally has several releases, also called product versions. Product versions are derived from the software component versions. In SAP Solution Manager, products are used to classify systems, for example, product SAP ECC with product version SAP ECC 5.0.

Project administration: A transaction for creating and managing projects in SAP Solution Manager (SOLAR_PRO-JECT_ADMIN). This entails defining general project data, such as the team members, standards, and system landscape that come into play for a given project.

Process chain: A sequence of processes that are scheduled to wait for an event in the background. Certain processes trigger another event, which, in turn, can start other processes.

Process step: The third level of the process-based structure in SAP Solution Manager. It represents an elementary activity that is performed by the system or an end user and runs in a specific software component. A process step contains implementation-relevant assignments, such as documentation, IMG activities, and transactions.

Process structure: A structure based on scenarios and processes that is created for an SAP Solution Manager project in the Business Blueprint transaction (SOLAR01). It consists of three levels: master data, organizational units, and business scenarios (level 1); business processes (level 2); and process steps (level 3). Together with their respective implementation-relevant assignments, these levels form the basis for subsequent configuration and testing activities. The process structure is also used in the solution directory, which lists production business processes that can be used as the basis for SAP Solution Monitoring.

Quality gate (Q-Gate): Type of project administration milestone in SAP Solu-tion Manager. Controls how project data is imported into subsequent systems: Data can be imported to subsequent systems only if the quality gate has the status "approved."

Query: A combination of characteristics and key figures (InfoObjects) that allows you to analyze the data in an In-foProvider. A query always corresponds to one InfoProvider, although you can define any number of queries for each InfoProvider.

Roadmap: Methodical, phase-based guidelines that list all of the procedures, activities, and deliverables needed to support a given software project. These include accelerators, in the form of templates or best practices, for instance, to add more value during a project. Roadmaps are available in SAP Solution Manager as project-specific working versions and on the SAP Service Mar-ketplace as display-only HTML versions. Types of Roadmap: ASAP Implementa-tion Roadmap, SAP Upgrade Roadmap, Global Template Roadmap. Roadmaps can have different versions.

Roadmap authoring environment: A transaction for structuring and mo-difying Roadmaps using appropriate documentation for methodical proce-dures, inputs, and outputs in the form of topics, and accelerators to speed up projects. Roadmaps must be defined in the Roadmap Repository. A graphical entry screen is optional, allowing quick access to selected activities (Transaction RMAUTH).

Roadmap Repository: A transaction in SAP Solution Manager for creating or copying Roadmaps to be customized

(Transaction RMDEF). This is where you manage header data for a Roadmap, such as name and attributes (flavors, roles, subject areas), which can be used for filtering information in SAP Solution Manager projects or in the display-only HTML version on the SAP Service Marketplace.

SAP global support backbone: Composed of SAP Solution Manager Enterprise Edition, the SAP Service Marketplace, and the SAP service infrastructure. It constitutes the technical foundation of SAP Enterprise Support.

SAP support services: SAP Active Global Support provides a list of services on the SAP Service Marketplace. You can view the current list at *http://www.service.sap.com/supportservices*.

SDCC: With certain session types, workbench sessions can be filled automatically with statistical data and other data that is supplied actively from the systems in the solution landscape that are being analyzed in a Service Session. The modules in your ABAP-based systems, which are responsible for collecting and transmitting data to your SAP Solution Manager system, are available in the ST-PI software package.

Service Desk: A function in SAP Solution Manager for processing internal customer problem messages.

Service Session: Certain SAP services (such as SAP GoingLive) consist of a number of smaller, shorter units, namely, Service Sessions, to optimize the service. For example, the SAP GoingLive service consists of SAP GoingLive Ana-

lysis (technology-related, before go-live date), SAP GoingLive Optimization (application-related, before go-live date), and SAP GoingLive Verification (after go-live date). Most SAP services, however, consist of just one Service Session, in which case the terms *service* and *Service Session* are virtually synonymous.

Software component: The smallest reusable part of a product. The modular approach enables such software parts to be installed, maintained via Support Packages, and upgraded. A software component is usually released for multiple databases and operating systems and for various languages or country versions. Software components are available in different component versions (also known as software component releases), for example, software component EA-APPL with component version EA-APPL 5.0 as part of the SAP ECC product.

Solution: A group of systems that are managed collectively in SAP Solution Manager. For example, all systems run by the same subsidiary.

System role: A purpose defined in SAP Solution Manager for a combination of system and client in a logical component's system group. It describes the role of a particular system-client combination in the customer-specific system landscape environment, for instance development or customizing, quality assurance, or production operation.

Task: An element within an issue or Top Issue that enables you to instruct users how to resolve the issue or Top Issue.

Technical bill of materials (TBOM): A bill of material that includes all objects that are linked to a specific transaction (or executable unit). The transaction is uniquely assigned to a specific scenario, business process, or process step in the Business Process Hierarchy.

Template: A container for bundling predefined global business scenarios and processes with documentation, transactions, configuration settings and documents, customer developments, and test cases. Templates can be reused in global rollouts to promote the use of harmonized, standard business processes.

Template collector: A wizard in SAP Solution Manager that consists of all the steps for gathering a template's content (process structure and implementation-relevant assignments) into one transport request. Once transported in this way, the template can be transported to a defined target system as part of a global rollout, for instance.

Top Issue: Describes management's view of a set of problems that threatens to jeopardize business processes in your SAP solution landscape, the solution for which requires management decisions. In general, such problems are viewed at the management level in your organization as being critical to the success of a project or a business process. As such, the Top Issue concept in SAP Solution Manager primarily addresses project managers with a nontechnical orientation.

Transaction type: Defines the properties and characteristics of a business transaction (such as sales order, service request, sales call) and specifies the control attributes (such as text determi-

nation procedure, partner determination procedure, status profile, organizational data profile). A transaction type controls how a particular business transaction is processed. It is assigned to one or more business transaction categories (such as activity, opportunity, sale, or service). This category determines the business context in which a transaction type can be used.

Transport request: A document for copying corrections between different types of systems. A transport request collects released corrections. The data is transported once the transport request has been released. For example, you can transport corrections from an integration system to a consolidation system.

Upgrade/Change Impact Analysis (UCIA): A function of the Custom Development Management Cockpit used to optimize custom developments. The Upgrade/Change Impact Analysis is used to identify the technical effects of an upgrade or Support Package on your custom developments and estimate the effort required to adjust these developments.

Upgrade indicator: A function available for upgrade projects in SAP Solution Manager. The indicator is set in the Project Administration transaction and, in the case of existing projects that are relevant for an upgrade, indicates in the Configuration transaction (SOLAR02) which configuration settings (IMG activities and configuration documents) are relevant for a given upgrade.

Workbench session: To increase the efficiency of many of the main types of Service Sessions, SAP Solution

Manager's integrated workbench tool is used to automate highly complex elements of a Service Session or elements that are repeated mechanically. This kind of automation substantially accelerates the Service Session. The workbench content is continuously being improved, so it is important that your SAP Solution Manager system always has the latest version of the ST-SER software package.

Workbook: A file with multiple worksheets (Microsoft Excel terminology). You insert one or more queries into a workbook to display them in the Business Explorer Analyzer. You can save a workbook in your favorites or roles.

C   Bibliography

BMC. *Maximizing DB2 Performance and Availability*. 2006.

Economist Intelligence Unit Ltd. *Coming to Grips with IT Risk*. March 2007.

Forrester Research Inc. *Optimizing SLA Performance*. 2006.

Föse, Frank; Hagemann, Sigrid; Will, Liane. *SAP NetWeaver ABAP System Administration*. 3rd ed. Boston: SAP PRESS, 2008.

Friedrich, Matthias, and Torsten Sternberg. *SAP Solution Manager 4.0 Service Desk – Functionality and Implementation*. Bonn: SAP PRESS, 2008.

Oswald, Gerhard. *SAP Service and Support*, 3rd ed. Bonn: SAP PRESS, 2006.

Schneider, Thomas. *SAP Performance Optimization Guide*: *Analyzing and Tuning SAP Systems*, 5th ed. Bonn: SAP PRESS, 2008.

Schöler, Sabine, and Liane Will. *SAP IT Service & Application Management. The ITIL Guide for SAP Operations*. Bonn: SAP PRESS, 2006.

Schröder, Thomas. *Business Process Monitoring with SAP Solution Manager*. Bonn: SAP PRESS, 2009.

The Standish Group International Inc. *Extreme Chaos*. 2000.

Weidmann, Corina, and Lars Teuber. *Conception and Installation of System Monitoring using the SAP Solution Manager*, 2nd ed. Bonn: SAP PRESS, 2009.

Will, Liane, and Sigrid Hagemann. *SAP R/3 System Administration*, 2nd ed. Bonn: SAP PRESS, 2003.

Woods, Dan. *Enterprise Services Architecture*. Bonn: SAP PRESS, 2004.

D   Authors (2nd Edition)

Marc Oliver Schäfer, Senior Product Manager, SAP AG

Marc Oliver Schäfer studied English and German literature and linguistics at the University of Tübingen, Germany. Prior to joining SAP in 2000 as product manager for the Customizing tools development group, he worked at DaimlerChrysler AG as a trainer in language courses and intercultural courses. Since 2004, Mr. Schäfer has been a product manager for SAP Solution Manager, where he is responsible for issues regarding SAP Solution Manager Enterprise Edition along with portfolio planning of SAP Solution Manager. You can reach Mr. Schäfer at *marc.oliver.schaefer@sap.com*.

Dr. Matthias Melich, Vice President, SAP Solution Manager Product Management, SAP AG

Dr. Matthias Melich studied English literature at the University of Rochester, New York, and mathematics and English philology at the University of Cologne, Germany, where he wrote his doctoral thesis on computer-based language acquisition in 1993. He began working for SAP in 1995, initially in the object modeling group, and then moving one year later to the data archiving team. In 1998, he assumed responsibility for product management for Customizing tools. Since January 2005, he has been responsible for global product management activities in E2E Solution Operations as vice president. Dr. Melich can be reached at *matthias.melich@sap.com*.

Suzanne Dietrich, Product Manager, SAP AG

Suzanne Dietrich studied English and American studies, romance studies, and adult education at the Chemnitz University of Technology, Germany, and the Università degli Studi di Modena e Reggio Emilia, Italy. She joined SAP in 2006 as a student employee, and supported SAP Solution Manager project management in creating the first edition of the SAP Solution Manager book. Since 2007, Ms. Dietrich has been a permanent employee at SAP and coordinates the SAP Solution Manager application documentation in product management. She is also responsible for customer success stories and overall project management of the second edition of the SAP Solution Manager book. Ms. Dietrich can be reached at *suzanne.dietrich@sap.com*.

Doreen Baseler, Product Manager, SAP AG

Doreen Baseler studied communication science (translation studies, English, and Spanish) at Magdeburg University of Applied Sciences, Germany, and the Universidad Complutense de Madrid, Spain. She joined SAP in 1999, starting in the ASAP department. Since 2000, she has been a product manager for SAP Solution Manager. Her work focuses on global rollouts, system landscape administration, support for upgrade projects, and, since 2006, SAP Solution Composer. You can contact Ms. Baseler at *doreen.baseler@sap.com*.

Marco Bertolini, Project Manager, SAP AG

Marco Bertolini studied computer science at Mannheim University of Applied Sciences, Germany. He started working for SAP AG in 1999, developing procedures for implementing and configuring SAP products efficiently. He participated in development projects for a range of implementation and configuration tools: from SAP Business Engineer to AcceleratedSAP and ValueSAP to SAP Solution

Manager. In the SAP Solution Manager development group, Mr. Bertolini leads the project office for product development. You can contact Marco Bertolini at *marco.bertolini@sap.com*.

Dr. Veit Eska, Senior Developer, SAP AG

Dr. Veit Eska studied physics at the University of Rostock and the Institute of Atmospheric Physics in Kühlungsborn, Germany, from 1989 to 1994. He then worked for six months as an assistant at the institute and, three years later, wrote a doctoral thesis on applied physics. He joined SAP in 1998, where he worked in the Technical Core Competence Team on the development of service tools for creating services such as SAP EarlyWatch Alert. With regard to SAP Solution Manager, he is responsible for managing development projects in the areas of monitoring, reporting, and business intelligence. Since 2007, Dr. Eska has managed the development of the SAP Engagement and Service Delivery and Business Process Operations work centers. You can contact Dr. Eska at veit.eska@sap.com.

Esther Hardt, Senior Product Manager, SAP AG

Esther Hardt studied business administration at the Universität des Saarlandes in Saarbrücken, Germany, and at the University of Southern Colorado (now CSU-Pueblo), USA. She began her career in management consulting at PricewaterhouseCoopers AG and joined SAP as a consultant in 2004. Since 2006, Ms. Hardt has been working as an SAP Solution Manager product manager. She is responsible for implementation, managing the Solution Documentation Assistant, and collaborating with SAP Consulting. She is also the SAP contact person for the SAP Solution Manager and Support Infrastructure work group of the German-Speaking SAP User Group e.V. (DSAG). Ms. Hardt can be reached at *esther.hardt@sap.com*.

Michael Klöffer, Expert Technical Support Consultant, SAP AG

Michael Klöffer studied information technology at the Berufsakademie Karlsruhe, Germany, prior to gaining five years of experience in various positions throughout the IT sector. He joined SAP in 2004, initially working in Strategic Research and Development in the areas of IT services and application management. Currently part of the Global Technology Center of Expertise within SAP Active Global Support, Mr. Klöffer now works on the rollout and further development of end-to-end solution operations with a focus on potential uses and procedures for end-to-end diagnostics. Mr. Klöffer can be reached at *michael.kloeffer@ sap.com*.

Claudia Pfeil-Biehl, Product Manager, SAP AG

Claudia Pfeil-Biehl studied linguistics and translation studies (English and Spanish) at Heidelberg University, Germany. She joined SAP in 1997 and was initially responsible for promoting the area of SAP Service & Support. Since 2001, she has been managing the SAP Service Marketplace and SAP Solution Manager as part of product management. Her focus is on ramp-up knowledge transfer for SAP Solution Manager. Ms. Pfeil-Biehl can be reached at *claudia.pfeil-biehl@sap.com*.

Dr. Peter Pieruschka, Development Manager, SAP AG

Dr. Peter Pieruschka studied theoretical physics at Munich's Technical University, Germany, and the University of Canterbury, UK. In 1994, he wrote a doctoral thesis on applied mathematics at the Australian National University and went on to work at European research institutes before working for the Australian government in the field of environmental policy. He joined SAP AG in 1999, initially as a CRM consultant in the support organization. Since 2003, Dr. Pieruschka has worked as a developer and project manager in the SAP Solution Manager development group, and since 2007, he has worked as a development manager in Bangalore, India. His work focuses on the service plan, Issue Management, Task Management, Downtime Management, and Self-Diagnosis in SAP Solution Manager. You can reach Dr. Pieruschka at *peter.pieruschka@ sap.com*.

Cay Rademann, Senior Product Manager, SAP AG

Cay Rademann studied business administration at the University of Mannheim, Germany, and the University of Wales, Swansea (now Swansea University). After graduating with a degree in commercial management, he joined SAP AG in 1994, where he has worked as a consultant, in development, and in product management. Since 2003, Mr. Rademann has been a senior product manager for SAP Solution Manager and subsequently for end-to-end solution operations. His responsibilities include presenting an overall picture of the solution and coordinating active rollouts. Mr. Rademann can be reached at *cay.rademann@sap.com*.

Martin Rink, Senior Product Manager, SAP AG

Martin Rink studied industrial engineering at the Karlsruhe University of Applied Sciences, Germany. Before joining SAP in 1998, he accumulated 15 years' experience managing IT projects. For seven years, Mr. Rink has worked as a product manager for SAP Service and Support Infrastructure. He is responsible for maintenance (Maintenance Optimizer) and integrating partners into SAP Service and Support Infrastructure. You can contact Mr. Rink at martin.rink@ sap.com.

Dr. Wolfgang Schatz, Support Architect, SAP AG

Dr. Wolfgang Schatz studied physics at the University of Regensburg, Germany, where he wrote a doctoral thesis in 1994. He joined SAP in 1998 after studying for several semesters in the United States and Berlin. Currently, he works in Active Global Support on application topics and performance optimization and develops expert services. In SAP Solution Manager, he developed the *Scoping* and *Cooperation Enabling* services, which provide support for organizations implementing SAP Solution Manager in complex enterprise structures. Since 2006, he has worked in the areas of end-to-end solution operations and Run SAP. You can contact Dr. Schatz at *wolfgang.schatz@sap.com*.

Patrick Schmidt, Service Architect, SAP AG

Patrick Schmidt studied information management at the Berufsakademie Karlsruhe, Germany. From 2000 to 2006, he worked as a consulting manager at REALTECH AG, where he was responsible for setting up software solutions in the SAP environment. He joined SAP in 2006 in the Center of Expertise for Software Logistics within SAP Active Global Support. You can contact Mr. Schmidt at *pat.schmidt@sap.com*.

Benjamin Schneider, Senior Product Manager, SAP AG

Benjamin Schneider studied German language and literature and political sciences for teaching at the University of Mannheim, Germany. During his study, he spent three years in SAP product management as a student employee. After completing his studies, he spent one year working in technical support for SAP add-on products at REALTECH AG before returning to SAP in 2007. Since then, he has been working as a product manager for SAP Solution Manager. He is responsible for Change Request Management and the work centers of SAP Solution Manager. Mr. Schneider can be reached at *benjamin.schneider@sap.com*.

Gergely Spiry, Service Architect, SAP AG

Gergely Spiry studied industrial engineering at the Universität Karlsruhe, Germany, and the University of Reading, UK. After completing his dissertation at Audi AG, he joined SAP in 1998, where he initially provided the SAP GoingLive Check, SAP EarlyWatch Service, and performance optimization services. He then worked in SAP Active Global Support, where he developed service content in the application and performance area. In SAP Solution Manager, he is involved in developing the service delivery platform (including Issue Management) and representing users. You can contact Mr. Spiry at *gergely.spiry@sap.com*.

Volker von Gloeden, Platinum Support Consultant, SAP AG

Volker von Gloeden studied mathematics at the University of Düsseldorf, Germany, from 1997 to 2002. After obtaining a master's degree in mathematics, he began working at SAP in 2003. He initially worked in the area of business process monitoring, before focusing on performance optimization in the business process context. Since 2006, he has held overall responsibility for business process monitoring in SAP Solution Manager, and also manages the project for Job Scheduling Management. Mr. von Gloeden can be reached at *volker.von.gloeden@ sap.com*.

Marcus Wefers, Senior Director of Product Management, SAP AG

As senior director of production management in the Active Global Support area, Marcus Wefers is responsible for tools, products, and positioning of test management as part of SAP Solution Manager. He has worked at SAP for 18 years, focusing on software development, consulting, project management, quality management, and product management. He has also been involved in the areas of Financial Consolidation, Profit Center Accounting, Analytics, Performance and Strategy Management, Business Planning, Corporate Governance, Test & Quality Management, and Application Management. Mr. Wefers has extensive experience from global customer projects in Europe, the USA, and Asia, and is a regular speaker at international conferences. Mr. Wefers can be reached at *marcus.wefers@sap.com*.

Henrik Zimmermann, Senior Product Manager, SAP AG

Henrik Zimmermann studied geography at Heidelberg University and the Freie Universität Berlin, Germany. In 2000, he joined SAP as a developer for Supply Chain Management. He has been involved in SAP Solution Manager product management since January 2002. His work currently focuses on monitoring, service delivery, and integrating partner products in testing, as well as Job Scheduling Management in SAP Solution Manager. Mr. Zimmermann can be reached at *henrik.zimmermann@sap.com*.

Index

Fundamental knowledge and in-depth administration advice

Expert advice on key areas like planning, administration, and development

Includes extra chapters on backup, recovery, restoration, SAP NetWeaver BI, and more

Michael Höding, André Faustmann, Gunnar Klein, Ronny Zimmermann

SAP Database Administration with Oracle

Oracle is one of the most significant, but also one of the most complex, DB platforms available for SAP systems---so why hasn't someone written a book on how to configure the interaction? Well, here it is: With this in-depth reference book, administrators get much needed background knowledge, as well as complete details on architectural and software/ logistics issues, in addition to step-by-step instructions for all of the most important administration tasks. Every aspect of system landscape planning and maintenance is covered, helping administrators hone their problem solving skills. Bonus chapters deal with Java, SAP NetWeaver BI, and the highly complex issues of Backup, Recovery, and Restoration.

818 pp., 2008, 89,95 Euro / US$ 89.95
ISBN 978-1-59229-120-5

>> www.sap-press.de/1386

Extended, updated 2nd edition with details on eCATT and SAP accelerated Data Migration

Comprehensive examples for Batch Input, eCATT, and LSMW

Valuable tips for planning a migration project

Michael Willinger, Johann Gradl

Migrating Your SAP Data

This completely revised and updated edition of our bestseller is a comprehensive practical companion for ensuring rapid and cost-effective migration projects. It illustrates the basic principles of migration, discusses preparatory measures for a project, and shows you how to migrate your data using the methods offered by your SAP system economically, rapidly, and without the need for programming. The new edition is up-to-date for ECC 6.0 and provides you with the latest available information on eCATT and SAP Accelerated Data Migration. An ideal companion for administrators and technical consultants, this book also serves as a helpful resource for power users in specialized departments.

373 pp., 2. edition 2008, 79,95 Euro / US$ 79.95
ISBN 978-1-59229-170-0

>> www.sap-press.de/1585

SAP PRESS

Revised new edition, completely
up-to-date for SAP ERP 6.0

New functions and technologies: Archive
Routing, Transaction TAANA, XML-based
archiving, and many more

New chapters on archiving in
SAP ERP HCM and SAP NetWeaver BI

Helmut Stefani

Archiving Your SAP Data

This much anticipated, completely revised edition of our bestseller is up-to-date
for SAP ERP 6.0, and provides you with valuable knowledge to master data
archiving with SAP. Fully updated, this new edition includes two all-new
chapters on XML-based data archiving and archiving in SAP ERP HCM and
contains detailed descriptions of all the new functions and technologies such as
Archive Routing and the TAANA transaction. Readers uncover all the underlying
technologies and quickly familiarize themselves with all activities of data
archiving—archivability checks, the archiving process, storage of archive files,
and display of archived data. The book focuses on the requirements of system
and database administrators as well as project collaborators who are responsible
for implementing data archiving in an SAP customer project.

405 pp., 2. edition 2007, 69,95 Euro / US$ 69.95, ISBN 978-1-59229-116-8

>> www.sap-press.de/1375

MDM technology, architecture, and solution landscape

Detailed technical description of all three usage scenarios

Includes highly-detailed, proven guidance from real-life customer examples

Loren Heilig, Steffen Karch, Oliver Böttcher, Christiane Hofmann, Roland Pfennig

SAP NetWeaver Master Data Management

This book provides system architects, administrators, and IT managers with a description of the structure and usage scenarios of SAP NetWeaver MDM. It uses three comprehensive real-life examples to give you practical insights into the consolidation, harmonization, and central management of master data. Plus, more than 120 pages are dedicated to an MDM compendium, complete with detailed information on individual components, data extraction, options for integration with SAP NetWeaver XI, SAP NetWeaver BI, and the SAP Portal (including user management), as well as on workflows and the Java API.

331 pp., 2007, 69,95 Euro / US$ 69.95, ISBN 978-1-59229-131-1

>> www.sap-press.de/1445

Interested in reading more?

Please visit our Web site for all
new book releases from SAP PRESS.

www.sap-press.com